To Elliot,

With best regards,

Dan

THE INSTALLATION
OF BAAL'S HIGH PRIESTESS AT EMAR

HARVARD SEMITIC MUSEUM
HARVARD SEMITIC STUDIES

Frank Moore Cross, editor

Syriac Manuscripts: A Catalogue	Moshe H. Goshen-Gottstein
Introduction to Classical Ethiopic	Thomas O. Lambdin
Dictionary of Old South Arabic	Joan C. Biella
The Poet and the Historian: Essays in Literary and Historical Biblical Criticism	Richard Elliot Friedman, Editor
The Songs of the Sabbath Sacrifice	Carol Newsom
Non-Canonical Psalms from Qumran: A Pseudepigraphic Collection	Eileen M. Schuller
The Hebrew of the Dead Sea Scrolls	Elisha Qimron
An Exodus Scroll from Qumran	Judith E. Sanderson
You Shall Have No Other Gods	Jeffrey H. Tigay
Ugaritic Vocabulary in Syllabic Transcription	John Huehnergard
The Scholarship of William Foxwell Albright	Gus Van Beek
The Akkadian of Ugarit	John Huehnergard
Features of the Eschatology of IV Ezra	Michael E. Stone
Studies in Neo-Aramaic	Wolfhart Heinrichs, Editor
Lingering over Words: Studies in Ancient Near Eastern Literature in Honor of William L. Moran	Tzvi Abusch, John Huehnergard, Piotr Steinkeller, Editors
A Grammar of the Palestinian Targum Fragments from the Cairo Genizah	Steven E. Fassberg
The Origins and Development of the Waw-*Consecutive: Northwest Semitic Evidence from Ugaritic to Qumran*	Mark S. Smith
Amurru Akkadian: A Linguistic Study, Volume I	Shlomo Izre'el
Amurru Akkadian: A Linguistic Study, Volume II	Shlomo Izre'el
The Installation of Baal's High Priestess at Emar: A Window on Ancient Syrian Religion	Daniel E. Fleming

THE INSTALLATION OF BAAL'S HIGH PRIESTESS AT EMAR

A Window on Ancient Syrian Religion

by
Daniel E. Fleming

Scholars Press
Atlanta, Georgia

THE INSTALLATION OF BAAL'S HIGH PRIESTESS AT EMAR

by
Daniel E. Fleming

Library of Congress Cataloging in Publication Data

Fleming, Daniel E.
The installation of Baal's high priestess at Emar : a window on ancient Syrian religion / by Daniel E. Fleming.
p. cm. — (Harvard Semitic studies ; no. 42)
Includes text and translation of the Akkadian cuneiform inscription on the nin.dingir ritual (Emar 369).
Includes bibliographical reference and indexes.
ISBN 1-55540-726-9
1. Baal (Deity)—Cult—Syria—Emar (Extinct city) 2. Emar (Extinct city)—Religion. 3. Syria—Religion. 4. Women priests—Syria—Emar (Extinct city) 5. Akkadian language—Texts.
I. Title. II. Series.
BJ1605.B26F54 1992
299'.21—dc20 92-15132
CIP

Printed in the United States of America
on acid-free paper

for Nancy

ACKNOWLEDGEMENTS

This book is revised from my 1990 doctoral dissertation, *The Installation of Baal's High Priestess at Emar: A Window on Ancient Syrian Religion*, written under the supervision of William L. Moran, Piotr Steinkeller, John Huehnergard, and Frank M. Cross. Each member of my committee read the material in various stages of preparation, and their collected insight will be found throughout the present work. It is my hope that this and all my future effort will do justice to their training.

I am also grateful to Frank Cross as editor for the opportunity to publish this book in the Harvard Semitic Studies monograph series.

With funding from a National Endowment for the Humanities Summer Stipend, I was able to collate many Emar ritual tablets at the Aleppo National Museum in Syria. The Syrian Department of Antiquities provided generous assistance at every level, and I would especially like to thank Dr. Ali Abou-Assaf, Dr. Adnan Bounni, and Dr. Kassim Toueir at Damascus, and Dr. Wahed Khayata and Mr. Hamido Hammade at Aleppo. Daniel Arnaud, the epigrapher of the Akkadian texts from Emar, supported my original choice of topic and has responded promptly and graciously to my further enquires. Both he and Jean-Claude Margueron, the director of excavations at Meskéné/Emar, made possible my visit to Syria by approving access to the Aleppo collections.

In the course of my work on this project I have received assistance from more people than I can thank individually in this space, but I wish to name a few. Gernot Wilhelm provided opportunity to air ideas for the revision by an invitation to visit Würzburg in June of 1991. He, Gary M. Beckman, and Edouard Lipiński kindly responded to questions about Emar culture, language, and religion. Manfried Dietrich and Oswald Loretz made available to me their collations of select Alalaḫ tablets, and Prof. Dietrich sent me an early copy of his new article on the installation text. Wolfgang Heimpel and Anne D. Kilmer offered their support in the use of the facilities at the University of California at Berkeley in 1989-1990. During the past year I have enjoyed the support and advice of my colleagues at New York University, especially Baruch Levine and Lawrence Schiffman.

Finally, I must thank my wife Nancy, who has made my project her own from start to finish. After all the effort she expended in various aspects of work on my dissertation, Nancy miraculously volunteered to superintend the production of camera-ready copy for the present book. I can only hope to return her love and care in kind.

In spite of the efforts of so many generous and knowledgeable benefactors, the final result will remain flawed, and these flaws remain the full responsibility of the author.

TABLE OF CONTENTS

ABBREVIATIONS

AAAS	*Annales archéologiques arabes syriennes*
AASOR	*Annual of the American Schools of Oriental Research.*
AEPHER	*Annuaire. Ecole pratique des hautes études; Ve section - sciences religieuses.*
AfO	*Archiv für Orientforschung.*
AHw	W. von Soden, *Akkadisches Handwörterbuch.*
ANET	J.B. Pritchard, ed., *Ancient Near Eastern Texts Relating to the Old Testament.*
AnSt	*Anatolian Studies.*
AOAT	Alter Orient und Altes Testament.
AOATS	Alter Orient und Altes Testament -- Sonderreihe.
AoF	*Altorientalische Forschungen.*
ARET	Archivi Reali di Ebla, Testi.
ARM(T)	Archives Royales de Mari (Textes).
ArOr	*Archiv Orientální.*
AS	*Assyriological Studies.*
ASJ	*Acta Sumerologica*
AT	D.J. Wiseman, *The Alalakh Tablets.*
AuOr	*Aula Orientalis.*
BDB	F. Brown, S.R. Driver, C.A. Briggs, *A Hebrew and English Lexicon of the Old Testament.*
BiOr	*Bibliotheca Orientalis.*
CAD	I.J. Gelb, et al., *The Assyrian Dictionary of the Oriental Institute of the University of Chicago.*
CBQ	*The Catholic Biblical Quarterly.*
CH	The Code of Hammurabi.
CRAIBL	Académie des Inscriptions et Belles-Lettres, *Comptes rendus.*

CTA	A. Herdner, *Corpus des tablettes en cunéiformes alphabétiques.*
CTH	E. Laroche, *Catalogue des textes hittites.*
DamM	*Damaszener Mitteilungen.*
EA	J.A. Knudtzon, *Die El-Amarna-Tafeln.*
Emar (VI)	D. Arnaud, *Recherches au pays d'Aštata: les textes sumériens et accadiens.*
GLH	E. Laroche, *Glossaire de la langue hourrite.*
Ḫḫ.	Lexical series ḪAR-ra = *ḫubullu.*
JBL	*The Journal of Biblical Literature.*
JCS	*Journal of Cuneiform Studies.*
JESHO	*Journal of the Economic and Social History of the Orient.*
JNES	*Journal of Near Eastern Studies.*
JNSL	*Journal of Northwest Semitic Languages.*
KAR	E. Ebeling, *Keilschrifttexte aus Assur religiösen Inhalts.*
KBo	Keilschrifttexte aus Boghazköi.
KTU	M. Dietrich, O. Loretz, J. Sanmartín, *Die keilalphabetischen Texte aus Ugarit.*
KUB	Keilschrifturkunden aus Boghazköi.
LB	Late Bronze (Age).
MA	Middle Assyrian (Akkadian).
M.A.R.I.	*Mari. Annales de recherches interdisciplinaires.*
MB	Middle Babylonian (Akkadian). Middle Bronze (Age), only in context of archaeology.
MDOG	*Mitteilungen der Deutschen Orient-Gesellschaft.*
MUSJ	*Mélanges de l'Université Saint-Joseph* (Beirut).
MVAG	*Mitteilungen der Vorderasiatisch(-Ägyptisch)en Gesellschaft.*
NA	Neo-Assyrian (Akkadian).
N.A.B.U.	*Nouvelles assyriologiques brèves et utilitaires.*

NB	Neo-Babylonian (Akkadian).
OA	Old Assyrian (Akkadian).
OAkk	Old Akkadian.
OB	Old Babylonian (Akkadian).
OLP	*Orientalia Lovaniensia Periodica.*
Or NS	*Orientalia* (Nova Series).
PRU	Le Palais royal d'Ugarit.
RA	*Revue d'assyriologie et d'archéologie orientale.*
RAcc	F. Thureau-Dangin, *Rituels accadiens.*
RAI	Rencontre assyriologique internationale.
RHA	*Revue hittite et asianique.*
RHR	*Revue de l'histoire des religions.*
RlA	E. Ebeling, et al., *Reallexikon der Assyriologie.*
RS	Ras Shamra excavation/tablet number.
SB	Standard Babylonian (Akkadian).
SEb	*Studi Eblaiti.*
SEL	*Studi Epigrafici e Linguistici sul Vicino Oriente Antico.*
SMEA	*Studi Micenei ed Egeo-Anatolici.*
StBoT	Studien zu den Bogazköy-Texten.
Syria	*Syria. Revue d'art oriental et d'archéologie.*
UET	Ur Excavation Texts.
UF	*Ugarit-Forschung.*
Ug 5	J. Nougayrol, et al., *Ugaritica* 5.
UT	C.H. Gordon, *Ugaritic Textbook.*
ZA	*Zeitschrift für Assyriologie und Vorderasiatische Archäologie.*
ZAW	*Zeitschrift für die alttestamentliche Wissenschaft.*

I. INTRODUCTION

The alphabetic cuneiform texts from the coastal city of Ugarit unveiled a previously unknown world of Syrian culture from the second millennium B.C.E., and these finds have dominated most recent study of ancient Syrian religion. Excavations in the 1970s at Emar, a 13th-century B.C.E. city in north-central Syria on the great bend of the Euphrates River, have yielded a collection of native ritual texts, recorded in Akkadian. Emar now represents a major new source for understanding early Syrian religion, a supplement and a balance to the data from Ugarit. The diverse collection reveals a cult and culture that is distinctly West Semitic but not Canaanite, and the site thus contributes to a more nuanced picture of Syrian culture and religion.

This study consists of three major parts: a revised text for an important event in Emar religious life, the celebration of the NIN.DINGIR-priestess installation; a detailed interpretive study; and discussion of the historical and cultural context. The original copies, transcription, and translation were published by Daniel Arnaud in 1986, without commentary, and my dissertation was completed before the appearance of Manfried Dietrich's recent article.[1] Although Dietrich's work will remain an important treatment of the NIN.DINGIR ritual, the study offered here attempts the broader scope and depth possible in a book-length project. My collated text and extended commentary should represent considerable progress in understanding the raw materials: the ritual and its components, the gods, the human personnel, the

[1] Dietrich, "Das Einsetzungsritual der Entu von Emar (Emar VI, 369)", *UF* 21 (1989) 47-100.

sacred sites, and all the elements that relate to each ritual action. Comparison of ritual terminology and pantheon both within the Emar texts and with material from neighboring lands displays a uniquely Syrian heritage with a long history of indigenous development. Though the Emar rites are recorded in Akkadian, they describe long-standing local practices that are dependent on neither Mesopotamian nor Anatolian ritual language and custom. Identifiable Canaanite or west Syrian features appear to belong to the last stage of Emar's religious history, the period of Hittite domination during the 13th century.

A. PROCEDURE

The results of any project are shaped significantly by the definitions of limits, focus, and approach which frame it. Moreover, the written results are understood best when these definitions are most explicit, and the following discussion is intended to make clear what choices undergird the present study of the NIN.DINGIR-priestess installation at Emar. I will deal with:

1. Choosing an approach,
2. Limiting the project,
3. Addressing broader issues.

1. Choosing an Approach

In 1985-1986, Daniel Arnaud published a large portion of the Sumero-Akkadian texts found at Meskéné/Emar, thus making available over 500 texts from a new Syrian site of the second millennium B.C.E. These texts included the archive of an Emar diviner (^{lú}ḪAL), found in the center-city temple M_1, and that archive included almost 200 fragments of ritual texts which have no parallel in known Akkadian literature. Most of the fragments are small and have been severely damaged, but we have sufficient remains to discover a range of ritual types: offering lists, rites tied to the calendar, and a set of rites called EZEN (Akkadian *isinnu*), roughly, "festival," associated with a variety of occasions. From the larger fragments we can piece together major sections of several ritual events. Altogether, the Emar ritual texts constitute an immense new resource for understanding ancient Syrian religion and placing it in the context of the larger ancient Near East.

At the time of my dissertation, only Daniel Arnaud, the epigrapher for the French excavation team, had published primary studies of the Emar ritual texts (see the *AEPHER* series), and these represent only preliminary reviews of their content, without detailed evaluation and commentary. Arnaud has been responsible for the entire body of Akkadian texts from Emar excavations,[2] and he has not pursued publication of further comment.[3] Even as this monograph comes to press, new studies of Emar ritual will be emerging, but very little has been completed to date. Before the Emar ritual texts are incorporated into the scholarly lore regarding ancient religion, this detailed interpretive study must be undertaken so that broader work will be adequately rooted in the reality of the primary data, the texts themselves.[4]

My own study of the Emar rituals therefore begins as a response to the urgent need for thorough interpretive study of the texts individually, and I have chosen an approach that reflects the central importance of this interpretive task. The work proceeds from the tablet copies published by Arnaud as Emar VI.1 and 2 (1985). Thus, in the first stages of my research I confined myself to reading, transliterating, and translating all the ritual fragments listed by Arnaud in Emar VI.3, numbers 369-535. This supplied a foundation for a more precise reading of the limited text base which I describe below. Then I

---

[2] Study of all Akkadian texts from Emar is complicated by the fact that excavations did not exhaust the epigraphic yield of the site, and significant numbers of tablets of identifiable Emar origin continue to appear in the possession of dealers or collectors outside Syria. Many of these remain unpublished, though Arnaud himself published 17 tablets from outside the excavation finds in *Aula Orientalis*, and Akio Tsukimoto is publishing 50 tablets from the "Hirayama collection" in *Acta Sumerologica* that include those already published by John Huehnergard and Gary Beckman. See Arnaud, "La Syrie du moyen-Euphrate sous le protectorat hittite: contracts de droit privé," *AuOr* 5 (1987) 211-241; Tsukimoto, "Sieben spätbronzezeitliche Urkunden aus Syrien, "*ASJ* 10 (1988) 153-189; "Akkadian tablets in the Hirayama collection (I)," *ASJ* 12 (1990) 177-259; Huehnergard, "Five tablets from the vicinity of Emar," *RA* 77 (1983) 11-43; Beckman, "Three tablets from the vicinity of Emar," *JCS* 40 (1988) 61-68. See also, M. Sigrist, "Miscellanea," *JCS* 34 (1982) 242-246; J.-W. Meyer and G. Wilhelm, "Eine spätbronzezeitliche Keilschrifturkunde aus Syrien," *DamM* 1 (1983) 249-261.

[3] Professor Arnaud kindly informed me that his plans preclude immediate work on the ritual texts (personal communication, November 7, 1988).

[4] Recent examples include the review article by Douglas Frayne on the sacred marriage and the *entu*, "Notes on the sacred marriage rite," *BiOr* 42 (1985) 20-21, and the paper on Syrian socio-political systems by J. Sapin, "Quelques systèmes socio-politiques en Syrie au 2e millénaire avant J.-C. et leur évolution historique d'après des documents religieux (légendes, rituels, sanctuaires)," *UF* 15 (1983) 188-189. These include versions of the NIN.DINGIR and *zukru* festivals, respectively, that are based on preliminary readings by Arnaud that are altered considerably by further study.

moved from text to commentary, developing models for the structures of the major rituals, comparing form, pantheon, ritual players, the language of offering, sacred sites, and other significant ritual elements (temporal phrases, prepositional phrases, conjunctions, etc.). My first resources for wider comparison were the rest of the Akkadian texts from Emar and the major Akkadian dictionaries (*CAD*, *AHw*).[5] Only after I had worked extensively with the Emar texts themselves did I expand my horizon to ritual texts from the neighboring lands, peripheral Akkadian texts generally, and a range of secondary literature dealing with problems that arise in study of ancient Syria and its religion.

My study of Emar ritual therefore has been text-centered, in accordance with the primary need for close study and interpretation of the ritual texts themselves as a foundation for future work on broader issues in Emar religion and culture. The treatment of these issues which follows my text and commentary is thus subsidiary to them -- a necessary foray, but dependent on the philological work.

2. Limiting the project

In the course of my study, I have attempted to penetrate the surface of the newly discovered Emar ritual, to get a view of its working parts -- the actions and events that compose the rituals and the language used to direct their execution. However, the body of rituals is so varied and large that I needed to limit my textual base to a major text or texts that would provide an adequate point of entry for understanding the entire group. I chose the installation ritual for the NIN.DINGIR-priestess of the storm god[6] (Arnaud's

---

[5] The relevant dictionary articles for the Akkadian words found in the NIN.DINGIR festival furnished a preliminary indication of known Akkadian use. It is possible to gain an initial impression of the periods, geographical regions, and genres in which each word occurs.

[6] In the NIN.DINGIR installation (Emar 369) the storm god is always spelled ^{d}IM, and this is the form which I will use throughout the text and commentary for the sake of precision. However, there is evidence that in 13th-century B.C.E. Emar the storm god was called Baal, so I have used this well-known form in the title of my study. Carlos Zaccagnini, "Golden cups offered to the gods at Emar," *Or* NS 59 (1990) 518-520 n.4 and 5, comments that F.M. Fales has "convincingly pointed out that ^{d}10//^{d}IŠKUR stands for Adad and not for Baal," but this work was unfortunately not yet available to me at the time of publication. See Fales, "Notes on the royal family of Emar," in *Mélanges P. Garelli*, forthcoming. For further discussion see "The storm god" in the commentary and "The Gods of the Installations" in the chapter on the Emar festival tradition.

Emar VI.3 369), one of the most prominent rites in the corpus. This text makes an ideal starting point because of several features. For one, the NIN.DINGIR installation involves a wealth of ritual players in a rich variety of events, with comparatively little repetition. Many features do not belong to the lexicon of familiar Akkadian terms and uses. Then, the installation is one of the longer Emar rituals, and one exemplar in two pieces constitutes a full text, with distinct beginning and end, and only a few significant gaps. These can be filled in part with the help of additional smaller fragments, so that we come close to possessing a complete text of the ritual. Whereas the other long rituals from Emar contain breaks that hamper evaluation of the overall structure, we can approach a full outline of the NIN.DINGIR installation. This rite therefore makes an appropriate object for comprehensive study.

Just as the text base must be limited, the range of issues treated in this study must be circumscribed as well, in order to achieve greatest control of the subject. As I have said, a foundation for interpretation of ancient religion must be thorough understanding of the textual evidence, and this requirement is all the more pressing at this early stage of Emar research. Therefore a fresh examination of the NIN.DINGIR installation text and a full commentary stand at the center of this work, and larger issues discussed at the end should be considered secondary in this context, no matter how interesting or important they may be.

The first major section consists of a new text, translation, and notes for the NIN.DINGIR ritual, Emar 369. Close study has suggested many new readings and has revealed a fifth fragment of the ritual: text E, Arnaud's Emar 402, Msk 74286e. Comparison with the ritual idiom of the entire corpus has allowed completion of several broken lines.

The second major section is the commentary, based on examination of each component of the celebration. My goal has been to develop a comprehensive picture of the religious event, and of the text as a manual for performance of that event. The text as a whole separates the ritual proper from administration of allotments at the end (lines 1-75, vs. 76-94). The ritual itself covers approximately nine days and may be divided into discrete segments, such as the *qaddušu* ceremony of lines 22-28. The installation involves a continuing interplay between the old and new homes of the priestess -- her father's house and her residence in the temple of the storm god. My study aims to illuminate the progression of ritual acts that carries the woman from one place in life to the other. In revision of the dissertation I attempted to penetrate more deeply these elements that carry the effect of the whole installation festival, and many of the changes introduced reflect new ideas regarding their significance.

The commentary is organized around the individual actions that make up this process, and discussion of individual terms is placed in the context of the associated verb. For instance, the NIN.DINGIR's Akkadian garment (TÚG.GAR URI) and her "bedroom" (*bīt urši*) are dealt with in the context of the associated action, "to lay out" (*muṣṣû*), lines 70-71.

3. Enlarging the scope

The first two sections form the core of this study, and in these sections I have attempted to define my subject somewhat narrowly and to examine this material systematically. However, many larger issues cry out to be dealt with, some of which require attention even in a preliminary study such as this. I have taken on two particular issues:

-- What complexities appear in the larger body of Emar ritual? What patterns and distinctions emerge? Where does the NIN.DINGIR-priestess installation fit in this larger scheme?

-- Do the rituals recorded in Akkadian at Emar reflect local practice, and do they offer hints of their ancestry? Do the Emar rituals borrow from neighboring cultures concepts, whole rituals, specific ritual actions, terminology, or pantheon? We know that the writing system ultimately derives from Mesopotamia,[7] and one set of rituals is explicitly devoted to the gods of the land of Hatti, the powerful empire that ruled Emar during this period.

Both sets of problems require investigation and response before the Emar rites can be used to contribute reliably to our understanding of ancient Syrian and wider Near Eastern religion of the second millennium B.C.E.

Each of these questions immediately draws us into fields of study involving work that exceeds the defined scope of this project, as well as a

---

[7] Note, however, that the only texts known to have been written at Emar come from the late second millennium, when the Hittites dominated the city. Along with the tablets from the Meskéné/Emar excavations, these evidently include three letters found at Ugarit and published by Daniel Arnaud, "La Syrie du moyen-Euphrate sous le protectorat hittite: l'administration d'après trois lettres inédites," *AuOr* 2 (1984) 179-188.

literature that spans many specializations. As a result, my contribution to these issues will be less systematic than the commentary for the NIN.DINGIR installation, and my work will at times involve me in specialties that reach beyond my own training in Semitic philology. I hope that scholars from several disciplines will take part in future evaluation of Emar religion and that on-going research will benefit from multiple perspectives and fields of expertise.

The question of patterns within Emar ritual is illuminated by the preparation of all the Emar ritual texts which I undertook as a basis for reading the one installation rite. However, this work is less complete and consequently more tentative than that involving the NIN.DINGIR ritual. My conclusions are based on comparison of overall format and function, as well as on compared ritual elements such as the pantheon, personnel, sacred locales, offering terminology, and so forth.

To answer the second question about derivation, I read texts and comment on the ritual traditions from Ugarit, Babylon and Assyria, and Hurro-Hittite Anatolia, and I pursued a range of sources for the Syrian pantheon of the third and second millennia. Again, I compared format and specific ritual elements, giving most weight to activities that are common to ritual from multiple cultural traditions, such as sacrifice and offering. Pantheons take on special significance in this sort of comparison, because data can be drawn from many literary genres and from sites with only a few textual artifacts.

I have arrived at preliminary conclusions regarding these and other questions which call for continued study. I present my views as suggestions and proposals -- certainly not as a final word. It is hoped that within this definition, the final section of the work also will prove useful to scholarship of ancient Near Eastern religion. I have tried to make the core of the study substantial and accurate so that it will contribute even to alternative views.

II. TEXT, NOTES, AND TRANSLATION

A. THE TEXT OF THE NIN.DINGIR RITUAL, EMAR 369

Daniel Arnaud published a composite text of the NIN.DINGIR ritual, Emar 369, based on six tablet fragments representing four manuscripts, which he labeled texts A, B, C, and D. I have added one further fragment, Msk 74286e (Arnaud's Emar 402), which I call text E. We now have the following manuscripts for the NIN.DINGIR ritual:

Text A: Msk 731027 (left side) and Msk 74245 (right side), lines 1-94;

Text B: Msk 731042, lines 20-70, 91, 94;

Text C: Msk 74286a, lines 1, 6-22, 69-91;

Text D: Msk 731061+74274 (Emar VI.1, pp. 85 and 137), lines 47-75;

Text E: Msk 74286e, lines 14-20.

The published edition of Arnaud will surely provide the standard of reference for all work with the Emar texts, so I have adopted his system as far as possible. However, I have made one significant change: because we do have one manuscript that is essentially complete, text A, I have used the lineation from that text as a base for the whole ritual, rather than following Arnaud's composite lineation. It is hoped that this will clarify the precise state of the tablets.

The limitation of the base for this study to one ritual permits the luxury of an expanded text, with all manuscripts presented side by side. Again, this should help the reader to identify fine variations more readily. The work for my dissertation was based entirely on Arnaud's copies, the reliability of which was suggested by the fact that they could correct his transliterations. Since that time I have had the opportunity to collate all the tablets of Emar 369, along with other ritual tablets from Emar, at the Aleppo National Museum in Syria, and the present edition reflects the improvements and precision made possible by that collation. Also, Manfried Dietrich has published his reading of the text since completion of my dissertation, and my new edition benefits from interaction with his work ("Das Einsetzungsritual der Entu von Emar (Emar VI/3, 369)," *UF* 21 (1990) 47-100).

Note that when no text is missing between the two halves of text A, as in line 3, the join is marked by a vertical line (¦). Broken text is placed within brackets ([]) to distinguish it from material that is simply absent. Brackets are closed at the beginning and end of each printed line even if only one break is indicated, in order to avoid ambiguity. The text within the breaks is only restored where specific readings are advocated, and I have made no attempt to fill in entire lines systematically.

1. A *ṭup-pu pár-ṣi* NIN.DINGIR ^{d}IM *ša* ^{uru}[*E-m*]*ar*
C [*š*]*a* NIN.DINGIR *ša* ^{d}IM

A *e-nu-ma* DUMU.MEŠ ^{uru}*E-mar* NIN.DINGIR *a-na* ^{d}IM
C *e-nu-ma* [ ]

2. A *i-na-aš-šu-ú* DUMU.MEŠ ^{uru}*E-mar pu-re-*⸢*e*'⸣ [*i*]*š-tu* É

A ^{d}NIN.URTA *i-laq-qu-ú a-na pa-ni* ^{d}IM

3. A *i-ṣa-ba-*tu_4 DUMU.MÍ *a-i-me-e* DUMU ^{uru}*E-m*¦*ar*

A *it-tar-ra-aṣ i-na* u_4*-mi ša-a-šu-ma* Ì.DU_{10}.GA *iš-tu* É.GAL-*lì*

4. A *ù iš-tu* É ^{d}NIN.KUR *i-laq-qu-mi a-n*¦*a*

A SAG.DU-*ši i-šak-kán-nu* 1 UDU 1 ^{dug}*qú-'u-ú* 1 *ḫi-zi-bu* KAŠ.GEŠTIN

5. A *a-na pa-ni* ^{d}IM *i-na-qu-ú* 1 GÍN KÙ.BABBAR ¦

A *a-na* ^{lú}ḪAL SUM 8 NINDA UD.DU.MEŠ 1 *ḫi-zi-bu it-ti*

A *pu-re-e*

6. A *a-na* É ^{d}NIN.URTA *ú-te-er-ru i-na qa-*¦⸢*du*⸣*-ši ša*

C [*i-na qa-a*]*d*(?)*-du-ši ša*

A *gal-lu-bi* DINGIR.MEŠ ^{uru}*E-mar* *gáb-bá iš-tu*

\-

C *gal-lu-bi* DINGIR.MEŠ ^{uru}[*E-ma*]*r* ⌈*gáb-bá iš*⌉*-tu*

\-

A NINDA.MEŠ KAŠ.MEŠ *ú-qa-da-šu*

\-

C NINDA.M[EŠ]

\-\-\-\-\-\-\-\-\-\-\-\-\-

7. A *i-na ša-ni-i* u_4*-mi gal-lu-bu ša* NIN.DINGIR 1 G[UD]
C *i-*[*na ša-n*]*i-i* u_4*-mi gal-lu-bu ša* NIN.DINGIR 1 GUD

A [6 UDU.ḪI.A]⌈SISKUR⌉[*ša*]⌈NIN.DINGIR *a-na*⌉ É ^{d}IM DU*-ku-ma*
C 6 UDU.ḪI.A SISKUR *ša* NIN.DINGIR *a-na* ^{d}[ ]

A ^{giš}TUKUL DINGIR.MEŠ
C ^{giš}TUKUL DINGIR.MEŠ

8. A *ù* NIN.DINGIR EGIR*-šu-nu* DU*-ku* $^{lú.meš}$*za-ma-*[*ru*]
C *ù* NIN.DINGIR EGIR*-ki-šu-nu* DU*-lak* $^{lú.meš}$*za-ma-ru*

A [ ]
C *a-na pa-n*[*i-š*]*u-nu* DU*-ku a-na* É ^{d}IM

A [*i*]-⌈*ka*⌉*-ša-*⌈*du*⌉*-ma* NIN.DINGIR
C *i-kaš-ša-du-ma* NIN.DINGIR

9. A *a-na pí-i* KÁ *ša ta-ar-ba-ṣi ú-gal-*[ ]
C *i-na pí-i* KÁ *tar-ba-*⌈*ṣi*⌉ [*ú-ga*]*l-la-bu-ši* [x x] x (x)

A [*a-na pa-ni* ^{d}]⌈IM *ep*⌉-[*pa*]*-šu*
C *ku-ba-da a-na pa-ni* ^{d}IM *ep-pa-šu*

10. A *a-bu-ši* ^{giš}TUKUL DINGIR.MEŠ *a-na ku-ba-dì*

\-

C *a-bu-ši* ^{giš}TUKUL DINGIR.MEŠ ⌈*a*⌉-[*na ku-ba-dì*] *ki-mu-ši*

A *i-na-aš-š*[*i*]

\-\-\-\-\-\-\-\-\-\-\-

C *i-na-*[*aš-ši*] *ki-i-me-e ku-ba-da* GAL *ú-gam*$_4$(KÁM)*-ma-ru*

A [x]⌈GÍN KÙ⌉.BABBAR *a-na* ^{lú}ḪAL SUM
C

11. A 1 GUD 6 UDU.ḪI.A *a-na pa-ni* ^{d}IM SISKUR-*u* UZ[U]
C 1 GUD ⸢6⸣ UDU.ḪI.A *a-na pa-ni* [^{d}IM]⸢*i*⸣-*na-qu-u* UZU

A
C G[UD] GARZA UZU UDU GARZA *a-na pa-ni* DINGIR-*lì*

A [*i-šak-ká*]*n-nu* 7 ^{ninda}⸢*nap*⸣-*ta-nu*
C *i-šak-kán-nu* 7 ^{ninda}⸢*nap-ta-nu*⸣

12. A 7 NINDA UD.DU.MEŠ 2 NINDA UD.DU GURUN.MEŠ
C 7 NINDA UD[.DU] ⸢1⸣-*en* NINDA UD.DU GURUN.MEŠ

A *a-na* IGI DINGIR-*lì* [ ]
C *a-na* IGI DINGIR.MEŠ GAR-*nu* KAŠ.GEŠTIN *ka-sà-ti*

A [*ú*]-*ma-lu-u* $^{lú.meš}$*šar*-⸢*ru*⸣
C *ú-ma-lu-u* $^{lú.meš}$⸢*šar*⸣-*ru*

13. A *na-di-nu-ti qí-da-ši* $^{lú.meš}$*ḫu-us-su*
C *na-di-nu qí-da-ši* $^{lú.meš}$*ḫu-us-su*

A 7 [*ù* 7 $^{lú.meš}$*ḫa-am-ša-ú*(?) NA]G-*u ù*
C *a-na* É ^{d}IM KÚ NAG-*u ù*

A LÚ.M[EŠ]
C LÚ.MEŠ *ša* [*qí-d*]*a-ši*

14. A 1 TA.ÀM ^{ninda}*nap-ta-ni* 1 TA.ÀM *ḫi-zi-bu* KAŠ[ ]
C 1 TA.ÀM ^{ninda}*nap-ta-ni* 1 TA.ÀM *ḫi-zi-bu* KAŠ.MEŠ.ŠE
E [*nap-ta-n*]*i* 1 TA.ÀM [*ḫi-zi-bu*]

A [ ] É *i-na-ki-i*[*s*]
C TI-*u* 1 UDU EN É *a-na* É-*šu i-na-ki-is*
E

15. A *ú-šab-šal-ma a-na* KÁ É ^{d}IM *a-na* É NIN.DINGIR
C *ú-še-eb-šal-ma a-na* KÁ É ^{d}IM *a-na* É NIN.DINGIR
E [*m*]*a a-na* KÁ É ^{d}IM ⸢*a*⸣-[*na*]

A [5 ^{giš}BANŠUR.MEŠ]*nap-ta-ni*
C 4 ^{giš}BANŠUR.MEŠ *ša* 3 TA.ÀM ^{ninda}*nap-ta-nu*
E

A *i-ša*[*k-kán-nu*]
C *i-šak-kán-nu*
E

16. A 1 ^{giš}BANŠUR *ša* NIN.DINGIR *ma-ḫi-ri-ti* 1 ^{giš}BANŠ[UR]
C 1 ^{giš}BANŠUR *ša* NIN.DINGIR *ma-ḫi-ri-ti* 1 ^{giš}BANŠUR
E [1 ^{giš}B]ANŠUR *ša* NIN.DINGIR *ma-*[ ]

A [$^{gi]š}$BANŠUR *ša* ^{f}*ma*[*š-ar-ti*]
C *ša* NIN.DINGIR ^{uru}*Šu-mi* 1 ^{giš}BANŠUR *ša* ^{f}*maš-ar-ti*
E

17. A 1 ^{giš}BANŠUR *ša* LÚ LUGAL KUR *ša* ^{uru}*E-mar* 1
C 1 ^{giš}BANŠUR LUGAL KUR
E [*š*]*a*(?) LUGAL KUR

A ^{giš}BAN[ŠUR *ša* LUGAL *ša* ^{uru}*Ša-tap-p*]*í i-na* ŠÀ-*šu-nu*
C *i-na* ŠÀ-*šu-nu*
E *i-na* ŠÀ-*š*[*u-*]

A UZ[U UDU]
C UZU UDU
E

18. A *ù* 1 TA.ÀM NINDA UD.DU SISKUR 1 TA.ÀM
C *ù* 1 TA.ÀM NINDA UD.DU GURUN.MEŠ GAR-*nu* 1 TA.ÀM
E

A DUG KAŠ.Š[E] *i-la-qu-ú*
C DUG KAŠ.MEŠ.ŠE 1 TA.ÀM ^{dug}*maḫ-ḫa-ri* KAŠ.MEŠ.ŠE TI-*u*
E [ ] KAŠ.MEŠ.ŠE TI-*u* [ ]

19. A *a-na* DINGIR.MEŠ *gáb-bi ša* ^{uru}*E-mar* 1 TA.ÀM

C *a-*⌈*na*⌉ [DINGIR].MEŠ *gáb-bi ša* ^{uru}*E-mar* 1 TA.ÀM
E

A ^{ninda}*nap-ta-*[Š]E
------------- -
C ^{ninda}*nap-ta-nu* 1 TA.ÀM *ḫi-zi-bu* KAŠ.MEŠ.ŠE

E [KA]Š.MEŠ.ŠE

A NINDA.GUR$_4$.RA Ì.GIŠ ^{g}[^{iš}ERIN.NA(?)]

C NINDA.⸢GUR$_4$.RA⸣ [Ì.GIŠ(?)] ^{giš}ERIN.NA GURUN.MEŠ

E NINDA.GUR$_4$.RA [ ]

A
C SISKUR *a-na* DINGIR.MEŠ *ú-za-zu*

E

20. A *a-na pa-ni nu-ba-at-ti* Ì.DU$_{10}$.GA *ša* É ^{d}NIN.KUR ⸢*ù*⸣
B [*a-na pa-ni nu-ba*]-⸢*at*⸣-[*ti*]
C *a-na pa-*[*ni nu-ba-a*]*t*(?)-*t*[*i*(?) ^{d}NI]N.KUR *ù*
E [^{d}NIN].KUR *ù*

A [*a-n*]*a* KÁ ^{d}IM ^{lú}ḪAL *i-*[*na*]
B [ ] ^{d}IM ^{lú}ḪAL [ ]
C É.GAL-*lì i-le-qu-nim-ma a-na* KÁ [ ]
E ⸢É⸣.[GAL-*lì*]

A [SAG.DU]
B
C
E

21. A *ša* NIN.DINGIR *i-tab-bu-uk ù* LÚ.MEŠ *ša qí-da-ši*

B
C [*i-tab-bu*]-⸢*uk*⸣ [*ù*] ⸢LÚ⸣.MEŠ *ša qí-da-ši*
E [L]Ú.M[EŠ *ša qí-da-ši*]

A *iš-t*[*u* É ^{d}IM È-*ma a-na* É *a-bi-ši ú-še-e*]*r*(?)-*ra-bu-ši*

---- ------------

B [*iš-t*]*u* É ^{d}IM *uṣ-ṣu-m*[*a*]

C

22. A *i-na qa-dú-ši ša ma-al-lu-ki* DINGIR.MEŠ
B ⸢*i*⸣-*na u$_4$-mi qa-ad-du*<-*ši*> *ša m*[*a-al-lu-ki*]
C

A ^{uru}*E-mar gá*[*b-bá iš-tu* NINDA.MEŠ KAŠ.MEŠ]
B
C

A [*ú-q*]*a-da-šu* ^{d}NIN.KUR.R[A]
B ^{d}NIN.KUR
C [*ú*]-⸢*qa-da*⸣-*šu* [ ]

23. A *i-na* É *a-bi-ši uš-na-al-lu ù* ^{túg}ḪÉ.ME.DA ≈*a* É
B *i-na* É *a-bi-ši* [ ]

A [^{d}NIN.KUR *i-laq-qu-u* (x x) *a-n*]*a* ⸢UGU⸣ ^{d}NIN.KUR
B *a-na* UGU ^{d}NIN.KUR

A ⸢*i*⸣-[*šak-kán-n*]*u*
B *i-ša*[*k-kán-nu*(?)]

24. A 4 ^{giš}BANŠUR *a-na pa-ni* DINGIR.MEŠ GAR-*nu* 1 ^{giš}BANŠUR
B

A *a-na* ^{d}[2 ^{giš}BANŠUR.MEŠ *i-n*]*a*
B *a-na* ^{d}IM 1 ^{giš}BANŠUR ^{d}[*Ḫé-bat*(??)]

A ⸢KI⸣ *qa*-⸢*qa*⸣-*ri*
B

25. A *a-na* DINGIR.MEŠ KI.TA *i-šak-kán-nu i-na* ŠÀ-*šu-nu*
B *i-na* ŠÀ-*šu-nu*

A 12 NINDA.MEŠ *e*-[*bu-u*(?) x NINDA.MEŠ *ra-qa-tu*$_4$(??)]
B 12 NINDA.MEŠ *e-b*[*u*(?)-*u*(?)]

A [x ^{ninda}*na*]*p-ta-ni*.MEŠ
B

26. A 4 TA.ÀM NINDA UD.DU.MEŠ 4 TA.ÀM NINDA UD.DU.MEŠ
B 4 NINDA UD.DU

A GURUN.MEŠ GAR-nu [(?) *k*]*a-sà-ti*
B GURUN GAR-nu U$_4$.7.K[ÁM]

A KAŠ.MEŠ.GEŠTIN
B

27. A *ú-ma-lu-ú* 1 GUD 1 UDU 7 *ḫi-zi-bu* KAŠ.MEŠ.GEŠTIN
B *ú-ma-al-lu-u* 1 GUD 1 UDU [ ]

A 2 ^{giš}PA Š[E *a-na* ^{d}NIN.KUR(??) SISKUR(?)]
B

28. A GARZA GUD GARZA UDU SAG.DU GUD SAG.DU 1 UDU

B

A *a-na* IGI [DINGIR.MEŠ *i-šak-kán-nu*(?) 7 *ḫi-zi-bu*(?)]

B *a-na pa-ni* DINGIR.MEŠ GAR-*nu* 7 *ḫi-z*[*i-bu*]

A [KAŠ.MEŠ].ŠE *i-šak-kán-nu*

B

29. A *i-na ša-ni-i* u_4*-mi ma-al-lu-ku ša* NIN.DINGIR 1 GUD
B *i-na ša-ni-i* u_4*-mi ma-al-l*[*u-ku*]

A ⸢6⸣[UDU.ḪI.A SISKUR *ša* NIN.DINGIR *a-na* É ^{d}IM DU-*k*]*u*
B

A ^{giš}TUKUL DINGIR.MEŠ
B ^{giš}TUKUL DINGIR.MEŠ

30. A *ù* NIN.DINGIR EGIR-*šu-nu* DU-*ku* *ù* $^{lú.meš}$*za-ma-ru*
B NIN.DINGIR EGIR-*šu-nu* D[U(?)-*ku* *ù* $^{lú.meš}$*za-ma-ru*]

A *a-n*[*a pa-ni-šu-nu* DU-*ku* *a-na pa-ni* ^{d}*IM ku*]*-ba-da* GAL
B [*a-na pa-ni-šu-nu* DU-*ku*(?) *a-na* É *tùk-li* KU_4-*ma*(?)]

A *e-pa-šu*
B

Lines 31-36: A and B diverge significantly.

Text A:

31 NIN.DINGIR ^{giš}TUKUL DINGIR.MEŠ *a-na ku-ba-dì*
ta-na-aš-ši ki-i-me-⸢*e*⸣ [*ku-ba-da ú-gam*$_4$*-ma-ru*
(5-7 signs)]-TE(?).MEŠ *ú-kap-pa-ru*

32 *a-na* É ^{d}IM ⸢*ú-še*⸣*-re-bu-ši* 1 GUD 6 UDU.ḪI.A *a-na*
^{d}[IM SISKUR-*u* (6-9 signs) *i-na/la*(?)]*-qú*(?)*-ú*

33 NIN.DINGIR *it-ti* ^{giš}TUKUL DINGIR.MEŠ *ù* ^{lú}*za-ma-ri*
i(?)-⸢*la*(??)⸣-[*ak*(?) *a-na* É *tu-uk-li* KU$_4$-*ma*(?) 1 SILA$_4$ *a*]-*na*
^{d}*A-dam-ma-te-ra*

34 *iš-tu* É *tu-uk-li uṣ-ṣu-ma a-na* É ^{d}*Ga-*| ⸢*ad-da*(?)⸣
D[U(?)-*ku* 1 SILA$_4$ *a-na* ^{d}IM SIS]KUR 1 SILA$_4$ ^{na4}*si-ka-ni*

35 *ša* ^{d}*Ḫé-bat i-na-qu-u* NIN.DINGIR Ì.DU$_{10}$.GA *a-na* |
SAG.DU ^{na4}*si-*⸢*ka-ni ša*⸣ ^{d}*Ḫé-bat i-tab-ba-ak*

36 *i-na u*$_4$*-mi ša-šu-ma a-na* É *Ga-ad-dá* KU$_4$-*ub ù* |
ap-pu-na NU-*ul te-er-ru-ub i-tu-ru-ma a-na* É ^{d}IM

Text B (31-36):

a. 1 SILA$_4$ *a-na* ^{d}*A-dam-ma-te-r*[*i* SISKUR(?) *iš-tu* É *tùk-li*
È-*ma*(?) *a-na* É ^{d}*Ga-ad-dá* DU-*ku*(?)]

b. 1 SILA$_4$ *a-na* ^{d}IM SISKUR-*u* 1 [SILA$_4$ (*a-na*)
^{na4}*si-ka-ni ša* ^{d}*Ḫé-bat* SISKUR(?) NIN.DINGIR
Ì.DU$_{10}$.GA(?)]

c. *a-na* SAG.<DU> ^{na4}*si-ka-ni ša* ^{d}*Ḫ*[*é-bat i-tab-ba-ak*
iš-tu É ^{d}*Ga-ad-dá* È-*ma*(?)]

d. *a-na* É ^{d}IM DU-*ku-ma i-na* [*u*$_4$*-mi ša-šu-ma a-na pa-ni*
^{d}IM *ku-ba-da* GAL *e-pa-šu*(?)]

e. NIN.DINGIR ^{giš}TUKUL DINGIR.MEŠ *a-na ku-ba-*[*dì*
ta-na-aš-ši i-na u$_4$*-mi ša-šu-ma* X *er-ru-ub/bu*(?)]

f. *ù ap-pu-na la-a er-ra-*[*ab*(?)]

g. *ki-i-me-e ku-ba-da ú-gam*$_4$*-ma-r*[*u* (8-12 signs) TE.MEŠ
ú-kap-pa-ru(?)]

h. *a-na* É ^{d}IM *ú-še-er-ra-*[*bu-ši* 1 GUD 6 UDU.ḪI.A *a-na* ^{d}IM
SISKUR GARZA GUD GARZA 6 UDU.ḪI.A]

37. A GARZA GUD GARZA 6 UDU.ḪI.A *a-na* IGI
B *a-na níg-na-ki ša pa-ni*

A ^{d}IM GAR-*nu* 7 ^{ninda}*nap-ta*|*-ni* 7 NINDA UD.DU
B ^{d}IM [ ]

A 2 NINDA UD.DU GURUN.MEŠ *a-na* IGI ^{d}IM GAR-*nu*
B

38. A *ka-sa-ti* KAŠ.MEŠ.GEŠTIN *ù* KAŠ.MEŠ.ŠE

B *ka-sà-ti* KAŠ.MEŠ.GEŠTIN : *ḫa-am-*[*ra*]

A *ú-ma-al-lu-ú* ¦ LÚ.MEŠ *qí-da-ši* $^{\text{lú.meš}}$*ḫu-us-su*

B

A $^{\text{lú.meš}}$*ka-WA-nu* $^{\text{lú.meš}}$*ta-ri-i*

B

39. A *ki-i ka-WA-ni-šu ù ta-re-e-šu* KÚ NAG-*ú* 5 $^{\text{g|iš}}$BANŠUR

B 5 ^{giš}BANŠUR

A *i-na* É *Bu-uK-Ki ša* NIN.DINGIR GAR-*nu* *ki-i ša* u_4*-mi*

B *i-na* É NIN.DINGIR ⸢*i*⸣-[*šak-kán-nu*(?)]

A *gal-lu-bi*

B

40. A *a-na pa-ni nu-ba-at-ti* NIN.DINGIR *a-na* ^{giš}GU.ZA-*šì*

B *a-na pa-ni nu-ba-at-ti* NIN.DINGI[R]

A *ú-š*[*e*]*-ša-bu-ma* ^{giš}BANŠUR GIBIL! *ša* É *a-bi-ši a-na*

B *ša* É *a-bi-ši a-na*

A *pa-ni-ši*

B *pa-ni-ši*

41. A *i-šak-kán-nu* NINDA *i-na* ŠÀ-*šu* <*i-*>*šak-kán-nu* 2

B *i-ša*[*k-kán-nu*]

A NÍG.GEŠTUG KÙ.GI ¦ ⸢*ša*⸣ É *a-bi-ši a-na* GEŠTUG.MEŠ-*ši*

B *ša* É *a-bi-ši a-na* GEŠTUG.ḪI.A-*ši*

A *i-šak-kán-nu iq-qu* KÙ.GI *ša* ^{d}IM

B GAR-*nu* [ ]

42. A *i-na* ŠU-*ti* ZAG-*ša i-šak-kán-nu* SAG.DU-*ša* ¦ TA

B *i-na* ŠU ZAG-*ši* GAR-*nu* SAG.DU-*ši* [ ]

A ^{túg}BAR.SIG ^{síg}ḪÉ.ME.DA *i-ra-ka-su* Ì.DU_{10}.GA ^{d}IM

B

A SISKUR-*u*
B

43. A 10 GÍN KÙ.BABBAR *a-na* ḪAR KÙ.BABBAR *a-na* ŠU-*ti*
B 2 ^{d}LAMA KÙ.GI *ša* 1 GÍN KÙ.GI *a-na* [ ]

A ^{lú}ḪA|L *i-šak-kán-nu* 2 ŠEŠ-*ša* *a-na bu-ú-di*
B 2 ŠEŠ.MEŠ-*ša a-na ti-ik-ki*

A *i-na-aš-šu-ši-ma i-na* É *a-bi-ši*
B *i-na-aš-šu-*[ ]

44. A DU-*lak* $^{lú.meš}$*ši-bu-ut* URU.KI *a-na* GÌR.|MEŠ
B *a-na* GÌR.MEŠ-*ši*

A *i-ma-qu-*tu_4 *tu-dì-it-*tu_4 KÙ.BABBAR 7 GÍN KÙ.BABBAR
B *uš-ḫé-ḫa-nu t*[*u*(?)-]

A *ú-qa-ia-šu-ni-iš-ši*
B *a-na* NÍG.BA-*ša ú-qa-ia-šu-n*[*i-iš-ši*]

45. A ŠEŠ.MEŠ-*ši* DIRI.MEŠ-*ši qí-ša-ti i-q*|*í-šu-ni-iš-ši*
B

A ^{giš}TUKUL DINGIR.MEŠ EGIR-*ša ta-a-lak*
B *ḫa-ṣi-in-nu ša* DINGIR.MEŠ EGIR-*ši* [ ]

A $^{lú.meš}$*za-ma-ru a-na pa-ni-ša* DU-*ku*
B

46. A *ù ki-i i-na* É *a-bi-ši* KU|$_4$-*ub* ^{giš}TUKUL
B *ḫa-ṣi-in-nu*

A DINGIR-*lì* *a-na* UGU ^{d}NIN.KUR U_4.7.KÁM
B DINGIR.MEŠ *a-na* UGU ^{d}[ ]

A *i-*<<*na-*>>*šak-kán-nu*
B

47. A *i-na* u_4*-mi ša-a-šu-ma* 1 T|A.ÀM ^{ninda}*nap-ta-nu* 1 TA.ÀM
B 1 TA.ÀM
D

A *ḫi-zi-bu* KAŠ.ŠE NINDA.GUR_4.RA.MEŠ UZU GUD *ša*
B *ḫi-zi-bu* KAŠ.MEŠ.ŠE NI[NDA]
D [KAŠ.MEŠ.Š]E

A ^{d}NIN.KUR SISKUR
B Ì.GIŠ.MEŠ SISKUR-*e*
D ^{giš}ERIN.NA [SISKUR(?)-]⸢*e*(?)⸣

48. A *a-na gáb-bi* DINGIR.MEŠ ^{uru}|*E-mar ú-za-a-zu i-na*
B *gáb-bá a-na* DINGIR.M[EŠ] *i-na*

D

A 3 u_4-*mi* EZEN *da-at-na-ti ša* NIN.DINGIR
B U_4.3.KÁM EZEN *dá-at-na-ti š*[*a*]

D [*d*]*a-at-na-ti š*[*a* NIN.DINGIR]

A ^{f}*nu-gag*^{ag}-*tu*$_4$ BÚN SUM
B
D ⸢^{f}⸣*nu-ga*$_{14}$(KA)-*ag-tu*$_4$ B[ÚN]

49. A U_4.7.KÁM 2 UDU *i-na u*|$_4$-*mi-ma a-na* DINGIR.MEŠ
B U_4.7.KÁM 2 UDU.ḪI.A *i-na* u_4-*mi-ma* [ ]
D

A *a-na* É-*ša a-na* ^{d}*Ḫé-bat* SISKUR-*u* GARZA UZU 2 SAG.DU
B
D [ ] GARZA UZU [ ]

A UDU *i-na* u_4-*mi-ma*
B
D

50. A *a-na* DINGIR.MEŠ *i-š*|*ak-kán-nu* ^{uzu}ŠÀ MUR *ša*
B *a-na pa-ni* DINGIR.MEŠ *i-šak-kán-nu* [ ]
D

A 1 UDU 1 ^{ninda}*nap-ta-nu* GAL 1 NINDA UD.DU GURUN
B
D [UD]U 1 ^{ninda}*nap-t*[*a-*]

A 1 DUG KAŠ.ŠE 1 ^{dug}*maḫ-ḫa-rù* KAŠ.GEŠTIN
B
D

51. A U_4.7.KÁM ⸢*i-na*⸣ ¦ *u_4-mi-ma a-na* É ^{d}IM SISKUR *ki-i*
B U_4.7.KÁM *i-na* *u_4-mi-ma a-na* É ^{d}[ ]
D

A NIN.DINGIR *a-na šu-kúl-ti-ša uš-šab* 2 ^{d}ALAM(?)
B
D [NI]N.DINGIR *a-na šu-k*[*úl-ti-ša uš-š*]*ab*

A KÙ.GI
B
D

52. A 1 GÍN K¦I.LÁ.BI *a-na* ^{d}IM *ù* ^{d}*Ḫé-bat ú-še-él-la*
B
D [*-š*]*e-el-la*

A [1(?)] UDU *a-na* ^{d}*Ša-aḫ-ri* SISKUR-*u*
B 1 $SILA_4$ *a-na* ^{d}*Ša-aḫ-ri* SISKUR-*u*
D [ ] x x ^{d}*Ša-aḫ-ri* SISKUR-[ ]

----

53. A 7 *ù* ¦ 7 $^{lú.meš}$*ḫa-am-ša-ú* U_4.2.KÁM *i-na* É NIN.DINGIR
B ⸢7(?)⸣[ ]
D [ ] x

A KÚ NAG-*u* 1 TA.ÀM 1 ^{giš}PA ZÌ ŠE 1 TA.ÀM ^{dug}*a-na-ti*
B 1 TA.ÀM 1 ^{giš}PA ŠE 1 TA.À[M]
D KÚ NAG-*u* 1 TA.ÀM 1 ^{giš}PA ZÌ [ ]

A KAŠ.Ú.SA-*a*
B
D

54. A *i-na-*⸢*di*⸣*-nu-ni-iš-ši ù* LÚ.MEŠ *ša qí-da-ši*
B *i-na-di-nu-ni-iš-ši* LÚ.MEŠ *ša q*[*í-*]
D [*i-n*]*a-di-nu-ni-iš-ši*

A U_4.7.KÁM *i-na* É-⸢*ša*⸣ KÚ NAG 7 TA.ÀM ^{ninda}*nap-ta-ni*
B
D [NA]G-*u* 5 TA.ÀM ^{ninda}*nap-ta-ni*

A 7 TA.ÀM *ḫi-zi-bu*
B
D 7 [TA.ÀM *ḫi-z*]*i-bu*

55. A KAŠ.[MEŠ.Š]E *i-laq-qu-u* NIN.DINGIR *ma-ḫi-ri-*tu_4
B NIN.DINGIR *ma-ḫi-ri-*tu_4
D KAŠ.ŠE TI-*u*

A NIN.DINGIR *ša* ^{d}KUR [E]N *Šu-ú-mi* ^{f}*ma-aš-ar-*tu_4 LUGAL
B NIN.DINGIR *š*[*a*]
D [LUGA]L

A KUR ^{uru}*E-mar*
B
D KUR

56. A [LUGAL *š*]*a* ^{uru}*Ša-tap-pí* ^{giš}BANŠUR.MEŠ-*šu-nu qa-du* UZU
B
D ^{giš}BANŠUR.MEŠ-*šu-nu qa-du* [ ]

A GUD UZU UDU 7 NINDA UD.DU GURUN.MEŠ
B 7! NINDA UD.DU.MEŠ GURUN.MEŠ
D [UZ]U UDU

A 7 DUG KAŠ.MEŠ.ŠE
B ⸢7(?)⸣ DUG.MEŠ K[AŠ]
D

57. A [7(?) ^{dug}]*maḫ-ḫa-ri* KAŠ.MEŠ.ŠE *ša* U_4.7.KÁM
B
D

A ^{uzu}*na-ag-la-bu* ⸢*a*⸣-*na* NIN.DINGIR *ša* ^{d}IM ^{uzu}*ka-bar-*tu_4
B
D

A *a-na* NIN.DINGIR ^{d}KUR EN *Šu-ú-mi*
B
D

58. A [^{uzu}*sí*]*l-qu a-na* ^{f}*ma-aš-ar-ti* ^{uzu}ELLÁG *a-na* LUGAL KUR
B LUGAL KUR
D [ ]x u_4(?)-*mi ma-qu-u* ELLÁG(?) GUD *ša a-na*

A ^{uru}*E-mar* ^{uzu}ELLÁG LUGAL *ša Ša-tap-pí*
B TI-*qé*
D ^{d}[IM(?) x x] x x

A
B *i-na* u_4*-mi* E[GIR(?)-*ki*]
D

59. A [*i-na* x u_4]-⌜*mi*⌝ 2 UDU *a-na* ^{d}IM SISKUR // *ta-ši-ia-ti*
B *ù* u_4*-mi* EGIR-*ki ú-ma-*x[ ]
D [ ]x KÙ.GI *i-na* u_4*-m*[*i*] x-*ri-i*

A *ú-ma-al-lu-ú* // É ^{d}IM KÚ NAG-*u* //
B
D [ ] IGI(?) DINGIR.MEŠ GAR-*nu i-na* u_4*-mi*

A
B
D *ša-a-šu*

60. A [^{d}NIN.KUR *ú-še*]*-et-bu-ú ù* ^{túg}ḪÉ.ME.DA *ša* ^{d}NIN.KUR
B *ú-še-et-bu-ú ù* ^{túg}[ḪÉ.ME.DA]
D [ ]NIN.KUR

A *it-ti* NINDA.MEŠ KAŠ.MEŠ *a-na* É ^{d}NIN.KUR *ú-ta-ru-šu*
B
D *it-ti* NINDA.MEŠ KAŠ.MEŠ *a-na* É ^{d}NIN.KUR

A
B NIN.DINGIR *iš-tu* É *uṣ-*[*ṣi-ma*]
D [ ] É È-*ma*

61. A 1(?) x [(x) ^{túg}ÍB.LÁ(?)] *bi-ir-mi ša* É *a-bi-ši* SAG.DU-*ša*
B
D TA ^{túg}ÍB.LÁ *bi-ir-mi ša* É AD-⌜*šu*(?)⌝

A *ki-i* É.GI_4.A *ú-kat-ta-mu*
B *ú-kat-ta-mu*
D [*ki-i* É.GI]$_4$.A *ú-kat-ta-mu*

62. A 2 $^{f.m}$[^{eš} *ta-(ap-)p*]*u-ta-ši ki-i-ma ka-al-la-ti e-pí-qa-ši*
B 2 ^{f}[ ]
D 2 ^{f}*ta-ap-pu-ta-ši ki-i-ma* É.GI_4.A

A *a-na pa-ni nu-ba-at-ti*
B
D [ ]*-ba-at-ti*

63. A 1 GUD 7 [UDU.ḪI].A 3 SILA$_4$.MEŠ
B 1 GUD 7 UDU.ḪI.A 3 SILA$_4$ [ ]
D 1 GUD 7 UDU.ḪI.A 3 SILA$_4$

A <<GIŠ>> KI GI.IZI.LÁ *ù* $^{lú.meš}$<*za-ma-ru*>
B
D KI GI.IZI.LÁ *ù* $^{lú.meš}$*za-ma-*[*ru*]

A *a-na pa-ni-ša* DU-*ku ù* ^{giš}TUKUL DINGIR.MEŠ
B *ša* DINGIR.MEŠ
D [*ḫa*]-*ṣi-in-nu ša* DINGIR.MEŠ

64. A EGIR DU-[*la*]*k a-na* É *tu-uk-li* KU$_4$-*ma* 1 SILA$_4$
B EGIR-*ši* DU-*lak* [ ]
D EGIR DU *lak a-na* É *tùk-li* KU$_4$-*ma* [ ]

A ^{d}*A-dam-ma-te-ra* SISKUR *iš-tu* É *tu-uk*<*-li*>
B *iš-tu* É *tùk-li*
D [^{d}*A-dam-ma-t*]*e-ri* ⌈SISKUR⌉-*u* TA É *tùk-li*

A È-*ma*
B È-[ ]
D È-*ma*

65. A *a-na* É ⌈^{d}⌉NIN.KUR DU-*lak* 1 SILA$_4$ *a-na* ^{d}NIN.KUR
B
D *ana*(DIŠ) É ^{d}N[IN].KUR DU-*lak* [.KU]R

A SISKUR 3 <^{ninda}>*nap-ta-ni*.MEŠ *a-na* DINGIR.MEŠ GAR-*an*
B
D BAL-*qí* 3 ^{ninda}*nap-ta-ni*.MEŠ *a-na* DINGIR.MEŠ GAR-*an*

66. A *iš-tu* <É> ^{d}NI¦N.KUR È-*ma a-na* É ^{d}IM *ta-al-la-ak*
B ⌈*iš*⌉-*tu* É ^{d}NIN.KUR ⌈È⌉-[ ]
D [ ]⌈È⌉-*ma ana* É ^{d}IM *ta-a-lak*

A 1 SILA$_4$ *a-na* <^{d}IM> SISKUR 7 ^{ninda}*nap-ta-ni*.MEŠ
B
D 1 SILA$_4$ *a-na* ^{d}IM BAL-*qí* [ME]Š

67. A *a-na pa-ni* DINGIR.MEŠ | GAR-*an ka-sa-ti*
B [*ka*]-*sà-ti*
D *a-na pa-ni* DINGIR.MEŠ GAR-*an ka-sà-ti*

A KAŠ.GEŠTIN *tu-ma-al-la* LÚ.MEŠ *qí-da-ši* $^{\text{lú.meš}}$*ši-bu-ut*
B KAŠ.GEŠTIN *t*[*u-*]
D KAŠ.GEŠTIN *tu-ma-al-la* [ ]-*ši* $^{\text{lú.meš}}$*ši-bu-ut*

A <URU.KI>
B
D <URU.KI>

68. A EGIR-*ki* DU-*ku a-na* | É ^{d}IM KÚ NAG 1 GUD *ša-a-šu*
B [GU]D *ša-a-šu*
D EGIR-*ki* DU-*ku ana* É ^{d}IM KÚ NAG-⌜*u*⌝ [ ]

A 7 UDU.ḪI.A *ša a-na pa-ni* NIN.DINGIR DU-*ku*
B 7 UD[U]
D 7 UDU.ḪI.A *ša a-na pa-ni* NIN.DINGIR DU-*ku* TA-*qú*

69. A *a-na* É EN É *ú-te-er-ru-šu-nu-*[*ti*]
B [-*e*]*r-ru-šu-n*[*u-*]
C [E]N(?) É
D x (x) DUB DIŠ x x [ ] [*ú-te-er-r*]*u-šu-nu-ti*

A *ki-i-me-e* $^{\text{lú.meš}}$*ši-bu-ut* URU.KI KÚ NAG 1 TÚG SIG$_5$
B
C
D *ki-i-me-e* $^{\text{lú.meš}}$*ši-bu-ut* URU KÚ NAG-u

70. A *a-na lu-bu-ši-ša i-na-da-n*|*u* 1 ^{giš}NÁ 1 ^{giš}GU.ZA
B
C [-*n*]*a lu-bu-ši-ša*
D [ ] *lu-bu-ši-ša i-na-da-nu* 1 ^{giš}NÁ 1 ^{giš}GU.ZA

A 1 ^{giš}GÌR.GUB *i-na-di-nu-ni-ši i-na* ŠÀ ^{giš}NÁ
B [-*n*]*i-iš-ši* [ ]
C [-*n*]*a* ŠÀ ^{giš}NÁ
D ^{giš}GÌR.GUB *i-n*[*a-*]

71. A *ša-a-šu* TÚG.GAR URI *ša* É x|*ur*(?)-*ši-ša* KÙ.GA
C *ša-a-šu* [TÚG] x x E [ ]
D *ša-a-šu* TÚG.GAR URI *ša* É *ur-ši-ša* KÙ.GA

A *ù-ma-aṣ-ṣu-u* ^{giš}BANŠUR *ša* ^{d}*Ḫu-le-e-li*
C [ ] ^{d}*Ḫu-le-li*
D *ú-ma-aṣ-ṣu-u* [ ]⸢^{d}⸣*Ḫu-le-e-li*

72. A *a-na* KÁ *re-ši-ša* GAR-*nu*
C *a-na* KÁ *re-ši-ši i-šak-kán-nu*
D *a-na* KÁ *re-ši-ša* GAR-*nu*

A 3 TA.[À]M ^{ninda}*nap-ta-ni* 1 NINDA UD.DU GURUN
C 3 [ ] [ ] ⸢NINDA⸣ UD.DU GURUN.MEŠ
D 3 TA.ÀM ^{ninda}*nap-*[ ]

A 1 *ḫi-zi-bu* KAŠ.GEŠTIN SÍG *zi-ir-tu*$_4$
C 1 *ḫi-zi-bu* KAŠ.MEŠ.GEŠTIN SÍG *zi-ir-tu*$_4$
D [GEŠTI]N SÍG *za-zi-tu*$_4$

73. A *i-na* ^{giš}BANŠUR *ša-a-šu* GAR-*nu* $^{\text{l|ú}}$*za-ma-ru* ^{d}*Ḫu-le-la*
C *i-na* ^{giš}BANŠUR *ša-a-šu* GAR-*nu* [ ]⸢*Ḫu-le*⸣*-la*
D *i-na* ^{giš}BANŠUR *ša-a-šu* GAR-*nu* ^{lú}*za-ma-*[ ]

A *i-za-am-ma-ru* GARZA ^{giš}BANŠUR *ša-a-šu*
C *i-za-ma-rù* GARZA ^{giš}BANŠUR *ša-a-šu*
D [*i-za-a*]*m-ma-ru* GARZA ^{giš}BANŠUR *ša-a-šu*

74. A *i-laq-qé ù* NIN-*ši* GÌR.MEŠ-*ši*
C ^{lú}*za-ma-ru* TI-*u* NIN-*ši* GÌR.MEŠ-*ši*
D TI-*u* NIN-*ši* GÌR.M[EŠ]

A ⸢*i*⸣-[*m*]*a-as-si ù i-na* A.MEŠ *ša* GÌR.MEŠ-*ša*
C *i-ma-as-si* ⸢*i*⸣-[*na*] GÌR.MEŠ-*ša*
D [ ]-⸢*ši*(?)⸣

A *i-ma-su-ú* 1 ŠU.GUR KÙ.BABBAR
C *ú-ma-as-su-u* ŠU.GUR KÙ.BABBAR
D ⸢*i-ma*⸣*-su-u*(?) x ⸢ŠU.GUR KÙ.BABBAR⸣

75. A 1/2 GÍN KÙ.BABBAR *i-šak-kán-nu* NIN-*ši* TA|-*qé*

C 1/2 GÍN KÙ.BABBAR NIN-*ši* TI-*qé*

D 1/2 GÍN KÙ.BABBAR ⸢*i*⸣-[ ]

A NIN.DINGIR *i-na* ^{giš}NÁ-*ša te-el-la-ma ta-at-ta-al*

C NIN.DINGIR *i-na* ^{giš}N]Á *te-la-ma ta-at-ta-a-al*

D

76. A *i-na* U_4.7.KÁM 1 GUD *ša a-na pa-ni* NIN.[DINGI]R DU-*ku*
C *i-na* U_4.8.KÁM 1 GUD *ša a-na pa-ni* NIN.DINGIR DU-*ku*

A *a-na* É *a-bi-ši* LÚ.MEŠ *qí-da-ši*
C *a-na* É AD-*ši*

77. A *i-pa-al-<la->ku-šu* *it-ti a-ḫa-mèš*
C *i-pa-la-ku-šu* LÚ.MEŠ *ša qí-da-ši it-ti a-ḫa-mèš*

A *ú-za-a-[zu]-šu* ^{uzu}ELLÁG GUD *ù* ḪA.LA-*šu* LÚ LUGAL KUR
C *ú-za-zu-šu* ^{uzu}ELLÁG GUD *ù* ḪA.LA-*šu* LUGAL KUR

A TI-*qé*
C TI-*qé*

78. A ^{uzu}*ḫa-ṣi-te ù* ḪA.LA-*šu* ^{uzu}SAG.DU ¦
C ^{uzu}*ḫa-ṣi-te ù* ḪA.LA-*šu* SAG.DU GUD

A x ŠÀ *ir-ri* ^{uzu}Ì.UDU ^{lú}ḪAL TI-*qé*
C ^{uzu}ŠÀ.MEŠ GUD ^{uzu}Ì.UDU GUD 1 KUŠ GUD ^{lú}ḪAL TI-*qé*

79. A ^{uzu}MUR : *ḫa-še-e ù* ḪA.LA-*šu* $^{lú.meš}$*za-ma-ru* [T]I-*qé*
C ^{uzu}*ḫa-še* *ù* ḪA.LA $^{lú.meš}$*za-ma-rù*

A *mi-ši-il* ^{uzu}ŠÀ *ir-ri-šu*
C *mi-ši-il* ^{uzu}ŠÀ.MEŠ-*šu*

80. A LÚ.MEŠ *qí-da-ši* KÚ 4 ^{giš}BANŠUR *ša a-ni*
C LÚ.MEŠ *ša qí-da-*⌜*ši*⌝ KÚ 4 ^{giš}BANŠUR.MEŠ *ša a-na*

A DINGIR.MEŠ ¦ GAR-*nu i-na* ŠÀ-*šu-nu*
C DINGIR.MEŠ GAR-*nu* ⌜*i*⌝-[*n*]*a* ŠÀ-*šu-nu*

A 2 ^{giš}BANŠUR KÙ.GA 2 ^{giš}BANŠUR
C 2 ^{giš}BANŠUR KÙ.GA 2 ^{giš}BANŠUR.MEŠ

81. A *la-a* KÙ.GA ^{lú}ḪAL ^{lú}*za-am-ma-rù it-ti a-ḫa-m*¦*èš*
C NU KÙ.GA ^{lú}ḪAL $^{lú.meš}$[ ] *it-ti a-ḫa-mèš*

A *i-zu-zu ù* KUŠ.MEŠ UDU.ḪI.A *gáb-bi*
C *i-za-az-zu ù* K[UŠ].⌜A⌝ *gáb-bá*

82. A ^{lú}ḪAL $^{\text{lú.meš}}$<*za-ma-ru*> *it-ti a-ḫa-mèš i-zu-zu*

C ^{lú}ḪAL $^{\text{lú.meš}}$*za-ma-rù* *i-za-zu*

A 3 KU¦Š GUD

C 1 KUŠ GUD *ša* [x (x)] x NIN.DINGIR *a-na* ^{d}NIN.KUR

A ^{lú}ḪAL *i-la-aq-qè*

C SISKUR-u ^{l}[^{ú}ḪAL] ⸢TI⸣-*qé*

83. A U_4.7.KÁM ^{lú}ḪAL $^{\text{lú.meš}}$*za-ma-ru* 1 TA.ÀM ^{ninda}*nap-t¦a-nu*

- -

C U_4.7.KÁM ^{lú}ḪAL $^{\text{lú.meš}}$*za-ma-rù* 1 TA.ÀM ^{ninda}*nap-ta-ni*

A 1 TA.ÀM DUG KAŠ.ŠE TI-*u*

- -

C 1 TA.ÀM 1 DUG KA[Š].MEŠ.ŠE TI-*u*

C ^{uzu}*ḫa-ṣi-ti* GUD.ḪI.A *ù* UDU.ḪI.A *ša gáb-bi* U_4.ḪI.A

C ^{lú}ḪAL TI-*qé* ^{uzu}MUR GUD.ḪI.A *ù* UDU.ḪI.A ⸢*gáb*⸣-*bi*

- -

C $^{\text{lú.meš}}$*za-ma-rù* TI-*qé* UZU SISKUR GUD *a-na* DINGIR.MEŠ

- -

C *ú-za-zu*

- - - - -

84. A *ki-i* NIN.DINGIR *i-na šu-kúl-ti-ša uš-šab*

C *ki-i* NIN.DINGIR *i-na šu-*⸢*kúl*⸣*-ti-ši uš-*[*ša*]*b* 5 GÍN

- -

A 1 GÍN K[Ù].BABBAR $^{\text{lú.meš}}$*za-ma-ru*

C NÍG.BA ^{lú}ḪAL 1 GÍN NÍG<.BA> $^{\text{lú.meš}}$*za-ma-ri*

- -

A TI-qé

C

85. A *i-na* MU SIG_5.GA 30 ^{giš}PA ŠE

C *i-na* M[U] SIG_5 30 ^{giš}PA ŠE ŠE.BA-*ši ša* NIN.DINGIR

A *iš-tu* É *tùk-li* *i-¦na-an-di-nu-ni-ši i-na*

C *iš-tu* É DINGIR-*lì* S[UM(?)-*n*]*u*(?) *ù šum-*[*ma*(?)]

A MU *la-a* SIG_5 15 ^{giš}PA ŠE TI

C [MU NU SIG_5 15 ^{giš}PA] ŠE ŠE.BA-*ši* x x

86. A 6 ME SÍG 2 ^{dug}*ḫi-it-tá* Ì.[G]IŠ 1 ^{dug}*za-du* Ì.GIŠ
C (traces)

A 4 *me-at* ^{giš}ŠIM
C

87. A 5 *ḫu-bu* KAŠ.GEŠTIN 2 ^{giš}*ku-du-* | *ru* GEŠTIN
C (broken)

A 2 ^{giš}*ku-du-ru* ^{giš}ḪAŠḪUR
C

88. A 2 ^{giš}*ku-du-ru* ^{giš}ḪAŠḪUR.KUR.RA 1 | DUG GA.MEŠ
C

A 1 GA.ḪAB GAL 1 ^{giš}PA ZÍZ 1 ^{giš}PA ŠIM
C [Š]IM

89. A 3 *qú-'u-ú* KAŠ.Ú.SA-*a* ⸢2⸣ | *ta-pal* ^{kuš}E.SIR
C 3 ^{dug}*qú-'u-u* K[AŠ(?)]

A 2 ^{kuš}ŠUḪUB 2 MAŠ.DÀ
C [ ] x MAS.DÀ

90. A 2 KU_6 4 MUŠEN.MEŠ *ša* MU.1.KÁM [*i*]*š-tu*

C 4 TU.MUŠEN.MEŠ *ša* MU.1.KÁM *iš-tu* [ ]

A É DINGIR.MEŠ *i-na-an-di-nu-ši*

C

91. A *ki-i-me-e* NIN.DINGIR EGIR[(-*ki*)] | *ši-im-*⸢*ti*⸣
B
C (edge) *ù ki-i-me-e* NIN.DINGIR EGIR-*ki* *ši-i*[*m-*]

A ⸢*ta*(?)-(*a*)⸣-[*l*]*ak* 1 GUD 1 UDU *i-na* É *i-pa-la-ku*
B (edge) [*ta-a*]-*lak*
C

92. A 1 UDU 1 ^{dug}*za-du* Ì.GIŠ ⸢1⸣ | *ḫi-zi-bu* 2 x x x -*ra*

A *a-na* ^{d}*Ša-aḫ-ri* SISKUR

93. A KUŠ GUD *ša-a-šu* ^{lú} | ḪAL TI-*qé* 1 UDU I ⸢BI⸣ AD TI

A *ú-nu-tù-ú*

94. A *an-nu-ti ša* É [*a*]-*bi-ši*
B É *a-bi-šu pár-ṣi-ša*

A URU.KI *ul mì-im-ma*
B *i-na-aš-ši* URU.KI *ú-ul mi-im-ma*

B. NOTES TO THE TEXT

The following notes deal with textual matters exclusively. Other problems and observations will be discussed in the commentary which follows. Diverse situations require textual comment:

-- all variations between manuscripts;
-- corrections to readings found in Daniel Arnaud's composite text or notes;
-- new restorations for manuscript breaks;
-- miscellaneous problems.

This text edition revises or supplements Arnaud's readings at many points. In order to help the reader identify these changes, entries involving new readings are marked with an asterisk (*). Differences with the readings from Dietrich's new article will be discussed where significant, but not specially marked. Finally, my own edition has been improved and corrected in revision, and these changes will only receive comment where based on notable observations in collation.

All NIN.DINGIR ritual manuscripts appear to consist of instructions for a single rite, not multiple installation traditions. Real variation in the events described is limited, and the wording is strongly fixed. Most differences involve single words, parts of words, or spelling. Texts C and D appear to concur with the order and wording of our primary manuscript, text A, in most cases, while text B strays furthest from the majority version. This manuscript offers the greatest number of alternative wordings, and in lines 31-36 places the *kubadu*-ceremony after the procession to visit Adammatera (presumably at the *bīt tukli*) and the *bīt Gadda*, reversing the order found in text A. The B version is simpler, since the A text requires a separate procession to these locales from ᵈIM's temple with return afterward (line 36). Text E is too short to evaluate. Dietrich (pp. 59-76) discusses the detail of this variation at some length.

At the important transition to the last day of the installation ceremony we find considerable variation between texts A, B, and D. Unfortunately, B and D are too broken to provide a coherent sequence of action. Text A shows signs of corruption, and the introductory time formula is broken away (line 59), so we are left with no coherent version.

Texts B and C display scattered small circular imprints which examination of the tablets shows to penetrate all the way through, apparently for more even baking. Not all the large ritual tablets from Emar have these holes, but all the ritual tablets were found already baked. All the texts indicate some major ritual units by horizontal dividing lines, though the choice of units varies. These lines are marked in my edition according to their actual extent; not all of them cross the entire tablet.

The sample sizes are unequal, but text A nevertheless displays a higher frequency of scribal errors than the other texts. Compare the following, which belong to text A unless noted otherwise:

- -- omitted sign: lines 41, 64, 65, 66, 77; text B, 22, (31-36)c; text C, 84(?);
- -- omitted word: lines 63, 64(?), 66, 67, 82; text D, 67;
- -- added incorrect sign: lines 46, 63;
- -- substituted incorrect sign: lines 18, 40, 51(?), 75(?); text D, 61, 68(?);
- -- other corruptions: lines 59-60, at least three truncated sentences.

This list does not include numbers, which can be difficult to evaluate. Collation clarified several problematic numbers and showed that these were written more consistently than apparent in the published copy. For instance the fourth wedge of the number "4" is placed below the first wedge, at the left, distinguishing it from NINDA/GAR. The number "7" is formed in the same manner, and all the wedges are consistently visible. The errors in text A do not mean the tablet is poorly written; on the contrary, all the manuscripts are remarkably clear and coherent. The quality of text A does seem to deteriorate somewhat toward the end, however.

The plural marker MEŠ offers a particular problem. Collation shows that all the Emar 369 tablets form MEŠ with one vertical wedge followed by two or three horizontals, often written almost directly over each other, and sometimes angled slightly downward. In many cases I was able to discern more horizontals than copied by Arnaud, and I was not always certain that I could identify every separate impression. Therefore, while Dietrich has carefully distinguished multiple forms of the plural marker, I prefer to identify all these by the single MEŠ-sign, in the belief that the variations were intended by the scribes to represent only MEŠ.

Arnaud does not mark the reverse of Emar 369, apparently because he produces a composite text. The actual reverse of the A text begins with line 59. On the other hand, although Emar 370 exists in only one copy, and the reverse begins with line 55, Arnaud marks the whole text with "prime" after each line number (so, 370.1'). Rather than reevaluate every text to determine where the reverse begins, I have referred to all Emar lines by number only, without "prime."

Line:

1. Note *ša* twice in text C.
   *Text C omits reference to Emar.
   Text C jumps from line 1 to line 6, omitting details of the NIN.DINGIR's selection.
5. Text A does show 8 dried cakes (NINDA UD.DU), but we expect 7, from lines 37, 56, etc.
6. *Either [-*a*]*d*- or [-*q*]*a*- may fit the traces in the copy for text C. I prefer the former, comparing Emar 370.2, 385.3, etc.
   *Both A and C read *ša gal-lu-bi*.
7. Text C omits É, the temple of ^{d}IM. This could be a scribal error, though the meaning is unaffected.
   The one significant gap in text A consists of a large block missing from the right-hand piece (Msk 74245) from line 7 to line 34, leaving only the far right margin intact.
8. Text C adds *-ki-* after EGIR, and uses the singular verb with plural subject, DU-*lak*. This could be either masculine or feminine.
   *Arnaud omits É (^{d}IM), of text C.
   *A break after DU-*ku* in text C has room for up to three more signs, at the end of the C line, but the context requires nothing. Dietrich adds [-*ma*], which is possible, though the conjunction is used irregularly in Emar 369.
   *Text C reads *i-kaš-ša-du-ma*, vs. -⸢*ka*⸣- in A. Dietrich reads -*kà*- (GA) for -*kaš*- in C but I see no verticals.
9. Text C reads *i-na* for *a-na* before *pí-i*.

*Text A reads KÁ *ša*..., and text C spells the courtyard, *tar-ba-*⌜*ṣi*⌝.

*Text C, the only textual witness for the *kubadu* in line 9, does have room for [*ù ki-i-me-e*] at the end of its line, though the traces are ambiguous.

The traces of one vertical and one horizontal do not disprove ⌜*-me-e*⌝, but the relation between them is not quite right.

The first vowel in the I-weak verbs of the ritual should be Assyrian /*e*/: see line 30A, *e-pa-šu* (cf. Babylonian *ippeš* and *ippuš*); 62A, *e-pí-qa-ši*.

*The right margin of text A shows a clear *-šu*, above BABBAR of line 10. The preceding traces show the upper parts of the IM- and IB-signs.

10. The NIN.DINGIR's father bears the weapon of the gods "for the *kubadu*" in text A, and this phrase fits the short break in text C as well, so that *ki-mu-ši*, "in her stead," should be a further qualification, not a substitute for *a-na ku-ba-dì*.

*Judging by the size of the gap in the A text after *i-na-aš-š*[*i*], the reference in C to completing (*gamāru*) the *kubadu* should precede the gift to the [lú]ḪAL. The clause fits in the gap, with room to spare. The A text traces should be read [x(some number)] ⌜GÍN KÙ⌝.BABBAR, according to the idiom found also in line 5.

11. *The logogram GARZA is formed by the signs PA+AN, and it appears twice in text C. Arnaud understands these to be scribal errors, but the best solution to these and other problematic examples of PA+AN is to read GARZA for the noun *parṣu*, perhaps "ritual portion" (see the commentary).

*Text A reads [ninda]⌜*nap*⌝*-ta-nu*. The traces in text C show *-nu* also, and we have no text with *-ni*.

12. Collation shows the number 7, not 6, in text C.

*Read NINDA UD.*DU* GURUN.MEŠ in texts A and C.

*DINGIR-*lì* is clear in text A (vs. DINGIR.MEŠ).

*GAR-*un* in Arnaud's edition appears to be a typographical error for GAR-*nu*.

Dietrich reads NAR?-*r*[*u*](A) and *n*[*a*]?-*ru*(C), but see the commentary.

13. *Text C omits *-ti* on *na-di-nu*.

The number 7 in text A suggests reference to the *ḫamša'u*-men who appear in line 53A, though this remains a guess.

14. Text C reads É-*šu*, while -*šu* is lacking in A.

15. Text C reads *ú-še-eb-šal-ma*, and *nap-ta-nu*.

The gap in text A contained mention of 5 tables, not 4, to match the extra table listed in line 17A and the added dignitary, the king of Šatappi, in lines 56A and 58A. This could indicate a connection between text A and the nearby cult center of ᵈKUR/Dagan at Šatappi, with its *kissu* ritual set.

17. *The title LÚ LUGAL KUR appears in text A both here and in line 79, during the apportionment of meats. We should not take LÚ to be a scribal error. The angle-wedge at the left margin of text E could belong to either -*ša* or LÚ, but the fact that E omits the king of Šatappi makes it unlikely that it follows A with LÚ LUGAL.

*Following lines 56 and 58, the fifth table belongs to the king of Šatappi, in text A. However, the omission of this table in text C is not accidental, and should not be restored. Line 15C mentions only 4 tables, and the addition of *ša* ᵘʳᵘ*E-mar* in line 17A is necessary only because a second king is introduced.

18. *The text A scribe introduces some confusion by substituting SISKUR for the similar sign, GURUN. The next sign (GAR? only one vertical is clear) is smudged, followed by 1 TA.ÀM. Perhaps the scribe began to write the expected GAR, saw that it made no sense after SISKUR, and erased it, going on to "1". This would explain why there is no -*nu*, as in C.

Text A uses no plural marker after DUG KAŠ.

*Read *i-la-qu-ú* in text A, not -*laq*-.

19. The horizontal divider below line 19 of A continues all the way across the tablet, but it dips somewhat to the right, and the scribe wrote the next two lines over it, so that on the right margin it emerges as an extension of the ŠI-sign in line 21.

*No text shows -*ni* with *nap-ta*-.

*No text reads GURUN.MEŠ Ì.GIŠ and only text C has both oil and fruit, ᵍⁱˢERIN.NA GURUN.MEŠ. Texts A and C may be equivalent, here. Dietrich suggests SI[SKUR...] at the end of text A, which could fit the one visible horizontal.

Text A probably has no room for the clause in C with the verb *zâzu*. The last sign in C is written with four horizontals, like SU.

20. Dietrich reads [*nu-ba-a*]*t-t*[*i*(?)] in B, which properly places the first traces. This fits the lineation of B in this section, where the break at the right would cover about 20 signs. This line of text B would then begin with line 20(A), and there should be a horizontal divider above, as in texts A, C, and E. Collation indicates the two lower horizontals and the vertical of the AD-sign, only.

*No version appears to have *i-li-qu*, and text C should read *i-le-qu-nim-ma*, not *-qu-u ù*.

Restore *i*-[*na* SAG.DU], following the anointing idiom of lines 4 and 35A.

21. Arnaud uses texts A and B to restore *iš-tu* É ^{d}IM *uṣ-ṣu-m*[*a a-na* É *a-bi-ši ú-še-e*]*r-ra-bu-ši*, and this restoration makes sense. The final verb indicates that the priestess is returned to her father's house, from which she departs on the next day in lines 29-30. The restoration is slightly long for the space, so I have guessed È for *uṣ-ṣu*, to gain a fraction.

22. Text B appears to omit <*-ši*> in *qadduši*, or *-ša* is substituted accidentally. Text A begins *i-na qa-dú-ši*, without affecting the meaning.

*The gap in line 22 can be restored by comparison with the *kissu* text, 385.4, which likewise involves setting tables for the gods and laying down ^{d}NIN.KUR on the sanctification day. The verb in text A is then [*ú-q*]*a-da-šu*, and the traces of text C suit this meaning. Collation shows the full signs for *-da-šu* in A, though the lower horizontals of each were smudged by angle wedges written in the line below.

Text A spells the divine name ^{d}NIN.KUR.R[A]. The leading four horizontals of RA are clear.

23. *Fill in the A text break with [^{d}NIN.KUR *i-laq-qu-u*], with reference to the ^{túg}ḪÉ.ME.DA in line 60 and the association of the verbs *leqû* and *târu* (D) in lines 2 and 6.

The NU-sign at the end of text A is visible after the break, wrapped around on the reverse of the tablet.

24. Text B indicates that ^{d}IM receives the first table, but we are left to guess the second deity -- perhaps Hebat? This text omits *a-na* after the second table, possibly using a simple genitive construction.

*The end of line 24 in text A should include "two tables" for the underworld gods, and Arnaud's *Ša-aḫ-ri* does not allow for this.

Comparison with 385.9 offers a likely parallel, and collation indicates the restoration, [2 ^{giš}BANŠUR.MEŠ *i-n*]*a* ⌜*ki*⌝ *qa*-⌜*qa*⌝-*ri*. Arnaud's copy omits the two visible horizontals and two verticals of KI.

25. *NINDA.*MEŠ* is found in both texts A and B.

*Only one attested Emar bread-type can begin with *e*-, and the fat and thin loaves of the *kissu* ritual, 388.11-12, would fit in the A-text break: *e*-[*bu-u*(?) x NINDA.MEŠ *ra-qa-tu*$_4$(??)], where "x" is some number. Dietrich suggests reading *nap*- for *e*-, but the E-sign is clear in both A and B.

*At the end of the break, [^{dug}*ḫi-it*]-*ta* is unlikely. This is written with -*tá* in line 90, and we should not find an oil listed before breads. The bread *naptanu* is expected before NINDA UD.DU, and we can read [*na*]*p-ta-ni*.MEŠ, as in lines 65A and 66A. The traces of a final horizontal and vertical before -*ta*- fit *nap*- but not -*it*-.

26. Text B omits TA.ÀM.

*Text B reads NINDA UD.DU GURUN, with no MEŠ.

*Arnaud's copy shows U$_4$.5.K[ÁM] in text B, but the tablet reads "7" clearly.

The break in text A has room for some action before the filling of cups and after the setting out of breads.

27. Note the shorter spelling of the verb *ú-ma-lu-ú* in text A.

This line is too short in text A to show at the end of the right-hand tablet, Msk 74245. We expect the verb *naqû* in the offering sequence of lines 27-28A.

28. *Text A reads *1* UDU.

Text A has *a-na* IGI for *a-na pa-ni*.

The longer spelling of the verb *šakānu* is suggested by the length of the break in A.

*We do not find KAŠ standing alone in the Emar 369 texts, and the traces in text A could be read [KAŠ.MEŠ.*Š*]*E*.

There is a horizontal divider below line 28 in text A, written over by line 29.

29. *This longer text better fits the break in text A, and is indicated by the parallel event on the preceding day in line 7.

*Text B does not diverge from the order of events in text A in lines 29-30. However, it does appear that the *kubadu* which is introduced in line 30A is not found in B until line (31-36)e.

30. Text B omits *ù* at the beginning of the line.
Based on the pattern of line 64, entry into the *bīt tukli* should precede the offering to Adammatera.

31. *Texts A and B diverge significantly between lines 31 and 36 (see above). It is best not to read them together.
*Following text B(31-36)g, read [*ku-ba-da ú-gam*$_4$*-ma-ru*] after *kīmê* in text A. The verb which concludes line 31A should be read *ú-kap-pa-ru*, following the idiom in Emar 452.53: URU.KI *ú-kap-pa-ru*, "They will purify the city." 369.31A shows [ ] x(TE?).MEŠ before the verb, with room for several signs preceding this. I have found no Emar or other Akkadian idiom that illuminates the broken text. Dietrich suggests [*ú-nu*]*-te*.MEŠ *ú-káp-pa-ru*, which would presumably represent ritual implements for the sacrifice.

32. *Arnaud and Dietrich suggest reading the last signs *-lu-ú*, for *umallû*, "they will fill (cups)." The offering-sequence begun by the sacrifice in this line is taken up in line 37, with filling of cups in the usual position, so this action is not expected here, where it would be isolated without any following feast. The sign at the margin resembles KU(*qú*?) more than LU, which could fit the verbs *leqû* or *naqû*. Ritual patterns offer no convincing parallel.

33. *The last sign on the left half of text A is not *ap-*, and appears rather to be *i-*; all five horizontals are visible. Dietrich proposes DU for *alāku*, and I can suggest no better verb. The gap is filled in from the pattern of line 64, since entry into the *bīt tukli* should precede sacrifice and exit.

34. *The verb *alāku* or *erēbu* should follow departure from the *bīt tukli*, as in the procession sequences of lines 64-66. One horizontal wedge is visible in what could be the start of the DU-sign. Otherwise, the A text is restored from B(31-36)b.

35. *The long final vowel is marked in *i-na-qu-u*. The U-sign is not used in Emar 369 for the conjunction, though this use does appear in other Emar rituals (e.g. ^{d}30 *u* ^{d}UTU in 373.27).

B(31-36). The various restorations are made from comparison to text A and to all the *kubadu* and procession sequences.

(31-36)a. *The last sign of the divine name is *-r*[*i*], not *-r*[*a*], so that Adammateri has the genitive case ending after *ana*. SISKUR(?) is restored in accordance with the pattern in (31-36)b, and the other two processional clauses should anticipate the next offering. Comparison between texts A and B before they diverge suggests that B is missing an average of 15-20 signs in the break, and this restoration would complete the line.

(31-36)c. Text B omits <DU> after SAG. Outside of this instance, the use of the logogram SAG.DU for "head" is consistent in Emar 369. Note that in Ugaritic Akkadian, SAG and SAG.DU alternate (John Huehnergard, *The Akkadian of Ugarit*, Atlanta: Scholars Press, 1989, 365). The restoration assumes departure from the *bīt Gadda* before procession back to the main temple of ^{d}IM.

(31-36)d. The idiom for performance of the *kubadu* with verb *epēšu* is restored in accordance with the sequence of actions attested in lines 9-10 and lines 30-31A.

(31-36)e. This restoration follows line 36A, where a statement that the stone is to enter the *bīt Gadda* precedes a prohibition against the entry of the priestess. While the appearance of the prohibition in (31-36)f provokes the comparison, the referents would have to be changed, since the procession has left the *bīt Gadda* and the stone of Hebat. Perhaps in the scheme of text B, the divine weapon enters the temple of ^{d}IM before the priestess, who is made to enter in line (31-36)h. In both texts A and B, the NIN.DINGIR bears the weapon "before ^{d}IM" in the *kubadu* before she has entered the temple (cf. 31-32A), indicating that the god may be brought out to the entrance area for the sacrifice.

(31-36)f. Some further qualification is given the *kubadu*, but we have no parallel to suggest what it might be.

(31-36)g. This line has room for the same broken idiom that appears after *ugammarū* in line 31A, followed by the entry of the priestess (Š, *erēbu*) into the temple in both texts.

(31-36)h. The restoration from lines 32A and 37A is necessary in order to bring the action to the presentation before ^{d}IM in line 37B.

37. If we consolidate texts A and B for line 37, we must account for placement of animal parts on an incense burner (*nignakku*), which would indicate that the GARZA is a very small portion. The *nignakku* only occurs in text B, with the associated offering lost in the break, but the same "ritual portions" are expected.

Text A has IGI for *pa-ni*.

38. Text B spells *kāsāti* with *-sà-*, and glosses KAŠ.MEŠ.GEŠTIN with *ḫa-am-*[*ra*].

*Tentatively read *ka-WA-nu*; this is the usual reading of the PI-sign at Emar.

39. Text B omits *Bu-uK-Ki ša*.

*Text B appears to spell the verb *šakānu* syllabically, where A uses the logogram GAR.

40. Text A has [giš]BANŠUR *EGIR*, which does not make sense. Arnaud correctly prefers the similar GIBIL (cf. 388.29).

41. The second use of *šakānu* in text A omits <*i-*>.

Text B uses a different plural marker and the logogram GAR: *a-na* GEŠTUG.*ḪI.A-ši* GAR-*nu*.

42. Text B uses the 3fs pronominal suffix *-ši* instead of *-ša*, GAR for the verb *šakānu*, and spells ŠU without *-ti*.

43. In text B, the payment consists of two figurines, 2 [d]LAMA KÙ.GI *ša* 1 GÍN KÙ.GI.

Text B substitutes *ti-ik-ki* for A's *bu-ú-di*.

*Text B adds the plural marker, 2 ŠEŠ.*MEŠ-ša*.

*The verb should be *i-na-aš-šu-ši-ma*.

44. There is no suffix on GÌR.MEŠ in text A.

Text B uses the verb *uš-ḫé-ḫa-nu* for *i-ma-qu-tu*$_4$, followed by a sign which should be *tu-*, but which looks more like IŠ.

The phrase *a-na* NÍG.BA-*ša* in B is not found in A.

45. *The beginning of text A is obscure: ŠEŠ.MEŠ-*ši* DIRI.MEŠ-*ši*, where DIRI should indicate some form of the verb *watāru*, perhaps simply the durative of the D conjugation in hendiadys with the verb *qiāšu* which follows: *uttarūši* (W.L. Moran, personal communication; alternatively, the Babylonian form would be *uwattarūši*). The suffix (*-ši*) rules out an adjective. The meaning should be "to lavish gifts," as attested in two Amarna letters from Mitanni (see *AHw* s.v. *(w)atāru(m)* D8, "reichlich beschenken," several times in EA 26 and 27, with suffix *-anni*). For the D of *watāru* in hendiadys, see *CAD* s.v. *atāru* 2a2'.

*Text A has [giš]TUKUL *DINGIR*.MEŠ, where B reads *ḫa-ṣi-in-nu ša...*

Where text A reads EGIR-*ša*, B uses the suffix *-ši*.

*Read *pa-ni-ša* in text A, not *-ši*.

46. Text A has ^{giš}TUKUL DINGIR-*lì* where B reads *ḫa-ṣi-in-nu* DINGIR.MEŠ.

Collation shows 7 clear wedges in the number, as expected from lines 49A, 54A, 57A.

Text A mistakenly introduces < <*na*-> > into the verb *šakānu*.

47. *The cedar mentioned in text D belongs at the end of the offering list, not at the beginning, and the two halves of text A join with no gap, reading 1 T|A (not DUG).

Text B adds KAŠ.*MEŠ*.ŠE.

The sign before ^{giš}ERIN.NA in D has three angle-wedges which best fits ŠE.

Dietrich reads SISKUR-*e* in texts B and D, which would indicate a singular verb-form where we have consistently seen general 3mp forms. This does seem to be the best solution to the difficult text in B.

48. Text B makes *gáb-bá* the direct object and moves it in front of *a-na*.

*Both texts A and B refer to *3* days, not 2: *i-na* 3 u_4-*mi*, in A; *i-na* U_4.3.KÁM, in B.

Text B uses *dá*(TA)- in the word following EZEN.

Note the two spellings of the *nugagtu*: ^{f}*nu-gag*^{ag}*-tu*$_4$, in A;⌈^{f}⌉*nu-ga*$_{14}$(KA)-*ag-tu*$_4$. Dietrich follows von Soden, *N.A.B.U.* 1987 Nr. 46 (p. 25), in reading GAG as *ga*$_x$ in A, so *nu-ga*$_x$*-ag-tu*$_4$.

49. All seven wedges are present in the number 7 in text B.

Text A omits the plural ḪI.A after 2 UDU.

*Observe UDU after SAG.DU.

50. Text B adds *pa-ni* after *a-na*.

*Read MUR for "lungs."

51. *The number 7 is clear in both texts A and B. Arnaud's copy shows only four wedges for the number in B.

"ALAM" in the A text is not the normal ALAM-sign, though it seems to be derivative. Some figurine appears to be intended (see below, Figurines for ^{d}IM and Hebat).

52. *Text A reads *ú-še-él-la*, versus *-el-* in text D.

The offering to Šaḫru consists of a sheep (UDU) in text A, as opposed to a lamb ($SILA_4$) in text B. Text D is damaged, but the line appears to have room for more than just a single direct object before ^{d}*Ša-aḫ-ri*. Dietrich reads [1] $SILA_4$ DIŠ ^{d}*Ša-a'-ri-ri*, but the traces before the divine name do not easily fit this reading. Also, the substitution of -*a'-ri-* for *-aḫ-* here and elsewhere depends on interpretation of one sign which is written consistently throughout all texts. This sign has one more wedge in the right half than the expected AḪ-sign, but one or two fewer wedges than A'+RI. I have considered the divine name Šaḫru to be more plausible than Ša'riru.

53. The two 7's in text A are clear, and one vertical is visible after SISKUR-*u* in B.

*Read *1 TA.ÀM* before gišPA in texts A, B, and D. Text D has 4 gišPA instead of 1 (A and B). I do not see the three upper verticals in text D to make 1 into 4 gišPA, as in Arnaud's copy.

Text B omits ZÌ before ŠE (vs. A and D).

54. *Text A substitutes the TI-sign (-⸢*dì*⸣-) for *-di-* in the verb *nadānu*.

Only text A places the conjunction *ù* after *nadānu*.

*Text D shows traces of the NAG-sign, with the long final vowel marked with *-u*. The number which follows is 5, not text A's 7.

55. There is a real space between KAŠ and ŠE of the left and right halves of text A, so that MEŠ is likely.

Text D writes TI-*u* where A uses the syllabic spelling, *i-laq-qu-u*.

*Text D represents the version of the ritual with only four tables and dignitaries, so that it omits uru*E-mar* of text A, as well as the king of Šatappi at the beginning of line 56.

56. *Read 7! NINDA UD.DU.*MEŠ* in text B. Six verticals in three columns are visible, and 7 is nearly certain.

Arnaud reads *ta-ás-s*[*i-*] at the end of the line in text B, and Dietrich proposes *dá-aš-š*[*u*(?!)*-pí*]. Collation shows that Arnaud's TA has the third vertical of DUG, and the final vertical belongs to MEŠ. Only one vertical is clear before DUG, but the sign is smudged, and 7 is expected from A.

57. Arnaud's copy omits the *-ú-* in *Šu-ú-mi* (text A).

*Texts B and D do not appear to have the same full listing of meat portions for dignitaries as text A.

58. The traces in Emar 370.36 suggest [*s*]*íl-qu* for the *maš'artu*, in a parallel list of meats. Although the sign here ends with an unexpected double-vertical, the scribe of the A-text previously substituted a double for a single final vertical in the GIBIL-sign (line 40).

*The textual confusion that accompanies the transition to the last day of the ritual begins at line 58, where text B introduces a time formula, apparently *i-na* u_4*-mi* E[GIR(?)-*ki*] (based on collation). Text D offers an extremely difficult statement with no parallel in the other versions or the rest of the ritual. The tip of a horizontal appears before u_4*-mi*, ruling out [*i-n*]*a*. Dietrich reads the noun *qu-u-pí* (from *kūbu*, fetus), but QU-U should represent the end of the word, not the beginning, since the U-sign is only used to mark final long vowels in Emar 369. I have read *ma-qu-u*, or the noun *maqqû*, "offering, sacrifice." Then, KAŠ is not expected before GUD, and this sign might better be read ELLÁG, "kidney," though the determinative UZU is expected. This reading is more likely than "beer (and) ox," though it still does not resolve interpretation of a line that does not match any other Emar ritual idiom. The wedges at the end of the line resemble GU-*u* or x-MU, but I have no solution.

Text B omits the king of Šatappi, the fifth dignitary found in text A.

59. *My numbering system diverges from that of Arnaud at this point because text A moves directly to [*i-na* x u_4]-⌜*mi*⌝ 2 UDU..., which Arnaud places in his line 60. The traces of *-mi* appear to confirm the expected time formula, but the actual reference is lost. This is the first line of the reverse for text A, which I label line 59.

*The material separated by double slashes (//) in text A represents fragments of known idioms that appear elsewhere in the ritual.

The verb *ú-ma-x*[ ] in text B should not be *umallû* or *umallakū*, familiar verbs from the ritual. The last sign begins with three horizontals and a vertical which would fit the pattern of signs such as MA, ŠA, DA, and GAL.

Text D includes the phrase u_4*-m*[*i*] x-*ri-i*, which Arnaud and Dietrich read *ma-ḫi-ri-i*. However, "*ma-*" has only two clear horizontals, with the tip of an angle extending below these, and "*-ḫi-*" has only the two angles of a gloss marker.

60. Comparison with the lines below, where we pick up the left fragment of text A once again, indicates that we are missing no more than 3 to 6 signs -- room for ᵈNIN.KUR, at most. Without a temporal phrase, the A text probably should be considered truncated, as in line 59A.

*Text A matches B, with [ ]-*et-bu-ú*, not *it-te-bu-ú*.

*The A text does not mention the departure of the NIN.DINGIR from her father's house, È/*uṣ*-[*ṣi-ma*] in texts B and D.

61. *Line 61 begins with a clear vertical wedge in text A (1?), which is not part of a MA-sign (Arnaud?) or a KI-sign (Dietrich). Text D begins with TA/*ištu*.

Text D seems to reads AD-⸢*šu*(?)⸣, though the suffix should be feminine.

62. *Text A includes MEŠ after the feminine marker MÍ, where D does not.

"Bride" is spelled *ka-al-la-ti* in text A, É.GI_4.A in text D.

63. Text A appears to contain two scribal errors: the GIŠ-sign before KI/*itti*, and omission of <*za-ma-ru*>.

The divine weapon is ^{giš}TUKUL DINGIR.MEŠ in text A, and [*ḫa*]-*ṣi-in-nu ša* DINGIR.MEŠ in text D. The *ša* in text B probably indicates the syllabic [*ḫa-ṣi-in-nu*].

64. *Both texts A and D omit the suffix -*ši* on EGIR.

*Text A spells *tukli tu-uk-li*, vs. *tùk-li* in text D, before entry. At the departure, text A omits <-*li*>, but still uses *tu-uk* for *tùk*.

*We do not find the preposition *a-na* before Adammatera, but it is not certain whether this is an error or a variation using the genitive. Text D uses the genitive -*ri* for -*ra* on the divine name. SISKUR is certain, though smudged (vs. Dietrich, B[A]L$^{!}$).

65. *Text D spells *ana* with the DIŠ-sign.

The verb *naqû* is spelled with the logogram BAL in text D.

*Text A omits <^{ninda}> before *naptanu*. Arnaud's copy has ^{ninda}AN-*ta-ni*.MEŠ, but collation shows the expected *nap*-.

66. *Arnaud's correct copy shows that <É> is omitted in text A.

*Text D writes the first *ana* with the DIŠ-sign. There is no TA É.

The verb *tallak* receives two different spellings: *ta-al-la-ak* (A), and *ta-a-lak* (D).

Text A omits <^{d}IM>, a scribal error.

In text D the verb *naqû* is written with BAL-*qí*, over against SISKUR in text A.

*The "3 NINDA" of Arnaud's note appear in line 65D.

67. Text B reads -*sà*(ZA)-, with text D, versus text A's -*sa*-, in *kāsāti*.

Both texts A and D have $^{lú.meš}$*ši-bu-ut*, without <URU.KI>. Apparently a scribal error was reproduced.

68. Text D writes the first *ana* with a single vertical wedge.

Only text D adds the vowel-marker -*u* to the verb NAG.

*The only witness for Arnaud's proposed **il-ta-qú* is text D, TA-*qú*. In line 75A, Arnaud reads TA-*qé* as *ta*-[*la*]-*qí*, again producing a syllabic spelling. An alternative to these emendations would be to see TA as another logogram for the verb *leqû*, which should be written with the TI-sign.

69. *Text A reads smoothly without the elements from text D, and the two should not be integrated into one. On the other hand, text D is confused, and the signs after TA-*qú* do not form a clear sequence. Neither *e-nu-um-ma* (Arnaud) nor (*ta-qú*)-*un*[!]-*um-ma* (Dietrich) fit the actual signs, which resemble IS U DUB/UM DIŠ(1) A(?) ḪA[L].

Text D has URU, without .KI, and adds the vowel marker on NAG-*u*.

70. *Text A repeats the number "1" after each item of furniture, whereas D only places the number before [giš]NÁ at the head of the set.

*Text B appears to record the ventive and suffix on the verb *nadānu* in expanded form, [-*n*]*i-iš-š*[*i*-] instead of -*ni-ši*.

71. *We have traces from text C for the signs following *ša-a-šu*, but they are not TÚG.GAR URI of texts A and D. Dietrich proposes [TÚG]⸢*bi-re-e*⸣, "a select garment," but BI and RI do not fit the first two signs. The first includes a horizontal and a vertical (not BI), and the second has two or three horizontals (not RI).

The sign after É in text A is obscured by the break between the left and right halves, and Dietrich seems correct in reading another sign before *ur-ši-ša*. His *ḫu-ur-ši-ša* fits the traces, but the word is somewhat unexpected (see the commentary, The *bīt urši*).

*The verb *ù-ma-aṣ-ṣu-u* in text A does have the final -*u*. The first sign is *ù*-, vs. *ú*- in text D.

The deity associated with the table is spelled [d]*Ḫu-le-li* in text C.

72. Text C uses the suffix -*ši* instead of -*ša* on the noun *rēšu*, and spells the verb *šakānu* syllabically.

Text C gives a longer form for "wine," KAŠ.*MEŠ*.GEŠTIN.

The gift of *zirtu*-wool in texts A and C becomes SÍG *za-zi-tu*$_4$ in text D.

73. Text C reads the shorter form of the verb, *i-za-ma-rù*.

74. Only text C inserts the subject [lú]*za-ma-ru* before the verb, *leqû*. Note the 3ms form, followed by the conjunction *ù*, in text A. Dietrich identifies the U-signs in texts C and D as the conjunction, but this sign is consistently used to mark final long vowels. Subject and verb do

not always agree in the case of the *zammārū* (see lines 79A, 83C, 84C), and the form TI-*u* appears with the singers in line 83A and C.

Traces suggest that text D may use the suffix *-ši* instead of *-ša* (A and C) after the second GÌR.MEŠ.

*The A-text does appear to agree with C in reading *i-* with the verb *mesû*, the first time. Text C switches to the D conjugation when the verb is repeated. The traces in text D indicate the G conjugation, with text A.

Text C omits the "1" before ŠU.GUR. The number before ŠU.GUR in text D is obscure; two verticals are visible, separated by a space too large to allow interpretation as the number "2".

75. Text C omits the verb *šakānu*.

*Text A appears to use the unusual logogram TA for the verb *leqû*, with the GI-sign for *-qè* (for */qe/* in *leqû*, see Huehnergard, *Akkadian of Ugarit*, 35, 52 n.83). Compare line 68D, above.

*It appears that text C does not use the 3fs suffix *-ša* with ^{giš}NÁ.

Texts A and C spell the last two verbs differently: *te-el-la-ma ta-at-ta-al* (A), and *te-la-ma ta-at-ta-a-al* (C).

76. Arnaud's copy shows "9" days in text C and "6" days in text A, but collation shows rather "8" and "7".

Note the logogram AD- in text C for *a-bi-*.

The subject LÚ.MEŠ (*ša*) *qí-da-ši* is used with the verb *palāku* in text A, and with *zâzu* in C (line 77). The correct original may not include the repeated subject, but just one or the other, since we have no version with both.

77. Text A adds *-al-* but leaves out <*la-*> in the verb *palāku*.

Text C uses a shorter spelling than A: *ú-za-zu-šu*.

*With line 17, text A gives the royal share to the *LÚ* LUGAL KUR.

78. Text A adds the determinative ^{uzu} to SAG.DU.

*At the join of the left and right halves of text A, only the first sign on the right is unclear, though there appears to be too little space for UZU. The MEŠ-sign appears only C. Text A uses the noun *irrū* in both lines 78 and 79, in contrast to C, and A omits the GUD specification found three times in text C, along with the fourth ox-part, the hide (1 KUŠ GUD).

79. Compare two spellings for the lungs, with a gloss in text A: ^{uzu}MUR : *ḫa-še-e* (A), and ^{uzu}*ḫa-še* (C).

Text C omits the suffix on ḪA.LA, and uses *-rù* instead of *-ru* in the title of the singers.

*The verb *leqû* is left out in text C.

*There is no mention of *irrū* in text C, which just has ^{uzu}ŠÀ.MEŠ-*šu*. The copy does not show evidence for text D beyond line 75.

80. Text A omits *ša* in LÚ.MEŠ *qí-da-ši*.

*Text A does not use MEŠ with the three occurrences of tables, while text C uses MEŠ with the first and the third.

*We have a scribal error in A, with *ša a-ni*, a mistake for *a-na* or perhaps *a-na pa-ni*.

81. *Text C begins, NU KÙ.GA.

*Note the determinative ^{lú} (without MEŠ) on *za-am-ma-rù* in text A.

Text A uses a shorter spelling with /u/ root vowel: *i-zu-zu*, vs. *i-za-az-zu* (C).

*Text C does not appear to have room for both plural markers found in A, KUŠ.MEŠ UDU.ḪI.A.

Text A uses the genitive form *gáb-bi*, where the accusative is expected.

82. The title <*za-ma-ru*> is missing from text A.

Text C omits *it-ti a-ḫa-mèš*.

Contrast the spellings, *i-zu-zu* (A) and *i-za-zu* (C).

*Text C mentions only one hide (KUŠ).

The hide in text C is further defined by the clause *ša* ... SISKUR-*u*, which does not appear in A. Dietrich suggests the reading 1 KUŠ GUD *ša*-[*a-šu ša*] NIN.DINGIR..., which fits the space and the traces quite well, though the reference to "the aforesaid ox" would be somewhat awkward. Line 76 (A and C) does not use this phrase, nor does it appear in mention of the ox between lines 76 and 82.

The verb *leqû* is spelled with the logogram TI in text C, with *-qé* for -*qè*.

83. Text C spells the singers' title with *-rù* and uses *-ni* instead of *-nu* for the *naptanu*-bread.

*Text C adds *1* DUG.

*Text A omits MEŠ in KAŠ.ŠE.

The next two lines in Arnaud's composite text (86-87) appear in text C only, so I have not incorporated them into my numbering scheme. This means that my line 83 covers Arnaud's lines 85-87, and my line 84 begins with his line 88.

*Read *ḫa-ṣi-ti*, not *-te*.

*Read UZU *SISKUR*, not AMAR. The term AMAR is not used in the NIN.DINGIR-ritual.

Note that the division of meat among the gods (verb, *zâzu*) is only attested in text C, here and in line 19.

84. *The text originally published for lines 84-90 (Arnaud's 88-94) is confused because lú.meš*za-ma-ru* TI-*qé* of line 84 in the right half of the A text was read with the same words at the end of the line 83 addition in text C. The alignment between the left and right halves of text A is then thrown off by one line throughout the section. This corrected version reads more smoothly: for example, the good year is discussed before the bad. I will not mention specific differences with Arnaud's text in this section, but refer the reader to his edition.

Text C uses the suffix *-ši* on the noun *šūkultu*.

The description of the payments associated with the feasting of the NIN.DINGIR varies sharply between texts A and C. Text A makes no mention of the lúḪAL and uses the term KÙ.BABBAR instead of the NÍG.BA found in text C. Text C describes the payment without using a verb (*leqû*, in A).

The genitive *za-ma-ri* properly occurs with the verbless construction in text C.

85. Text A uses the longer SIG_5.*GA*, and omits the descriptive phrase, ŠE.BA-*ši ša* NIN.DINGIR.

The *bīt tukli* of text A is equated with the É DINGIR-*lì*, *bīt ili*, of text C. The verb should be in the break in text C, and the traces would fit SUM. After the break, traces could fit either *-nu* or perhaps *-ši*, though we expect the former, given the space requirements.

Text C begins *ù šum-*[*ma*(?)], an alternative to the temporal construction with *i-na*. Again, text C adds the term, ŠE.BA-*ši*, and the verb is lost in a break.

86. Line 86 begins the list of allotments to the NIN.DINGIR, and this new section is indented in the A text.

*Read 6 *ME* SÍG in text A, not *me-at*. The traces in text C do not match the material in A and I cannot decipher them. Dietrich reads S[UM] after ŠE.BA-*ši*, then [*me-a*]*t*(?) SÍG[ ], but collation does not support these proposals.

88. *Read gišḪAŠḪUR.*KUR*.RA.

*Read 1 *GA*.ḪAB.

89. *Text C adds the ^{dug} determinative before *qú-'u-u* and spells that word with *-u* instead of *-ú*. Both texts show 3, not 2 vessels.

*The noun *šēnu* is spelled ^{kuš}E.*SIR*; *AHw* s.v. *šēnu(m)* shows that the SIR-sign is an alternative to SÍR. Read *ta-pal*, "pair."

*Instead of KUŠ EME$_5$ (*mašak atāni*), read ^{kuš}ŠUḪUB (*šuḫuppatu*) in text A.

90. *Text C omits 2 KU$_6$.

Text C has *TU*.MUŠEN.MEŠ.

91. Text A omits *ù*.

*Arnaud correctly reads *-in-*, not *-im-*, at the right edge of text C.

Dietrich suggests that the line written on the edge of text B jumps from the statement of the priestess' death to the inheritance instructions.

92. *Read the number "1" before *ḫi-zi-bu*.

*The A text is not clear after "2". Dietrich suggests NINDA$^{!}$.G[UR]$_4$.RA[.MEŠ], but the space before RA is too large, and the traces do not easily fit NINDA. There is nothing between RA and *a-na*.

93. The signs I ⌜BI⌝ AD TI are quite clear, though the meaning remains obscure (see the commentary, The diviner).

94. The last line of the text is straightforward in A, using verbless sentences to assign "these items" (*ú-nu-tù-ú an-nu-ti*) to the house of the NIN.DINGIR's father, with nothing for the city. The words *pár-ṣi-ša i-na-aš-ši* in text B appear to follow *tallak* of line 91 (see above).

*Text B uses the 3ms suffix, *a-bi-šu*.

*Text A writes just *ul* for the negative.

Note the use of *mì*(ME)- in *mimma* of the A text.

C. TRANSLATION

Most of the textual variations between the five manuscripts of the NIN.DINGIR ritual do not affect the translation. Therefore I have produced a composite translation, with separate versions only provided where differences in meaning appear. When the attested manuscripts are fundamentally in agreement, a single translation is given, with the contributing texts identified by the appropriate letters in parentheses: e.g., (A,C). When there is significant variation, the texts are translated separately, and each is identified by an underlined letter followed by a colon: e.g., A:. Notes to the translation will only deal with matters that do not fall within the scope of the commentary, including points of divergence from Arnaud's translation that do not simply reflect our different readings of the text. Dietrich's treatment will be discussed as appropriate in the commentary.

1. (A,C) Tablet of rites for the NIN.DINGIR of ^{d}IM of Emar. When the sons of Emar elevate the NIN.DINGIR
2. (A) to ^{d}IM, the sons of Emar will take[1] the lots(?) from the temple of ^{d}NIN.URTA (and) manipulate them before
3. (A) ^{d}IM. The daughter of any son of Emar may be identified. On that same day they[2] will take fine oil[3] from the palace
4. (A) and from the temple of ^{d}NIN.KUR, and put (it) on her head. They will offer before ^{d}IM one sheep, one *qu'û*-jar, (and) one *ḫizzibu* of wine.
5. (A) They will give the ^{lú}ḪAL one shekel of silver. They will send back to the temple of ^{d}NIN.URTA eight dried cakes (and)
6. (A,C) one *ḫizzibu* along with the lots(?). During the shaving sanctification they will sanctify[4] all the gods of Emar with bread (and) beer.

---

[1] I use the future tense to translate the standard ritual durative, since to my ear this communicates the tone of instruction better than the English present.

[2] Arnaud uses the 3mp "ils" through line 6, except for the giving of silver, where he switches to the impersonal "on." The subject in lines 3-6 is somewhat ambiguous because of the specific subject in line 2, but even this should not be taken to indicate a distinct set of people. In most cases, I have translated the 3mp verbs in the ritual with English "they," understood to have an indefinite subject.

[3] The translation comes from von Soden, "Feinöl" (*AHw* s.v. *šamnu(m)* 3c). It is possible that what was called "sweet oil" did not have oil as its liquid base, but rather beer. Robert M. Whiting, *Old Babylonian Letters from Tell Asmar*, *AS* 22, Chicago: The Oriental Institute, 1987, 107-108, argues from recipes for three types of *šamnum ṭābum* that this substance "was an aromatic unguent made of a complicated mixture of ingredients, none of which was ì or ì-giš."

[4] The Emar verb *qaddušu* appears to mean "to treat as holy, or sacred," not "to consecrate, or purify." Gods do not need to be made pure. Translation with the entire English idiom is prohibitively cumbersome, so I have resorted to an older use of the English religious term, "sanctify," which could have the holy God as its object. The King James Version preserves this use in Deut 32.51, "...because ye *sanctified* me (Yahweh) not in the midst of the children of Israel," with the Hebrew verb *qiddaštem* (Piel conjugation). The King James also translates the Hiphil conjugation of *qādaš* with "sanctify" in Isa 8.13 and 29.23. See also the commentary, The Sanctification Ceremony.

7. (A,C) The shaving of the NIN.DINGIR is on the next day.[5] One ox (and) six sheep, the offering[6] of the NIN.DINGIR, will go to the temple of ^{d}IM, and the divine weapon[7]

8. (A,C) and the NIN.DINGIR will go behind them, (while) the singers will go ahead of them. When they reach the temple of ^{d}IM, they will shave the NIN.DINGIR

9. (A,C) at the opening of the courtyard gate. [When(??)] they perform the *kubadu*-ceremony before ^{d}IM,

10. A: her father will carry the divine weapon for the *kubadu*. [When they finish the great *kubadu*,(?)] they will give the ^{lú}ḪAL [x] shekel(s) of silver.

C: her father will carry the divine weapon [for the *kubadu*] in her stead. When they finish the great *kubadu*, [...]

11. (A,C) They will offer the one ox and the six sheep before ^{d}IM. They will place before the gods a beef ritual portion(?) (and) a mutton ritual portion(?). They will

12. (A,C) place before the gods seven dinner-loaves, seven dried cakes, (and) two dried cakes (with) fruit. They will fill goblets with wine. The officials

13. (A,C) who give the *qidašu*,[8] the *ḫussu*-men,

A: (and) seven [and seven *ḫamša'u*-men(?)]

(A,C) will eat and drink at the temple of ^{d}IM, and the men of the *qidašu*

14. (A, C,E) will get one dinner-loaf each (and) one *ḫizzibu* of barley-beer each. The *bēl bīti* will slaughter one sheep at his (C) house.

15. (A, C,E) He will cook (it), and then at the gate of the temple of ^{d}IM, in the house of the NIN.DINGIR, they will set up four (C; A: [five]) tables with three dinner-loaves each.

---

[5] With Arnaud, I take this as a complete sentence, though I translate *šanî* as "next" instead of "second." Reading "second" again, Arnaud makes the same construction a circumstantial phrase in line 29, but the nominative cases of *gallubu* and *malluku* indicate that the full sentence is preferable.

[6] Arnaud translates SISKUR as a finite verb, but the genitive-marker *ša* which follows suggests that it is best understood as a noun in this context.

[7] In lines 45, 46, and 63, ^{giš}TUKUL varies with syllabic spellings of *ḫaṣṣinnu*, and both terms should represent the same item in the ritual. Thus the actual weapon is apparently an axe, though it is often called simply "the weapon" (*kakku*). W.L. Moran (personal communication) suggests that ^{giš}TUKUL may even be a Sumerogram for *ḫaṣṣinnu* at Emar.

[8] On this group of men, see the commentary. Arnaud translates *šarrū* as "chanteurs."

16. (A, C,E) One table (will be) for the previous NIN.DINGIR.[9] One table (will be) for the NIN.DINGIR of Šumi. One table (will be) for the *maš'artu*.

17. A: One table (will be) for the man of the king of the land of Emar. One table (will be) [for the king of Šatappi].
C,E: One table (will be) for the king of the land.
(A,C,E) On them

18. (A, C,E) they will set out (A: offer) the mutton and one dried cake (C, E: (with) fruit) each. They[10] will get one (regular) jar of barley-beer each (and) one *maḫḫaru*-jar of barley-beer each.

19. (A, C,E) They will offer to all the gods of Emar one dinner-loaf each, one *ḫizzibu* of barley-beer each, *kerṣu*-bread, cedar oil,
C: (and) fruit, (and) they will distribute (them) among the gods.

20. (A, B,C,E) Just before the evening watch, they will take fine oil of the temple of ^{d}NIN.KUR and of the palace, and at the gate of ^{d}IM the ^{lú}ḪAL

21. (A, B,C,E) will pour (it) on the NIN.DINGIR's [head], and when the men of the *qidašu* leave the temple of ^{d}IM, they will [brin]g her [into the house of her father].

22. (A, B,C) On the day of (B) the sanctification of the installation, they will sanc[tify] all the gods of Emar [with bread (and) beer]. They will

23. (A,B) lay down ^{d}NIN.KUR in the house of her father, and [they will take] the red wool vestment belonging to the temple [of ^{d}NIN.KUR]. [They will plac]e (it) on ^{d}NIN.KUR.

24. (A,B) They will set up four tables before the gods. They will set up one table for ^{d}IM, one table for [Hebat(??)], (and) [two tables o]n the ground

25. (A,B) for the underworld gods. They will set out on them twelve th[ick(?)] loaves, [(x) thin loaves(??), (x) di]nner-loaves (each?),

26. (A,B) four dried cakes each, (and) four dried cakes (with) fruit each.
A: (something in the break)

---

[9] This explanation of the arrangement of tables and dignitaries could also be treated as epexegetical: "... they will set up four tables with three dinner-loaves each: one table for the previous NIN.DINGIR, one table for the NIN.DINGIR of Šumi...," and so on.

[10] In this case, the specific "ils" would seem to be preferable to Arnaud's "on."

B: For seven days ... (some unknown action)
(A,B) They will fill goblets with wine.

27. (A,B) [They will offer(?)] one ox, one sheep, seven *ḫizzibu* of wine, (and) two *parīsu* [of barley to ᵈNIN.KUR(??)].

28. (A,B) They will place before the gods a ritual portion(?) of the ox, a ritual portion(?) of the sheep, the head of the ox, (and) the head of one sheep, (and) they will place seven *ḫiz*[*zibu* of barley-be]er(?).

29. (A,B) The installation of the NIN.DINGIR is on the next day.[11] One ox [(and) six sheep, the offering of the NIN.DINGIR, will go to the temple of ᵈIM]. The divine weapon

30. (A,B) and the NIN.DINGIR will go behind them,
A: and the singers [will go] ah[ead of them]. They will perform the great [*ku*]*badu* [before ᵈIM].
B: [and the singers will go ahead of them(?). They will go into the *bīt tukli*(?), and]

31-36(A):

31A The NIN.DINGIR will carry the divine weapon for the *kubadu*. When [they finish the *kubadu*,] they will purify the [(?)],

32A (and) they will bring her into the temple of ᵈIM. [They will offer to ᵈIM] the one ox and the six sheep, (and) [they will ...].

33A The NIN.DINGIR will go(?) with the divine weapon and the singer(s), [they will go into the *bīt tukli*, and one lamb (will be) f]or Adammatera.

34A When they leave the *bīt tukli*, the[y will go] to the *bīt Gadda*. They will [offer one lamb to ᵈIM, (and)]

35A they will offer one lamb of the *sikkānu* of Hebat. The NIN.DINGIR will pour fine oil on the top of the *sikkānu* of Hebat.

36A On that same day it will go into the *bīt Gadda*; however, she must not go in. They will go back, and at the temple of ᵈIM,

31-36(B):

a [they will offer(?)] one lamb to Adammatera. [When they leave the *bīt tukli*(?), they will go to the *bīt Gadda*(?).]

---

[11] See the note for line 7.

b They will offer one lamb to ^{d}IM, (and) [they will offer(?)] one [lamb (to) the *sikkānu* of Hebat(?). The NIN.DINGIR will pour fine oil(?)]

c on the top of the *sikkānu* of H[ebat. When they leave the *bīt Gadda*(?),]

d they will go into the temple of ^{d}IM, and on [that day(?) they will perform the great *kubadu* before ^{d}IM(?).]

e The NIN.DINGIR [will carry] the divine weapon for the *kuba*[*du*. On that day (it/they) will go in (?);]

f however, she(?) must not go i[n.]

g When they finish the *kubadu*, [they will purify(?) the ... (?),]

h (and) they will bring [her in]to the temple of ^{d}IM. [They will offer to ^{d}IM the one ox and the six sheep, and a ritual portion(?) of the ox (and) a ritual portion(?) of the six sheep]

37. A: they will place before ^{d}IM a ritual portion(?) of the ox (and) a ritual portion(?) of the six sheep.

B: [they will place] in[12] the incense burner which is in front of ^{d}IM ...

A: They will place before ^{d}IM seven dinner-loaves, seven dried cakes, (and) two dried cakes (with) fruit.

38. (A,B) They will fill goblets with wine and barley-beer. The men of the *qidašu* (and?) the *ḫussu*-men are to be the *kawanū* (and) the attendants;

39. (A,B) as his[13] *kawanū* and his attendants they will eat and drink. They will set up five tables in the house of weeping(?) (A) of the NIN.DINGIR. (Just as for the shaving day.)

40. (A,B) Just before the evening watch, they will seat the NIN.DINGIR on her throne and set up before her a new table of her father's house,

41. (A,B) (and) place bread on it. They will put on her ears two gold earrings of her father's house, put on her right

42. (A,B) hand the(?) gold ring[14] of ^{d}IM, (and) wrap her head with a red wool headdress. They will offer fine oil of ^{d}IM.

---

[12] Arnaud translates "devant," since meat would not belong in an incense burner, but this may only be a problem with a composite text (see text notes).

[13] "His" presumably refers to ^{d}IM.

[14] I have taken *iqqu* as a Syrian equivalent for Akkadian *unqu* (W.L. Moran, personal communication); see *AHw* s.v. *unqu(m)* I, "Ring; (Stempel-)Siegel." The form *uqqu* is attested in the Neo-Assyrian period. Arnaud translates, "matériel."

43. (A,B) They will put into the ^{lú}ḪAL's hand
A: ten shekels of silver in (the form of) a silver coil.
B: two gold *lamassu*-figurines of one gold shekel.
(A,B) Two of her brothers will carry her on (their) shoulders (B: necks), and she will go to the house

44. (A,B) of her father. The city elders will fall at her feet, (and) give her a seven-shekel silver *tudittu*-pin as her gift.

45. (A,B) Her brothers will give her gifts lavishly.[15] The divine weapon (B: axe) will go behind her, (and) the singers will go ahead of her.

46. (A,B) Then when she has entered the house of her father, they will put the divine weapon (B: axe) on ^{d}NIN.KUR for seven days.

47. (A,B) On that day, they will offer one dinner-loaf each, one *ḫizzibu* of barley-beer each,
A: *kerṣu*-bread, (and) the meat of the ox of ^{d}NIN.KUR,
B: *ke*[*rṣu*-bread(?)...], (and) oils,
D: (and) cedar,

48. (A, B,D) (and) distribute (them) among all the gods of Emar. On the third day of the *datnātu*(-)festival[16] of the NIN.DINGIR, the *nugagtu* will give forth (her) cry.

49. (A, For seven days, two sheep on each day[17] they will offer to the

---

[15] Arnaud translates "autant qu'elle en a" for ŠEŠ.MEŠ-*ši* MAL.MEŠ-*ši*. See the text notes.

[16] Arnaud: "Pendant ces trois jours de la fête de la prêtresse-*entu*...". Arnaud translates *datnātu* as "these" and understands the temporal phrase to indicate three days' duration (length of time) as opposed to the third day in a sequence (the time when). The temporal phrase with *ina* should mean "on the third day," not "for three days," and I do not understand the analysis of the form *datnātu* which underlies Arnaud's translation as "these." See the introduction to the commentary, below.

[17] The temporal phrase with no preposition should indicate seven days' duration, in contrast to the construction with *ina* noted above. The unusual idiom *ina ūmīma* should indicate a point in time rather than duration: "on the day." Within the context of the seven-day period, this would mean, "on each day," or "daily," as in EA 147:7 (*i-na* u_4-*mi-ma*; see W.L. Moran, *El-Amarna*, "jour par jour," with reference to the rising of the sun). Arnaud translates Emar 369.49, "le septième jour, le jour même." "Le septième jour" of lines 49 and 51 thus stands in contrast to his translation of the expression U_4.7.KÁM in line 54 (and cf. 83), "pendant sept jours." However, all the instances of this temporal phrase should have the same meaning. Huehnergard, *Akkadian of Ugarit*, 204, observes that the enclitic *-ma* at Ugarit "may be broadly described as a focussing morpheme," and I would take this Emar use to fall within that definition, though I have no close parallel. See also *GAG*, par. 123a.

B,D) gods on behalf of Hebat at her (the NIN.DINGIR's) house.[18] Every day they will place before

50. (A, the gods a ritual portion(?) of the meat (and) the two heads of
B,D) the sheep. For seven days, every day they will offer at the temple of ^{d}IM the

51. (A, heart (and) the lungs of one sheep, one large dinner-loaf, one
B,D) dried cake (with) fruit, one (regular) jar of barley-beer, (and) one *maḫḫaru*-jar of wine. When the NIN.DINGIR is enthroned at her feast, she will present

52. (A, to ^{d}IM and Hebat two gold figurines of one shekel weight. They
B,D) will offer one sheep (A; B: lamb) to Šaḫru.

53. (A, The seven and seven *ḫamša'u*-men will eat and drink for two days
B,D) in the house of the NIN.DINGIR, (and) they will give her one *parīsu* of barley-flour (B: barley) each (and) one *anati*-jar of malt beer.

54. (A, Also the men of the *qidašu* will eat (and) drink for seven days in
B,D) her house, (and) will get seven

55. (A, dinner-loaves each (and) seven *ḫizzibu*'s of barley-beer each. As
B,D) for the previous NIN.DINGIR, the NIN.DINGIR of Dagan, lord of Šumi, the *maš'artu*,
A: the king of the land of Emar,
B,D: the king of the land:

56. A: (and) [the king o]f Šatappi:
(A, their tables, together with beef, mutton, seven dried cakes (with)
B,D) fruit, seven (regular) jars of barley-beer,

57. A: (and) [seven(?)] *maḫḫaru*-jars of barley-beer (will be) for seven days. The haunch (will be) for the NIN.DINGIR of ^{d}IM. The hock (will be) for the NIN.DINGIR of Dagan, lord of Šumi.

58. A: The boiled-meat(?) will be for the *maš'artu*. The kidney (will be) for the king of the land of Emar. The kidney (will be) for the king of Šatappi.[19]
B: ... the king of the land will get. On the l[ast(?)] day ...

---

[18] See the commentary. Arnaud identifies "her house" as the temple of Hebat.

[19] Arnaud's translation is based on finding the verb *leqû* at the end of this sequence ("[prenn]ent").

D: [The (last?)] day (is) the offering(?). The kidney(?) of the ox which to ^{d}[IM(?)...]

59. A: [On the (last?) da]y, they will offer two sheep to ^{d}IM [...]. They will fill chalices// temple of ^{d}IM will eat and drink//

B: On the last day they will [...]

D: On the ... day, a gold ... on the ... day ... They will place before the gods ... On that day ...

60. (A, B,D) They will make [^{d}NIN.KUR] rise, and then they will send back to the temple of ^{d}NIN.KUR the red wool vestment of ^{d}NIN.KUR along with bread (and) beer.

B,D: When the NIN.DINGIR leaves the house,

61. (A, B,D) they will cover her head as a bride with (D; A: one ...) a colorful sash of her father's house.

62. (A, B,D) Her two maids will embrace her as a bride. Just before the evening watch,

63. (A, B,D) one ox, seven sheep, three lambs, along with a torch[20] and the singers, will go ahead of her, and the divine weapon (B? and D: axe)

64. (A, B,D) will go behind her. She will go into the *bīt tukli*, and offer one lamb to Adammatera. When she leaves the *bīt tukli*,

65. (A, B,D) she will go to the temple of ^{d}NIN.KUR. She will offer one lamb to ^{d}NIN.KUR, (and) place three dinner-loaves for the gods.

66. (A, B,D) When she leaves the temple of ^{d}NIN.KUR, she will go to the temple of ^{d}IM. She will offer one lamb to ^{d}IM,

67. (A, B,C) place seven dinner-loaves before the gods, (and) fill goblets with wine. The men of the *qidašu* (and) the <city->elders

68. (A, B,D) will go afterward, (and) eat (and) drink at the temple of ^{d}IM.

A,B,C: They will send back to the place of the *bēl bīti*

/69. the aforesaid ox (and) the seven sheep which went ahead of the NIN.DINGIR.

D: They will take [the aforesaid ox (and)] the seven

/69. sheep ... . [they will send] them [back].

---

20 See the commentary for GI.IZI.LÁ.

(A,D) When the city elders have eaten (and) drunk,
70. (A, they will give one fine garment as her garment,
B,C,D)(and) give her one bed, one chair, and one footstool. On that bed
71. (A, they will lay out one Akkadian (A and D; C: ?) blanket of her
C,D) pure bedroom. They will set up
72. (A, the table of Hulelu at the gate of(?) its head,[21] (and) place on that
C,D) table three dinner-loaves each(?),[22] one dried cake (with) fruit,
73. (A, one *ḫizzibu* of wine, (and) a *zirtu*-garment (A and C; D: *zāzītu*).
C,D) The singers will sing for Hulelu, (and) the singers (C) will perform the rites
74. (A, of that table.[23] Then (A) her sister will wash her feet, and
C,D)
A,D: they will place one silver ring of 1/2 shekel of
/75. silver in the water that washed her feet, (and) her sister will get (it).
C: [from the water that] washed her feet, her sister
/75. will get a silver ring of 1/2 shekel of silver.
(A,C) The NIN.DINGIR will ascend her (A) bed and lie down.

76. A: On the seventh day, the men of the *qidašu* will slaughter at the house of her father the one ox that went ahead of the NIN.DINGIR,
C: On the eighth day, they will slaughter at the house of her father the one ox that went ahead of the NIN.DINGIR,
77. A: (and) divide it among themselves.
C: (and) the men of the *qidašu* will divide it among themselves.

---

[21] Arnaud's "juste à son chevet" makes sense, though *ana bāb rēšīša* is difficult. The phrase *a-na* KÁ is not an attested Akkadian compound preposition, and the 3fs suffix *-ša* could have either the priestess or the bed (*eršu*, a feminine noun) as its antecedent. Since SAG.DU/*qaqqadu* is used for the priestess' "head" elsewhere in the ritual (lines 4, 42), the bed seems the more likely referent, and this seems a more likely location for a table. For the "head" of a bed in Akkadian, see *AHw* s.v. *rēšu* B3c, "Kopfseite v Bett" (NB texts).

[22] It is not clear to whom or what the distributive "each" (TA.ÀM) may refer.

[23] Arnaud translates, "Le plateau de la table un chanteur prend." Elsewhere in this festival the word GARZA/*parṣu* represents some part of the meat which is placed (*šakānu*) before the gods in offering (see the commentary, the GARZA/PA+AN), but the idiom *parṣī leqû*, "to perform a ritual," is well-established in later Akkadian texts (see *CAD* s.v. *leqû* 5a; *AHw* s.v. *parṣu(m)* B3 "Kult(ordnung) aufnehmen"), and makes sense in conjunction with the ritual singing.

(A,C) The man of (A) the king of the land will get the kidneys of the ox plus his share.[24]

78. A: The ^{lú}ḪAL will get the *ḫaṣītu*-meat plus his share, the head, the intestines, (and) the fat.

C: The ^{lú}ḪAL will get the *ḫaṣītu*-meat plus his share, the head of the ox, the intestines of the ox, the fat of the ox, and the one hide of the ox.

79. A: The singers will get the lungs plus their share.

C: The lungs plus their share (are) for ("of") the singers.

80. (A,C) The men of the *qidašu* will eat half of its intestines. As for the four tables which they set up for the gods: among them (there were) two pure tables and two impure

81. (A,C) tables. The ^{lú}ḪAL and the singer(s) will divide (them) among themselves; the ^{lú}ḪAL (and) the singers

82. (A,C) also will divide among themselves the hides of all the sheep.

A: The ^{lú}ḪAL will get three ox hides.

C: The ^{lú}ḪAL will get the hide of the ox ... that the NIN.DINGIR(?) offered to ^{d}NIN.KUR.

83. (A,C) For the seven days, the ^{lú}ḪAL and the singers will get one dinner-loaf each (and) one jar of barley-beer each.

C: The ^{lú}ḪAL will get the *ḫaṣītu*-meat of the oxen and the sheep for all the days. The singers will get the lungs of all the oxen and the sheep. They will share the meat of the offering(?) of the ox among the gods.

84. A: When the NIN.DINGIR sits down at her banquet, the singers will get one shekel of silver.

C: When the NIN.DINGIR sits down at her banquet, five shekels (are) the gift for ("of") the ^{lú}ḪAL (and) one(?) shekel (is) the gift for ("of") the singers.

85. A: In a good year, they will give her from the *bīt tukli* thirty *parīsu* of barley. In a bad year, she will get fifteen *parīsu* of barley.

---

[24] There is a problem with translating "his" because the last "share" goes to the plural "singers." Arnaud renders ḪA.LA-*šu* "leurs/ses parages," an alternative, though he translates "le chanteur." However, *zittu* should indicate portions allotted to people, and the plural desigation for the singers is not consistent (see lines 73 and 74).

C: In a good year, th[ey will gi]ve(?)] from the divine (store)house thirty *parīsu* of barley as the barley allotment of the NIN.DINGIR. And i[f (it is) a bad year, she will get(?) fifteen *parīsu*] of barley as her barley allotment.

86. (A) They will give her from the divine (store)house six hundred (shekels?) of wool, two *ḫittu*-jars of oil, one *zadu*-jar of oil, four hundred (shekels?) of aromatics,

87. (A) five *ḫubu* of wine, two racks of grapes, two racks of apples(?),

88. (A,C) two racks of apricots(?), one jar of milk, one large (jar) of soured milk, one *parīsu* of emmer, one *parīsu* of aromatics,

89. (A,C) three *qu'û*-jars of malt beer, two pairs of sandals, two pairs of boots, two gazelles,

90. (A,C) two fish, (and) four pigeons (C; A: birds)--for ("of") one year.

91. (A, B,C) When the NIN.DINGIR goes to her fate,

A: they will slaughter one ox (and) one sheep in the house.

92. (A) They will offer to Šahru one sheep, one *zadu*-jar of oil, [( )] *ḫizzibu* <?> (and) two ...

93. (A) The ^{lú}ḪAL will get the hide of that ox. One sheep ... ??

94. A: These items are for ("of") the house of her father. The city (gets) nothing.

B: The house of her father will take her ritual appurtenances(?), (and) the city (gets) nothing.

III. THE NIN.DINGIR INSTALLATION (EMAR 369): COMMENTARY

A. STRUCTURE

1. The NIN.DINGIR Installation as Festival

Emar text 369 is one of two rituals for installation of a high priestess at Emar; text 370 is the installation of the *maš'artu*, a priestess important enough to join two NIN.DINGIR's at the special banquet tables in 369.16-17, 55-58. These two rituals stand out from most of Emar ritual in that while the gods are naturally key players, the focus is on a human participant who is not the king.

To those who recorded Emar ritual instructions, these two installations belonged to the class of "festival": EZEN, properly *isinnu*, but not attested at Emar with syllabic spelling.[1] I have chosen the English translation, "festival," in spite of the ambiguity of the term.[2]

---

[1] Note the polyglot vocabulary from Ugarit, Ug 5 137 iii.6, (Sumerian) EZEN = (Akkadian) *i-sí-nu* = (Hurrian) *e-⌈li?⌉*= (Ugaritic) *da-ab-ḫu*; S[a] Vocab, 197.1, in John Huehnergard, *Ugaritic Vocabulary in Syllabic Transcription*, Harvard Semitic Studies 32, Atlanta: Scholars Press, 1987, 42-43. We cannot be certain that any of these represents the true Emar reading for the Semitic term.

[2] Jack M. Sasson, "The calendar and festivals of Mari during the reign of Zimri-Lim," in Marvin A. Powell and Ronald H. Sack, eds., *Studies in Honor of Tom B. Jones*, AOAT 203, Neukirchener: Neukirchen-Vluyn, 1979, 123, observes that the word can refer to either a periodic celebration or any time of celebration marked by feasting, ceremonies or other observances. He notes that at Mari the Akkadian word *isinnu* is not restricted to events tied to the calendar. Of the Emar "festivals," only the *zukru* is explicitly cyclical.

The festivals included the installations (369.48; 370.41); the *zukru* (373.36, 65, 174, 210), a New Year festival tied to a seven-year cycle; the *kissu* "throne"(?)[3] feasts for various gods;[4] and some set of festivals which seems to end with the *ḫenpu* of oxen (394.26-44, especially line 39, *i-na gáb-bi* EZEN.MEŠ *an-na-ti*, "in all these festivals"). Breaks in the tablets prevent sure distinction of these "festivals" from rituals not given that definition, but some fairly complete ritual texts do not receive it. These include Emar 452, a cycle of offerings in the month of Abû which has some special relation to the dead; text 460, the offering set for *Aštartu tāḫāzi* along with other gods and human officials; and the intact rite for the Hittite gods, Emar 471. It is likely that the term EZEN/*isinnu*(?) referred to a particular subset of Emar ritual, though our NIN.DINGIR installation shows that the word did not have to appear in the heading of a "festival."

The heading in 369.1 follows a pattern found in both the festivals and other rituals, using an incomplete sentence (with no verb) which begins *ṭuppu* (or *ṭuppi*) *parṣī* ("tablet of rites"), and then defines the occasion or player at the center. In text 369, this is a player, the NIN.DINGIR of the storm god at Emar. It is the festival itself in 385.1, a heading which may refer to the whole set of *kissu* feasts. Likewise, the rites are of "the *imištu* ceremony of the king," in 392.1.[5] On the other hand, Emar 471 is defined in terms of the deities, "the gods of Hatti" (line 1).

In light of these patterns, the titles in lines 1 and 48 in the NIN.DINGIR installation should be roughly equivalent:

-- *pár-ṣi* NIN.DINGIR ᵈIM *ša* ᵘʳᵘ[*E-m*]*ar* (1)
-- EZEN *da-at-na-ti ša* NIN.DINGIR (48)

---

3 See below, The *kissu* Festivals.
4 385.1, 2, Dagan; 385.27, ᵈEREŠ.KI.GAL; (386.1), Ea; 387.1, Išḫara and ᵈNIN.URTA; 388.1, all the *kissu* festivals; and 370.113 in the *maš'artu* installation.
5 Another ritual which is introduced by the term *ṭuppu*, "tablet," is 460.1, *ṭup-pu an-nu-ú* (with copy), for the rites of *Aštartu tāḫāzi*. After *ṭuppu annû*, Arnaud reads *ša ṣi*ˡ*-ra-ḫi* ᵈINANNA MÈ, "Cette tablette est du cri d'Astarté du combat," based on the Akkadian noun *ṣerḫu* (cf. *ṣiriḫtu*). As Arnaud states in his note to the text, his *ṣi*ˡ is in fact the AD-sign, and I find no other instance of **ṣiraḫu* to support such a reading here. One expects a noun in genitive relation to Aštart of Battle. Perhaps read *ša-aṭ*(?)*-ra-ḫi*, as a (Hurrian?) formation of *šaṭru* (cf. 373.194, *ki-i ša i-na ṭup-pí ša-aṭ-ru*, "just as written on the tablet"); so, "the recorded (things) of Aštart." In the *zukru* instance, the tablet that is written refers to instructions for offerings to the gods (line 195). The Hurrian formation is not confirmed by other features of the text, and this remains only a guess, based on the *zukru* line.

The obscure term *da-at-na-ti* may be part of a title for the installation, "the festival of the *datnāti* of the NIN.DINGIR." Its meaning is unknown, and the word likely belongs to the local dialect.[6] Although Arnaud translates *datnāti* as a demonstrative pronoun modifying *ūmi*, "pendant *ces* trois jours," the plural *datnāti* would not modify the singular "third day" of 369.48, *i-na* 3 u_4-*mi* ("on the third day").[7]

In spite of the uncertain interpretation of line 48, the installation of Baal's NIN.DINGIR displays closest kinship with the other Emar festivals, especially the *maš'artu* installation and the *kissu* festivals. Comparison with other texts from this family of rituals consistently illuminates Emar 369.

2. Outline

The NIN.DINGIR installation covers approximately nine days. Based on a preliminary reading, Arnaud suggests that the festival covers seven days, and several other have followed him.[8] Perhaps comparison with the week-long Israelite festivals or simply the magic of the number itself produces a disposition toward the seven-day length, but various details of the text suggest the alternative scheme elaborated below.

The NIN.DINGIR installation tablets unfortunately do not supply easy headings: "day 1," "day 2," "day 3," etc. Various temporal phrases define the movement of time through the festival, but the fundamental units in the text itself are determined by topic as well as time. The tablets themselves provide some indication of major units by means of horizontal dividing lines that fall at logical boundaries. These are helpful for identifying what the Emar scribes

---

[6] Perhaps the term could be a noun derived from the verb *nadānu*. The Assyrian form of the verb, *tadānu* (see *AHw* s.v. *tadānu(m)*), might yield the noun *tadittu* for the Babylonian *nidintu*, with the plural *tadnātu*, "gifts." (See *AHw* s.v. *nidintu(m)*, *nidittu(m)* I, and *CAD* s.v. *nidintu*; this possibility was suggested by J. Huehnergard, personal communication.) Dietrich, *UF* 21 82 n.78, adopts this interpretation. Line 48 would read, "On the third day of the festival of gifts (or Dietrich, das Festes des Übergabe) of the NIN.DINGIR...," referring to the presentations that take place during the first day of the *malluku* (see the text, and commentary below). However, it seems awkward to use the term EZEN, which should belong to the entire installation, for a subset of the whole.

[7] See the text, above, for the variant readings.

[8] See Arnaud, "Religion assyro-babylonienne," *AEPHER* 84 (1975-76) 223. The others include Sapin, *UF* 15 (1983) 188-189; Frayne, *BiOr* 42 (1985) 20-21; Eiko Matsushima, "Les rituels du mariage divin dans les documents accadiens," *ASJ* 10 (1988) 96-97; Dietrich, *UF* 21 (1989) esp. 87-89.

themselves saw as points of transition, but they do not display a consistent regimen, and we cannot develop an outline strictly based on scribal dividers. Horizontal markers are found in the following places:

After lines:	6	10	19	21	28	39	48	54	58	75	83	84	90	94
Text:														
A (1-94)	x	x	x	x	(space)	x	-			x	x	-	x	x
B (19-69, 94)					?	x	x	x	x	-	-			
C (5-22, 70-91)	x	-	x	?						x	x	x	x	
D (48-75)							x	x	x					
E (14-21)			x											

Working from both the horizontal dividers and considerations from context, the structure of the festival may be outlined as follows:

- 1 Heading.
- 2-6 The day of selection.
    - 6 The *qaddušu*-ceremony for the next day.
- 7-28 The day of consecration by shaving (*gallubu*).
    - 7-19 Shaving, sacrificial procession ending at the ^{d}IM temple, offering and feast.
    - 20-21 That evening: return to the father's house.
    - 22-28 The *qaddušu*-ceremony for the installation (*malluku*).
- 29-58 The installation (*malluku*).
    - 29-39 Sacrificial procession ending at the ^{d}IM temple, offering and feast.
    - 40-48 That evening: enthronement and return to the father's house.
    - 49-58 Seven days of feasting (*šūkultu*) at the *bīt* NIN.DINGIR, with the new priestess at the father's house; counted to include the enthronement.

59-75 The final day.

59-62 The NIN.DINGIR leaves the father's house for the last time, as a bride.

63-75 That evening: the last procession ending at the ^{d}IM temple (63-68), preparation and mounting of the bed (69-75).

76-94 Administration.

76-83 Allotments for ritual players.

84-90 The annual allotment for the NIN.DINGIR.

91-94 Ritual and inheritance after her death.

3. The Calendar of the Festival

The calendar of the NIN.DINGIR installation is entirely internal, covering roughly nine days that begin with the confirmation of a new candidate. That is, the festival is in no way linked to the annual calendar, unlike the *zukru* (Emar 373), for instance. Arnaud considers that a new priestess was likely chosen every year, and the allotment of the priestess "for one year" (*ša* MU.1.KÁM, line 90) would cover that term.[9] If, however, the installation represents a major annual rite at Emar it is difficult to explain why it is not explicitly linked to the annual calendar and thus tied to the regular order of ritual time, at a significant season.

Lacking any reference to the external calendar, it is natural to conclude that the festival is occasional rather than regular, and the expected occasion would be the death of the previous priestess. The process of selection and installation of Baal's NIN.DINGIR-priestess would be set in motion when the old one dies. One barrier has blocked this interpretation: the previous priestess (NIN.DINGIR *maḫirītu*) is provided a table for receiving ritual meat portions in lines 16 and 55. In the context of ancient Near Eastern religion,

---

[9] Arnaud, *AEPHER* 84 223; cf. Arnaud, "Les textes suméro-accadiens de Meskéné (Syrie) et l'Ancien Testament," *Bulletin de la Société Ernest Renan*, 1979 (*Revue de l'Histoire des Religions* 197 [1980]), 117. He is followed by the same scholars who speak of a seven-day festival (see above).

death should not be perceived as an absolute barrier to participation in the affairs of the living, and in fact a number of rites in the NIN.DINGIR installation make good sense when understood as mourning for the departed office-holder. It appears that the festival balances the focus on the new priestess with a secondary attention to the needs of the old, and this balance will be examined further, below.[10]

The opening three days of the NIN.DINGIR festival are bound together by a set of tightly interlocking events, and corresponding descriptions in the text. The ritual links are the two *qaddušu*-ceremonies, which take place on the evening before the event each "sanctifies": the *gallubu* (shaving), 369.6, and the *malluku* (installation proper), (369.22-28). These two ceremonies perform the same function (see below, Special Festival Rites), though the first is portrayed as a single offering, and the second details a more elaborate feast involving ᵈIM and ᵈNIN.KUR. Each new day then begins *ina šanî ūmi*, "on the next day (or morning)" (lines 7, 29), with action divided between the daytime and the evening, the latter introduced by *ana pānī nubatti*, "just before the evening watch" (lines 20, 40).

On both the day of consecration by shaving and the day of enthronement,[11] the NIN.DINGIR sets out for the temple of ᵈIM and then returns to her father's house in the evening. Within this larger scheme, the two days' activities are similar at several points, giving considerable help to reconstruction of broken sections of the text. Parallels include the following:

-- *ina šanî ūmi gallubu/malluku ša* NIN.DINGIR (7, 29).

-- One ox and six sheep, the NIN.DINGIR's offering, go to ᵈIM's temple. The weapon of the god (*kakki ili*) [12] and the NIN.DINGIR go behind them, and the singers (*zammārū*) go ahead of them (7-8, 29-30).

-- The *kubadu*-ceremony is performed (*epēšu*), with the divine weapon carried (*našû*) by the father on the first day, but by the NIN.DINGIR on the second (9-10, 30-31).

---

[10] This aspect of the ritual was observed independently by W.L. Moran and P. Steinkeller (personal communications).

[11] The first day of the seven-day *malluku* or "installation" will be referred to as the "enthronement day," from the central event in the NIN.DINGIR's progress, that evening.

[12] The most common form is ᵍⁱˢTUKUL DINGIR.MEŠ (see below), but the MEŠ may simply mark the logogram as such.

-- When the *kubadu* is finished (*gamāru*), the seven animals are sacrificed to ᵈIM (10-11, 31-32A).
-- The same meal that is set out for the gods on the first day (11-12) is set out for ᵈIM on the second (37-38): the GARZA/*parṣu* of the sacrificed sheep and ox are placed before the god(s) (*šakānu*), followed by equivalent amounts and types of bread (also *šakānu*), and finally cups are filled with wine and barley-beer (38, just wine in 12).
-- The men of the *qidašu* and the *ḫussu*-men (see below) eat and drink in ᵈIM's temple (13, 38). On the day of enthronement, two more groups of feasters are added.
-- Five tables (text A) are set for the same five local dignitaries mentioned in lines 55-58 (15, 39).
-- The remainder of the second day is "just as for the shaving day" (*kî ša ūmi gallubi*, 39), and thus repeats lines 15-19.

The differences between the sections are highlighted by the common framework. Most striking are the special role of the *bēl bīti* on the *gallubu*-day (lines 14-15) and the side trips made to the *bīt tukli* and *bīt Gadda* on the enthronement day (lines 33-36). These will be discussed further in the sections dealing with players and places of the festival. The prohibitions against the NIN.DINGIR herself entering these sacred locations are dropped for the similar visits made during the final day procession, when she is the one to prepare a feast for the gods (lines 64-68).

The evening of the *gallubu*-day is still part of the NIN.DINGIR's selection and preparation, linked by repetition of the anointing ritual which was performed after her designation (lines 3-4, 20-21). However, the next evening marks her real installation into office (*malluku*) by enthronement, in spite of the fact that her transfer into ᵈIM's household is not yet accomplished. The detail of lines 40-48 reflects the importance of this third day. All the rites performed before the procession returns from the ᵈIM temple to her father's house proclaim the NIN.DINGIR's new position. She is seated on a throne (or chair) of office (40) and given special gifts (40-42). Though one more return to her father's household is required, this time the new NIN.DINGIR is carried on her brothers' shoulders, presumably on her chair (43-45). Imbedded in the description of the procession back to the father's house are instructions for obeisance from the city elders and gifts from these and her brothers (44-45).

By the evening of the third festival day, the NIN.DINGIR has been enthroned, but she remains at her father's house for seven days, apparently counted from the day of her enthronment. During this time, a feast is held at the *bīt* NIN.DINGIR in the temple of ^{d}IM, before she is finally installed there in her new home. As with the *maš'artu* installation (see 370.41), the term *malluku* appears to refer to the full seven-day period, inaugurated in Emar 369 by the enthronement day, and celebrated with offerings and feasting. Although the seven-day period is already mentioned in line 46, when the divine weapon is girded on ^{d}NIN.KUR, and it is probably anticipated by the "seven days" of line 26B, description of the enthronement day continues through line 48. The subsequent offering associated with ^{d}NIN.KUR is made "on that same day" (*ina ūmi šâšūma*, 47), and the crying of the *nugagtu* is "on the third day" (48). Moreover, the apportionment to the gods of Emar (48) is a closing act for two previous sections (line 19, and 39 implied; see *zâzu*, below). The description of rites for the period of celebration opens with the phrase U_4.7.KÁM, "For seven days...," and this unit of time is repeated in lines 51, 54, and 57, always with the same meaning. These phrases must be distinguished from those that begin with *ina*, such as *ina* U_4.3.KÁM (B; A, *ina* 3 u_4*-mi*), "on the third day." In the Emar rituals, temporal phrases introduced by the preposition *ina* consistently indicate "time when" (and thus ordinal numbers, as "third"), rather than "how long" (so cardinal numbers, as "three").[13]

The time formulae in the NIN.DINGIR text through line 58 therefore move the ritual through nine days, if the selection is counted separately based on the phrase *ina šanî ūmi*, "on the next day," in line 7. The timing of the last day of the festival is difficult to fix because the formula at the transition in line 59A is lost in a break, and the texts of B and D offer no absolute reckoning. Text B refers (twice?) to some *ūmi arki*, which might be translated as "the last day" -- of the seven-day sequence? Text D provides only a garbled phrase in line 59 (see text). The one piece of evidence that could confirm the suggested interpretation of the phrase *ūmi arki* is found at the beginning of the administrative section. Line 76 accounts for the ox which went with the priestess in the last day's procession (line 63) but was returned to the house of the *bēl bīti* without being sacrificed (lines 68-69A). It is to be slaughtered "on

[13] See 369.7, 29, 76; the *maš'artu* seven-day sequence, 370.41, 48, 51, 60, 63, 66; and the formula that occurs repeatedly in the sequence of month dates in 452.3, 7, 8, 9, 30, 31, 36, 43, cf. 53.

the seventh (A), or eighth (C) day." The seventh day in text A is surely counted from the start of the *malluku*, and the eighth day of text C could either count the festival as eight days (shaving day plus seven-day *malluku*) or envision slaughter on the first day after the completed *malluku* (possibly a separate "final day").

The seven-day unit is not primarily a standard festival length. Rather, it is the basic unit of feasting and celebration for various ritual occasions and is incorporated into larger festival complexes. At Emar, this can be seen in the NIN.DINGIR installation, the *maš'artu* installation (Emar 370), and the *zukru* festival (Emar 373; see below on both). The *maš'artu* consists of a seven-day feasting sequence, with a preliminary (eighth) sanctification day (*qaddušu*). The *zukru* festival involves rites for the preceding month and preceding year in a seven-year cycle, but the *zukru* proper occupies seven days counted from the fourteenth day of the first month in the seventh year. Although the Israelite festivals are commonly perceived as seven days long, the priestly writings of the Torah describe both the spring and autumn festivals as seven-day periods with added rites for an eighth day. The seven-day feast of Unleavened Bread is introduced by the preceding day of Passover. The feast of Booths includes seven days of offerings followed by an eighth day for special assembly (see Lev 23.5-6, 34-36; cf. Num 28).

The NIN.DINGIR festival is therefore approximately nine days long, depending on whether the final day is the last day of the seven-day *malluku* or the following day. The administrative section (after line 76) does not extend the festival proper. The allotments for the diviner and the singers in line 83 specify their portions as for "the men of the *qidašu*" for the seven days of the major feast (see line 54, and more below). A list of goods for the priestess represents her annual allotment for her term of office, and the calendar of rites for the NIN.DINGIR concludes with the end of that term, at her death. The last lines (91-94) of the text anticipate the closing of her affairs "when she goes to her fate."

4. Literary Considerations

The NIN.DINGIR installation was likely an occasion of high drama, but the installation text is a dry manual focused entirely on the mechanics of the event.[14] Surely the celebration of this event included prayers, spoken instructions, or explanatory story, but the text has no liturgy and is composed by and for administators. Emar 369 was found among all the other ritual tablets and fragments in an archive which also included the personal records of a diviner's family (the temple M_1). The diviner is shown throughout the temple and ritual texts to be an administrator and supervisor of various religious affairs (see the lúḪAL, below), so both composition and any use of the installation text likely would have remained within the diviner's circle.

The NIN.DINGIR text, with the other rituals, is not presented as a record of a particular festival's execution but is rather prescriptive. The verbs are universally present/future, without reference to any event beyond the scope of the festival. We find specific place-names but no personal names. Emar ritual is conducted from the perspective of the impersonal "they." The general 3mp view is demonstrated in 369.8-9, with the consecutive verbs *ikaššadū* and *ugallabū*. Those who "arrive" in line 8 are the animals, the divine weapon of the god, the singers, and the NIN.DINGIR herself, yet line 9 indicates that the priestess is now the object of shaving with no identification of a new subject. She is shaved by unspecified ritual personnel, and we have no grounds for picking out any one group. (Compare other major ritual texts such as 370, 373, 385, 446, and 452 for the same phenomenon.)

The installation text appears to have been composed by building a framework out of the distinctive ritual events and then clothing the frame according to detail that could not be remembered automatically. Lists of participants at different meals and the amounts and types of provisions would vary from rite to rite, for instance. Occasionally, specific details can be explained as expressions of this method. The return of the *purû* (lots?) may have been considered automatic except for the specific offering that must accompany it (lines 5-6). Only the NIN.DINGIR installation mentions the carrying (*našû*) of the divine weapon in the *kubadu*-ceremony, but we should not conclude that all other *kubadu*'s lack this element. The detail

[14] B.A. Levine separates descriptive from prescriptive Ugaritic ritual texts. Descriptive ritual records the details from actual performance of rites, while prescriptive texts offer a program for any performance. See Levine, "The descriptive ritual texts from Ugarit: some formal and functional features of the *Genre*," in Carol L. Meyers and M. O'Connor, eds., *The Word of the Lord Shall Go Forth*, Winona Lake, IN: Eisenbrauns, 1983, 467; cf. Levine, "Ugaritic descriptive rituals," *JCS* 17 (1963) 105-111. The Emar rituals appear to be prescriptive.

communicates an important movement in the progress of the priestess, when her father must perform this rite the first time, before she takes over the role on the enthronement day (lines 10, 31A, B(31-36)e).

Whether or not the text was consulted for performance of an installation, composition itself would have served as an aid to memory. At Emar, the diviners dominated both religious and scribal affairs, and scribal training that involved copying rituals would have prepared apprentices for both areas of responsibility.

B. THE PLAYERS

1. The Gods

The storm god

Emar 369 records the rites for the festival of the NIN.DINGIR of ^{d}IM, the storm god at Emar (369.1). ^{d}IM is thus the central god of the ritual, and he is the most frequent individual recipient of offerings (lines 5, 11, 24, (32A), 34A, 37, 52, 66, not counting the *kubadu*). However, he plays no active role (vs. ^{d}NIN.KUR and Hebat): his statue is not moved or adorned, and the description of the final night is concluded without mentioning him. Perhaps it is appropriate for the great god to remain in royal state in his court while provision is made for his marriage to the human priestess. This static role makes a vivid contrast to the mobility of Dagan and ^{d}NIN.URTA during the *zukru* festival's chariot processions, and works within the fixed setting of the temple.

Throughout the NIN.DINGIR festival and the rest of the Emar ritual texts the name of the storm god is written ^{d}IM, with no instances of syllabic spelling or phonetic complements. Residents of Emar would have been familiar with the storm gods of the Hurrians, Canaanites, and Assyrians, and ^{d}IM could be read Teššub, Ba^{c}lu/Haddu, or Adad. Identification of the storm god at Emar and evaluation of his place in the Emar pantheon requires consideration of materials and issues involving deities not present in the NIN.DINGIR's installation. In order to avoid redundancy, I have gathered all the evidence bearing on these problems in the final section of this study, which deals with patterns and development in the Emar cult, chapter IV.

The storm god appears in several Emar documents relating to temple affairs. Four of these are from the southern temple of the pair found in chantier E:[15] Emar 42.4, 12, 17, 21 (all ^{d}U);[16] 45.1 and 52.1, headings of weapon assignments for the storm god's temple; and 59.1-2, gold belonging to the storm god (these three written ^{d}IM). From temple M_1, there is a legal document that refers to a tablet of ^{d}IM's temple (202.13), a list of sheep that mentioned ^{d}IM (326.3), and the list of personnel, 275.1, 6 (see below).

All the gods of Emar

The gods *en masse* are never long neglected in the NIN.DINGIR installation. They are sanctified with offerings[17] during the *qaddušu*-ceremony on the first day (369.6), apportioned beef after it is over (line 83C), and receive food throughout: lines 11, 12, 19, 22, 24 (four gods are specified), 28, 48, 49, 50, 58-59D(?), 65, and 66. These offerings are made when the celebrants are at ^{d}IM's temple (11, 12, 19, 66), the father's house (24, 28, 48), the *bīt* NIN.DINGIR (49, 50), and ^{d}NIN.KUR's temple (65).

While the gods are prominent through the whole festival, they remain a nebulous entity at many points in the event. In two idioms they are described as "all (*gabbu*) the gods of Emar": all the gods are sanctified with bread and beer in the *qaddušu* preparation (lines 6, 22), and distribution of offerings by the verb *zâzu* is for all the gods (see below, Provision). This longer phrase is quite common in the *zukru* festival text (see below, Binding the Community), and it appears in the line that introduces the exhaustive offering list of 373.66-167: DINGIR.MEŠ [^{uru}]*E-mar gáb-bá i-pa-al-*[*la-ḫu*], "they will give cult to all the gods of Emar" (line 65). The list is surely intended to name all the gods who will receive offerings under the auspices of the general phrase. When the NIN.DINGIR installation uses the same phrase, a similar long list should be indicated.

In contrast to the inclusive "all the gods of Emar," the four tables set before "the gods" (DINGIR.MEŠ) during the sanctification of the

---

[15] Jean Margueron, "Les fouilles françaises de Meskéné-Emar (Syrie)," *CRAIBL* 1975, 208.

[16] Three votive offerings from the king; see Daniel Arnaud, "Traditions urbaines et influences semi-nomades à Emar, à l'âge du bronze récent," in Jean Margueron, ed., *Le Moyen-Euphrate, zone de contacts et d'échanges*, Strasbourg: Université des Sciences Humaines de Strasbourg, 1980, 253.

[17] See the note with the translation. In this context the verb *qaddušu* means "to treat as

enthronement day (lines 24-25) involve a limited group: ^{d}IM and a partner (Hebat?), and "the gods below" (DINGIR.MEŠ KI.TA). Here, "the gods" represent a balanced combination of heavenly and underworld deities (two tables for each). Is this the intended reference group when the phrase appears so often through the rest of the ritual? The evidence does not provide an answer, but this one case of a more limited definition suggests that "the gods" and "all the gods of Emar" may not indicate the same groups.

The *zukru* liturgy says there are seventy gods in the Emar pantheon (373.38), a traditional figure, though it goes on to include many more than that in the elaborate list of lines 66-167. Either the figure is thought of as no more than a customary round number, or it refers to less than the whole pantheon.[18] Instructions are given to offer "seventy pure (KÙ.GA) lambs," presumably to the same seventy gods of Emar (373.37). This recalls the distinction between the pure and impure tables of the NIN.DINGIR festival *qaddušu*-ceremony (369.80-81, see lines 24-25), where the impure (*la-a* KÙ.GA) tables are for the underworld gods. Perhaps the seventy gods do not include underworld deities: for example, Alal and Amaza in the *kissu* festival, 385.9, parallel to the NIN.DINGIR festival's DINGIR.MEŠ KI.TA (369.25) and high on the *zukru* offering list (373.73).

The number "seventy" appears in other ritual texts. Seventy birds are distributed (*zâzu*, D) to the gods in the offering cycle, 463.6, and ^{d}EREŠ.KI.GAL's *kissu* festival may indicate a tradition of seventy underworld gods. Seventy *kirru*-vessels are filled with beer before her (385.33), and seventy portions of *ḫukku*-bread and *maš'irtu*-meat are set "before them" (line 34) -- seventy gods?

We also find the "gods of Hatti," DINGIR.MEŠ ^{kur}*Ḫat-ti*, at Emar (271.3; 471.1 *Ḫa-at-ti*). See below, in chapter IV.

^{d}NIN.KUR

^{d}NIN.KUR and ^{d}IM are the only prominent Emar gods in the NIN.DINGIR festival. Hebat, Adammatera, and Šaḫru all belong to a fairly narrow setting, but ^{d}NIN.KUR appears throughout Emar ritual and other temple texts. These appearances include the following:

---

holy," which I translate with the single English verb "to sanctify."

[18] Arnaud suggests that the long list may indicate seventy consorts or goddesses to parallel the seventy gods, but the figure is more likely just a round number. See Arnaud, in *Le Moyen Euphrate*, 254, n.44; *Bulletin de la Société Ernest Renan*, 1979, 117; "La

- -- the *zukru*, 373.11, 76, 154, 155, 160, 164
- -- the *kissu* festivals, 385.5, 7, 21; 388.2
- -- the cycle of offerings for the month of Abû, 452.33
- -- the *Ar'uri* ritual, 393.2-3, 7
- -- first in the offering lists, 379.1 and 382.1, and present in others, 378.12, 14, 16, 46; 380.6; 381.5
- -- her priesthood in a letter, 268.7, 9, 23
- -- inventory of her silver possessions, text 284; cf. 287.1-5, gold and bronze

^{d}NIN.KUR has several cults at Emar, reflected in various compound names: ^{d}NIN.KUR ^{uru}*Ú-ri*, 287.5;[19] ^{d}NIN.KUR GAŠAN *na-aḫ-li*, "mistress of the wadi," 373.154; ^{d}NIN.KUR GAŠAN *ka-ak-ka-ri*, 373.155 and 378.16, "mistress of the environs ('circle')," cf. the bread, 387.5; 434.8; 460.21, 24, 29;[20] ^{d}NIN.KUR GAŠAN *iš-pa-(a-)at*, "mistress of the quiver," 373.160 and 378.46; ^{d}NIN.KUR *ša* KÁ *Li-'i-mi Šar-ta*, "of the gate of the Šarta clan" (*CAD* s.v. *līmu* C, only lexical, including the spelling *li-'-mu*; cf. Ugaritic *lʾim*, Hebrew *lĕʾôm*), 373.164 and 378.14. All the last four involve terms known to occur in the Syrian or western regions,[21] and all these names except the first are in lists associated with the *zukru* festival (text 378 leads with Dagan *bēl bukari*, found nowhere else but the *zukru*).

^{d}NIN.KUR is involved in the NIN.DINGIR's installation from the time of anointing (oil comes from her temple, line 4) to the final day (receiving offering during the final procession, line 65). This activity is discussed under "^{d}NIN.KUR's Role," below.

The gods below

In line 25, these receive two tables (cf. 80-81, "impure" tables) with a set of offerings during the sanctification ceremony for the enthronement day at the father's house. Alal and Amaza take this position in the *kissu* for Dagan, 385.7-9. See the discussion of the *kissu* in chapter IV. The *ilāni šaplûti* are attested in Neo-Babylonian ritual, TuL 130/3, etc.; see *AHw*, s.v. *šaplû(m)* 5e.

---

bibliothèque d'un devin Syrien à Meskéné-Emar (Syrie)," *CRAIBL* 1980, 385.

[19] The city-name ^{uru}*ú/u-ra-a* is found at Ugarit with the alphabetic equivalent *hry*, see J. Huehnergard, *Ugaritic Vocabulary in Syllabic Transcription*, Harvard Semitic Studies 32, Atlanta: Scholars Press, 1987, 252 and n.264.

[20] Hebrew *kikkār* signifies both a geographical circle or district and a circular loaf of bread.

[21] "Wadi" (*naḫlu/naḫallu*) occurs in texts from Mari and Nuzi; "quiver" (*išpatu*) appears at

The Hittites have the terms *siunes ERṢETI* and *siunes katteres*, "deities of the earth" and "lower deities."[22]

Adammatera

Adammatera receives a single lamb during the processions to the temple of ᵈIM on the enthronement and final days (369.33 and 64), both times at the *bīt tukli*. Close association with this storehouse for offering materials raises the possibility that Adammatera could be a god of stores, though this would require confirmation from other evidence.

Outside this festival, he only makes one appearance, receiving one sheep in the annual offering cycle, Emar 446.77, during the month of Anna, before an offering is made to the *abû* of the *bīt ili* (=*bīt tukli*?, see below). The involvement of the *abû* indicates some attention to the underworld in this ritual sequence.[23] The sheep is given by the *nupuḫannu*-men and the *ḫamša*-men. The *ḫamša'u*-men participate in the feasting at the *bīt* NIN.DINGIR in 369.53-54, as noted above, and the *nupuḫannu*-men supply a sheep for an offering to the *abû* of the *bīt tukli* on the 25th day of the rites in the month of Abû, the day when a *kubadu* is performed "at the gate of the grave" (452.32).

Adammatera is surely a longer name for the ancient Syrian god Adamma,[24] who is often paired with Rašap at Ebla, further strengthening his underworld associations.[25] This pairing recalls the juxtaposition of ᵈ*A-dam-ma-te*-[*ra*] and ᵈNÈ.IRI$_{11}$.GAL EN KI.LAM (*bēl maḫīri*, "lord of commerce") in adjacent segments of the broken offering list, Emar 465.2 and 4. The presence of Adamma in the Hurrian pantheon probably results from adoption by incoming Hurrian populations rather than Hurrian exportation.[26]

Hebat and her sikkānu

Hebat is ᵈIM's consort in the NIN.DINGIR installation and in the Emar god lists, though evidence which we will examine in a later section (see The

---

Alalaḫ, Nuzi, and in EA 29 from Mitanni.

22 See Volkert Haas, *Or* NS 45 (1976) 205.

23 See the Appendix on the *abû* in Emar 452.

24 I have not found the shorter form at Emar, except in the personal name *A-dam-ma*, Emar 14.8.

25 See Alfonso Archi, "Die ersten zehn Könige von Ebla," *ZA* 76 (1986) 214 and n.6; for example, the offering list ARET 7 150 IV:3-6 includes sheep for ᵈ*Ra-sa-ap wa* ᵈ*A-dam-ma*.

26 Archi, "Les dieux d'Ebla au IIIᵉ millénaire avant J.C. et les dieux d'Ugarit," *AAAS* 29-30 (1979-80) 171, following Emmanuel Laroche's comments at the 1977 Rencontre assyriologique; Haas, "Substratgottheiten des westhurrischen Pantheons," in *Les Hourrites*, RAI 24, *RHA* 36 (1978) 67-68; Gernot Wilhelm, *Gründzuge der Geschichte und Kultur der*

Gods of the Installations) points to an association between ᵈIM and Aštart/Ištar in 13th-century Emar. The relationships between these deities are discussed in chapter IV, below. Although Hebat is best known as the high goddess of the Hurrian pantheon borrowed by the Hittites in the mid-second millennium B.C.E., she has deep roots in northern Syria and a particular connection with Halab (see below). She is always paired with ᵈIM, whether the Hurrian Teššub or West Semitic Haddu, and they are divine spouses in the NIN.DINGIR festival as well. When the NIN.DINGIR presents ᵈIM and Hebat two figurines in 369.52, some kind of reference to marriage may be involved. When the priestess enters the household of ᵈIM as its human head, she enters a special relationship with Hebat as well, who is the divine (female) head of his household. An offering is made to Hebat (and the gods) daily throughout the seven-day feast before the final day (line 49).

The *sikkānu* of Hebat enters the *bīt Gadda* in the NIN.DINGIR's stead during the enthronement-day procession, after the priestess has offered it a lamb and anointed it just as she herself was anointed (369.34-36). When we combine this fact with the pairing in the *zukru* festival god list, we see that this *sikkānu* is a particular symbol of Hebat that inhabits the *bīt Gadda* with a statue of ᵈIM (373.165-166):

ᵈIM *ša* É *Gad-da*
ᵈ*Si-ka-ni ša* ᵈ*Ḫé-bat*

The *sikkānu* of Hebat may be indicated in a broken context in the ritual fragment, 444.3, [*si-ka-ni š*]*a*ꜝ ᵈ*Ḫé*-[*bat*].

Use of the term *sikkānu* for "stele" may be a West Semitic Syrian trait; the word does not appear in northern peripheral Akkadian texts with the strongest influence from the Hittite and Hurrian cultures, such as Boghazkoy, Nuzi, and Alalaḫ. Akkadian *si(k)kanu(m)*, "rudder," may be related through their similar upright form, but the more immediate equivalent is the term for "stele" found at Ugarit and Mari, *skn* and *sikkānum*.[27] Use of standing stones

---

Hurriter, Darmstadt: Wissenschaftliche Buchgesellschaft, 1982, 78.

[27] The Ugaritic term *skn* appears in two much-discussed contexts: the inscribed Dagan stele, KTU 6.13/UT 69, and the opening of the legend of ʾAqhat, KTU 1.17 I 26-28. In the first case the word should refer to the stone artifact itself, which records an offering to Dagan by *ṯryl*; the ʾAqhat instance speaks of the duties of a son, who should "set up the stele of his ancestral god(s)," *nṣb skn ʾilʾibh*. The interpretation of *skn* as "stele" is widely accepted: see Meindert Dijkstra and Johannes C. de Moor, "Problematical passages in the legend of Aqhatu," *UF* 7 (1976) 175; de Moor, "The ancestral cult in KTU 1.17:I.26-28," *UF* 17 (1986) 407; Manfried Dietrich and Oswald Loretz, "Bemerkungen zum Aqhat-Text. Zur ugaritischen Lexikographie (XIV)," *UF* 10 (1978) 67-68 and n.28, 29; Jean-Michel de

as focal points of the divine presence was a feature of Hittite practice as well. These *ḫuwaši*-stones were sometimes set up in temples, or could serve as the center of rural shrines without buildings.[28] Stelae have been found at several archaeological sites in the Syro-Palestinian region, including Ugarit (see above), Hazor, and Byblos/Gubla.[29] The stele also forms part of the late first-millennium Phoenician cult of Astarte.[30]

Tarragon, *Le culte à Ugarit d'après les textes de la pratique en cunéiformes alphabétiques*, Paris: J. Gabalda, 1980, 68-69; Marvin H. Pope, "The cult of the dead at Ugarit," in Gordon D. Young, ed., *Ugarit in Retrospect: Fifty Years of Ugarit and Ugaritic*, Winona Lake, IN: Eisenbrauns, 1981, 160-161; Paolo Xella, *I Testi Rituali di Ugarit I*, Roma: Consiglio Nazionale delle Ricerche, 1981, 297-299.

In his recent work, *Ugaritic Vocabulary in Syllabic Transcription*, 157, Huehnergard observes the term ZI-GA/QA-ni-ma in Ug 5 96.0,17, in a phrase which probably corresponds to Ugaritic *gt sknm*, and translates "statue(??)." This follows Edouard Lipiński, "*Skn* et *sgn* dans le sémitique occidental du nord," *UF* 5 (1973) 200-202, 207, who translates "substitut" or "image." J.F. Healey, "The underworld character of the god Dagan," *JNSL* 5 (1977) 46, does not consider the identification settled, but adopts "stele" for *skn*; cf. "The Ugaritic dead: some live issues," *UF* 18 (1986) 29, and "The 'pantheon' of Ugarit: further notes," *SEL* 5 (1988) 107, for further discussion of the Dagan stelae.

The interpretation of the Ugaritic word as a standing stone receives support from the Mari archives, which attest the noun *sikkānum*, "bétyle." J.-M. Durand devotes an entire article to treatment of this phenomenon, "Le culte des bétyles en Syrie," in Durand and J.-R. Kupper, eds., *Miscellanea Babylonica: mélanges offerts à Maurice Birot*, Paris: Editions Recherche sur les Civilisations, 1985, 79-84. The Mari item is usually spelled with doubled *-kk-*, often with the determinative NA_4, and sometimes associated with a specific deity, as in Emar 369. Compare ^{na4}*sí-ik-ka-nu-um ša* ^{d}IM, M. 7014, lines 5' and 13', and ^{na4}*sí-ik-ka-nu-um* [*ša* ^{d}]*Da-gan*, lines 3'-4' and 11' (page 83). These stones are 4 and 5 cubits (*ammatum*) long -- quite large. Durand observes that nothing indicates that the stones are used after the religious rites are completed, whereas the Emar *sikkānu* of Hebat resides in a shrine and appears to be a permanent fixture. It is interesting that the Mari stones are delivered from upstream at Lasqum, very near Emar on the Euphrates River.

28 See Hans G. Güterbock, "The Hittite temple according to written sources," in *Le temple et le culte*, RAI 20, TE ISTAMBUL: Nederlands historisch-archeologisch Instituut, 1975, 127; O.R. Gurney, *Some Aspects of Hittite Religion*, Oxford: The University Press, 1977, 36-38. Yazilikaya, the great rock shrine outside the Hittite capital of Boghazkoy/Hattuša, may have been associated with a *ḫuwaši*, according to Gurney, 40, and Itamar Singer, *The Hittite KI.LAM Festival*, I, Wiesbaden: Otto Harrassowitz, 1983, 101. In some cases, the *ḫuwaši* may have been a model or cult-object, since they may be made of wood or silver. See Güterbock, "Hethitische Götterbilder und Kultobjekte," in R.M. Boehmer and H. Hauptmann, eds., *Beiträge zur Altertumskunde Kleinasiens: Festschrift für Kurt Bittel*, Mainz am Rhein: Verlag Philipp von Zabern, 1983, 215; Muhibbe Darga, "Über das Wesen des *ḫuwaši*-Steines nach hethitischen Kultinventaren," *RHA* 27 (1969) 11, n.6.

29 For Hazor, see André Caquot, "Problèmes d'histoire religieuse," in M. Liverani, ed., *La Siria nel tardo bronzo*, Roma: Centro per le antichita e la storia dell'arte del vicino oriente, 1969, 62. On Byblos, see Maurice Dunand, "Byblos et ses temples après la pénétration Amorite," in Hans-Jörg Nissen and Johannes Renger, eds., *Mesopotamien und seine Nachbarn*, RAI 25, Berlin: Dietrich Reimer Verlag, 1982, 195-197.

30 Brigitte Soyez, "Le bétyle dans le culte de l'Astarté phénicienne," *MUSJ* 47 (1972) 149-

At Emar, we know that the *sikkānu* can function outside the strict limits of the cult, since it appears in curses from legal documents with the meaning, "boundary marker": ^{na4}*sí-kà-na a-na É-šu li-iz-qú-up*, "may (the gods) erect a *sikkānu* on (or, for) his house" (Emar 125.40-41; cf. 17.39-40).[31] The noun *sikkatu* ("peg") can be used of property markers in the ground, which would have been pounded in with an action corresponding to the Emar use of *zaqāpu*, "to implant."[32] The Emar curse seems to refer to taking over property, and *sikkatu* and *sikkānu* should be related terms.[33]

The *sikkānu* is most prominent in ritual at Emar, with special connection to the gods. A *sikkānu* of ^{d}NIN.URTA makes an appearance at the beginning of the *zukru* festival (375.16), and the gate of the *sikkānu*'s (KÁ $^{na4.meš}$*si-ka-na-ti*) is perhaps the central sacred site for the whole feast. This gate is where the gods are brought out from the city,[34] and a chariot bearing statues of the gods is driven "between the stelae" (*bērat sikkānāti*) at several points in the ritual (verb, *etēqu*).[35] They are anointed with oil and blood at least twice.[36] A *kubadu*-ceremony is performed at this gate for Dagan (373.177-178).

169, especially 149-150.

[31] W. Mayer, in M. Dietrich, O. Loretz, and W. Mayer, "*Sikkanum* 'Betyle'," *UF* 21 (1989) 136-137, presents three new attestations of this formula from Mumbaqat, a Late Bronze I site several miles north of Emar on the Euphrates: ^{na4}*sí-kà-na a/i-na* É(*-ti*)*-šu li-iz-qú-up*, (anyone who changes these words), "may (DN$_1$ and DN$_2$) erect a *sikkānu* on his house." The deities of the curse are ^{d}IM and ^{d}*Da-gan* in MBQ-T 36:14-19 and MBQ-T 73:8-11, and ^{d}*Da-gan* and ^{d}*Ba-aḫ-la-ka* in MBQ-T 69:25-29. The verb remains singular in spite of the dual subject, so the subject of the Emar idiom should likewise be the gods from the preceding curse on seed and name. Mayer, "Der antike Name von Tall Munbāqa, die Schreiber und die chronologische Einordnung der Tafelfunde: Die Tontafelfunde von Tall Munbāqa 1988," *MDOG* 122 (1990) 45-66, places the texts in the period at the end of the 16th and beginning of the 15th centuries B.C.E., which would show a remarkable continuity in even the spelling of the curse formula over two to three hundred years. Mumbaqat was probably called Ekalte, according to Mayer, and he has published only the tablets that indicate this identification (*MDOG* 122 51-63).

[32] See *CAD*, s.v. *sikkatu* A1c; and Piotr Steinkeller, *Sale Documents of the Ur III Period*, Stuttgart: Franz Steiner Verlag, 1989, 239.

[33] At Mari the word *sikkānum* is consistently spelled with a doubled *-kk-*, and association with the noun *sikkatu* would give further reason for expecting the same doubled *-kk-* in the Emar term, in spite of the common use of defective orthography. The form *si-ik-ka-na-ti* occurs once in the *zukru* festival (373.179) and is likely indicated in the fragment 422.4, ^{na4}*si-ik-*[*ka-nu*]. A similiar case would be the *ḫizzibu*-vessel, which is spelled *ḫi-zi-bu* except in the list Emar 274.1, etc., where it is spelled *ḫi-iz-zi-bu*. Text MBQ-T 35:25-27 from Mumbaqat doubles the last consonant, ^{na4}*sí-kan-nu-mi*, the only evidence for *-nn-*.

[34] Emar 373.27, 45, 185-186, 192-193, cf. 23.

[35] Emar 373.168, 179, 188, 197, 207-208; cf. 205 (*našû*), and in broken context, 375.6, 7, 8, (13), 24.

[36] In 373.57-58 the *sikkānātu* are "anointed" (*pašāšu*); in 373.32 the NA$_4$.MEŠ are "rubbed" (*ṭerû*/*ṭarā'u*). Compare 375.14, where we should read UŠ.ḪI.A Ì.GIŠ *ú-pa-ša-šu*, "they will anoint (the *sikkānātu*) with blood and oil." The D conjugation of *pašāšu* is

We also find a *sikkānu* present at a key moment in the *maš'artu* installation. At the head of the cycle of offerings made to various Emar gods at their own temples (370.45-68), a stele is put on the roof of some building (line 41) and presented with offerings (line 43, verb *naqû*). The setting described in lines 20 and following suggests that the place should be the *bīt maš'arti*, the house of the priestess, and the stele might belong to *Aštartu tāḫāzi* (20-21).

The stelae appear in several fragments of ritual texts, 422.4, 424.4; 448.3, 26 (text A), 9(B).

Šaḫru

Šaḫru appears to be part of dIM's temple and ritual circle. He does not appear outside the NIN.DINGIR installation except in the fragment 371.10, which is part of neither installation, but is clearly from the same sphere as 369.[37] In the NIN.DINGIR festival, Šaḫru receives a sheep during the seven-day period just before the *ḫamša'u*-men are said to eat and drink in the NIN.DINGIR's residence (369.52), and Šaḫru is the only god to get an offering after the NIN.DINGIR dies (369.92). The latter offering appears to place Šaḫru with Adammatera in the sphere of death and the underworld. The earlier offering may play a part in recognizing the previous priestess' continuing residence in the *bīt* NIN.DINGIR until the last day of the festival. Note that Šaḫru is not present in the *qaddušu*-ceremony of lines 24-25 (see text and notes). The Ugaritic text KTU 1.23 treats the birth of the twin gods, Šaḥar and Šalim (lines 52, 53), and Šaḥar could be the same god.

However, KTU 1.23 places Šaḥar in a mythic sphere of El which makes no mention of Baal, while Emar's Šaḫru belongs entirely to the storm god's circle.[38] In the Ugarit god lists, on the other hand, *šḥr wšlm* tend to appear in texts that also associate *b'l* and *dgn*.[39]

---

attested at Boghazkoy; see *AHw* s.v. *pašāšu(m)* D1.

[37] Note the gods Šaḫru, dNIN.KUR, and dIM, 371.10, 11, 16, and the *zammārū*-singers and men of the *qidašu*, lines 2 and 17.

[38] See B. Cutler and J. MacDonald, "On the origin of the Ugaritic text KTU 1.23," *UF* 14 (1982) 33-34.

[39] See de Moor, "The Semitic pantheon of Ugarit," *UF* 2 (1970) 215, number 216. These include his list numbers 35, 36, and 37; list 36 is Ug 5 number 8:13-18, composed largely

2. Human Participants

The NIN.DINGIR of ᵈIM

This phrase encapsulates the fundamental uncertainties about our important Emar festival. Who is the god who is so central to Emar religion? And who is the high priestess? In Mesopotamia, the NIN.DINGIR of a god (*ša* DN) would be the *entu(m)*, high priestess of a temple, wife of a male deity.[40] A second possibility could be the reading *ugbabtu(m)*, known at Mari. However, these appear as a group or class, not a single priestess of a god, and according to *AHw*, s.v. *ugbabtu(m)*, the title is written NIN.DINGIR.TUR after the OB period. Given the number of new terms for cultic personnel found at Emar, it would not be surprising to find a different Semitic reading for NIN.DINGIR, though we have no spelling but the Sumerogram in the Akkadian texts from current Emar life (those published in the volume Emar VI.3).

One of the scribal texts from Emar supplies a possible solution.[41] William L. Moran has observed that the lexical text published by Arnaud as Ḫḫ. XIX, Emar VI.4, no. 556 (text D, Msk 74149), provides a syllabic Sumerian reading for the term NIN.DINGIR: i-ri-iš-ti-gi-ra (lines 43 and 47).[42] This text actually includes an Akkadian word as the third entry for lines 43 and 47, which has not been discussed by Moran or Arnaud. Arnaud has placed the Akkadian entry for line 43D after line 44 in his composite text, which somewhat obscures the relationship between the three columns. We should read lines 43-47 in text D as follows:

---

of double names, and offering the combined *bʿl wdgn* along with *šḥr wšlm*.

[40] See Douglas R. Frayne, "Notes on the sacred marriage rite," *BiOr* 42 (1985) 13-22; J. Renger, "Untersuchungen zum Priestertum in der aB Zeit," *ZA* 58 (1967) 134-144. Durand "Les dames du palais de Mari à l'époque du royaume de Haute-Mésopotamie," *M.A.R.I.* 4 (1985) 397, n.69, even suggests that at Mari NIN.DINGIR.RA might be read *aššat ilim* because of its variation with the writing, DAM + DN ("wife of DN") in ARM X. The term DAM.DINGIR follows a personal name in one Ebla text (SEb 3 34ff). The original Sumerian term (NIN.DINGIR) does not have the genitive (-a(k)), and would have meant "lady-god," not "lady of the god," but the spelling i-ri-iš-ti-gi-ra in the Emar lexical text 556.43 (see below) appears to indicate the Sumerian genitive.

[41] See Daniel Fleming, "The NIN.DINGIR/*ittu* at Emar," *N.A.B.U.* 1990, 5 (No. 8).

43	gad-za-x nin-dingir-ra	ka-ad-ka-(PA+X) [(x)] ri?-iš i-ri-iš-ti-gi-ra	*še-ši-[x]-ta-at* ⌜*i*⌝*-ti*
44	gad-šu-šu-ub	ka-ad-šu-šu-ub	*šu-šu-pu*
45	gad-šu-šu-ub dingir-ra	ka-ad-šu-šu-ub ti-gi-ra	*šu-šu-[up] i-li*
46	gad-šu-šu-ub lugal	ka-ad-šu-šu-ub lu-ga-al	*šu-šu-u[p] šar-[ri]*
47	gad-šu-šu-ub nin-dingir-ra	ka-ad-šu-<šu->ub i-ri-iš-ti-gi-[ra	*šu-šu]-up i-ti*

In lines 43 and 47 the Akkadian equivalent for nin-dingir-ra = i-ri-iš-ti-gi-ra is *i-ti*, which should be read *itti*, the genitive of *ittu*, which appears to be a form of the Akkadian *entu*. The usual Akkadian term displays both the *e*-vowel and the unassimilated *-n-* quite consistently,[43] and another Emar lexical text shows the expected form: Emar VI.4, no. 602, "Série lú-*ša*" (text D, Msk 74148b), line 236, has MIN *en-ti* DINGIR.MEŠ in the right-hand entry, after a broken Sumerian entry. The previous entry is MIN LUGAL, recalling the order for Emar 556.46-47, above.

Because this is a version of a Mesopotamian lexical text, we cannot assume that the word *ittu* represents the appropriate reading for the Emar NIN.DINGIR of the installation celebration and other Emar ritual and temple texts (see below). However, the form *i-ti* is sufficiently unexpected to indicate that this could be a local adaptation, originally derived from the Mesopotamian *entu*, but reflecting an independent Syrian development. The accompanying Akkadian word in Emar 556 is given a spelling only attested in a peripheral dialect, that of Nuzi.[44] Frayne points out that the word *entu* virtually dies out

---

[43] See *AHw* and *CAD*, s.v. *entu(m)*; compare *e-en-ti*, HSS 15 188:5 (Nuzi); *(e)-en-ti* as an Akkadogram at Boghazkoy (*CAD*); *en-ti*, YOS 1 45 i 26 (NB, Nabonidus); *e-ne-tum*, SB Legend of Sargon, CT 13 42:2, 4; *e-ne-ti*, Maqlû VI 28, 39. Perhaps the Mesopotamian word retained the spelling with *en-* by association with the male *ēnu*, who is not attested in the west (J. Huehnergard, personal communication).

[44] See *AHw* s.v. *šuš/sippum* 2, *šu-šu-up-pu(-ú)*, HSS 14 6:9 and others. In Emar 556.43D Arnaud restores *še-ši-[ik]-ta-at* for *sissiktu*, "hem." This likewise represents an unusual spelling, since the form *šiššiktu* is only known in NA Akkadian texts (see *CAD* and *AHw*, s.v. *sissiktu(m)*). On *sissiktu* as some sort of loin-cloth or lap-garment rather than "hem," see Meir Mallul, "'*Sissiktu*' and '*sikku*' -- their meaning and function," *BiOr* 43 (1986) 20-36.

in Mesopotamia proper after the OB period, surviving only in omen texts, showing that the institution was no longer active.[45] In the west, the office seems to take on a life of its own during the following period. The Emar *ittu* may be part of a larger pattern, in which Hurrian, Hittite, and Syrian cultures took on both word and institution at a time when they were integral to Mesopotamian religion (the OB period or earlier). The nature of the NIN.DINGIR would have developed along different lines in each region and culture.

The texts from Nuzi display an active role for the NIN.DINGIR in this MB period city.[46] The Hittites also had a NIN.DINGIR-priestess of similar high rank in the religious hierarchy. She joins the king (and queen) in several Hittite rituals, once bowing to him[47] and once receiving a cup together with him.[48] The Hittite NIN.DINGIR appears in association with various ritual personnel, but I am not familiar enough with their significance to take advantage of this information. Most of the texts are severely damaged, and it does not seem that Hittitologists have found sufficient data to produce a coherent picture of her office.[49]

---

45 Frayne, *BiOr* 42 22, based on the *CAD entu* article. Brigitte Menzel, *Assyrische Tempel*, Rome: Biblical Institute Press, 1981, 249, finds that the only firm evidence for the NIN.DINGIR in the Assyrian sphere is from the MA period.

46 All the examples (over 20) are gathered in Karlheinz Deller and Abdulillah Fadhil, "NIN.DINGIR.RA/*entu* in Texten aus Nuzi und Kurruḫanni," *Mesopotamia* 7 (1972) 193-213.

47 KBo XXII 189 Ro.II 9-16, in René Lebrun, "Deux textes hittites représentant la version impériale tardive de fêtes anatoliennes," in Guy Jucquois and R. Lebrun, eds., *Hethitica 2*, Louvain: Editions Peeters, 1977, 8-9. Lebrun tentatively identifies the text as part of the AN.TAḪ.ŠUM^{ŠAR} festival at the temple of Inara.

48 No. 24 in KBo XXVII 42 of Singer, *KI.LAM* I, page 76. Other rituals that involve both the NIN.DINGIR and royalty are KUB II 3 II 1-2, in the *KI.LAM* I, page 78; StBoT 25 No. 12 Rs III 19' and No. 32 3', of Erich Neu, *Althethitische Ritualtexte in Umschrift*, StBoT 25, Wiesbaden: Harrassowitz, 1980, pages 35 and 86.

49 Laroche lists the texts that involve the NIN.DINGIR in CTH par. 649 and 738, and Franca Pecchioli Daddi, *Mestieri, Professioni e Dignità Nell'Anatolia Ittita*, Roma: Edizioni Dell'Ateneo, 1982, 419-424, organizes all attestations by form, locations, and associations. A few scholars comment briefly on the priestess without much detail: Güterbock, RAI 20, 130, n.23 (=*entu*, he says); Lebrun, "Considérations sur la femme dans la société hittite," in Laroche et al, eds., *Hethitica 3*, Louvain: Peeters, 1979, 115, n.26 (of high rank, and "soeur du dieu"); Singer, *KI.LAM* I, 28 (her associations with equally obscure cultic personnel and objects); A. Kammenhuber, *Materialen zu einem hethitischen Thesaurus*, Lieferung 6, Heidelberg: Carl Winter, 1977, 304-305 (especially in Hattian cult, speaking only Hattic). Perhaps further systematic study of all texts and associations, carried out by a trained Hittitologist, would advance the state of our knowledge.

One indication of a basic difference in the nature of the NIN.DINGIR at Emar is found in Emar 276, a list of priestly personnel which includes the NIN.DINGIR *ša* ^{d}*Iš*$_{8}$*-tár* (line 8). The connection with the goddess shows that the priestess at Emar may not be seen primarily as the wife of the god she serves, but as the head of any divine household.[50] In OB Mesopotamia, the EN (*ēnu/entu*) occupies the highest priestly rank in the major temple of a central cult-place, while the NIN.DINGIR is the high-priestess of either a subsidiary temple at a central cult-place or the high temple at a secondary cult-place.[51] At Emar, we find a NIN.DINGIR for ^{d}IM at what seems to be the central shrine of the city (see below), with no candidate for a higher temple.[52] The NIN.DINGIR of ^{d}IM leads the lists of dignitaries during the installation of the new priestess (369.16, 55), as well as at the installation of the *maš'artu* (370.33 and 35). In the *kissu* festival of Dagan, she precedes the NIN.DINGIR's of the towns of Šumi and Šatappi (385.16). On the other hand, her contingent of personnel is listed after those of the *zābiḫu*'s of ^{d}IM, ^{d}KUR/Dagan, and ^{d}NIN.URTA in the temple list, Emar 275.1-6.

In spite of her importance, the NIN.DINGIR of ^{d}IM is not selected from the royal family. She may be the daughter of "any son of Emar," though we do not know how wide a social circle the term "son of Emar" (369.3) emcompassed in practice. The NIN.DINGIR is never given a personal name in the Emar texts, and only once a relationship to another person. A certain ^{m}Alal-abu seals a legal document and is identified as the brother of the (or, "a"?) NIN.DINGIR (213.27, 34). Unfortunately, the name is a common one, and it is not possible to connect this man with a title or status. We have no indication that he belongs to the royal family or the clan of the ^{lú}ḪAL of Emar, though his place among the signatories shows some social standing.

We have no mention of any NIN.DINGIR's child (see the treatment of Emar 275, below); in OB Mesopotamia, we find only occasional instances.[53] There is no indication that the NIN.DINGIR had a human husband. It is not

---

[50] Frayne, *BiOr* 42 19, emphasizes the centrality of the marriage image, but observes that some early texts do show *entu*'s for goddesses such as Baba, Gatumdug, and Ninisinna. This suggests that the marriage aspect may not be intrinsic to her role.

[51] See J. Renger, "Ortliche und zeitliche Differenzen in der Struktur der Priesterschaft babylonischer Tempel," in *Le temple et le culte*, RAI 20, TE ISTAMBUL: Nederlands historisch-archeologisch Instituut, 1975, 111-114.

[52] Dagan's temple appears to be located in the neighboring town of Šatappi (see below).

[53] See Renger, *ZA* 58 140-141.

clear how this would have worked with betrothal practices. If girls were betrothed in childhood, as Kemal Balkan suggests for OA Kultepe, perhaps some children were set apart for later temple service.[54] In spite of the apparent selection at the time of the installation (369.3), the choice may have been limited by earlier decisions.

The NIN.DINGIR also appears in broken contexts in Emar 276.6; 286.19; and the ritual fragment 399.8.

Excursus: Emar 275

Text 275 deserves separate comment because it is the only Emar tablet that could be seen to furnish a personal name for a NIN.DINGIR-priestess: ^{m}*I-ba* DUMU DINGIR-*lì-a-bi* NIN.DINGIR *ša* ^{d}IM (line 6). However, the name Ilī-abī is used consistently for males at Emar,[55] and Ilī-abī should not be the name for the female NIN.DINGIR of ^{d}IM. The tablet bears a list of personal names that includes several titles for temple personnel. A simplified presentation of the contents, with each name (with patronym) shortened to "*PN*," helps follow the scheme:

275.1. 4 ZA *PN* ^{lú}*za-bi-ḫu ša* ^{d}IM

----

2. 4 ZA *PN* ^{lú}*za-bi-ḫu ša* ^{d}KUR

----

3. 2 ZA *PN*/1 ZA *PN*
4. /1 ZA *PN* ^{lú}*za-bi-ḫu ša* ^{d}NIN.URTA

----

5. 1 ZA *PN*/1 ZA *PN*
6. /1 ZA *PN*/1 ZA *PN* NIN.DINGIR *ša* ^{d}IM

----

[54] Balkan, "Betrothal of girls during childhood in ancient Assyria and Anatolia," in Harry A. Hoffner and Gary M. Beckman eds., *Kaniššuwar: A Tribute to Hans G. Güterbock*, *AS* 23, Chicago: The Oriental Institute, 1986, 5.

[55] The male gender may be marked either by the DIŠ-sign before the name or by DUMU ("son of") and a patronym. Compare the following: ^{m}*Ì-lí-a-bi* DUMU *Ḫa-at-ta*, Emar 8.14 and 9.13; *Ì-lí-a-bi* DUMU *Ia-ri-x*, 20.37; *Ì-lí-a-bi* DUMU *I-ri-ia*, 52.69; ^{m}DINGIR-*lì-a-bi* DUMU *Še-i-*^{d}KUR, 121.17; *Ì-lí-a-bi* DUMU *A-bi-ḫa-mi-is*, 126.28; *Ì-lí-a-bi* DUMU *Da-da*, 176.10; ^{m}DINGIR-*lì-a-bi*, 285.19; ^{m}DINGIR-*lì-a-bi* DUMU *A-bi-ka-pí*, 325.12.

7. 2 ZA *PN*
8. /2 ZA *PN* ^{lú}*wa-bi-il i-la-i*[56]

----

9. 3 ZA *PN*
10. /1 ZA *PN*

----

11. 2 ZA *PN* ^{lú}ḪAL
12. /1 ZA *PN*

----

13. 7 É.MEŠ UGULA ^{d}IM-UR.SAG
14. ^{lú}*el-lu-tu*$_4$

The ZA-sign following each number is obscure. Arnaud tentatively transcribes "4", which would be conceivable if each section deals in fractions, though the number should not be written with the ZA-pattern. All but the seventh division (lines 11-12) add up to four. Durand proposes that ZA abbreviates the vessel *zadu*, known in the NIN.DINGIR installation and other Emar rituals.[57] If this hypothesis is correct, the text should be a list of oil rations, since the *zadu* is used only for oil, where the contents are known (see below, Provision). Failure to mention the oil would be somewhat surprising, but is possible.

In line 13, PA may be UGULA,[58] so that the last lines would mean, "the 7 houses of the overseer ^{d}IM-UR.SAG; the pure men," where the ^{lú}*el-lu-tu*$_4$ are those listed above in the seven sections of the text, and each section represents a "house" administered by ^{d}IM-UR.SAG.[59] ^{d}IM-UR.SAG DUMU *Zu-Ba-la*, the *PN* of line 11, is the name of a well-attested ^{lú}ḪAL (diviner) at Emar,[60] so

---

56 See also Emar 63.3, ^{lú}*wa-bíl i-*[*la-i/ú*]; 276.10, [^{lú}]*wa-bíl i-la-ú*. Arnaud's translation is a good suggestion: "porteur d'idoles," or "bearer of gods." One wonders whether the spelling could reflect the pronunciation /*ilāhī*/, with comparison to the Hebrew plural *ʾĕlôhîm* (J. Huehnergard, personal communication). The initial *w-* appears elsewhere in Emar texts: KÁ *ša Wa-ar-da-na-ti*, 137.1, cf. 168.8; ^{d}*Wa-ad-ḫa*, 137.6; *wa-aš-ba-*[*at*], 196.1; ^{lú}*wa-ra-ša* (heir), 213.6; *wa-aš-ḫa-zu* (item of silver), 284.5; *wa-ar-da*, 363.2; [*w*]*a-ar-di-ti*, 454.12; *wa-lu-ḫi ša* ^{d}IM, 461.8, cf. 454.7, 8. At least in personal names, initial *y-* is spelled with the IA-sign: *Ia-aq-ri* (52.10), *Ia-tu-ur-a-ḫu* (52.27), etc.

57 Durand, review of Emar VI.1-3, *RA* 84 (1990) 80.

58 We have the form ^{lú}UGULA in Emar 289.4.

59 Arnaud, "Les hittites sur le moyen-Euphrate: protecteurs et indigènes," in *Hethitica VIII, Acta Anatolica E. Laroche Oblata*, Louvain: Peeters, 1987, 12, remarks that the term *ellūtu* should have the Anatolian meaning, "franc de charges."

60 See below, The diviner.

in section 7 (lines 11-12) the title surely describes the *PN*. However, this is the only title in text 275 which does not come at the end of the section, and since section 6 (lines 9-10) includes no title at all, these last two sections may not follow the pattern of the first five. The lúḪAL is also different in that he may be the same dIM-UR.SAG who administers the whole list of personnel.

Given the problem of the female NIN.DINGIR following the masculine personal name Ili-abī, it seems best to understand the titles in the first five sections to identify houses in which the listed men serve. This would suit the placement of the titles at the end of each section. We know there is a *bīt* NIN.DINGIR from her festival (e.g. 369.15) and a *bīt maš'arti* from hers (e.g. 370.21). The three *zābiḫu*-priests[61] and the lú*wa-bi-il i-la-i* may well have had special temple residences as well.[62]

Whatever the precise intent of this tablet for administration of temple personnel, I prefer to interpret the NIN.DINGIR *ša* dIM as a reference to the temple residence in which the four men serve, so that we remain without any instance of a NIN.DINGIR identified by personal name.

The sons of Emar

These appear only at the beginning of the ritual (369.1-3) and are also the celebrants of the *zukru* festival (373.174). The "sons of Šatappi" perform the *kissu* for Dagan (385.2). Michael Heltzer has studied the titles which define the population at Ugarit, and the term *mārū Ugarit*, "the sons of Ugarit," identifies the mass of the freeborn populace of the land, including the neighboring villages.[63] At Ugarit, this group stands in contrast to the "servants of the king" and the servants of those servants.[64] It is significant that the Emar rituals are celebrated by the populace of the city as such, not "the servants of the king."

---

61 The first three titles of text 275 give us three leading deities at Emar, with the *zābiḫu* of dIM listed before that of Dagan and dNIN.URTA. The root consonant *ḥ* is spelled with *ḫ*; compare the Hebrew root *zbḥ* and Ugaritic *dbḥ*, and note that *ḏ* is written "z" at Emar in the *Zū*-DN theophoric names. The personnel listed for the Astarte temple at Kition (400-350 B.C.E.) include the *zbḥm*, "sacrificateurs"; M. Delcor, "Le personnel du temple d'Astarté à Kition d'après une tablette phénicienne (CIS 86 A et B)," *UF* 11 (1979) 154, line 8.

62 The residences of these personnel could accomodate either groups with these titles or merely individuals.

63 Heltzer, "Problems of the social history of Syria in the Late Bronze Age," in M. Liverani, ed., *La Siria nel tardo bronzo*, Roma, 1969, 35, and *The Rural Community in Ancient Ugarit*, Wiesbaden: Reichert, 1976, 4-6.

64 Heltzer, in *La Siria...*, 35: see PRU 4 RS 17.238.

The diviner[65]

The diviner plays a leading role in both the installation of the NIN.DINGIR and a wide range of Emar affairs. He appears often in ritual, and various individuals are identified by this office in all sorts of Emar texts. Family records from a single diviner's clan (Emar texts 199-226) appear to indicate that the archive and temple M_1 were under the supervision of the head of this family, "the ^lú^ḪAL of the gods of Emar" (see below). Based on the role of the elders and ^d^NIN.URTA in many land sales, W.F. Leemans proposes that the temple M_1 was the temple of ^d^NIN.URTA, administered by the elders, but this surely underestimates the overwhelming presence of the diviner displayed in both the personal documents and the religious and literary collection.[66] The temple M_1 should rather be the diviner's temple, perhaps the temple of "the gods of Emar."

The diviner's title is ^lú^ḪAL in the installation and most other ritual texts, as well as in many administrative texts. We find the old Sumerian spelling ^lú^MÁŠ.ŠU.GÍD.GÍD in the annual calendar ritual 446.39, 51, etc., as well as outside the rituals. The form DUMU.ḪAL (22.1; 99.4, 11; etc.) may indicate sons of a ^lú^ḪAL, a diviner of junior rank (a position naturally held by sons of the ^lú^ḪAL), or the title may simply indicate membership in the diviner's profession. Although the Emar lexical texts attest the spelling *ba-ru-u* for ḪAL (Syllabaire Sa, Emar 537.290) and máš-šu-gíd-gíd (Ḫḫ. II, Emar 542.167), showing familiarity with the standard Mesopotamian word *bārû*, we have no examples of syllabic spellings from the texts not related to Mesopotamian canons. We should consider the actual local reading unknown, at present.

In Mesopotamia, the *bārû* is a practitioner of divination, and when he takes part in ritual, it is with that function (see *CAD* s.v. *bārû* a4'a'). At Emar, we have no certain reference to the ^lú^ḪAL performing divination in the ritual texts, and his participation in those suggests other roles. On the other hand, the diviner's archive of the temple M_1 included a large cache of treatises

---

65 I translate "diviner" in spite of the fact that divination was only one part of the ^lú^ḪAL's responsibilities at Emar. A collection of Hurrian divination texts was found in the temple M_1, apparently reflecting the specialty indicated by the Mesopotamian Sumerogram. Although the title "diviner" does not adequately express the whole function of the ^lú^ḪAL, use of another English word would obscure his abiding association with divination.

66 See W.F. Leemans, "Aperçu sur les textes juridiques d'Emar," *JESHO* 31 (1988) 234-235, 240-241.

dealing with theoretical hepatoscopy (*bārûtu*) and medical prognostics. These are recorded in the Hurrian language typical of the Hittite empire, reflecting the technical vocabulary of Boghazkoy/Hattuša.[67] One of the texts recently published from the "Hirayama collection" records the rewarding of Mašruḫe "the diviner (lúMÁŠ.ŠU.GÍD.GÍD) of the king and of the city" for a successful act of divination (*ba-ru-tu₄-šu*) when Emar was threatened by the "Hurrians."[68] Mašruḫe's title contrasts with that of the diviner who superintends the temple M_1, who is "the lúḪAL of the gods of Emar," and he does not appear to be part of the group associated with that temple.

The skills of the lúḪAL in Mesopotamian divination lore do not seem to penetrate the fabric of Emar religion, at least by the evidence of extant texts. It is possible that line 94 in our NIN.DINGIR installation should read in part, 1 UDU *i-pí-at-ti*,[69] "he will open one sheep," with *petû* used in a technical sense for performing divination (see *AHw* s.v. *petû(m)* II G14), but there is such a striking absence of similar use elsewhere at Emar that this reading is tenuous. At least it is certain that if this set of signs is a verb form, the lúḪAL should be the subject (see line 93).[70]

Note that the Hittite LÚḪAL likewise may show a drift away from the precise function originally pertaining to his office in Mesopotamia: he serves as an incantation priest, according to Güterbock.[71] However, we have so little data for the Mesopotamian practices of the same (MB) period that no definitive statement should be made.[72]

---

67 This is the evaluation of E. Laroche based on preliminary readings; see "Emar, étape entre Babylone et le Hatti," in Margueron, ed., *Le Moyen Euphrate*, 244. The Hurrian texts from Emar have not yet been published.

68 HCCT-E 10 (Text 7) rev. 31-33, in Akio Tsukimoto, "Akkadian tablets in the Hirayama collection (I)," *ASJ* 12 (1990) 190.

69 Another possibility would be *i-pé-et*!(AT)-*ti*.

70 Dietrich, *UF* 21 75, advocates this reading of the line and proposes that the divination is for choosing the next candidate, if the priestess dies within her-one year term of office. If true, this interpretation would fit even better into the model of a lifetime term for every NIN.DINGIR.

71 See Güterbock, RAI 20, 130. R. Lebrun, *Šamuḫa: foyer religieux de l'empire hittite*, Louvain-la-neuve: Insitut Orientaliste, 1976, 43, emphasizes his multiple roles which encompass divination, magic, offering, and other ritual tasks.

72 Jean Nougayrol, "Trente ans de recherches sur la divination babylonienne (1935-1965)," in *La divination en Mésopotamie ancienne et dans les regions voisines*, RAI 14, Paris: Presses Universitaires de France, 1966, 12-13, finds that the divination from the archives of Boghazkoy and Ras Shamra should give us information about MB practices as well as the OB sources. He notes as an example that one person serves as both diviner and *šangû* of Adad, according to PRU 4 201, line 16 (Nougayrol, page 14 and n.4). This evidence could reflect western developments as well, however, adapted from the Mesopotamian original.

The principal activity of the ^{lú}ḪAL in the NIN.DINGIR festival and other rituals is collection of silver payments and allotments in animal parts. In the NIN.DINGIR installation the timing of payments suggests various ritual roles. He anoints the new priestess twice (369.5, 20-21), receiving a one-shekel fee in connection with the first instance; he gets a similar payment after the hair-preparation (369.10); and he receives a silver coil during the enthronement ceremony (line 43). Perhaps he oversees the last two events as well as the first. The administrative section of the festival records numerous animal portions allotted to the ^{lú}ḪAL (lines 78, 81, 82, 83, 83C, and 93), and he gets five shekels for participation in the feast as a whole (line 84). Other rituals follow the same pattern. He only appears at the end of the *maš'artu* installation, receiving this same general fee (370.108; cf. 369.84), and he joins the king and the chief scribe in "sanctifying" the gods ("them") in the *kissu* for Dagan (385.25-26; see *qaddušu*, below). The ^{lú}ḪAL receives allotments repeatedly during the annual ritual cycle, Emar 446 (lines 39, 44, 53, 81, 94, 101, 104; cf. 28, 75), and he is one of several recipients of bread and beer in 460.10. See also fragmented appearances in 385.2 (text E; = 385.4, A); 386.22; 393.5; 406.4 (here, [^{lú}MÁ]Š.ŠU.GÍD.GÍD).

One ritual act from the annual cycle stands out against this background of payment for unspecified services: in 446.51, the diviner (^{lú}MÁŠ.ŠU.GÍD.GÍD) scatters (*nadû*) seed on the ground after a sheep has been slaughtered for the garden of the *bi-ri-ki*[73] of ^{d}IM and for Dagan, "Lord of the seed" (*be-el* NUMUN.MEŠ, lines 48-50). This appears to take place on the fifteenth day of the first month, in conjunction with offerings made at the cattlepens and the stables (É GUD.MEŠ and É ANŠE.KUR.RA, lines 45-47). These are rites to ensure the productivity of animals and fields, part of a spring New Year. The ^{lú}ḪAL is playing a major role that has nothing to do with divination.

Outside of the Mesopotamian learned collection (Emar VI.4, versus VI.3), the title of the diviner is never linked to a place or god that might

---

[73] ARMT 23 284 now attests the *bi-ri-ki-im* of Dagan, in a text which also mentions the *sikkānum*; see Durand, "Bétyles," 81. Durand left the word untranslated, but in his more recent review of Emar VI.1-3 (*RA* 83 179) he reads *i-na pí-ri-ki*-ma** in text 28.5 and says that the *pirikkum* is a sacred place and symbol found in Syrian temples; cf. his comment in ARMT XXI, *Textes administratifs des salles 134 et 160 du palais de Mari*, Paris: Paul Geuthner, 1983, 25-26. At Emar, we also find Aštart (*^{d}Iš$_{8}$-tár*) (*ša*) *bi-ri-GA-ti*, which could be read *pí-ri-kà-ti*.

further identify his role. This information is provided in the colophons of the scholarly texts, where we find a whole hierarchy of diviner-scribes. The highest rank belongs to the ^{lú}ḪAL *ša* DINGIR.MEŠ ^{uru}*E-mar*, "the ^{lú}ḪAL of the gods of Emar." Only two men possess this title in the colophons, a grandson and a grandfather: Baʿlu-malik and Zū-Baʿla.[74] The family archive of the diviners (Emar 199-226) shows a sequence of family members inheriting the title ^{lú}ḪAL, from Zū-Baʿla to Baʿlu-qarrād (^{d}IM/U-UR.SAG) to Baʿlu-malik (^{d}IM/U-*ma-lik*).[75] It appears that this longer title represents a unique position in the city of Emar, head of the temple M_1 with its scribal academy. Lower ranks in the diviners' hierarchy are represented by other titles in the colophons: Ì.ZU TUR, "lesser diviner," and Ì.ZU TUR.TUR, "lowest diviner."[76]

The city appears to have more than one ^{lú}ḪAL. In addition to Mašruḫe the ^{lú}MÁŠ.ŠU.GÍD.GÍD, one witness to a legal proceeding in the diviners' family archive is called ^{lú}ḪAL although he has no apparent connection to the dominant clan of Zū-Baʿla (^{m}EN-^{d}IM, in 212.28 and the accompanying seal). In the ritual texts we never find more than one ^{lú}ḪAL mentioned, and we cannot tell whether any ^{lú}ḪAL may fill this role, or whether it must be the ^{lú}ḪAL *ša* DINGIR.MEŠ ^{uru}*E-mar* who is known from the colophons.

---

74 Arnaud gathers all the information from the scribal colophons in one place, Emar VI.4, no. 604. The many examples of Baʿlu-malik appear in the subheading 1, while the instances of Zū-Baʿla are in subheadings 4 and 6.

75 Zū-Baʿla as ^{lú}ḪAL: 201.24; 202.4; 205.2; 206.13; 207.12, 26; he is ^{lú}MÁŠ.ŠU.G[ÍD.GÍD] in 201.4. Baʿlu-qarrād, son of Zū-Baʿla, as ^{lú}ḪAL: 211.15; 214.3; 215.4; he is DUMU.ḪAL in 212.3, perhaps as son of Zū-Baʿla. Baʿlu-malik, son of Baʿlu-qarrād, as ^{lú}ḪAL: 225.5; in the family archive, he is much more often called DUMU.ḪAL, 213.12; 221.1; 225.1; 226.1.

76 ^{md}IM-EN is Ì.ZU TUR in Emar 604, subheading 2; three different men are given the title Ì.ZU TUR.TUR in subheadings 3, 5 and 7. Other spellings for "diviner" (probably *bārû* in this context) appear in the colophons, none referring to the chief diviner: (^{lú})MÁŠ.ŠU.GÍD.GÍD in subheadings 2 and 8; ^{lú}Ì.ZU in subheading 2 (this heading refers to ^{md}IM-EN); ^{lú}UZÚ in subheading 6, speaking of a son and grandson of Zū-Baʿla, who bears the full title with ^{lú}ḪAL; ^{lú}A.[ZU] and ^{lú}ZU.[ZU] in the colophon for the Mesopotamian literary text, Emar 767; compare Emar 229.6 for ^{lú}A.ZU.

Most of these spellings are attested in Mesopotamia. MÁŠ.ŠU.GÍD.GÍD is an old Sumerian writing, with long use that includes Mari (see Adam Falkenstein, "'Wahrsagung' in der sumerischen Überlieferung," in RAI 14, 45-46, and Finet, "La place du devin dans la société de Mari," in RAI 14, 87). Ì.ZU appears at Mari and in lexical texts (Finet, RAI 14, 87, and Falkenstein, RAI 14, 52). A.ZU is found in later cult-songs, and probably is equated with *asû*, "doctor" (Falkenstein, RAI 14, 51). At Alalaḫ, the *bārû* is indicated by the spelling ^{lú}UZÚ (D.J. Wiseman, *The Alalakh Tablets*, London: The British Institute of Archaeology at Ankara, 1953, 158; texts 180:20; 274:29; 378:21; 424b:11).

A further line of evidence for the nature of the diviner's office is found in the temple administration documents. The diviner is a temple administrator with responsibility quite similar to that of the *šangû*, known in various cultic roles in Mesopotamia. Texts 285 and 287 are similar inventories of temple valuables. Emar 287.6-7 records three silver beads (*ḫiddu*) belonging to the god Halma, and the LÁ of PN, the *šangû*-priest, where LÁ may stand for *ṣimittu*, which refers to silver scrap in one Mari text (see *CAD* s.v. *ṣimittu* 6, *AHw* s.v. *ṣimittu(m)* 4; vs. Arnaud, *piqittu*). The precise intent of these last two lines of the text is not certain, but the *šangû* is somehow responsible for the items listed above. Emar 285.16-18 describe the administrator's responsibility more clearly, this time for the diviner:

> *ú-nu-tu-ú an-nu-tu*$_4$
> GIBIL *ša* ^{m}[^{d}I]M-*ma-lik* DUMU.ḪAL
> *ip-qi-du*$_4$
>
> These new items
> are those which PN the diviner('s son)
> has deposited.[77]

One difference between the ^{lú}ḪAL and the *šangû* may be that the first serves multiple cults while the second is an administrator of a single temple, though not every *šangû* at Emar is identified by divine name. The *šangû* in 287.7 may be a temple administrator distinct from priests who are called ^{lú}SANGA *ša* DN, for only the latter appear in Emar ritual texts. However, the specific temple affiliation of the simple ^{lú}SANGA is unknown. Judging by grain allotments, these may be the higher *šangû*-officials. Even the servant of the *šangû* gets ten *parīsu* of barley annually (319.8), whereas a *šangû* of Dagan gets four (279.21) or five (319.4?, ^{lú}[SANGA *š*]*a* ^{d}KUR), and the *šangû* of Sîn is likely in the same low range (279.48, at the end of a list).[78] A ^{lú}ḪAL's son receives eighteen (279.16) or twenty *parīsu* (279.5) in a system where thirty is the maximum, the amount the NIN.DINGIR gets in a good year

---

[77] See *AHw* s.v. *paqādu(m)* G I "übergeben." Durand, *RA* 84 81, translates the verb, "a mis en dépôt."

[78] Dominique Charpin, *Le clergé d'Ur au siècle d'Hammurabi (XIXe-XVIIIe siècles av. J.-C.)*, Genève-Paris: Librairie Droz, 1986, 240-241, wonders whether two SANGA's without identification by associated deity belong to the principal god of Ekišnugal, Nanna, in texts from OB Ur. It is possible that the *šangû* of Emar 287 likewise belongs to the high temple (^{d}IM?). Evidence in both cases is incomplete.

(369.85). The entire letter, Emar 268, is addressed to the diviner Zū-Baʿla for the purpose of getting him to appoint a *šangû* to the service of ^{d}NIN.KUR -- clear indication of his superior station in the specific case.[79] Evidence from ritual is mixed but does not contradict these observations. The priest of Alal comes last after both the ^{lú}ḪAL and the singers in the payments of the *maš'artu* installation (370.108-110). The priest of *Aštartu tāḫāzi* is listed first in the offering list 460.7-9, but he has a special place because the whole cycle is dedicated to that goddess. Note that a *šangû* (no DN) is a witness alongside a ^{lú}ḪAL in 212.27.

The diviner is thus a cultic official with a wide range of responsibilities and high social standing in Emar society. He is a wealthy man, too, given the payments he receives over the course of his activities. His NIN.DINGIR installation fee is five times that of the singers (369.84). The ^{lú}ḪAL also has a connection with the high priestesses that goes beyond the rituals themselves. A man listed in the diviner family archive is the NIN.DINGIR's brother (213.27, 34), and non-ritual texts mention the diviner in proximity to the NIN.DINGIR (275.6, 11), the *maš'artu* (345.4, 6) and both (286.11, 19). This high status might correspond to the well-documented situation at Mari, where the diviner Asqudum held an exalted position in the court of Zimri-Lim. He even marries the king's sister.[80]

The singers (zammārū)

The singers of the NIN.DINGIR festival, the *zammārū* ($^{\text{lú.meš}}$*za-ma-ru*), are a group attested only in a few texts, mostly Middle and Neo-Assyrian (see *CAD* s.v. *zammāru*, and in *rab zammārī*; *AHw* s.v. *zammāru*). In OB Mari and SB practice, the *zammeru* "was either an untrained singer or a singer of popular songs, etc.," in contrast to the *nāru*, "who performed in palace and temple" (*CAD* s.v. *zammeru*). When we consider the prominence of the *zammārū* in the Emar festivals against the backdrop of this scanty

---

[79] Arnaud observes this situation in *AEPHER* 84 221.

[80] See Charpin, "Les archives du devin Asqudum dans la residence du 'Chantier A'," *M.A.R.I.* 4 (1985) 457. He observes that the same marriage between *bārû* and king's sister appears to occur at Tell Rimaḫ/Karana. The ^{lú}ḪAL seems to have a much lower status in the Hittite cult, where the SANGA/*šankunniš* holds the leading position; see Güterbock, RAI 20, 129. Singer, *KI.LAM* I, 105, determines the hierarchy for the personnel at Arinna and Zippalanda from a list of garments given to cult functionaries (KBo XXV 176). Neither religious center includes a diviner/^{lú}ḪAL among its principal personnel, led by the SANGA in both cases.

Mesopotamian evidence, the class seems much more at home in Syria. They are not only present in temple ritual; they play important regular roles. First, they lead ritual processions, always *ana pānī*, "ahead of," any other participants: 369.8, 30 (cf. 33), 45, 63; 385.31; cf. 370.78?; 388.40?; (391.2?, in broken context).[81] It is likely that this involved singing and/or playing instruments, though no mention is made. The second role focuses on the singing itself; they perform hymns for specific gods (see below, The Final Day).

Like the lúḪAL, the importance of the singers to the temple cult is seen in the payments and portions they receive for participation in ritual. In the three-way division of meat-parts in the NIN.DINGIR festival, the singers make the third party after the king and the lúḪAL (369.79). The administrative section goes on to specify the shares of the singers, alongside the lúḪAL (369.81, 82, 83, 83C), and a gift in silver for general participation (line 84). They come behind the lúḪAL in standing, but with him they form a key part of the official cult, probably the "men of the *qidašu*" (see below). For further receiving of shares, see 369.74; 370.109 (cf. 369.84, silver); 371.2; 394.23, 25; 431.4?.

There are also female singers (*zammirātu*) who feast (370.59) and receive portions (388.67, cf. 410.4), as well as a group of singers known from Aššur and Nuzi, the *nuāru*.[82] The lúŠÌR.MEŠ of Emar 460.30 are probably the *zammārū*, not usually spelled logographically at Emar (cf. 255.9; 278.5; note syllabic lú*za-ma-ru*, 337.5).

In the NIN.DINGIR festival a 3ms form of the verb *leqû* may be used when the group takes a single share alongside the lúḪAL (369.79, 83C), and the confusion of number in 369.73-74 might result from the same collective function. There, the plural verb *izammarū* probably indicates lú*za-ma-ru* is

---

[81] During the Babylonian *akītu*-festival, singers lead a procession of the gold chariot and the silver chariot of Anu to his upper *bīt akītim*: RAcc 89 3, lúNAR.MEŠ *ina* IGI-*šu-nu* DU-*lak*, "the singers (*nārū*) will go ahead of them." Note the singular verb with plural subject.

[82] Emar 336.83 and 426.2; see *CAD* s.v. *nâru* c7'b', 8' and final note, maybe not the same as *nâru*; but *AHw* s.v. *nāru(m)* II, ass., Nuzi *nu'āru(m)*. M. Roth, "Age at marriage and the household: a study of Neo-Babylonian and Neo-Assyrian forms," in *Comparative Studies in Society and History* 29 (1987) 38-46, finds that some later references to *nu'ar(t)u* are probably West Semitic, "youth." See also Roth, *Babylonian Marriage Agreements: 7th - 3rd Centuries B.C.*, AOAT 222, Neukirchen-Vluyn: Neukirchener, 1989, 6-7.

plural in both lines, and the form *ilaqqe* reflects the single portion, as in 369.79 and 83C.

The NIN.DINGIR's father

The father of the NIN.DINGIR is only named as an actor when he substitutes for his daughter in the first *kubadu*, holding the divine weapon (369.10). The C text, *kīmūši*, "in her stead," accents this place-holding role.

The men of the qidašu

The group which appears most often in the NIN.DINGIR festival is the most difficult to identify. Their full title occurs in 369.12, $^{\text{lú.meš}}$*šar-ru* (or, LÚ.MEŠ *šar-ru*) *na-di-nu*(*-ti*) *qí-da-ši*. The final syllable *-ti* is present in text A, but dropped in C, and the same variation is found in other Emar ritual.[83] Two of the terms that make up the title are obscure: *šarru* and *qidašu*. Neither fits known Akkadian usage.

The form of the title is fluid, and this flexibility helps our analysis considerably.[84] The NIN.DINGIR installation most often abbreviates the formula to LÚ.MEŠ *ša qí-da-ši*,[85] "the men of the *qidašu*" or "those of the *qidašu*." In this version LÚ.MEŠ (*amīlû*) is not a determinative, though the full title is least awkward when we interpret it as such (see below). There is an intermediate form which omits only *šarru*, [LÚ.]MEŠ *na-di-nu qí*-[*da-ši*], 446.114,[86] and one of the long versions adds *ša*, [LÚ.MEŠ *šar-r*]*u na-di-nu ša qí-d*[*a-ši*], 395.12. In this grammatical context, *nādinū(ti)* only makes sense as the substantive of a plural participle. The plurals *nādinū* and *nādinūtu* are biforms.[87] When we read LÚ.MEŠ as a determinative the whole formula then means, "the *šarrū* who give the *qidašu*."

It remains to pin down the two difficult words, *šarru* and *qidašu*. Arnaud understands the former to be singers, but this does not suit the West Semitic middle-*yod* root for "sing" (*šyr*). One Emar text uses the LUGAL

---

83 With *-ti*, 385.14 (text A; E has *-ta*), 36 and 37 (A); without *-ti*, 372.6; 385.14 (F, G), 24 (A, C); 386.11 (H), 20 (F); 387.22 (F, J); 388.18 (K), 51 and 53 (F), 60 and 65 (K); 395.10, 12 (add *ša* before *qidaši*); 446.114.

84 Dietrich, *UF* 21 79, interprets the elements of the long title in line 12 as three separate groups, the singers ($^{\text{lú.meš}}$NAR(?)-r[u], in A), the donors (*nādinūtu*), and the consecrated (*qiddāšu*). The various forms are more simply explained in terms of a single group.

85 369.13, 21, 54, 77, 80 text C; cf. 371.17; 446.104, 116, cf. 61, omit MEŠ, but are plural; without *ša*, 369.38, 67, 76, 80A.

86 Arnaud's text for 395.10 misses *šar-ru*.

87 Cf. Huehnergard, *Akkadian of Ugarit*, 146.

(*šàr*) sign for the term, which suggests the translation "kings" (372.6, 10). But who would these be? We have no evidence to connect them with the kings of the Emar region who are honored as (absent) dignitaries who receive portions at tables in the NIN.DINGIR festival, and *šarru* "king" is not generally spelled syllabically at Emar, though there are occasional instances of phonetic complements for the last syllable, and one text speaks of a town as URU (^{uru})*ša-ar-ri*, "the city of the king" or "the city Šarru."[88] The best possibility may be that the LUGAL-sign is used because the words sound the same, and we have the West Semitic word from the same root, meaning "lord" or "official."[89] The distinction from Akkadian "king" might usually be made by the syllabic spelling.

The noun *qidašu* (the lengths of the vowels are not certain) is found in only one Emar context outside this formula, and not at all outside Emar. In the ritual fragment 396.5, something is for (*ana*) ^{d}KUR EN *qí-da-*[*ši*]. At Emar, the verb *qadāšu* (D) means "to sanctify with offerings" (see below). Unlike the usual Akkadian *quddušu*, it has nothing to do with one-time purification as initiation into cultic service (i.e. "consecration").[90] Rather, it seems to refer to offerings that prepare gods or human personnel for participation in a single festival or rite. The noun *qidašu* has some association with the installation as a whole. We should look for a concrete referent, especially with the verb *nadānu*; perhaps the *qidašu* is an offering -- one that initiates festivals at Emar (see the *ūmi qadduši*, below). The *zukru* festival is "given" in the fragment that records its beginning (*nadānu*, 375.2), and Mari now attests the word *zukrum* in a join to a letter to Zimri-Lim, A 1121 + A 2731, lines 6, 8, and 10. In the Mari letter, the *zukrum* (not indicated as a festival) is given (*nadānum*) to ^{d}IM.[91] Perhaps the word *zukrum* is fundamentally an offering term: at the end of the Emar *zukru* festival text, where all the animals offered are totaled, the execution of the festival may be defined by the verb *qaddušu*, [*z*]*u-*⌜*uk*⌝*-ra ú-qa-*[(*ad-*)*da-šu*(?)] (373.210).

---

88 E.g., Emar 17.4, LUGAL-*ri*; 69.11, the name ^{m}SUM-^{d}*É-a*-LUGAL-*ri*, etc. For the city, see Arnaud, *AuOr* 5 (1987) 224-225.

89 Compare Hebrew *śār*, Ugaritic *šr*, "prince"?, and *šarrum* at Mari for "Kleinkönig od Schech" (*AHw* s.v. *šarru(m)* A3e).

90 In the context of our installation festival, we might wonder whether the noun *qidašu is* intended to carry some nuance of this Akkadian meaning (initiation into cultic service). However, the men of the *qidašu* are not specially identified with the installation rituals, to the exclusion of the rest of Emar ritual, so such a definition for *qidašu* seems unlikely.

91 See Bertrand Lafont, "Le roi de Mari et les prophètes du dieu Adad," *RA* 78 (1984) 9.

In sum, our ritual staff might be "the officials who give the sanctification-offering." Dagan of 396.5 would then be "the lord (or possessor) of the sanctification-offering."

In the NIN.DINGIR festival, the men of the *qidašu* most often head a list of feasters (see *akālu/šatû*, below), 369.12-14, 38, 54, 67, cf. 79. Beyond that, they conduct the priestess to her father's house in the one case where no formal procession is described, after the day of shaving (369.21), and they begin the apportionment made in the administrative section (lines 76-77, see text notes). The instructions for the last event seem to equate this group with the individual recipients of portions. The phrase *itti aḫāmeš* with *zâzu* should mean, "to divide (equally) with each other" (*CAD* s.v. *aḫāmeš* 3; see *zâzu*, below), and the object of *zâzu* in lines 76-77 should be the same ox whose parts are taken by the king('s man), the lúḪAL, and the singers in a series which repeats the order, meat-portion, "his share" (*zittašu*), subject, verb *ilaqqe* (lines 77-79). When the lúḪAL and the singers divide portions "with each other" in lines 81 and 82, they are themselves clearly the recipients. The lúḪAL and the singers are never among the feasting personnel, yet their seven-day portion promised in line 83 is the precise match of the portions for the men of the *qidašu* during the seven-day feast of the NIN.DINGIR installation (lines 54-55). Perhaps they are *among* the *amīlû ša qidaši*, those who administer the ritual, or even make up the whole of this group. The men of the *qidašu* are never found outside the ritual texts, unlike the lúḪAL (*passim*) and the singers (see above). The *ḫussu* and *ḫamša'u* participate in feasting but may be specially associated with the mourning aspect of the installation. They are absent from the assignment of rations.

The ḫussu-men

This class of participants only feasts with the men of the *qidašu* during the NIN.DINGIR installation (369.13, 38), and their presence is only certain here.[92] The cycle of offerings for the month of Abû begins, *ina ūmi ḫu-us-si*, "on the day of recollection(?)" (452.1), where *ḫussu* might be related to *ḫasāsu*, "to think of a god," etc. This word should be related to the festival participants, another term for celebration of rites, like *qidašu*. See also 459.3, *ana ḫussi ša* [...], "for the recollection of(?)," and ritual fragments 502.4 and

[92] The form *ḫa-as-su* of 388.61 in Arnaud's edition is one possible reading of a broken text; the temple inventory 332.17 mentions [*ḫ*]*u-us-su*, but this may not be the men.

515.3. There is no evidence for *ḫussu* in Akkadian texts elsewhere. Since Emar 452 deals with offerings for the dead, the term *ḫussu* may refer particularly to recollection of the departed. Dietrich calls the *ḫussu*-men "die Ritualmeister," based on the adjective *ḫassu*, "klug, verständig." The *ḫussu* could only be ritual supervisors if the title is understood as an extension of the preceding men of the *qidašu*.

The bēl bīti.

The phrase *bēl bīti*, "lord of the house," is common throughout Mesopotamia, but in Emar ritual the title appears to define a particular function or office, not attested elsewhere. In Mesopotamian law and divination texts, the *bēl bīti* is the head of a household (*CAD* s.v. *bēlu* 1d, and house-owner, 2a; *AHw* s.v. *bēlu(m)* I B1a). The early first-millennium Babylonian boundary stones use the term for the "tribal chief" ("lord of the house," *CAD* s.v. *bēlu* in *bēl bīti*).

In the NIN.DINGIR installation, he slaughters and cooks a sheep at his house (following the parallel, 385.29) before the banquet for dignitaries at ᵈIM's temple on the first full day of the NIN.DINGIR festival (369.15). The verbs *nakāsu* and *bašālu* (Š) (see below) are especially associated with this player and his place of work (the *bīt(i) bēl bīti*, É EN É, see below). On the last day of the festival, the ox and the seven sheep from the last procession to the temple of ᵈIM are returned to the house (É)[93] of the *bēl bīti*, 369.68-69 (text A), and the ox is slaughtered by the men of the *qidašu* after the installation is over (*palāku*, not *nakāsu*, 369.76-77). If the ox and the sheep from the last procession return to the *bēl bīti* because they came from him, the animals from the other processions likewise might have come from his place.

The *bēl bīti* as supplier, butcher, and preparer of sheep and cattle for offering is found mainly in the NIN.DINGIR festival and the *kissu* set at Emar. The entire first day (*ūmi ša qadduši*) of the text for all *kissu* festivals is spent at the *bēl bīti*'s house (388.1, 10), until the action moves to the gate of the *sikkānu*'s on the next day (line 13-14). In the NIN.DINGIR festival (369.15), the ᵈEREŠ.KI.GAL *kissu* (385.29), and the text for all *kissu*'s, the *bēl bīti* plays an active role only on the first full day of the festival, and this may be true for the broken text of the Ea *kissu* rite as well (386.3-4). At the end of

---

[93] This could be either a separate building or a room inside another building.

that day(?) in the same text, the *bēl bīti* joins the men of the *qidašu* in giving a gift of silver to the god Ea (lines 10-11). See also the ritual fragments 396.10 (feasting at his place, cf. 388.18?); 409.4; 410.6 (*bēlet bīti*, with ᵈNIN.KUR laid down at her house, *niālu*, Š).

The *bēl bīti* does not appear in non-ritual texts,[94] including the various records for temple administration, so that there is no clear record that this is a professional title. Perhaps the NIN.DINGIR installation and the *kissu* festivals were supplied with animals for offering by wealthy heads of clans, who were not religious professionals. Confirmation of this scenario might be found in the fact that the texts for these two rituals never mention the sources known from the other major Emar rituals for sacrificial animals. Compare:

-- *ša* URU.KI, "of the city": 370.48, cf.51 (*maš'artu* installation); 373.24, 50, etc. (*zukru* festival); 446.99, 103;
-- *ša* LUGAL, "of the king": 373.20, 24, etc.; 452.13(?), 34; 463.20;
-- *ša nupuḫanni*, "of the *nupuḫannu*-men": 446.9, 14, etc.; 452.17, 29, etc.; 463.12(?);
-- *ša* LÚ.MEŠ *ša im-ma-ri*, "of the men of the sheep(?)": 452.36.

Conversely, none of the rituals which give these sources for animals has a *bēl bīti*. This is most striking in the other festivals, the *maš'artu* and the *zukru*.

The maš'artu

The *maš'artu* is a priestess unknown to other Akkadian literature, but at Emar she is only just behind the NIN.DINGIR in rank, listed after the NIN.DINGIR-priestesses of ᵈIM and *Dagan bēl Šumi* in the portions for dignitaries during both installation festivals (369.16-17, 55-58; 370.33, 35). The NIN.DINGIR and *maš'artu* are also juxtaposed in lists of personnel (276.6) and property (286.19), and they are associated more generally in one ritual fragment, 399.4 and 8. In spite of the fact that the two move in the same religious sphere, they have no recorded interaction. Each is provided a table and a meat portion at the other's installation, but this honor may not have required their actual presence.

---

94 Dietrich and Loretz discuss the Ugaritic administrative text KTU 4.15 in "Neue Studien zu den Ritualtexten aus Ugarit (I)," *UF* 13 (1981) 75. This text lists a series of *bʿl bt* in lines 2-9, 11, sometimes before personal names, and the authors translate the term "Bauarbeiter" (workmen). These men were associated with the *bt ʾil* -- a temple, or a storehouse as at Emar?

The *maš'artu* installation shows that she has some role in the military fortunes of Emar (see below, in section IV), and appropriately, her "mistress" (*bēltīya*) is Aštart/Ištar (370.84; also 71, 73), and *Aštartu tāḫāzi* in particular (line 20). *Aštartu tāḫāzi* is one of the major gods of the Emar cult. She and ᵈNIN.KUR are last in the offerings made on the 24th day of the month of an unspecified month near the beginning of the *zukru* festival (373.11-12; the goddesses are placed last?), though she is not in the *zukru* god-list or the related text 378 (in the breaks?). However, *Aštartu tāḫāzi* joins ᵈNIN.KUR and ᵈNIN.URTA in the first line of the god-list Emar 379, appears in most of these short sacrifice-lists (380.2; 381.11; 382.6), and the *ša-aṭ*(?)*-ra-ḫi* rites of *Aštartu tāḫāzi* are the occasion for the offerings of Emar 460 (especially lines 1, 6, 9).[95]

While *maš'artu* is not a known Akkadian word, the verb *ša'āru*, "to conquer," is attested for the OAkk and NB dialects (*AHw* s.v. *ša'āru(m)* II), and the title itself may carry a military tone. She can have children (124.25-26, a son), and both a son and a brother are identified by their relation to her, and are of sufficient social standing to be witnesses for legal documents (124.25-26, the son; 209.20, the brother). This characteristic may set her apart from the NIN.DINGIR. Note the occurrence of the *maš'artu* in 345.4; 432.3.

The king of Emar.

During the NIN.DINGIR installation, the king of Emar only takes part (perhaps *in absentia*) in the banquets for dignitaries (369.16-17, 55-58), and the precedence of the priestesses in this setting is expressed by placement of the king last in the lists (see below, the king of Šatappi). He has the same part in the *maš'artu* installation (370.36) and the ritual fragment, 371.7. At the end of Emar 369, the king receives the first portion when the ox is divided (line 77). Beyond this, the king's only ritual role is in the obscure *imištu* for the

---

[95] The goddess Ištar MÈ, "Ištar der Schlacht," is attested in Asia Minor, in KUB XV 20 III 4 and MIO 9.214; see Ilse Wegner, *Gestalt und Kult der Ištar-Šawuška in Kleinasien*, AOAT 36, Neukirchen-Vluyn: Neukirchener, 1981, 33. According to Laroche, CTH 590, KUB XV 20 belongs to "fragments de songes et d'ex voto," in the broader category of "divination." This ritual might thus share the Syrian/West Hurrian religious traditions of Kizzuwatna (see below).

LUGAL KUR *ša* ^{u}[^{ru}(*E-mar?*)].[96] He is a principal source of animals and vessels (see below, the *bīt ili*) for the *zukru* offerings but plays no personal role.

This minor ritual role contrasts with the practice of various neighboring cultures. The king serves as the central human player in the cults of Ugarit, Hatti, and Assyria.[97] Perhaps we should understand the absence of the king from Emar ritual activity to be a sign that Emar religion taps cultural sources outside the major urban centers.

It is possible to put together a sequence of Emar kings from the non-ritual texts. Only three men are explicitly called the king of Emar,[98] and it is likely that the bulk of our Emar inscriptions are from their reigns. They are:

^{d}IM-GAL (*-kabar*), son of Iaṣi-Dagan? (1.8; 14.26; 144.27; 156.28), 42.8, 20; 256.34.

Zū-Aštarti, son of ^{d}IM-GAL, 17.1-3, 12-13, 17; 256.33; HCCT-E 29, rev.23.[99]

---

96 Arnaud, "Religion assyro-babylonienne," *AEPHER* 85 211, proposes that *imištu* might be the Emar equivalent of *amertu*, "inspection." He observes that this is the only ritual to take place in the palace precincts, but it was only found in one copy and does not seem to have been important.

97 J. Sapin, *UF* 15 (1983) 181, states that at Ugarit, "le culte est lui-même fondamentalement un culte de royauté/royaume." The "priests" (*khnm*) appear in administrative texts but not in the rituals (page 180; e.g. KTU 1.43; 1.91:10-11; 1.148:18-22). Sapin then compares the unusual CTA 32, which involves "foreigners" and "citizens," to the Emar *zukru*, suggesting that both reflect older (pre-monarchic) political systems. See also J. de Tarragon, *Le culte à Ugarit*, 78-90, 92-96.

Likewise in Hatti, the great festivals take place in the presence of the royal couple; see Hatice Gonnet, "Rituel des fêtes d'automne et de printemps du dieu de l'orage de Zippalanda," *Anadolu* 19 (1975-1976) 151; R. Lebrun, "Les hittites et le sacré," in Julien Ries et al, eds., *L'expression du sacré dans les grandes religions*, I, Louvain-la-neuve: Centre d'histoire des religions, 1978, 170. See also Lebrun, *Šamuḫa*, 43 (at IŠTAR's festivals, there). The prominent role of the queen alongside the king sets the religion of Hatti apart from its ancient Semitic neighbors.

The king is at the very center of attested Assyrian ritual, though we lack texts for the daily temple routine. G. van Driel, *The Cult of Aššur*, Assen: Van Gorcum and Company, 1969, 170, notes that "the presence of the king is perhaps the very *raison d'être* of the Neo-Assyrian cultic rituals we have," placing extreme demands on his time, if in fact all the rituals were performed as described; see also Paul Garelli, "Les temples et le pouvoir royal en Assyrie du XIVe au VIIIe siècle," in RAI 20, 116.

98 Arnaud, "Les textes d'Emar et la chronologie de la fin du Bronze Récent," *Syria* 52 (1975) 88-89, adds Elli, the son of Pilsu-Dagan, and "Bisu-Dagan" from Emar 42.1-3; 11 and 20. Pilsu-Dagan and Bisu-Dagan should be the same figure (see below, The Gods of the *zukru* Festival).

99 Tsukimoto, *ASJ* 12 193, text 8.

Pilsu-Dagan, (younger) son of ^{d}IM-GAL, 42.1-3; HCCT-E 10, rev.34.[100]

The title "king of the land of Emar"[101] is not found outside of ritual, though we find "the king of the land of Carchemish."[102] Outside ritual the royal title is rarely used: it is LUGAL ^{uru}*E-mar* in 42.3, 9, and 20, a record of three votive offerings at the temple of ^{d}IM/U; and LUGAL ^{uru}*E-mar*^{ki} in 17.2, 13, and 17, acknowledgement of the loyalty of one ^{m}*Ku-na-zu* (line 10, cf. 22, 31) in reporting a treasonous plot to his sovereign. These are documents in which the king acts in his official role; when kings take part in legal transactions (often as witnesses), no title is used.[103] The Emar king is also a citizen, at one level.

As mentioned above, many legal transactions are witnessed by the king and members of the royal family, and these give us further information about the royal line at Emar. There is no certain evidence for ^{d}IM-GAL's father, though a ^{d}IM-GAL son of Iaṣi-Dagan is the first witness in two real estate documents (144.27 and 156.28, see above). The king Zū-Aštarti is ^{d}IM-GAL's son, listed with two (younger?) brothers, Abī-Rašap and Abbanu (17.41-43; 256.33-36). Oddly, Zū-Aštarti and Abī-Rašap disappear from the scene, and there are texts that make Abbanu the first brother, followed by Pilsu-Dagan and EN-malik (2.31-33; 11.37-39; 126.22-24). Then several lists of witnesses put Pilsu-Dagan at the head (e.g., 125.23; 146.24; 157.7; 158.24), and others, his first son Elli (e.g., 9.37; 94.23; 139.43). Elli is never explicitly called king, but the formula at the head of the votive offering, 42.1-3, and the juxtaposition of his offering with the official royal offerings of Pilsu-Dagan, indicate that he is at least crown prince. The next generation includes sons ^{d}IM-GAL (again!) and Asdi-aḫi (141.26; 147.37-38), but there is no sign that these reigned during the period of extant Emar inscriptions.

In the NIN.DINGIR festival administrative section, the king's portion might be assigned to a royal representative, LÚ LUGAL KUR (369.77, text

---

[100] *Ibid*, 190, text 7.

[101] LUGAL KUR (*ša*) ^{uru}*E-mar* 369.17, 55, 58; cf. LUGAL KUR, 369.77C; 370.36; 371.7.

[102] LUGAL KUR ^{uru}*Kar-ga-miš*, 201.20, cf. 16, 35; without URU, 18.1; 202.1, 2, 3; cf. 177.2; 201.23.

[103] Examples with witnesses from the royal family include Emar 2, 3, 4, 10, 11, 14, and others. Because no titles are used, it is difficult to tell if a given figure is serving as the current king.

A). The appearance of two of these together in the ritual fragment 399.4 shows that this is more than an alternate writing for the royal title.[104]

The king of Šatappi

Only text A of the NIN.DINGIR festival adds the king of Šatappi to the set of banquet dignitaries in 369.16-17, 55-58. The others end the list with the short form, LUGAL KUR, no further definition being necessary: text B (line 58); C (17); D (56, [LUGA]L KUR); E (369.17, = 402.4). Šatappi is the home of the *kissu* festival group (385.1, 2, 11, cf.16; 388.5), located at the temple of Dagan there (see below). The king and elders are mentioned in 257.4, and other citizens appear in 217.1 (cf. 218.4; 219.3); 251.1; 261.22; and 361.11.

The kawanu(?) and tārû.

These terms appear to represent functions of the *qidašu*-men and the *ḫussu*-men rather than separate personnel (see the translation, above). During the feast on the day of enthronement (369.38-39), the men of the *qidašu* and the *ḫussu*-men "are to be the *kawanū*(?) and the *tārû* (attendants)."[105] The repeated words without the determinative LÚ.MEŠ, *kî kawanīšu u tārêšu* ("as his *k*... and his *t*...") refer to the function alone. The verb *tarû* (*AHw* s.v. *tarû(m)* II G2, of slaves and servants) means "to pick up, to be in attendance" (so the noun, *tārû*, "attendant"[106]), but *kawanu*[107] is unknown in Akkadian.[108] We are intended to understand that the *qidašu*-men and the *ḫussu*-men are to belong to ᵈIM's entourage for this feast at the storm god's temple. The new role of these ritual personnel as servers would reflect the fact that ᵈIM himself receives offerings on the enthronement day, whereas on the preceding day of shaving the actual offerings for the feast go to the gods.

---

104 Dietrich, *UF* 21 50, etc., treats LÚ as a determinative.

105 This interpretation was suggested to me by W.L. Moran, personal communication.

106 This noun appears at Alalaḫ in AT 378:7, in a list of people giving wedding gifts: *A-ia-an* ˡᵘ*ta-ru-ú*.

107 The second sign is generally *-wa-* at Emar, not *-pi-*.

108 Potential comparisons include the Hebrew root, *k-w-n* (for, "to prepare"?), Sabaean *kwn* and modern Yemeni Arabic *kāwana*, "join, be allied with, support"; personal communication, John Huehnergard. Derivation from the Akkadian *kawû* ("to be outside"?) remains another possibility, though Akkadian intervocalic *-w-* is generally written *-m-* at Emar: 213.22, *ú-maš-šar*; 264.29, *ú-maš-šar-šu* (*wuššuru*, "to release"); 18.23, *a-ma-te*.MEŠ (*awatu*, "word, affair"), in a document that may be from Carchemish. One exception is found in the curse formula of Emar 125.35, *a-wa-ti*. Dietrich, *UF* 21 81 and n.74, derives a noun *kawânu*, "Gast," from *kawû*, and the idea of "Aussenstehender."

Neither of these groups is found anywhere else in the Akkadian Emar texts.

The NIN.DINGIR's brothers

Two of these carry the NIN.DINGIR in the last procession to her father's house (369.43), and as a group her brothers give gifts (line 45). There is quite a lot of family participation in the NIN.DINGIR festival: father, brothers, and a sister, though no mother. I have found no parallel to this phenomenon.

The elders of Emar.

The city elders pay homage and give a seven-shekel silver *tudittu* as a gift before the procession to the father's house on the day of enthronement (369.44). Then, they take part in the last feast after the NIN.DINGIR has finished preparations (line 67), and the elders begin bed chamber preparations by giving a "fine garment" (line 69). Their primary function is "giving," and this probably served as an official sanction from the city government. Note that it is the elders, not the king, who provide this government blessing. The elders have no ritual role except in the two installation festivals (see 370.18), and they are found elsewhere mainly in land sales from the city to private citizens, where they are the sellers with the god ^{d}NIN.URTA[109] or with the $^{lú.meš}$*aḫ-ḫi(-a)*, "brothers(?)."[110]

The city-elders, *šībūt āli*, are a common Mesopotamian group, but von Soden (*AHw* s.v. *šību(m)* C3) wonders whether they are not found in MA texts; he observes them at Ugarit and Alalaḫ, but not in the Akkadian texts from Nuzi and Boghazkoy. The elders of the Mari texts have received abundant attention because the institution might be a carry-over from the non-urban cultures of some Mari kingdom peoples.[111] It is generally agreed that the *šībūtum* serve as local leaders at Mari, taking part in various local roles, including taking the census. They do not have high rank, standing below the provincial governors and mayors who are responsible to the central

---

109 Emar 1.17-19, 26-27; 2.17-19, 26-29; also texts 3, 4, 9, 12, 139, 144, 146-153, 155. In 123.9, the tablet for the previous sale of the land was sealed with ^{d}NIN.URTA's seal.

110 E.g. Emar 109.25-26; 110.29-30; 130.22-24.

111 Horst Klengel, "Zu den *šībūtum* in altbabylonischer Zeit," *Or* 29 (1960) 363, understands this to be the case for the entire institution as attested in Mesopotamia through OB times.

government of the kingdom.[112] Kupper observes that so far the elders have not been found in the capital of Mari itself, but only the district centers and outlying areas.[113] Perhaps the elders did not originate in nomadic societies exclusively, but belong to non-urban settings more broadly.

The elders of Emar are entrenched in both the religious and economic life of the city, and might play a more prominent role in Emar culture than at Mari.

The nugagtu

This female player has one function, to give cries (see below, special ceremonies). She is not known outside Emar, but the title suggests a link with the Babylonian verb *nagāgu*, "to bray," which can refer to human wailing.[114] As observed above, the *nugagtu* thus appears to be some kind of lamentation priestess.

The ḫamša'u

"Seven and seven" of these men take part in the seven-day feast at the house of the NIN.DINGIR residence, but only for two days, and they give the priestess flour and malt-beer (369.53-54). The amount of flour is remarkably large: one *parīsu* each makes fourteen *parīsu*, nearly the fifteen *parīsu* of barley that represents the whole annual ration of the priestess in a bad year. Outside the NIN.DINGIR installation, they join the *nupuḫannu*-men in giving a sheep to Adammatera in the annual cycle 446.77-78, and they appear to be involved in some activity in the temple of ᵈIM in the broken ritual, 371.16. The *maš'artu* installation includes an interruption in the feast cycle (370.45-68) after the fourth day, in lines 55-59. Line 55 states that "seven and seven" of some group go to the temples for all seven days of the cycle, and we find

---

112 André Finet, "Les autorités locales dans le royaume de Mari," *Akkadica* 26 (1982) 10-15; see also Victor H. Matthews, "Government involvement in the religion of the Mari kingdom," *RA* 72 (1978) 153.

113 Jean-Robert Kupper, "La cité et le royaume de Mari: l'organisation urbaine à l'époque amorite," *M.A.R.I.* 4 (1985) 463.

114 The *nugagtu* could also be a loan-word from the Sumerian nu-gig, a female cult functionary (P. Steinkeller, personal communication). A text from Ebla has NÍG.GIG = *ni-gi-tum* = (Sumerian) ne-ki-ki, where *ni-gi-tum* may be *ni/nugigtum*, or even *nugagtum*; see Pettinato, *MEE* 4 207, line 100. The nu-gig is said to screech "like a young Anzud" in A. Berlin, *Enmerkal and Ensuḫkešdana*, 1979, 44, line 97. W. von Soden, "Kleine Bemerkungen zu Urkunden und Ritualen aus Emar," *N.A.B.U.* 1987, 25 (no. 46), suggests that *nugagtu* is probably *noggagtu*, from **naggagtu* (root *ngg*?).

"seven and seven" $^{\text{lú.meš}}$*ḫ*[*a*-...] in line 30, so that restoring *ḫa-am-ša-ú* seems likely in both cases. The [^{l}]$^{\text{ú.meš}}$*ḫa-am-ša-ú* appear without the numbers in line 58, where the two days of feasting, this time at the temples of ^{d}IM and ^{d}NIN.URTA, and the gift(?) of some drink (DUG [ ]) and flour (lines 57-58) parallel the NIN.DINGIR festival role.

The *ḫamša'u*-men are not known outside these Emar ritual texts, and the derivation of their title is uncertain. Arnaud translates "cinquanteniers" (cf. Dietrich, "50iger"), following the most straightforward derivation. The *aleph* is surprising, however, and it is not clear what would be the significance of a numerical root. The appearance of the *ḫamša*-men in text 446 with Adammatera and offering to the *abû* indicate a possible connection with mourning and the dead. Outside that context the group is found only in the two installations, both of which likely involve mourning for the previous priestess.

The two companions (see below *epēqu*).

The NIN.DINGIR's sister (See below, *leqû*, and above, the brothers.)

C. THE ITINERARY: PROCESSION AND SACRED SITES

At one level, the whole scheme of the NIN.DINGIR installation festival is organized by units of time, three separate days, a seven-day feast, and one final day (probably the last of the seven). However, the time framework is overlaid with a spaçial framework, movement between the temple of ^{d}IM and the house of the NIN.DINGIR's father. This movement is accomplished in the Emar rites by formal procession of the ritual players from one sacred locale to the next, and Emar has a language of procession which reflects the various aspects of the movement. The verbs carry the action of this and other ritual events, and make a good point of departure for discussing the processions of the NIN.DINGIR festival. Sacred sites visited will be treated separately.

1. Procession

Description of procession in the NIN.DINGIR festival falls into two classes. One focuses on the point of origin or (more often) the destination, and simply moves the players from and to temples and other festival locales. This class makes use of the verbs *alāku*, *erēbu*, *kašādu*, *târu*, and *(w)aṣû*, usually with *ištu* (*(w)aṣû*), *ana*, or substitute *ina*,[115] and reference to the relevant place. The other class is concerned with the execution of the procession itself, using the verb *alāku* with prepositions that fix the relative order of the participants; *ana pānī-*, "ahead," and *arki-*, "behind." Only one further detail is provided when the brothers carry (*našû*) the NIN.DINGIR back to the father's house. Note that Assyrian ritual texts use similar procession terminology, including *erēbu* and *(w)aṣû* for entering and leaving sacred sites,[116] and *târu* for returning to them.[117] However, Akkadian has few other verbs that would express these basic actions, and any procession between sacred sites probably must use *alāku*, *erēbu* and *(w)aṣû* for the primary movements.[118]

Focus on place

alāku, G

The generic verb for moving to a new festival location is *alāku*, "to go" or "walk." Most often, the destination is the temple of ᵈIM: 369.7, (29, from line 7), and 66. Processions to ᵈIM's temple from the father's house make stops at other sites; with *alāku*, these include the *bīt Gadda*, 369.(34A), from the pattern in lines 65-66, and the temple of ᵈNIN.KUR, 369.65. This use of *alāku* is less common in other rituals at Emar: 370.8; 373.169?, 208? (*ana muḫḫi*?); 392.4; 409.5?; 446.108.

erēbu, G

The verb "to enter" offers a detail not inherent in the verb *alāku*; the subject actually goes into the building, the *bīt Gadda* (369.36A), the father's house (line 46), and the *bīt tukli* (line 64). We should not make too much of the distinction, however, since the last use (line 64) has the same function in the procession series as *alāku* in lines 65 and 66. On the other hand, the specific entrance is very much the point when the NIN.DINGIR(?) is kept from going into ᵈIM's temple(?) on the enthronement day.[119] Note the

---

115 On *ana* for *ina* at Ugarit, see Huehnergard, *Akkadian of Ugarit*, 184 and 186.

116 E.g. *erēbu*, MVAG 41/3 8 I.27; 12 II.44 (MA); KAR 215 I.15 (NA); *(w)aṣû*, MVAG 41/3 12 II.39 (MA).

117 E.g. KAR 154 Rev 6' (MA).

118 We might consider the verb *saḫāru* for "to turn," and other verbs of movement express nuances not appropriate to entering, leaving, and going between sacred sites: *ṭeḫû* "to approach" (for offering), *etēqu* "to pass (by, through)," *ezēbu* "to abandon."

119 See line B(31-36)f. Both the person and place must be guessed from context.

emphasis in the form *appūna* with the negative. Outside the NIN.DINGIR festival, see 370.82; 388.58(?); 449.6.

erēbu, Š

The NIN.DINGIR is brought into some place (probably her father's house) at the end of the shaving (*gallubu*) day (369.21, see text). She is brought into the ^{d}IM temple precincts (line 32A; cf. B(31-36)h) the next day, though she is kept outside the *bīt tukli* and *bīt Gadda* (see above). The Š conjugation of *erēbu* may serve as the causative for both *alāku* and *erēbu* at Emar. It is unusual to find a person as the object of a causative verb of procession, though the use makes sense in the context of installation. When the object is clear in other Emar ritual instances, it is the gods who are conducted here and there, presumably in the person of their statues. Compare *erēbu* (Š), 370.21; cf. 101; 452.19, 20; *(w)aṣû* (Š), 373.45, 176, 193, 195; cf. 182, 184; 375.7; 386.17; 452.21, 25, 55; *elû* (Š), 373.58; *(w)arādu* (Š), 446.45.

kašādu, G

This verb only appears once in the NIN.DINGIR festival (369.8; see also 373.171). It zeroes in on the point of arrival at the temple of ^{d}IM, where the shaving is the first rite performed.

târu, G

In 369.36A, the verb *târu* is used without preposition and place, but the reference is the temple of ^{d}IM, after offerings are made at the *bīt tukli* and *bīt Gadda*.

(w)aṣû, G

The verb *(w)aṣû* is the only one in this set which focuses on the point of departure, not the destination, and in the language of procession, this is the beginning of the action, not the end. Thus, the verb always appears in the NIN.DINGIR festival with *-ma*, as the preliminary to another action, usually procession to another location. In the cases of continued procession, *(w)aṣû* is accompanied by the preposition *ištu*, with the place of exit: the temple of ^{d}IM, 369.21; the *bīt tukli*, lines 34A and 65; and the temple of ^{d}NIN.KUR, line 66. On the last day, the departure is the occasion for covering the priestess like a bride (line 61). It appears that *-ma* serves to subordinate the clause with *(w)aṣû* to the following action, so we might translate, "when (they) leave...". The bridal covering best demonstrates this, because the actual procession does not begin until line 63 (*ana pānī nubatti*), and lines 61-62 describe actions that coincide with the NIN.DINGIR's final departure for the temple of ^{d}IM.

The processional verb *(w)aṣû* is more common than any other at Emar; see 370.82; 373.15, 40, 202; 446.12, 24, 57, 59, 86, 107; 448.5; 452.27; 454.11.

Focus on execution

alāku, G

The main concern of the NIN.DINGIR festival instructions is to set the order of procession, and the verb *alāku* is used for the time spent *en route* (369.8, 30, 45, 63, 64, 67, 68, 76). We find no mention of further details (perhaps singing, playing of instruments, etc.). The order for the installation does not vary, though participants do: the singers are first, always "ahead," *ana pānī-*, lines 8, (30), 63 (with the animals and the torch, GI.IZI.LÁ[120]); from lines 7 and 29, the sacrificial animals come second (cf. 63); the NIN.DINGIR is third, and the divine weapon[121] is last, according to the division in lines 63-64, and the weapon is always "behind," *arki-* (lines 7-8, 29-30, 64). This pattern is similar to that found in other Emar ritual. In the *zukru* festival, the animals precede the gods (373.16, 28, using *ana pānī*); in the *kissu* for ^{d}EREŠ.KI.GAL, the singers go before the offering (*ana pānī* SISKUR),[122] and the divine axe goes behind (*arki-*) the offerings (446.43; 447.14; with the sheep in 446.87-88) and behind the god Halma (446.102-103) during the rites of the annual cycle.[123] The idiom also appears in broken contexts in 392.9 and 446.25.

našû, G

Two of the NIN.DINGIR's brothers carry her in the procession back to their father's house following her enthronement, presumably on her chair

---

120 Note that the Emar version of one lexical text (Ḫḫ. VIII-IX, Emar 546.9-10) gives two readings for this logogram: min(for GI)-izi-lá = *gi-zi-lu-u* : *šab-bu-ṭu* (line 9); ... = *di-pa-rù* (line 10). The term *šabbuṭu* is one of the scattered glosses to Akkadian entries, and should represent a local term for "torch." Compare *AHw* s.v. *šabbiṭu*, "Stab, Szepter."

121 On the meaning of ^{giš}TUKUL, see George C. Moore, "^{GIŠ}TUKUL as 'oracle procedure' in Hittite oracle texts," *JNES* 40 (1981) 49-52, covering the various Hittite meanings.

122 The usual Akkadian for SISKUR would be *niqû*, but occurrence of an equivalent noun *maqqû* from the same root in line 58D suggests this as a possible alternative.

123 Singer observes that the Hittite KI.LAM festival is organized as a series of processions, and each day there is a procession of cult symbols reviewed by the king. The order places the king first, followed by the queen, then the dancers, singers and priests, then the various symbols, including the central "animals of the gods" (*KI.LAM* I, 89-90). The participation and leadership of the Hittite king especially stands out from the Emar procession format.

(369.43, cf. line 40). Something or someone is carried between the stelae (*sikkānu*) during the *zukru* festival (373.205; cf. 374.6, from the *zukru* sphere but not the *zukru* festival itself).

2. Sacred Sites.

The following collection of NIN.DINGIR festival locations includes only sites visited by festival personnel as part of the event's itinerary, not cities or regions (e.g., Emar). Some of the places function only as sources for materials (the palace and the temple of ^{d}NIN.URTA), and some are both sources and itinerary points (the temple of ^{d}NIN.KUR, the *bīt(i) bēl bīti*, the father's house, and the *bīt tukli*). However, we have no evidence for the term É/*bītu*, "house," as the recipient itself of offerings or payments. The frequent substitution of *ana* for *ina* accounts for offerings made *ana* ("at"!) sacred sites (e.g. 369.13, 14, 15, feasting; 49, offering). Sites are listed in order of appearance.

The temple of ^{d}NIN.URTA

^{d}NIN.URTA's temple is the source of the lots(?) (*purû*) for identifying the new NIN.DINGIR (369.2, 6). ^{d}NIN.URTA has a special connection with civic affairs (see above, the elders of Emar), and he appears to function as a city-god, in spite of the prominent roles of Dagan and ^{d}IM. W.F. Leemans suggests that the temple M_1 is ^{d}NIN.URTA's temple, based on his importance in contracts, which Leemans believes were registered in this building.[124] This hypothesis seems unlikely (see above, The diviner). For an extensive discussion of ^{d}NIN.URTA's identity and role at Emar, see below, Chapter IV.

The palace

It is interesting that the only role of the palace in the NIN.DINGIR festival is as a source of fine oil for anointing the priestess (369.3, 20, with the temple of ^{d}NIN.KUR). One wonders whether this points toward anointing Emar kings as well. In the *zukru* festival, the palace and king are a frequent source of sacrificial animals and ritual vessels (see above, the king). The equivalence of king (LUGAL/*šarru*) and palace is evident in the identification of the *kurkurru*-vessel (^{dug}KUR$_4$.KUR$_4$) as either *ša* LUGAL (373.17, 20, 25,

---

[124] W.F. Leemans, *JESHO* 31 234-235.

47, 51, 53) or *ša* É.GAL-*lì* (373.67). This vessel belongs only to these sources, which are logically the same. (See below, The *bīt tukli* and the *bīt ili*, for further discussion of vessels in the *zukru*.) In Emar real estate transactions, the fee for a future claim is often paid to the palace when the witnesses are headed by the royal family (e.g. 8.40; 10.18, where the king acquires the land; 137.60; 138.46, a prince; 94.21; 97.16, other people). Note the list of palace goods 321.1-4, which includes animals garments, and *oil*.

The temple of ᵈ*NIN.KUR*

ᵈNIN.KUR's temple is the second source of oil for anointing (369.4, 20). This goddess has a key place in the *kissu* "throne(?)" festivals, which are somehow associated with the two high priestess installations (see below); the relation of ᵈNIN.KUR to anointing may forge another link in this chain. The ᵗᵘ́ᵍḪÉ.ME.DA which is placed on ᵈNIN.KUR in the father's house for the period of her residence there is also from ᵈNIN.KUR's temple (369.(23), 60). This red wool garment only appears here and on the first day of the *maš'artu* installation, laid out(?) on the bed(?) given to the priestess (370.17). Thus it may belong to the particular sphere of installation (and mourning?). Finally, ᵈNIN.KUR's temple is the last place visited by the final day procession before arriving at ᵈIM's temple (369.65, 66).

The temple of ᵈ*IM*

This is the central site for the whole NIN.DINGIR festival. It appears only as the location of various ritual activities, never as a source of materials. The temple is the destination of processions on each day, 369.7, 8, (29), 32A, 66, 67, and once the point of departure, line 21; it is the location of feasting (*akālu*/*šatû*), line 13, 59A; and it is where offerings are made, lines 36A and 51. The gate of the temple is the place of anointing (KÁ/*bāb*(*i*) ᵈIM, 369.20), and the residence of the NIN.DINGIR is apparently part of the gate complex (KÁ É ᵈIM, 369.15; see below, *bīt BuKKi*). On the first full day of the festival, the NIN.DINGIR is shaved at the opening of the courtyard gate, *ana pî bāb*(*i*) *tarbāṣi* (369.9), on arrival at ᵈIM's temple (line 8). Texts 42-62 were found in a building identified as ᵈIM's temple, based on the following texts: Emar 42, a series of three votive offerings to ᵈU; Emar 45, a tablet of "weapons of ᵈIM"; and Emar 52, a list of seventy-three archers who receive bows at (*ana*) the temple of ᵈIM (É ᵈIM). The inheritance document, Emar 202, also refers to a "tablet of the ᵈIM temple" which apparently recorded a previous legal agreement (202.13).

The house of the bēl bīti

The "house" (É/*bītu*) of the *bēl bīti* may be some sort of compound for holding and preparing sacrificial animals, or it may be the house of whoever serves in the *bēl bīti* role, providing animals for festivals (see above). Emar 369.69 indicates that the house of the *bēl bīti* is the source of the animals for the last day's procession (line 63). The three lambs are sacrificed along the way to Adammatera, ᵈNIN.KUR, and ᵈIM (lines 64-66), leaving the one ox and seven sheep (see text notes, line 63). Processions on the shaving and enthronement days (lines 7 and 29) include a similar combination of ox and sheep, perhaps from the same supplier. In line 15, one sheep is slaughtered and cooked there, apparently to provide the meat portions for the five dignitaries' tables (line 17, UZU UDU; cf. lines 57-58 for the individual portions).

The NIN.DINGIR's residence and the bīt BuKKi(?)

During the shaving and enthronement days, five tables are set up so that the high priestesses and kings of the Emar area may take special feast portions. The rites for these two days follow parallel courses, and the text for one can illuminate the other, as with the opening procession (369.7-8, 29-30). The location of the five tables receives slightly different descriptions which should refer to the same place: line 15, *a-na* KÁ É ᵈIM *a-na* É NIN.DINGIR; line 39, *i-na* É *Bu-uK-Ki ša* NIN.DINGIR. There is no Akkadian parallel for the *bīt BuKKi*; the terms *puqqu*[125] and *pukku*[126] are possible, but the best guess may be a noun *bukkû* "mourning," derived from the root *bky* "to weep, mourn."[127] In the Atraḫasis epic the goddess Nintu declares that her grief over the Flood's devastation is "like inhabiting the house of moaning," *kî ašābi ina bīt dimmati* (Atraḫasis III iii:47). The Emar *bīt bukki*(?) might represent a similar place of mourning within the NIN.DINGIR residence, or might describe the *bīt* NIN.DINGIR itself when it is given over to mourning rites. The *bīt BuKKi ša*

125 "Devotion(??)," from the verb "to pay attention to"; see *AHw* s.v. *puqqu(m)*, which can have a god for its object. Dietrich, *UF* 21 82, works from this root and calls the *bīt puqqi* "der Klause," from "Haus der Verwahrung."

126 The drum or hoop that serves as a game for Gilgamesh; see *AHw* s.v. *pukku*, and *CAD* s.v. *mekkû*, Gilg XII:4, 8, 56, 63.

127 Long final vowels are not consistently marked at Emar; see the discussion of the term *kissu/kussû* in chapter IV. For nouns related to the Akkadian verb *bakû*, compare *bakkā'u* "wailer, professional mourner," *bakkītu* "wailing woman," *bakkû* "squalling, crying" (English definitions from the *CAD*). This possibility and the *pukku* from Gilgamesh were suggested to me by P. Steinkeller, personal communication.

NIN.DINGIR could be equivalent to the *bīt* NIN.DINGIR of lines 15 and 53. According to the first phrase of the line 15 description, the *bīt* NIN.DINGIR is at the gate of ᵈIM's temple, an appropriate location for the human mistress of his house.

The seven-day feast of the NIN.DINGIR festival actually takes place at the *bīt* NIN.DINGIR as well, though the new priestess still waits at her father's house. One sheep is offered to the gods and to Hebat respectively at "her house" -- best understood as the NIN.DINGIR's residence (369.49). "Seven and seven" *ḫamša'u*-men eat and drink there for two days (line 53), and the men of the *qidašu* for seven days (line 54, "at her house"). It makes sense that the tables for Emar dignitaries are thus set in the same place as on the two previous days. The whole installation festival is summed up with a statement taken from the description of this seven-day period: *kî* NIN.DINGIR *ina šūkultīša uššab* (line 84; cf. line 51, with *ana*). However, we should not translate, "when the NIN.DINGIR sits down at her banquet," understanding this to mean that she joins the participants of lines 53-58. Rather, the temporal clause defines the occasion for the offering of the gold figurines to ᵈIM and Hebat, "when the NIN.DINGIR is enthroned at her feast," where *šūkultu* is a near synonym of *isinnu*/EZEN. It is the deceased NIN.DINGIR who still takes the first table at the feasts in the temple of ᵈIM (lines 16, (39), 55, and 57).

The *maš'artu* installation likewise provides for seven days of feasting at the *bīt maš'arti*, with the same tables and portions for the same dignitaries (the four-person version), and the *previous maš'artu*.[128] This is her official residence, not the private home of her family, just as with the NIN.DINGIR.[129]

The father's house

Although the temple of ᵈIM is certainly the focal point of the NIN.DINGIR installation, since it is her new home, the old home of the priestess serves as a counterpoint. She returns there after enthronement, carried by her brothers (369.43, cf. 46), stays for seven days, and begins the

---

128 370.20-40; see especially lines 21, 31, 33, 34 for the *bīt maš'arti*; lines 23, 28, 29 for the seven days; and lines 33-36 for the dignitaries.

129 If the office of the NIN.DINGIR does derive from the Mesopotamian *entu*-priestess, this official residence represents a contrast to terminology for the residence of the Mesopotamian *entu*, the *gipāru*; see *CAD* s.v. *gipāru* 1; *AHw* s.v. *gipa(r)ru* 1 (m/spB, but a Sumerian loan from earlier times); Charpin, *Clergé*, 192, 200-201, 204, etc. This seems to mark a substantial change in the Mesopotamian institution, in its western expression.

final day with a formal departure "as a bride" (lines 61-62; *ištu bīti* refers to the father's house). It is likely that she spends the night there on the two previous evenings as well (so, line 21), and ᵈNIN.KUR is moved there to join her until the final day (line 23). After the festival is over, the ox from the final procession is slaughtered and divided at the father's house (line 76), and the sacrifice required at her death may be performed there also (*ina bīti*, line 91; note the verb *palāku* in both lines 76 and 91).[130] This means that we can place both offerings to the god Šaḫru in the father's house, and he acts as some sort of family god for the NIN.DINGIR (see lines 52 and 92).

The father's house is responsible for supplying the NIN.DINGIR with a new table and gold earrings at her enthronement (lines 40 and 41) and a colorful sash for a bridal covering (line 61). A certain wealth is assumed, and the priestess must come from a prominent Emar family. The father's house receives the animals slaughtered after her death.

It is not surprising that the father's house is a ritual site only in the two installation festivals, but it is not clear why the family is so much more prominent in the NIN.DINGIR rites. We find the father's house mentioned only on the consecration day of the *maš'artu* installation, as a procession destination (370.8) and perhaps a place where beer is offered (line 9?). Perhaps the family plays a primary role in the NIN.DINGIR installation because a wedding is involved, and this shows the NIN.DINGIR to be a bride in a way that the other female initiate is not.

The bīt tukli and the bīt ili

The procession to the temple of ᵈIM on the final day makes stops at the *bīt tukli* and the temple of ᵈNIN.KUR before arriving at its final destination (369.64-66). On the enthronement day, there is a similar tour of other sacred sites, though it seems to take place after arrival at ᵈIM's temple (text A; in B it seems to precede the arrival). This version stops at the *bīt tukli* and the *bīt Gadda* (lines 33A-36A), though the point of departure from the ᵈIM temple(?) and the arrival at the *bīt tukli* are somehow lost and there is a break in the text between lines 32 and 33. Both times, Adammatera receives an offering (lines 33, 64), and the site should be his residence. The priestess, weapon, and singers are kept from entering on the enthronement day.

---

130 Another possible location is the É NIN.DINGIR.

The list of allotments for the NIN.DINGIR offers a further clue to the function of the *bīt tukli*. All the provisions of lines 86-90 are given from the É DINGIR.MEŠ, "divine (store)house."[131] However, the annual barley allotment is given (the same verb, *nadānu*) from the *bīt tukli* in the A-text, but the *bīt ili* (É DINGIR-*lì*) in the C-text (line 85). At least as sources of allotments for personnel, the two places seem to be equivalent.

In the *zukru* festival (373) and the offering cycle for the month of Abû (452), various vessels belong to either the palace (É.GAL-lì or LUGAL, see above) or the *bīt ili* (É DINGIR-*lì*). The dugPIḪÙ (see *AHw* s.v. *pīḫu(m)*, only Babylonian, no MB; OB includes Mari), the dug*ḫu-bar*,[132] and the *ḫi-zi-bu* (new word) can come from either the palace[133] or the *bīt ili*.[134] The dugḪA (unknown) comes from the *bīt ili* only.[135] Animal offerings have only two sources in the *zukru* festival, the king[136] and the city.[137] In the Abû cycle, animals are taken from the king,[138] the shepherds,[139] and the *nupuḫannu*-men.[140]

The *zukru* festival also provides information that might locate the *bīt tukli* -- not in the temple of dIM but in that of dNIN.URTA, notwithstanding the place's association with Adammatera. Something (statues of gods?) is brought out, [*i/a-n*]*a* É dNIN.URTA *i-na* É *tùk-li*, "to (*ina* for *ana* with *(w)aṣû*, versus *ištu*) the temple of dNIN.URTA, to the *bīt tukli*" (373.183).[141] This description by paired phrases matches the pattern of 369.15, which locates the *bīt* NIN.DINGIR in the gate of dIM's temple, *a-na* KÁ É dIM *a-na* É NIN.DINGIR. Perhaps the *bīt tukli* shares dNIN.URTA's place in the

---

131 *bīt ili*, in line 90A; the MEŠ may just mark the logograms, and not signify a true plural; compare 446.79, É DINGIR. This characteristic is also found at Ugarit; see Huehnergard, *Akkadian of Ugarit*, 89.

132 The Emar dug*ḫu-bar* recalls the Hittite vessel, *ḫuppar*. This is a large vessel (Singer, *KI.LAM* I, 162 and n.34), used at Zippalanda for carrying hand-washing water and for holding wine (Gonnet, *Anadolu* 19 157). Similar terms for vessels appear at Qatna (*ḫu-up-pa-ta-ru*, I:4; see Jean Bottéro, "Les inventaires de Qatna," *RA* 43 (1949) 7) and perhaps in the Hurrian *ḫubrušḫi*, "creuset" (Laroche, *GLH*, 109).

133 *pīḫu*, 373.30, 56; *ḫubar*, 373.33; *ḫizzibu*, 452.38.

134 *pīḫu*, 373.49; 452.29, 31, 47; *ḫubar*, 373.18, 21, 51 (read [1 dug*ḫu*]-*bar*); 452.3, 54; cf. 463.24; *ḫizzibu*, 452.22, 24.

135 373.26, 48.

136 E.g. 373.15-16, 24, 28, 37, 46, 52; corresponds to the palace.

137 URU.KI, e.g. 373.24, 46, 50, 52.

138 452.12, 34, cf. the offering cycle, 463.20, 29.

139 LÚ.MEŠ *ša im-ma-ri*?, 452.36.

140 Unknown word, 452.17, 29, 32, 36, (54).

141 See also 373.110, in the *zukru* god list: dx [x x x x] É *t*[*u-u*]*k-li*; the name of the deity is not legible.

economic affairs of the city government. We should recall that the god and the city elders are sometimes joint sellers of property held by the city and are to be joint recipients of claim payments. If the *bīt ili* is identical or closely related, it might correspond to "the city" in the *zukru*, as the second source of animals and vessels for offerings.

Another possible connection between the *bīt tukli* and the *bīt ili* arises from the offerings made to the *abû* (ritual pit)[142] of the *bīt tukli* in 452.32 and 52, first and last in a set of *abû* offerings. One such offering appears in the annual cycle, made to the *a-bi* É DINGIR, *abû* of the *bīt ili* (446.79), conceivably the same as the *abû* that framed the offerings of the last three days of the Abû cycle.

Neither the *bīt tukli* nor the *bīt ili* play familiar Mesopotamian roles in ritual. The word *tuklu* is rare, and the Emar use is the first known second millennium occurrence outside of personal names (see *AHw* s.v. *tuklu*, "Hilfe"). We should consider the Emar meaning of *tuklu* unknown.[143] It is odd to call the *bīt ili* a non-Mesopotamian term,[144] but the Emar use is specific and without parallel. The *bīt ili* shows no features of a temple proper but only appears as a warehouse for materials used in offerings. The *bīt tukli* has broader use, and is a storehouse only in the two installations (see 370.79-80, cf. 16).

The bīt Gadda[145]

This sacred site makes one appearance in the NIN.DINGIR festival on the day of enthronement, when the *sikkānu* of Hebat is anointed to enter the *bīt Gadda* in the place of the priestess (369.34A, 36A). As opposed to the *bīt tukli* and *bīt ili*, which have no special relation to ᵈIM, the *bīt Gadda* is a particular home of ᵈIM. The *zukru* festival god-list pairs ᵈIM *ša* É *Gad-dá* and ᵈ*Si-ka-ni ša* ᵈ*Ḫé-bat* (373.165-166), indicating that the *sikkānu* of 369.34-35 is taken out for anointing by the NIN.DINGIR and sent back into its home with ᵈIM. This action is preceded by a pair of offerings to ᵈIM and the *sikkānu* of Hebat, the two inhabitants of the *bīt Gadda* (369.34A-35A). One other

---

142 See the Appendix on text 452 and the term *abû*.

143 Dietrich, *UF* 21 81, translates *bīt tukli* as "Voratshaus" and bases this on "Haus des Vertrauens, gesichertes Haus."

144 The Mesopotamian use to mean "temple" is shared by the Hittite *É DINGIR-LIM*; see Güterbock, RAI 20, 125.

145 I have capitalized the term *Gadda* because it is preceded by the divine determinative in 369.34A.

attestation in Emar ritual keeps up the connection with ^{d}IM: some offerings are made there in the fragment 461.4 and 5, and ^{d}IM is the sole god mentioned in the offering list (lines 6, 8, 9, and 12). Dietrich equates the deity Gaddu with Mesopotamian PAP.SUKKAL and identifies the temple M_2 as the Gaddu-temple, but the argument is in a forthcoming article.[146] If this solution works, it must account for the special association with the divine couple ^{d}IM and Hebat.

The consonants of *Gadda* are fairly certain. Emar 369.34A and 36A use the GA-sign, and there is a personal name in the ration list, 336.89, spelled *Ga-ad-da*. The word is not Akkadian, and the "Gad" of later Syrian texts may reflect the same term.[147] Note the Israelite tribal name, Gad, and Daniel Sivan observes the personal name *gu-ud-da-n*[*a*?] at Ugarit.[148]

The bīt urši

Careful preparations are made for the NIN.DINGIR before she can climb onto her bed. One step is to spread out on the bed an Akkadian blanket (TÚG) *ša* É *ur-ši-ša*, "belonging to her (pure) place of repose(?)" (line 71). The *bīt erši*, "bedroom," is a familiar location in Mesopotamian palaces and temples (see *AHw* s.v. *bītu(m)* B4, mostly first millennium), but *uršu* is a distinct, if related, term, and there is a separate *bīt urši* found only at Amarna and Ugarit (see *AHw* s.v. *uršu(m)* I "Schlafgemach," 1, EA 84:13f and PRU 4 109, line 5). Dietrich introduces a third related possibility by reading É *ḫu-ur-*

---

146 Dietrich, *UF* 21 68 n.49, refers to the new article, "Die akkadischen Texte der Archive und Bibliotheken von Emar," *UF* 22 (1990).

147 The name *Gaddi-* is found at Palmyra, for instance in the name of a city group called the Bene Gaddibol. Javier Teixidor, *The Pantheon of Palmyra*, Leiden: E.J. Brill, 1979, 27, finds that the name belongs to the religious traditions of the (Phoenician) west, as does the name Baalatga = *bʿlt-gd*. The "Gad" was a fixture in the religion of Roman period Palmyra, often addressed to specific deities in requests for favor (page 60, especially Astarte/Allat), but functioning as general representatives of providence (see page 92). This term may come from the west, but it might be better to identify it as a long-standing part of central Syrian religion, given the new attestation at Emar. According to Koehler and Baumgartner (*gād* II) the term is found in Middle Hebrew, Punic, Jewish Aramaic, Egyptian Aramaic, Nabataean, and at Hatra, as well as at Palmyra.

148 Ug 5 6, line 29, in Sivan, *Grammatical Analysis and Glossary of Northwest Semitic Vocables in Akkadian Texts of the 15th-13th C.B.C. from Canaan and Syria*, AOAT 214, Neukirchen-Vluyn: Neukirchener, 1984, 221. Further evidence for the root in southern Syria might include the Iron II jar handles from Gibeon marked with stamps that may display the word *gdd* (the last letter is uncertain). In the personal name Gaddi-El ("El is my fortune"?), the Bible appears to provide attestation of the meaning "fortune" that predates the Palmyrene material. The last two comparisons were brought to my attention by F.M. Cross, personal communication.

ši-ša in text A (see the notes for the text) and then translating "Vorratskammer."[149] Akkadian *ḫuršu* does not usually occur with *bītu*/É,[150] and as a storehouse or storeroom it is particularly associated with foodstuffs and kitchens, as opposed to clothing. In our festival, it is not clear whether this is in fact the bedroom ("place of repose"?),[151] where the Akkadian blanket is laid, or a holy wardrobe from which it is taken. The frequent use of *ša* to indicate the source of ritual materials suggests the latter.

3. Procession in the Festival Progress

An important part of the installation's drama is carried by the processions between the father's house and the temple of ᵈIM. There are five, four of which are described in detail (the first return is stated without elaboration in line 21). The priestess goes to the storm god's temple on the days of shaving and enthronment, and each evening she is returned to her father's house for the night. After she spends the seven days of the enthronement feast at her old home, she is conducted to the temple a third time, to take up permanent residence.

The processions have a dual purpose. Altogether, they move the NIN.DINGIR through each stage of her transition to her new role and residence in service of ᵈIM. Introduction to the storm god's sacred domain is treated as a delicate process that cannot be accomplished in one motion with full assimilation achieved on the first visit. However, at the same time as they attend to the progress of the priestess, the processions to the temple are framed as sacrificial processions, focused on the animals that are led to slaughter. This aspect is expressed in the description of the participants' order for the *gallubu-* and enthronement-day processions (lines 7-8, 29-30): in both cases the sacrificial animals are given first mention, and the others are said to go in front of or behind them. During the procession on the final day, the animals once again receive first mention, but the order is defined by relation to the NIN.DINGIR (lines 63-64). The change reflects not only the ascendance of

---

149 Dietrich, *UF* 21 62, 85.
150 *CAD* s.v. *ḫuršu* lists only KAH 2 34:17.
151 William L. Moran, *Les lettres d'El-Amarna: correspondance diplomatique du pharaon*, Paris: Les Éditions du Cerf, 1987, translates the *bīt urši* in EA 84 as "la chambre à cou[cher]," and notes Nougayrol's translation in PRU 4 109, line 5, "maison privée."

the new priestess but the peculiar fact that the ox and sheep that walk in the procession are not sacrificed but returned to the *bēl bīti* (lines 68-69). Only the three lambs are offered to the gods.

As sacrificial processions, the three processions to dIM's temple begin a larger sequence. At the temple the ox and the six sheep are sacrificed after a *kubadu*-ceremony, and then offering and feasting follow. The last procession omits the major sacrifice and therefore the preparatory *kubadu* as well. The processions of the enthronement and final days make two intermediate stops each, where the NIN.DINGIR participates actively in various rites for Adammatera, Hebat, and dNIN.KUR.[152]

In both cases, the first stop is a simple sacrifice at the *bīt tukli*, and the second stop involves rites at a second site that is particularly relevant to that stage in the festival. Offering at the *bīt tukli* encourages Adammatera to ensure abundance for the place of the NIN.DINGIR's provision. On the enthronement day, the day of her first entry into dIM's temple (line 32A and B(31-36)h), the priestess must stop at the *bīt Gadda*, the shrine for the storm god and Hebat as a couple. Before the NIN.DINGIR can sit on her throne of office, she must dedicate a new *sikkānu* for Hebat, her divine counterpart, to serve the same term, through her lifetime (see above, Hebat and her *sikkānu*).[153] On the final day, the priestess herself makes the offering at the *bīt tukli* and the temple of dNIN.KUR. It seems that she acknowledges dNIN.KUR's stay at her home for the seven days of the celebration, where the goddess kept the divine weapon for the last procession to the storm god's temple.

Walter Burkert draws together aspects of animal sacrifice in ancient Greek religion that are relevant to the sacrificial procession at Emar. Burkert proposes that animal sacrifice originated in the hunt, which was laden with religious awe and carried out as ritual.[154] "Sacrificial killing is the basic

---

152 By contrast, the priestess remains a passive bystander on the shaving day and is not even allowed to enter dIM's temple. She is shaved when she arrives and anointed before she leaves.

153 The force of this act is not altered significantly by the variation between texts A and B. In text B, these affairs are to be settled before the priestess may be brought into dIM's temple. In A, the priestess is allowed to enter that temple and the animals are sacrificed before dIM, but the offering and feast must wait until after stops at the *bīt tukli* and the *bīt Gadda*.

154 See Walter Burkert, *Structure and History in Greek Mythology and Ritual*, Berkeley: University of California Press, 1979, 54-56; Burkert, Peter Bing tr; *Homo Necans: The Anthropology of Ancient Greek Sacrificial Ritual and Myth*, Berkeley: UC Press, 1983. *Homo Necans* represents a full development of this idea.

experience of the 'sacred.' *Homo religiosus* acts and attains self-awareness as *homo necans*."[155] Domesticated animals would have replaced the wild game, and in the Greek world the ox or bull became the supreme animal for sacrifice.[156] The animals given to the gods for maintaining human life and welfare were made to enter the sacred domain in a physical rite of passage, by procession. Ideally the victims went to the altar as if of their own will.[157] In second-millennium Minoan and Mycenaean ritual, as known from iconographic evidence, the sacrifice of the ox or bull is carried out in the presence of a double-axe, perhaps the weapon of the storm god.[158] A double-axe appears on a gold ring from Mycenae at the center of a procession toward a goddess,[159] and a "lentite steatite" from Knossos shows a female figure (a priestess?) carrying a double-axe, apparently in some ritual.[160]

It is apparent that the NIN.DINGIR festival's sacrificial processions stand in a long and widespread tradition of sacrificial ritual. Both Burkert and Arthur Cook find parallels for the axe and the ox-sacrifice in Hittite Anatolia, which in turn shares many cultural links with northern Syria.[161] The Emar sacrificial procession likewise prepares for an ox-sacrifice which is executed in the presence of a sacred axe, which goes with the NIN.DINGIR to the sacrifice. When the animals are presented to ^{d}IM in the *kubadu* (see below), it is the role of the priestess to bear this axe before the god (line 31A, B(31-36)e). The two great sacrificial rites of the shaving and the enthronment days lay the groundwork for the rites that move the priestess into office.

---

[155] Burkert, *Homo Necans*, 3.
[156] Burkert, *Structure and History*, 55; Burkert, John Raffan tr., *Greek Religion: Archaic and Classical*, Oxford: Basil Blackwell, 1985, 55.
[157] Burkert, *Structure and History*, 56; *Homo Necans*, 3.
[158] Burkert, *Greek Religion*, 36-38; cf. *Homo Necans*, 138-141, 183. See Arthur B. Cook, *Zeus: A Study in Ancient Religion*, Vol.2, New York: Biblo and Tannen, 1965, 513-548, for review of the evidence, with photographs. The axe is often shown between the horns of a bull, which Cook (p.539) interprets as the horns of the ox offered to the sky-god. Burkert follows Martin P. Nilsson, *The Minoan-Mycenaean Religion*, New York: Biblo and Tannen, 1971, 222-227, in identifying the axe as the (symbolic) sacrificial weapon rather than the weapon of the storm god (against Cook). Nilsson argues that the axe is never shown held by a male deity, though Cook, 544 and fig. 419, would dispute this.
[159] Burkert, *Greek Religion*, 38; he refers to a photograph in M.P. Nilsson, *Geschichte der Griechischen Religion*, Pl.17.1.
[160] Cook, *Zeus*, 623, fig. 523, cf. fig's. 520, 524.
[161] Burkert, *Greek Religion*, 37-38; Cook, *Zeus*, 620 (axe in worship).

D. THE PROVISION

A. Leo Oppenheim begins his discussion of the Mesopotamian cult with the apt heading, "the care and feeding of the gods."[162] The NIN.DINGIR festival at Emar displays a complementary aspect of ancient Near Eastern religion: events of the cult are also the occasion for the care and feeding of the priests, all the human players in the cult. The verbs which carry the action of this festival reflect this twofold purpose. Because the materials of care and feeding are not fundamentally different for gods and their human servants, we treat these as one group, but divide the actions according to divine and human realms.

1. Actions

Provision as offering

"Offering" is any gift to the gods, but in the NIN.DINGIR festival it is almost entirely provision of food and drink. The one verb that encompasses all such offering in the festival is *naqû*, which either means "to sacrifice" an animal[163] or "to offer," more generally. The verb is used of listed provisions which include both animals (or meats) and other foods, including oils.[164] This broad use is rare but present in Mesopotamia.[165] Inclusion of beverages that are apparently not libated is unique.[166] Offering, *naqû*, is usually directed "to" (*ana*) a god, most consistently when an animal is sacrificed,[167] but it may be "before" (*ana pānī*) a god[168] or "of" a god.[169] Line 51, *ana bīt* ᵈIM, is ambiguous, and I have taken it as a reference to place (so, *ana* for *ina*), not to the temple as a recipient. Either way, the phrase is unique in relation to *naqû*,

---

162 A. Leo Oppenheim, *Ancient Mesopotamia: Portrait of a Dead Civilization*, revised ed. prepared by Erica Reiner, Chicago: The University of Chicago Press, 1977, 183.
163 Emar 369.11, (32A), 34A, 35A, B(31-36)a, b, 49, 52, 59A, 64, 65, 66, 82; *AHw* s.v. *naqû(m)* G4; cf. *CAD* s.v. *naqû* 3.
164 369.5, 19, 42, just Ì.DU$_{10}$.GA "fine oil," 47, 50-51, 92.
165 See *CAD* s.v. *naqû* 3b, AfO 24 88:11 and *passim* (MB Elam); flour, beer and sheep are offered (*naqû*); cf. animals and lapis lazuli in Rost Tigl. III p. 10:47.
166 369.5, 19, 47, 50-51.
167 Lines (32A), 34A, B(31-36)a, b, 49, 52, 59A, 64, 65, 66; for general offering, line 92.
168 Line 5, general; 11, sacrifice.
169 Lines 35, 46, genitive with *ša*; line 42, without *ša*.

a verb that always refers directly to the god intended, in the NIN.DINGIR festival (see 370.48-49 for the same situation).

Another pattern in the installation is the avoidance of the verb *nadānu* for offering, though other Emar texts have *nadānu* with divine indirect objects.[170] The verb *nadānu* replaces *šakānu* in the J-text of the *kissu* to Išḫara and ᵈNIN.URTA (387.10, 12, 16, cf. 15), in context of offering. The verb *naqû* is found throughout Emar ritual.[171] Only in the rites for the Hittite gods does *naqû* plainly refer to libation, where the object is cups of drink (*kāsu*), and the verb is not used for sacrifice or general offering in those ritual texts.[172] One possible exception is the oil offering in line 42.

Although *naqû* is widely used, there are patterns in Emar ritual terminology that are worthy of note. The verb *pa'ādu* appears in the *zukru* festival[173] and the annual offering cycle,[174] with the same general application as *naqû*. The latter ritual makes use of the verb *ṭabāḫu*, "to slaughter," for sacrificing animals to the gods,[175] mostly clustered about the New Year's (fifteenth day) events of 446.45-57. There is no burning of offerings in the installations or the *kissu* festivals, but the *zukru* rites connect burning (*qalû*) with a *kubadu* for all the gods,[176] and the verb *šarāpu* occurs outside the festivals.[177] Other verbs represent specific acts of offering:

---

170 In ritual, 373.195; 385.26; 393.12, 15(?); 395.13; 452.33, 52, cf. 16; see the short offering lists, 363.3; 364.4.

171 E.g. 371.10; 373.19, 21, 26, 29; 385.5; 388.2; 391.3(?); 396.11; 409.6; 414.4, 5; 446.33, 42, both unique D conjugation (see Huehnergard, *Akkadian of Ugarit*, 173, on Akkadian verbs at Ugarit found with unexpected D forms); 452.37, for *zâzu*, to all the gods, 45-46, object *kubadu*; 463.7, 16.

172 471.27; 485.4 (fragment); cf. 472.2, 3, 4, 8?

173 373.9, 13, 38; line 41, *i-pa-'a-a-du*, shows the middle-aleph; 375.3, 11, 21, all G; 373.15(?); 375.9(?); 392.4(?), D; and the noun *pa-a̰-da-t*[*i*], 373.191. In an Emar legal document we find the expression, KÙ.BABBAR.MEŠ *a-na* PN *i-pa-a-da-šu*, "(if) someone offers(?) PN silver..." (to pay off his slave-debt), 16.10. The ending *-aššu* includes the ventive *-am-*. From this text it seems the verb *pa'ādu* can be used for giving something to people as well as to gods. Durand, *RA* 83 174, states that this verb is not mid-weak but rather *padûm*, known from Mari to mean, "verser le prix d'une rançon, racheter" (cf. Durand, ARMT XXI, p.3, on *pidîtum*). The Mari comparison is valuable, but the abundant Emar use of the verb in the ritual texts must be accounted for, and the middle-weak character there is certain.

174 446.18, 23, 59, 106, all G.

175 446.50, 54, cf.41, 46-47, 116.

176 373.35, 60; the latter includes a *ḫubar*-vessel of some drink(?); this may be another Akkadian word used generically for all offering.

177 The annual cycle, 446.91, 98; offering cycle 463.9(?), all G; especially ritual for Hittite gods, using both D (see Huehnergard, *Akkadian of Ugarit*, 173, n.266) and G conjugations, 471.33; 472.1(?), 14, 15, 18, 24, 28 (2 times).

-- *šarāku*: Two[178] brides (*kallatu*) "give" something, possibly to ᵈNIN.KUR (385.21).
-- *našāru*: They libate beer and wine in the broken 393.28.
-- (*nakāšu*): In the annual cycle, one ox is "slaughtered" (446.31); this may be sibilant confusion of *š* and *s* in the verb *nakāsu*.[179]
-- *(w)abālu*: "to bring" an offering, 446.93.
-- *kasāpu*, D: The rites for Hittite gods include breaking *turubu*-bread as an offering.[180]

While the verb *naqû* is the primary word for "to offer" in the NIN.DINGIR festival, the installation instructions give us a quite detailed view of the intended offerings. Two main sequences emerge. One has to do with offerings provided in conjunction with temple feasting, and the other entails tables set out for honored guests -- divine or human.

The shaving and enthronement days each begin with a procession to ᵈIM's temple with one ox and six sheep. These are sacrificed and become the centerpiece for feasts at the temple, supplemented by offerings of food and drink (369.11-13; 32A, 36-39). The feast on the last evening follows this order (lines 66-67) and the fragmented A-text for line 59 bears witness to the same scheme. All four examples are protocol for ᵈIM's temple particularly. Procedure for the offering begins with slaughter of the animals (*naqû*) "for ᵈIM," lines 11, 32A, 59, and 66. Then, offerings are "placed before" the gods (11, 66) or ᵈIM (36-37). The idiom is *ana pānī* DN *šakānu*, indicating proximity to the actual statues. If both meat portions (see GARZA/*parṣu*, below) and breads are involved, the two groups of offerings are listed separately and the verb *šakānu* repeated (lines 11-12, 36-37; line 66 has *šakānu* only once, and only bread is placed before the gods, the lamb being entirely for ᵈIM). The beverages are not included with the meat and bread; after those are placed before the god(s), cups are filled (*mullû*) with wine (lines 12, 67) or wine and barley-beer (line 38). Line 59A, *tašiāti umallû* is a variation, but the text is flawed, and the contents of the goblets are omitted, as is placement of offerings (*šakānu*). Note how the confused state of the text in lines 31-36 is reflected in the separation of sacrifice from placement of meat in

---

178 It is not clear what is the significance of finding two brides together.
179 Text 446 displays the reverse confusion of *š* for *s* in lines 17, 40, 91, 98, 100 (ŠA/sa_{10}). Durand, *RA* 83 165, observes another variation of this phenomenon in Emar 202.4, in the expression *ri-ik-sa ir-ku-uš*.
180 471.27; 472.74; 473.21; cf. 474.7.

lines 32 and 36 (text A). The list of feasters, those who "eat and drink in the temple of ᵈIM,"[181] properly belongs to the offering sequence, and the combination of offering and ritual eating is a signal case of care and feeding for priests along with gods.

The *naqû-šakānu* set appears also at the end of the consecration rites of 369.27-28 (*naqû* is restored). The verb *šakānu* is repeated for meat and bread, though there seems to be a problem with the text, indicated by the placement of the cup-filling before the sacrifice.[182] It is also odd to find *ḫizzibu* (line 28?) included in a listing that usually places drinks with *mullû*, not *šakānu*. Offerings for Hebat in lines 49-50 are carried out by sacrifice (*naqû*) and presentation (*šakānu*) of the meat-portions. This pairing of verbs is only found in the two installations and the *kissu* festivals, and these likewise make use of the larger sequence as well. The repeated feasts of the *maš'artu* festival all follow the pattern, *naqû-šakānu-mullû-akālu/šatû*. No single day contains the whole unbroken, but the pieces of the pattern can be fitted together when all the days are consulted.[183] The *kissu* festivals use similar terminology for offering, but only the Dagan *kissu* consistently follows the same order, *naqû-šakānu*(meat portions)*-akālu/šatû*, 385.12-14, and *naqû-šakānu*, 385.5-7 (with the cries of the *nugagtu* inserted). ᵈEREŠ.KI.GAL's *kissu* includes a sequence with sacrifice, presentation of meat and bread, filling of cups, and feasting, but *mullû* precedes *šakānu*, and division for human participants is inserted (385.31-37). Likewise, we find *mullû* (twice, again) before *šakānu* (of meat and bread) in the Ea *kissu*, 386.7-9. The Išḫara and ᵈNIN.URTA *kissu* replaces *šakānu* with *nadānu* for describing presentation of offerings, giving the sequence *naqû-nadānu*(meat portions)*-nadānu*(bread), 387.12-15.[184] Finally, the text for all the *kissu* festivals makes use of the pair *naqû-šakānu* (meat), 388.2-3, but another offering-feast sequence has the meat, bread, and beer taken (*leqû*) directly by the bakers[185] before they eat and drink, 388.11-

---

181 *ana* (for *ina*) *bīt* ᵈIM *ikkalū išattû*, lines 13, 67; 38-39, no locative; and 59A, missing *ina* and the list of subjects.

182 Or, the order could indicate that the offering sequence in this event comes from a different ritual context -- the *kissu*.

183 *naqû* (with animals, only), 370.46, 49; *šakānu* (meat-portions and bread combined), lines 46, 49, 52, 61, 64; *mullû* (cups with wine), lines 47, 50, 53, 62, 65, 68; *akālu/šatû*, line 54 (subject LÚ.MEŠ *ta-ḫa-zi*, lines 62, 65, 68, cf. 47, 50).

184 Line 14 [ ]-*nu*, should not be *šakānu*, but rather [SUM]-*nu*; the verb *nadānu* is used in text J; text F uses *šakānu*, making a closer parallel with the NIN.DINGIR festival sequence.

185 ˡᵘMU.NINDA.DÙ.DÙ, (*nuḫatimmu*) *ša muttaqi*, "the bakers of sweet cake"; see Huehnergard, "Five tablets from the vicinity of Emar," *RA* 77 (1983) 35 and n.10. The form ˡᵘ.ᵐᵉšMU.NINDA.DÙ.DÙ appears in Huehnergard's text 5, line 14 (page 25).

13. Otherwise, only the fragment 391.3 may contain the *naqû-šakānu* combination.

The first two full days of the NIN.DINGIR festival also include a rite that resembles a feast, the setting out of tables and provisions for Emar dignitaries (369.15-18, 39 implied), the previous (deceased) NIN.DINGIR (of ᵈIM), the NIN.DINGIR of the local town Šumi,[186] the *maš'artu* priestess, the king of Emar, and in text A, the king of Šatappi.[187] This group does not overlap with those who feast with the storm god after the great sacrifices -- the men of the *qidašu* and the *ḫussu*-men. Also in contrast to those feasts, the dignitaries are never said to eat and drink (KÚ NAG, *ikkalū* (*u*) *išattû*), and this banquet may not even require an actual gathering; the previous NIN.DINGIR, at least, is served *in absentia*. Portions were likely set aside on their behalf, or in their honor.

The table-setting sequence involves two more uses of the verb *šakānu* and a list of figures to whom each table belongs. I include the event in discussion of language for offering because the same terminology is used when the dignitaries are divine, during the *qaddušu*/sanctification of the enthronement day (369.24-26). First, the tables are "set-up" (*šakānu*).[188] Then, the text lists the participants, with (line 25) or without (16-17) repeating the verb *šakānu*. Finally, food is "set out" onto the tables (*ina libbi-... šakānu*, lines 17-18, 25-26). This double use of *šakānu* with tables need not be associated only with groups of dignitaries, since it is used of the table and bread for the NIN.DINGIR at her enthronement (lines 40-41) and of Hulelu's table set on the wedding evening.[189]

Ritual table-setting is found in roughly the same group of Emar festivals as the offering-feasting sequence. The first part of the *maš'artu* installation is broken, and these two uses of *šakānu* are not visible, but tables "on the ground" (*ina qaqqari*; for underworld gods?, 370.12), and *ša pānī* ("before") someone (gods?, line 27) suggest the verb may belong in the text. There are tables for the high priestesses and king of Emar, just as in the NIN.DINGIR

---

186 See the inheritance document 225.7 for another reference; the towns of Šumi and Šatappi, 217.1; 218.4; 219.3, are both mentioned in texts from the diviner's family archives, Emar 199-226.

187 See above; the five tables of the seven-day period in text A explain the "five" in the earlier rites, where the text is broken.

188 *šakānu*, lines 15, 24, 39; the rest of the process is indicated by the phrase, *kî ša ūmi gallubi*, "just as for the shaving day," in line 39.

189 Lines 71-73, with *ina* alone (no *libbi*-), and wool among the provisions, ˢⁱᵍ*zirtu*.

installation, though the verb is not used for setting them out (370.34). Meat portions are placed "before them," *ana pānīšunu išakkanū* (370.37; vs. *ina libbi-*). While the parallels with the *maš'artu* rites are hazy, there is an identical use of the *šakānu-šakānu* combination in the Dagan *kissu* festival (385.7-9). The similarity to the set-up in 369.24-26 is strong enough to help reconstruct the 369 text: four tables are set out for gods, two for heavenly gods (Dagan, Išḫara and ᵈNIN.URTA) and two for underworld gods (Alal and Amaza), "on the ground." Both setting up tables and setting food onto them (*ina libbīšu*?) are actions performed in the last *kissu*, 388.4 and 10, but they do not make a single coherent event. Note that the festival for oxen 394.31 refers to setting out a table, and the offering list 434.1-5, cf. 11, has no verb, but describes tables with bread "on them," *ina libbīšunu*.

A third offering sequence in the NIN.DINGIR festival is the combination of *naqû* and *zâzu*(D) separating the content of offering (*naqû*, with meat, bread, beer, etc.) and the recipients (*zâzu*, "to distribute" among the gods). This offering is the last event before evening on the shaving and enthronement days in text C (369.19, 39 implied), and there is another made in conjunction with the arming of ᵈNIN.KUR on the evening of the NIN.DINGIR's enthronement (lines 47-48). The verb *zâzu* is used without *naqû* in the administrative section of the installation (line 83), though the object is the noun *niqû* (UZU.SISKUR). Again, the language of the *kissu* for Dagan shows a remarkable resemblance to that of the NIN.DINGIR festival; the *naqû-zâzu* combination appears in 385.10-12, directed toward the gods of Šatappi. In other Emar ritual, the D conjugation of *zâzu* covers the items offered as well as "the gods" receiving them.[190] This verb only applies to distribution among the gods, not offering to individual deities. As observed above, the expression "all the gods of Emar" seems to apply quite literally to every recognized cult, so the offerings described with the verb *zâzu* represent by far the largest outlay of provisions in the NIN.DINGIR installation. This is particularly apparent with the bread and beer distributed "one each" in lines 19 and 47-48.

Elements of the offering-feasting sequence occur singly in various Emar festivals, not tied to the order of actions found in the NIN.DINGIR installation. Presentation of offerings before gods (*ana*, or *ana pānī* DN

---

[190] 370.40; 373.8, 192, 201; 388.62; 394.11(?); 396.9(?); 452.2, 7; 463.6, 30, cf. 4(?).

šakānu), filling cups with a beverage (*mullû*), and eating and drinking as a sacred rite (*akālu/šatû*) each appear separately in a variety of Emar ritual:

- *šakānu*, 370.26, 29; 371.4; 392.11; 394.32, 34; 472.14, 22, 25; cf. (400.3); 437.9, 12; 446.17, 40; 474.5.
- *mullû*, 393.21, 22; 446.97-98; 463.7; 472.19.
- *akālu/šatû*, 371.3; 373.32, 57, 178; 396.10; 422.8; 448.5(A); 471.25; 472.73; 472.14 has a unique prohibition against eating.

The activity of the *bēl bīti* in 369.14-15 properly belongs to the table-setting for human dignitaries in lines 15-18, since the meat portions provided for them presumably come from the sheep which he slaughters and cooks, *nakāsu-bašālu*(Š). The use of *nakāsu* ("to cut off") for "to slaughter" may be primarily western in this earlier period (see *AHw* s.v. *nakāsu* GII2b). During the *kissu* for ^{d}EREŠ.KI.GAL, one ox and three sheep are slaughtered (*nakāsu*) at the "house"/É of the *bēl bīti* (385.29). After slaughter, the verb *bašālu* may describe roasting as well as boiling (see *CAD* s.v. *bašālu* 7). In the final *kissu*, the bakers ($^{lú.meš}$MU.NINDA.DÙ.DÙ, see above) cook various breads, flour, fruit, and birds at the gate (KÁ/*bābu*) of the *bēl bīti*. Other references to cooking (*bašālu* Š) include 371.6; 429.3; and 472.11.

Provision as allotment

The instructions for performing the NIN.DINGIR festival are very much concerned with concrete matters, and at one level they comprise an economic text, apportioning food, clothing, and precious metals to divine and human participants. "Offering" is provision for the gods, and provision for the human players is "allotment" that contributes to the income of the ritual personnel. Only the NIN.DINGIR's full income is described; other gifts include fees associated with specific ritual services (e.g., anointing) and portions of food assigned to participants in sacred meals.

Although the festival makes provision for the needs of both gods and humans, the two classes are by no means put on the same level. The terminology for the actions of giving and receiving by ritual personnel is completely different from the language of offering. "To give" may be expressed by *nadānu*,[191] *qiāšu*, and *ana qāti-*... *šakānu*. "To receive" is expressed by the verb *leqû*, and the formula *itti aḫāmeš*...*zâzu* (usually G), "to divide," covers distribution carried out both by and for human personnel.

---

[191] To gods in other Emar ritual, but not here; see above.

nadānu, G

As noted above, the verb *nadānu* does occur at Emar for offering, but in the NIN.DINGIR installation it is reserved for non-cultic giving. The verb appears with an array of gifts, from clothing and furniture on the final day (369.70, two verbs) to annual allotments, also for the NIN.DINGIR priestess (lines 85 and 90), to shekels for specific services performed by the lúḪAL.[192]

Each of the three groups represents a different nuance of the verb *nadānu*. The first refers to specific items that appear to make up a sort of trousseau for the priestess, a set of valuable possessions that will make the core of her personal property, to be transferred by legal testament to next of kin. These are a "fine garment" (TÚG SIG_5), a bed, a chair, and a footstool.[193] One Emar will begins an inheritance list with a bed and accompanying Akkadian blankets (TÚG.GAR URIki.MEŠ, 31.4) for a woman (a prostitute, fKAR.KID).[194] The NIN.DINGIR also receives an Akkadian blanket, which is spread out on her bed (369.70-71). Beds are particularly important for women in the Emar texts; there is another will where a bed heads the list of a daughter's inheritance, again (176.13), this time with its mattress and a delicate blanket (túg*ṣu-ba-tu* SIG). Furniture appears in property lists from both legal texts (69, 186, *RA* 77 text 4) and temple inventories (296, 303).[195] The verb *nadānu* here means, "to endow with gifts of office," or perhaps "with a woman's bridal inheritance." It is not clear whether the subject is the elders as representatives of the city (see 369.17), or the city via the general 3mp subject of all ritual action.

The second use of *nadānu* likewise has to do with the NIN.DINGIR's office, in that the items derive from her place in the temple household, but these are perishables for consumption, not permanent possessions, and *nadānu* here means "to give an allowance of provisions." As above, the NIN.DINGIR is the only recipient, and the allowance is specially linked to her priesthood.

---

192 This occurs in lines 5 and 10, for anointing and shaving; association with the *gallubu* of lines 8-9 is more likely than with the *kubadu*, lines 9-10, since there is no payment to the lúḪAL mentioned in connection to the enthronement day *kubadu*, lines 30-31).

193 On "footstool"/*gištappu* at Amarna, see Moran, EA 24, n.40; this is a word largely lost to 14th-century Babylon, but used widely in the west.

194 Durand, *RA* 83 181, states that the TÚG.GAR URIki is equivalent to TÚG.NÌ.*BÀR (his reading) of Emar 176.13 or *AuOr* 5 (1987) 6: "Il s'agit d'un lit comportant de grandes tentures. Des habits *ša* túg *akkadîte* sont encore attestés dans les textes médio-assyriens." (I do not see TÚG in Arnaud's copy for 176.13, R.3.)

195 Emar 69.13-14, table, (bed), stool; 186.13, table (and chair?), 20, 27-28, table and chair; *RA* 77 text 4:21-22, two chairs and an inlaid stool; 296.6-8, bed and stool, stools, chairs; 303.3-4, chair, table (and a garment).

The annual allotment of foodstuffs, wool, oil, and perfumes is intelligible from the phrase *ša* MU.1.KÁM, "for one year" (369.90), but a second gift is more obscure: the *ḫamša'u*-men each provide an additional *parīsu* of barley-flour and some malt-beer during the seven-day feast (lines 53-54), a significant supplement to her regular allotment, since fourteen units nearly double her allowance for a bad year.[196] It is not certain who the *ḫamša'u*-men represent in giving such a large part of the NIN.DINGIR's grain allowance.

The third use of *nadānu* has neither heritable property nor perishable goods as the object, but silver shekels, "paid" to the lúḪAL as a fee given for particular temple services (lines 5 and 10; vs. *leqû*, below).

These three uses of *nadānu* are accompanied by differences in orthography. The last is spelled with the logogram, SUM, whereas the other two use syllabic spellings.[197] The one instance of the irregular vocalization, *i-na-da-nu* (369.70), is also the only example of syllabic orthography without the ventive and suffix, *-nišši* (369.54, 70, 85, 90, in all texts).[198]

qiāšu, G~D

This verb is most nearly related to the first *nadānu* definition, to endow with gifts of office. Perhaps *qiāšu* means "to give outright," with no strings attached, not requiring or expecting a counter-gift.[199] The elders give the NIN.DINGIR a *tudittu*,[200] and her brothers give unspecified gifts (369.44 and 45). All are in recognition of her new office.[201] The Akkadian idiom nearest

---

196 See line 85, fifteen *parīsu*, vs. thirty in a good year; see also the fragment 372.13; the 3fs ending *-ši* indicates a priestess as recipient, perhaps the *maš'artu*, from the martial phrase [*n*]*akrūti ikkir*, "he has engaged in hostilities(?)," not a known Akkadian idiom.

197 See also 370.89 and 394.12, SUM-*nu*, for paying silver; but 370.117, SUM, for the annual allotment of the *maš'artu*, 388.69 for food "of twelve (shekels) silver," for the potter.

198 The vocalization *inaddan* does occur in some OAkk and early OB texts (see *nadānu* in the dictionaries).

199 W.L. Moran, personal communication.

200 See Harald Klein, "Tudittum," *ZA* 73 (1983) 257: "toggle-pin/Gewandnadel." They are most often made of metal, with 68% made of gold, silver, or both. Walter Farber, "Tamarisken-Fibeln-Skolopender," in Francesca Rochberg-Halton, ed., *Language, Literature, and History: Philological and Historical Studies Presented to Erica Reiner*, New Haven: American Oriental Society, 1987, 96-99 and n.36, suggests that Klein has neglected the first-millennium data, which shows a connection between *dudittu* (Farber) and *kirissu*, "(gerade oder gekrümmte) Gewandnadel." He proposes for first-millennium *dudittu* the tentative translation "Fibel," as opposed to the second-millennium "Verschlussnadel" (toggle pin).

201 The noun *qīštu* is used in the Amarna letters for wedding gifts specifically, but the term is not confined to this meaning, and the context from Emar 369 suggests that the wedding imagery may apply exclusively to the final day of the ritual, or part of it. See *CAD* s.v. *qīštu* 2c, and Pinḥas Artzi, "The influence of political marriages on the international relations of the Amarna-Age," in J.-M. Durand, ed., RAI 33, 25.

to the Emar instances uses the cognate plural object *qīšāti* with the ("pluralic") D conjugation in first-millennium texts (see *CAD* s.v. *qâšu* 3; *AHw* s.v. *qiāšu(m)* D2). Specific gifts are not identified. The Emar examples are slightly different: it is the G conjugation that is found with the plural direct object *qīšāti* (line 45), whereas the D includes both the specific gift (the *tudittu*) and the cognate by means of the formula, *ana qīšti-*, "as a gift."

The verb *qiāšu* is rare in the Akkadian Emar texts. One ritual fragment may include [*ú-q*]*a-ia-šu-ú* in broken context (399.1), associated with NIN.DINGIR festival players such as the priestess herself (line 8), the *maš'artu* (line 3), and the [lú]ḪAL (line 11).

ana qāti-... šakānu, G.

The [lú]ḪAL receives a fee in connection with the NIN.DINGIR's enthronement, given in the form of a silver coil, with the formula, *ana qāti* [lú]ḪAL *išakkanū*, "they will place in (*ana* for *ina*) the [lú]ḪAL's hand."[202] In fact, the use of *šakānu* here for payment is secondary to the basic meaning, to place (an ornament) on the body. Immediately before the payment to the [lú]ḪAL, the NIN.DINGIR is adorned with gold earrings placed on her ears (*ana uznīši išakkanū*, 369.41) and a gold band placed on her right hand (*ina qāti imittīša išakkanū*, line 42). These are gifts also, but they are part of the clothing that accompanies the enthronement of the priestess (see below, the NIN.DINGIR's progress, with *rakāsu*). This idiom does not occur elsewhere at Emar.

leqû, G

To some extent, giving and receiving are two sides of the same coin, the same ritual act, but the verbs *nadānu* and *leqû* are not interchangeable in the NIN.DINGIR text. They express equivalent events in one case only: the ration for the bad year in 369.85 uses the verb *leqû* (TI alone) as the exact counterpart of *nadānu*, which was used for the good year (also line 85). Payment and receipt of silver shekels may be described with either verb, but *nadānu* is used with specific ritual services (369.5, 10), and *leqû* seems to have to do with payment for participation in the festival generally. The latter verb occurs with the gifts to the [lú]ḪAL and singers, "when the NIN.DINGIR is enthroned at her feast" (369.84). Similar gifts are assigned to the [lú]ḪAL, the

---

202 The B-text for line 43 has LAMA/*lamassu* for ḪAR/*šemeru*. This should be a protecting figurine, cf. 282.7-8. Note that one Emar lexical text gives the Akkadian *se-e-mi-rù* as one reading for ḪAR (Emar 537.65, Syllabaire Sa).

singers, and the priest of Alal at the end of the *maš'artu* installation, "when the *maš'artu* sits (is enthroned) on her throne" (370.108-110; cf. 372.3?). The NIN.DINGIR's sister gets a silver ring in connection with washing the feet of the priestess (line 75).

Most instances of *leqû* in the NIN.DINGIR festival have to do with allotment of animal portions during the ritual or of meal portions for feasting. Assignment of animal parts belongs to the administrative section of the text, lines 76-94, where the lúḪAL (lines 78, 82, 83C, 93) and the singers (lines 79, 83C) dominate the apportionment. The one other recipient is the king of Emar (line 77). Meal portions as such are received (*leqû*) by the men of the *qidašu* during the ritual (lines 14 and 55), and the seven-day portions of line 83 in the administrative section match those of line 55 in the ritual itself. This suggests that the lúḪAL and singers (line 83), who are never united in the festival proper, together comprise the men of the *qidašu* (line 55), or are the major part of that group in this festival. Finally, the banquet tables of the shaving (and enthronement) day receive portions (line 18) destined for the dignitaries associated with each.

The verb *leqû* never has a god as subject, and this pattern is conspicuous in the rest of Emar ritual. Occurrence is frequent throughout the rituals that mention the human participants.[203] However, the *zukru* festival and the rites for the Hittite gods[204] focus on divine players only, and do not make use of the verb *leqû*. The cycle for the month of Abû (452) and other offering cycles (especially 460-463) likewise omit *leqû*. Texts 460-462 use verbless sentences and are hardly more than lists. Emar 452 and 463 are more complex, and properly belong with the *zukru* and Hittite deity rites, because human characters are only mentioned as the source of animals for offerings,[205] not as active participants.

Instances of *leqû* in Emar ritual outside the NIN.DINGIR installation include receipt of meat portions[206] as well as allotments of both food and drink.[207] The *maš'artu* gets something during the *kissu* festival that is

---

203 E.g., the NIN.DINGIR and *maš'artu* installations, the *kissu* festivals, and the texts for the annual cycle.
204 Especially 471, 472, and 473; note the personal name in 472.6, never part of other Emar rituals.
205 E.g. lú.meš*nu-pu-ḫa-nu*, 452.36 and 463.12; LUGAL, 452.34 and 463.20.
206 370.36; 388.63; 394.24, 25, 38; 446.27, 37, 39, 81; cf. 447.5.
207 370.15, 38; 371.2, 8; 385.18, tables, 24, for the men of the *qidašu*, 38, tables; 386.21, tables; 387.19, 21; 388.13; 395.2-3.

associated with her installation (370.113), as well as two bowls (line 114). Note that there is one case of *nadānu* with assignment of meat portions, in the annual cycle, 446.35.

leqû, G, and *târu*, D

One special use of the verb *leqû* deserves to be treated separately. Parts of the NIN.DINGIR installation require obtaining from a temple items that are not for offering. Twice, the object is fine oil (Ì.DU$_{10}$.GA/*šamnu ṭābu*, 369.4 and 20), taken (*leqû*) from the palace and ^{d}NIN.KUR's temple for anointing the NIN.DINGIR. It is not said whether any oil remained that should be returned to the source, but other temple property did have to be taken back, and the use was by loan, or better, by rental. The obtaining (*leqû*) and returning (*târu*, D) make a single ritual event, incomplete until the borrowed item was restored to the temple with offerings as a kind of user-fee. On the first day of the installation, the citizens of Emar take lots(?) (*purû*) from the temple of ^{d}NIN.URTA (369.2) in order to identify the new NIN.DINGIR. After she has been selected and anointed, bread and some beverage are returned to the temple "with the *purû*" (*itti*, lines 5-6). The return of ^{d}NIN.KUR's red wool garment to her temple with bread and beer (*itti*, this time attached to the offering, line 60) closely resembles the return of the *purû*, and we can reconstruct its obtaining in line 23.

On the final day of the festival the verb *târu* (D) occurs without a preceding reference to "taking" (*leqû*, 369.69). The objects are one ox and seven sheep, returned to the place of the *bēl bīti*, suggesting this is their source as well as destination. This use of *târu* lacks the offering which accompanies return of the *purû* (line 6) and the red wool garment (line 60), and at least the ox is slaughtered later (line 77), so we do not have return for reuse. Nevertheless, the verb should indicate restoration to the place from which the animals were obtained.

Only one other Emar rite may deal with removal and return of cultic materials: the F-text for 385.22, in the Dagan *kissu*, reads *ú-te-er-ru-ú* for the line following the statement, "the brides will give...," É.GI$_4$.A *i-šar-ra-ka$_4$*.[208] Unfortunately, the text is corrupt. In text A, line 21 reads, "at the evening vigil, two brides will give," with no break in the tablet, but some object has likely dropped out. This should be the object of *târu* in 385.22 (text F, line 11) also, but text F is broken, and text A offers a jumble of elements from two

[208] Text F is broken before É.GI$_4$.A; I derive the plural from text A, 2 É.GI$_4$.A.

different idioms: *iš-tu* NINDA.MEŠ KAŠ.MEŠ// *a-na* É ^{d}UD.ḪA *ú-še-ra-bu*. The first is found only with the verb *qadāšu* (D), though the return of the red wool garment is with bread and beer (*itti*, not *ištu*). Entrance into the temple of ^{d}UD.ḪA represents a separate idiom entirely, with unknown object.

The verb *târu* may be used for paying back silver shekels in legal documents, side by side with the verb *nadānu*, "to pay" (30.25, 27, *ut-te-er*, D perfect).

zâzu, G~D

Not all provisions are allotted to human participants with language of giving and receiving. In the administrative section of the NIN.DINGIR festival the men of the *qidašu* and the ^{lú}ḪAL plus the singers (overlapping groups, at least?) "divide" materials from offerings "with each other," *itti aḫāmeš zâzu*: 369.77, D, the men of the *qidašu*; lines 81 and 82, G, the ^{lú}ḪAL and the singers. Restriction of such distribution to these officials may be the rule; two more occurrences of division in broken ritual texts seem to make the men of the *qidašu* and the ^{lú}ḪAL/singers combination the subject of *zâzu*, at least by implication. Sheep skins are divided by someone in Emar 394.23 (*zâzu*, G, with no sign of *itti aḫāmeš*), and then the ^{lú}ḪAL and the singers each take (*leqû*) meat portions (lines 24-25), in a scheme very like that of 369.77-79 and 81-82. The LÚ.MEŠ *šar-*[*ru na-di-nu qí-da-ši*] appear to be the subject of *zâzu*, G, in the fragment 395.4-5.

Outside of ritual, this language is found in legal documents for fair division of inherited property.[209] The idiom *itti aḫāmeš zâzu* (D) occurs at Nuzi and Ugarit.[210]

Giving and receiving in Emar economic texts

The language of giving and receiving in the Emar NIN.DINGIR festival is similar to that of the economic and legal texts at many points. The verbs *nadānu* and *leqû* are the most common terms, just as in the installation. In exchanges involving real estate, slaves, and silver, *nadānu* represents whatever is given up by either party, and *leqû* whatever is received. Thus, *nadānu* can mean "to sell[211] (a slave)," Emar 7.7; 16.4; "to pay (silver)," 5.21, 26; 16.9;

---

209 *itti aḫāmeš zâzu*, 29.10, G; cf. 112.12; 93.8, N; *aḫu kî aḫi zâzu*, 34.22-23, G; cf. 31.19, D?; *aḫu kīma aḫi zâzu*, *RA* 77 text 1:31; just *zâzu*, 5.16; 183.13-14(?), G.

210 See *CAD* s.v. *aḫāmeš* 1a, *AHw* s.v. *itti* 3b for Nuzi; *AHw* s.v. *zâzu(m)* D4c for Ugarit; see also *CAD* s.v. *zâzu* 5c.

211 This idiom requires *ana* plus a price: i.e., *ana šīmi nadānu*, *ana kaspi nadānu*; P. Steinkeller, personal communication.

24.10, 14; and *passim*; "to bequeath (as inheritance)," 31.7, 10; 69.5; 91.5; and *passim*; or simply "to trade" (property for other property, usually real estate), 8.37; 10.14. One also "gives" a tablet as a legal record 6.19; cf. 18.24, a prohibition against acquiring (*leqû*) a tablet and the legal rights recorded therein. On the other hand, *leqû* covers receiving property in trade (8.33; 10.11), land confiscated because of some crime (1.16; cf. 11.21), or the legal share of an inheritance (5.25, ḪA.LA-*šu*; cf. 30.7, 16). Two verbs not used in the NIN.DINGIR festival are *šaqālu* (Ì.LÁ.E), "to weigh out (silver)," for paying the cost of redemption (2.30; 3.35; 4.25; and *passim*) and *maḫāru* for receiving payment (35.5).

palāku and lone akālu, both G

Two actions from the administrative part of the NIN.DINGIR festival fall outside the ritual proper and so belong to the allotment of rations, though the actions resemble those of the cult. Most interesting is the verb *palāku*, "to slaughter" (*AHw* s.v. *palāq/ku(m)*), because it is reserved for butchering animals in the house of the priestess' father, after the installation is over (369.77) and upon her death (line 91). The sheep which heads the list of offerings for Šaḫru in line 92 is not the sheep slaughtered with an ox in line 91, since there is no mention of meat or parts. The verb *palāku* appears nowhere else in the Emar texts, and it is not used elsewhere in the G conjugation with slaughter of animals until the first millennium.[212]

Whereas *palāku* has no direct cultic association in our text (i.e., as offering), the verb *akālu* is usually linked with *šatû* to encapsulate sacred feasting. However, in 369.80 *akālu* alone is much like *leqû*, and describes an action pertaining to allotment of meat parts once the ritual is over. One half of the intestines are to be eaten by the men of the *qidašu* in connection with the distribution of their official portions. In the annual cycle (446.104, cf. 22), instructions are given that the men of the *qidašu* are to eat (*akālu*) the sheep of the city (from line 99), while the ^{lú}ḪAL in particular gets the bread and beer. This appears to be a similar direction for allotment and not necessarily part of rites performed for Dagan (line 99) and Halma (line 102). Otherwise, *akālu* occurs alone in the cultic command, "no one shall eat," in the *maš'artu* installation (370.25) and one ritual for the Hittite gods (472.14), *lā ikkal*.

212 The D conjugation is used in the MB period.

2. The Materials

Whereas the actions of offering to the gods and allotment to human beings are expressed by largely distinct sets of verbs, there is much more overlap in the content of the provision throughout the NIN.DINGIR installation. For instance, staples of the divine meals such as the festival-bread (*naptanu*), wine (KAŠ.GEŠTIN/*ḫamru*) and barley-beer (KAŠ.ŠE/?) are also provided for the human players (see 369.18, 54-57, 83, 87-88, for the humans, and discussion of offerings below for the gods). The final administrative instructions assign to the lúḪAL and the singers the breads on the four tables of offerings from the consecration ceremony of the enthronement day (line 81, cf. lines 24-26). Hides (lines 81-82) and other animal parts (line 83C) from animals sacrificed as offerings end up in the possession of the same officials. There is no absolute separation of materials designated for divine and human consumption.

In spite of the foregoing tendencies, there are distinct patterns. Most of the overlap of human portions and divine offerings appears in the ritual feasting by various personnel, where they truly share in the meal for the gods. On the other hand, the tables set for Emar VIP's hold cuts of meat that do not occur in offering lists, and the NIN.DINGIR's annual allotment principally consists of items not found in festival provision for the gods. Likewise, some gifts are for gods only: especially lambs and the ritual portions of animal sacrifices (GARZA/*parṣu*, see below).

In order to highlight this continuing distinction between provision for divine and human players, discussion of materials follows the same two classes. Offerings which also may be given to humans are observed where relevant. Vessels are treated along with the materials they contain.

Offerings

Most of the materials for Emar offerings are objects of the verb *naqû*. Objects of *mullû* (wine and beer) and *nakāsu* (sheep) simply repeat items that are commonly "offered" (*naqû*). The verb *zâzu* (D) takes as its objects materials that have just been "offered." Only *šakānu* indicates a few offerings that are different. In the discussion, offerings are organized by class, and ordered as they appear in the lists with *naqû*. Where items occur with *šakānu*, this is noted, along with any other significant patterns.

Animals

Three types of animals are offered during the NIN.DINGIR festival at Emar: oxen (GUD/*alpu*), sheep (UDU/*immeru*), and lambs (SILA$_4$/*puḫādu*). Emar sacrifices are not limited to this small group. Elsewhere we find the calf (AMAR/*būru*, 373.15, 19, etc.), the she-goat (^sal^ÁŠ.GÀR/*unīqu*, 370.23, 42, etc.), the ewe (UDU.U$_8$/*laḫru*, 373.33, 34, etc.), the he-goat (MÁŠ.GAL/*mašgallu*, 471.29; 472.16, etc.), the gazelle (MAŠ.DÀ/*ṣabītu*, 452.39), various birds,[213] and unidentified animals (ŠÀ.DA?, 388.9; *bu-qá*(GA)-*ra-tu*$_4$, cow?, or firstborn?, 446.85). Oxen are never offered without sheep (369.11, 27, 32), though sheep may be sacrificed without oxen (lines 5, 49, 52, 59A, 92). These may be offered with or without other foodstuffs. Lambs are only sacrificed singly, during the cycles of temple visitation on the enthronement and final days, with neither other animals nor bread and drink (lines 33, 34, 35, 64, 65, 66). Parts of the oxen and sheep are presented to the gods (*šakānu*) and human participants eventually take many of them, but no such division or distribution of the lambs is mentioned.

On the whole, the number of animals offered in the NIN.DINGIR installation is not that large, compared to the *zukru* feast.[214] The largest clusters are the one ox and six sheep which go in the processions to ^d^IM's temple (369.11, 32, cf. 63, seven). This is a combination found in other Emar ritual (373.24) and in Middle Assyrian royal ritual.[215] The same numbers are even found in the Bible, in texts that suggest a Mesopotamian rather than a West Semitic/Canaanite source. One offering for Ezekiel's envisioned cult is made by the prince on the Sabbath: six male lambs and a ram (Ezek 46.4); a young bull, six lambs, and a ram (v.6). Nehemiah's personal ration from the Jews was one ox, six choice sheep, and some poultry. Ezekiel was a prophet who lived in Babylon, and Nehemiah was a Persian official on assignment in Palestine.

Meat Portions

Although many cuts of meat and body parts from sacrificed animals are found in the NIN.DINGIR installation, most of these are not given to the gods. The heart and lungs of one sheep are part of the daily offering to ^d^IM during

---

213 MUŠEN/*iṣṣūru*?, bird," 380.(1)-20; 388.9; TU.MUŠEN/*wattu*(?), "dove," 388.9; 452.1, etc.; MUŠEN A.MEŠ/*iṣṣūr mê*?, "water-bird," 463.9; MUŠEN *aṭ-ṭu-ḫi*, some bird, 371.13.

214 373.211, seven hundred lambs and fifty calves (not oxen; collated).

215 MVAG 41.3.I.42, to Aššur; IV.1, to Marduk.

the seven-day period (369.50), and an offering to ᵈNIN.KUR on the first day of that period includes the meat of her ox (line 47A, cf. line 27?). The second instance is unusual in that meat (UZU/*šīru*) is nowhere else the object of *naqû*, and one expects the meat to be listed first, as are animals, but instead it is last.

Portions of meat are more often described as part of the presentation before the god (*šakānu*) after the sacrifice is performed (*naqû*), and these consist of the head and the "ritual portion(?)" (GARZA/*parṣu*(?)) only:

-- line 11, UZU [GUD] GARZA UZU UDU GARZA
-- line 28, GARZA GUD GARZA UDU SAG.DU GUD SAG.DU 1 UDU
-- line 37, GARZA GUD GARZA 6 UDU.ḪI.A
-- line 49, GARZA UDU 2 SAG.DU UDU

The head is treated as a favored part of the sacrificed animal, reserved for the honored deity.[216] It is given to Marduk in one Middle Assyrian (MA) ritual (*ZA* 50 194:22), and to Yahweh in the biblical instructions for the burnt offering, Lev 1.8 and 12, where the head is the first portion to be placed on the altar. In Exod 12.9, the head is the first part of the Passover lamb to be eaten. At the end of the NIN.DINGIR festival, the ˡᵘ́ḪAL receives the head of the slaughtered ox (369.78, to eat?), underlining his importance to the ᵈIM cult at Emar. The lungs likewise may be for human as well as divine consumption, since they are also included in division of the same ox, given to the singers (line 79, cf. 83C for the whole festival).

These portions appear in other Emar ritual as well. The meat (*šīru*) of an ox or sheep is offered to gods in the *maš'artu* installation (370.40, object of *zâzu*, D; cf. 38, *naqû*?) and the *kissu* festivals (386.9, object of *šakānu*; cf. 388.45). The head is presented to the gods in the *maš'artu* ritual (*šakānu*, 370.61) and may be offered in the fragment 395.11. The heart (393.14) and the lungs (412.3) appear in fragments of ritual which belong to the installation and *kissu* festival sphere.

The noun *maqqû* in line 58D appears in a difficult line whose context is not clear, but it seems to be a general term for "offering" or "sacrifice"; the latter, if it refers to the ox(en) that follow. (See the Notes to the Text).

---

216 It is odd to find the head treated this way. We would not consider it a delicacy, and it is not treated as a desirable human food in Akkadian texts generally. Walter Burkert, *Homo Necans*, 7, observes that in Greek ritual the gods are given only "the bones, the fat, and the gall bladders," which are not the most desirable portions, and this becomes a joke in Greek comedy.

The "ritual portion(?)"

One prominent element of NIN.DINGIR festival offerings is completely new in Akkadian writings: some portion of meat represented by the signs PA+AN. The best reading of the signs is GARZA/*parṣu*(?), which would have some previously unattested meaning.[217] The problem is that the GARZA appears to be treated as a specific cut of meat, perhaps associated with the head (above), but I have not been able to pinpoint what this is. I translate "ritual portion(?)" in an attempt to relate the term to Akkadian *parṣu*. If the offered animal-head is not actually eaten by cult personnel, in contrast to other offerings, perhaps the GARZA represents a portion of meat that is likewise not to be for human consumption. Somehow a "ritual portion" should be different from the other offerings, which equally pertain to the *parṣu*/ritual.

We know the logogram GARZA/*parṣu* is found at Emar in the heading of the ritual for the *imištu* of the king, [*ṭup*]-*pu* GARZA (PA+AN), 392.1. Headings for rituals otherwise use the syllabic *pár-ṣi*: 369.1 and 471.1, *ṭup-pu pár-ṣi*; 385.1, *ṭup-pí pár-ṣi*. But is the PA+AN of animal sacrifices the same word? Arnaud translates "les avants," presumably treating the word as a syllabic spelling of the noun *pānu* "face, front" in bound form. However, in line 11 the PA+AN is placed *after* the nouns to which it seems to relate (UZU GUD, UZU UDU), and is not in a genitival construction. Arnaud emended the text to remove both instances of PA+AN from line 11 as scribal errors, but their presence in the line is rather one indication that PA+AN is a logogram. A further piece of evidence that the word is not *pānu* is the plural PA+AN.MEŠ, which would be **pa-ni*.MEŠ with syllabic orthography (a nonexistent form): GARZA.MEŠ *a-na pa-ni* DINGIR.MEŠ GAR-*nu*, "they will place the GARZA's before the gods," 388.3, cf. 391.3. In the fragment 404.7 GARZA.MEŠ *an-nu*-[*ti*] may refer to meat portions or be another example of GARZA for *parṣu*, "rites," with 392.1. The form PA+AN precedes *ša* in the fragment 371.13, GARZA *ša* MUŠEN *aṭ-ṭu-ḫi*, and line 12, GARZA *ša pa-ni* DINGIR.MEŠ. Line 13 could refer to "rites of the *aṭṭuḫu*-bird," though this sort of general reference to rites is usually restricted to headings.[218] The GARZA of line 12 must be something concrete, with the verb *šakānu*.

---

217 The use of PA+AN (read GARZA) for the Akkadian word *parṣu* is not new; it is the application to offering and ration terminology in ritual that has not been attested elsewhere. See *AHw* s.v. *parṣu(m)*.

218 Exceptions are 373.198 and 203, which concern rites for another day.

Use with the verb *šakānu* leads us back to the NIN.DINGIR festival itself, where PA+AN/GARZA must refer to part of the sacrificed animals in lines 11, 28, and 37, which separate meat from bread by repeating the verb *šakānu* for each group. In the *naqû-šakānu* offering sequences, GARZA is usually the *nomen regens* in bound form with the slaughtered ox or sheep (see lines 28, 37, 49, above). Likewise, the cycle of offerings and feasting in the *maš'artu* installation, which follows the same sequence (*naqû-šakānu-mullû-akālu/šatû*, 370.45-68), makes GARZA the *nomen regens*, with varying genitive nouns: GARZA GUD UDU salÁŠ.GÀR, line 46, referring to the three animals just sacrificed; and GARZA UZU, lines 52 and 67, cf. GARZA UZU.MEŠ, line 49 and perhaps 60-61. The examples from the *maš'artu* festival illuminate the difficult 369.11, UZU G[UD] GARZA UZU UDU GARZA; all of the expressions of the two installations should describe the same offering portion, so the long UZU UDU GARZA is really the equivalent of GARZA UZU. It is "the GARZA of the meat," or "the GARZA of the ox/sheep/kid," or an apposition which makes an equation of these, "the meat of the ox/sheep, (which is) the GARZA" (line 11).

We are dealing with some part of the meat, but the logogram GARZA indicates the noun *parṣu*, usually "office" (see *AHw* s.v. *parṣu(m)* A), "cult" (see definition B), "regulation" (see C), or "custom, command" (see D, from Boghazkoy and at El Amarna). How can *parṣu* be a meat portion? Since the rituals in which this use is found are themselves called *parṣu*, "rites," the meat should be essentially "ritual" meat -- thus the translation "ritual portion." Perhaps this signifies a first cut for the gods from any Emar ritual sacrifice. The noun *parṣu* takes on similar derived meanings when it becomes a cultic object (*AHw* s.v. *parṣu(m)* B13) and a ritual tax (B12?, only Old Assyrian); that is, some part of the cult takes on the term "cult" itself.[219]

In all these cases, the derived use is vague unless context further defines the specific function in the cult. The meat portion is some part of the meat (from GARZA UZU, "the *parṣu* of the meat") which is often placed alongside the head (369.28, 49; 370.61). In the ritual texts, the meat-*parṣu* occurs almost entirely with the verb *šakānu*; it is placed before (*ana pānī*) deities.[220]

---

219 Note that the scribal text Emar 560.66 (Ḫḫ. XXIII) has ninda-garza = NINDA.MEŠ *pár-ṣi*.

220 The NIN.DINGIR installation, 369.11, 28, 37, 49; the *maš'artu* installation, 370.46, 49, 52, (60-61), (63), 67; the *kissu* festivals, 385.6, 13 (to Dagan); 387.12 (*nadānu* with *ana*, substituting the F-text for J, *šakānu*; to Išḫara and dNIN.URTA); 388.3 (for all the *kissu*'s); cf. 371.12; 391.3; 399.2, for "before" (with *pānī*).

This pattern might narrow the definition to "presentation meat," perhaps a first cut for the gods from any ritual sacrifice.

Lines 73-74 of the NIN.DINGIR festival speak of the singers "taking" (*leqû*) a GARZA/*parṣu* of Hulelu's table, but this should represent a known Akkadian idiom for "to perform a ritual," and I have translated, "the singers will perform the rites of that table" (GARZA ᵍⁱˢBANŠUR *ša-a-šu*).[221] If this interpretation is correct, the idiom would supply a more certain attestation of the equation GARZA = *parṣu* within the NIN.DINGIR installation. The same idiom appears in the Dagan *kissu* with reference to Šuwala and ᵈU.GUR,[222] GARZA-*šu-nu* TI-*u*, "they (the singers) will perform their (the two gods') rites," 385.23.

At the end of the NIN.DINGIR festival, text B diverges from A and introduces the clause (É *a-bi-šu* (for *-ši*?)) *pár-ṣi-ša i-na-aš-ši* (line 94). The noun *parṣīša* should be plural if it is indeed the direct object (vs. **parassa*), but it is not certain what action the verb describes. The verb *našû* defines the occasion for the festival in 369.1-2, but the object is the priestess, not the rites. Moreover, the context of line 94 indicates that the statement with *našû* should have something to do with inheritance rights, and could have something to do with "taking."[223] But this Akkadian use generally communicates that the taking

---

221 See the note to the translation for lines 73-74. Dietrich, *UF* 21 85, translates this idiom, "Die Vorderseite desselben Tisches wird der Sänger einnehmen," explaining in n.88 that "er wird an der Vorderseite des Tisches stehen." This interprets PA-AN as *pānu*, so "Vorderseite."

222 At Emar, Hurrian gods are largely confined to the rites for the gods of Hatti (471-473, etc.), so the appearance of Šuwala and Ugur in one of the *kissu* rituals is surprising. Šuwala is the short form of Šuwaliyat(ti), the "pure brother of the storm god," husband of Hurrian Nabarbi, and equated with the Mesopotamian name NIN.URTA; see Laroche, *GLH*, 174, and *Recherches sur les noms des dieux hittites*, Paris: Librairie Orientale et Américaine (Maisonneuve), 1947, 60. ᵈU.GUR is a logogram that is identified as Nergal in early texts from Samarra (Haas, RAI 24, 61) and Ari-šen (A. Kammenhuber, "Neue Ergebnisse zur hurrischen und altmesopotamischen Überlieferung," *Or* NS 45 (1976) 142). However, the texts from Nuzi include personal names showing the syllabic form (see Haas, above, and Wilhelm, *Grundzüge*, 76), Tell Rimaḫ supplied the name *U-gur-a-tal* (Haas, 61 n.9), and now the Emar archives have given us a copy of the AN = Anu god list with U.GUR = ᵈ*U-ku-ru-un* (no. 204; see Laroche, *GLH*, 278).

Haas concludes that Ugur is one of the core Hurrian deities attested in the eastern Hurrian texts, perhaps even part of the early level of "Substratgottheiten" (RAI 24, 61; *Hethitische Berggötter und hurritische Steindämonen: Riten, Kulte und Mythen*, Mainz am Rhein: Philipp von Zabern, 1982, 35). The new attestation at Emar might cast some doubt on that hypothesis.

The presence of these deities in Emar 385 should be considered the primary instance of Hurrian features in the Emar festivals, and is striking in a pantheon which does not show heavy Hurrian influence.

223 See *CAD* s.v. *našû* A 4b, "to take away, to appropriate, to take over, to carry off."

is either by force or somehow irregular. If *našû* just means "to carry" (for ritual) as it does in the *kubadu* (see below), the *parṣū* could be symbols of office (*AHw* s.v. *parṣu(m)* A3), but no ritual appears to be taking place in this section. We are left with no satisfactory solution at this point.

A few other occurrences of GARZA/*parṣu* remain. The ritual fragment 535.5 reads [P]A?-AN x(LÚ?), with too little context to allow certainty.[224] The *parṣu* of a man would be new at Emar. One temple list seems to make GARZA *ša* x [...], "the ritual portion of the ..." (63.2), the heading for payments in shekels to sacred personnel, including the ^{lú}*wa-bíl i-*[*la-i*] (line 3) and the ^{lú}*za-bi-ḫ*[*u*] (line 5). Compare the lists with headings, 45.1; 46.1; 48.1; 290.1; 296.1; 319.1. Emar 326 appears to be an offering list of sheep for (*ana*) various gods (from ^{d}IM, in line 3). The signs MAŠ ZUM in line 8 are most likely *pár-ṣu*, perhaps for ritual portions of sacrificed sheep. If so, this would be a unique case of that use of *parṣu* with syllabic writing, but the context is uncertain.

Bread

Four types of bread make up the principal NIN.DINGIR festival repertoire of baked goods for offering. Most common is the festival ("meal"/feast) bread, ^{ninda}*naptanu* (with *naqû*, 369.19, 47, 51, (GAL/*rabû*); *šakānu*, before gods, lines 11, 37, 65, 66; *šakānu*, on tables, lines 25, 72, cf. 15). The dried breads, plain and with fruit, are equally characteristic of the NIN.DINGIR installation: NINDA UD.DU/*aklu ablu*[225] and NINDA UD.DU GURUN.[226] Finally, the *kerṣu*-bread NINDA.GUR_4.RA is associated with the division among the gods (*naqû-zâzu*), 369.19, 47. It appears that two other terms occur in the listing for the four sanctification day tables for the gods (line 25), "thick loaves," NINDA.MEŠ *e-*[*bu-u*], and perhaps the corresponding "thin loaves," [NINDA.MEŠ *ra-qa-*tu_4], following the *kissu* text, 388.11-12 (see text notes). Simply "bread," NINDA/*aklu*, is placed on the NIN.DINGIR's new table at her enthronement (line 41, *šakānu*), and note

---

224 One possibility would be PA-AN-LUGAL for Mesopotamian PA-LUGAL/*parṣu*; J. Huehnergard, personal communication.

225 With *šakānu*, before gods, 369.12, 37; *šakānu*, on tables, line 26; see *CAD* s.v. *ablu*, for UD.DU/*ablu*; cf. *AHw* s.v. *ablu*.

226 With *naqû*, line 51; *šakānu*, before gods, lines 12, 37; *šakānu*, on tables, lines 18, 26, 72. Perhaps this longer name is to be read *aklu ablu qadu inbi*, following the form of Emar 460.3, NINDA UD.DU *qa-du in-bi-šu-nu*, and line 8, NINDA UD.DU *qa-du* GURUN. Some preposition appears to be appropriate. Dietrich, *UF* 21 79, translates "Süssbrot(e)" based on his reading of *dá-aš-š*[$u^{?!}$*-pí*] "sehr Süsses" after NINDA UD.DU GURUN.MEŠ in line 56B; collation shows that *daššupu* is unlikely (see text and notes).

the combination "bread and beer" from the sanctification ceremony heading (see *qaddušu*, lines 6 and (22)) and from the return of ᵈNIN.KUR's red wool garment (*târu*, D, line 60), both NINDA.MEŠ KAŠ.MEŠ.

The *naptanu*-bread belongs especially to the sphere of the two installations and the *kissu* festivals.[227] Appearance in the fragments 371.7; 393;[228] 394.32; 409.7, 10 (without the determinative, NINDA), helps place these in the same family as the three major festivals. The basic meaning of *naptanu* is "meal" (see *AHw* s.v. *naptanu(m)*; cf. *CAD* s.v. *naptanu*; often for meals served to the gods), and the term may cover food allotments for meals (*CAD* s.v. *naptanu* 1a), but the Emar bread was unattested in Akkadian texts until the Assyrian examples recently observed by Deller.[229] The *naptanu* may be given to gods for offering or to human participants in feasting. When the latter, they are always served one each, so that a *naptanu* seems to be a portion of bread sufficient for one meal.[230]

The dried breads are confined to the same group of Emar ritual texts, except for the offerings for the *ša-aṭ(?)-ra-ḫi* of *Aštartu tāḫāzi*, 460.3, NINDA UD.DU *qa-du in-bi-šu-nu*, "dried loaves together with their fruit," cf. line 8, and 460.18, some ⁿⁱⁿᵈᵃ*qa-du-ú*, with (*qadu*) NINDA UD.DU. These are not part of the regular scheme of offerings, and are assigned only to the sanctification ceremony (line 3), the priest of the goddess (line 8; remember that this is the *maš'artu*'s mistress), and the ˡᵘ́ḪAL (line 18, prominent in the installations). Besides the *maš'artu* and *kissu* festivals, compare the following occurrences: without fruit, 394.33; 405.3, 6; 434.10; 438.6 (NINDA UD.DA); 442.9; with fruit, 371.9; 394.33. The term *aklu ablu* is always spelled logographically at Emar. "Dried bread" is known in Neo-Babylonian and Hittite (Boghazkoy) ritual (*CAD* s.v. *ablu* b2'; cf. *AHw* s.v. *ablu* 1), though the addition of fruit seems to be a local specialty.

The logogram NINDA.GUR$_4$.RA is usually read as the noun *kerṣu*, which means "pinched off" (*AHw* s.v. *k/gerṣu*, *CAD* s.v. *kirṣu* 1), derived from the verb *karāṣu*. The word *kerṣu* can refer to a lump of dough (*AHw*, 3; *CAD*, 1b), and may be identified with NINDA.GUR$_4$.RA, "a preparation of cereal," attested only in one Old Babylonian letter, Kraus AbB 1 81:6, 19, 43,

227 The annual cycle, 446.92, appears to read ⁿⁱⁿᵈᵃ*na-ap-ta-ni*, though the bread is otherwise always spelled with *nap-*.
228 GAL, "large," lines 7, 8, 17, 20; TUR, "small," lines 9, 10, 11, 19.
229 Deller, in K. Deller, W.R. Mayer, and W. Sommerfeld, "Akkadische Lexikographie: *CAD* N," *Or* NS 56 (1987) 182-183.
230 See lines 14 and 83; cf. line 54 for the same seven-day period mentioned in line 83.

48.[231] The dictionary comments, "The reading of NINDA.GUR$_4$.RA as *kirṣu* is based only on the bil(ingual) text cited in lex(ical) section, whose Sum(erian) version is not reliable" (*CAD* s.v. *kirṣu*). A different equivalence in the Emar lexical text 545.359 (Ḫḫ. V-VII) indicates that the OB reading may not hold for Emar. Unfortunately, the text is damaged, but the first and last signs of the key word are clear: mar-ninda-gur$_4$-ra = *mar BE*-⌈x⌉-*ti* (Arnaud, *pè*-[*e*]*t*-*ti*). This item has a wider use in Emar ritual than the other three breads. The *zukru* festival mentions two pair of NINDA.GUR$_4$.RA.MEŠ *pa-pa-sí*, *kerṣu* of barley mash (see *AHw* s.v. *pappāsu(m)*, "ein Gerstenbrei od Pudding"), 373.33, cf. 37, 171. It also appears in the door ritual, 463.5, the fragment 458.3, and one of the rites for the Hittite gods, 473.18, NINDA.KUR.RA ^{zì}BA.BA.ZA (*pappāsu*). Hittite NINDA.GUR$_4$.RA is "thick bread," ^{NINDA}*ḫarši*,[232] and the Emar item could be the same.

All of these breads remain strictly within the realm of cult offering in the NIN.DINGIR festival. Only the *naptanu*-bread is received by human participants, and that is as an allotment for sacred feasting (*akālu*/*šatû*, 369.14, 55, cf. 83.

Drink

There are two beverages given to the gods in the NIN.DINGIR installation, wine[233] and barley-beer, KAŠ.GEŠTIN[234] and KAŠ.ŠE.[235] Barley-beer, but not wine, is received by ritual personnel for feasting, with *naptanu*-bread (thus, "feast-bread"?), lines 14, 18, 55, cf. 83. The NIN.DINGIR is given wine, but not barley-beer, as part of her annual allotment (line 87). Both drinks appear throughout Emar ritual, with the notable exception of the rites that work from annual cycles, the *zukru* (373), which has neither, and text 446, which has only wine (line 97). One Emar letter summarizes a delivery of offering materials as NINDA.MEŠ KAŠ.ŠE.MEŠ KAŠ.GEŠTIN.MEŠ UDU.ḪI.A Ì.GIŠ.MEŠ *ša* DINGIR.MEŠ, "the breads, the barley-beers, the wines, the sheep, (and) the oils of the gods," 264.13-15.

---

231 NINDA.GUR$_4$.GUR$_4$ is now attested in Presargonic Mari in the bread list T 68; see Charpin, "Tablettes présargoniques de Mari," *M.A.R.I.* 5 (1987) 75, no.10, with NINDA.SIKIL.

232 See Hoffner, *Alimenta Hethaeorum: Food Production in Hittite Asia Minor*, New Haven: AOS, 1974, 200; Haas and L. Jakob-Rost, "Das Festritual des Gottes Telipinu in Ḫanḫana und in Kašḫa: ein Beitrag zum hethitischen Festkalender," *AoF* 11 (1984) 227.

233 De Tarragon, *Le culte*, 43-44, says that wine (*yn*) is rarely found as a ritual offering at Ugarit, in contrast to oil, which is common.

234 With *naqû*, 369.4, 27?, 51; *šakānu*, on a table, line 72; *mullû*, lines 12, 27, (32), 38, 67.

235 With *naqû*, 369.19, 47, 51; *šakānu*, before gods, line 28; *mullû*, line 38.

Neither the writing KAŠ.GEŠTIN nor KAŠ.ŠE is attested in Akkadian, as far as I can determine. "Wine," *karānu*, is GEŠTIN, not KAŠ.GEŠTIN,[236] and I can find no instances of KAŠ.ŠE. "Barley-beer" is never written with syllabic spelling but KAŠ.GEŠTIN is the West Semitic word *ḫamru*, attested in Ugaritic (*ḫmr*),[237] biblical Hebrew (*ḥemer*, Deut 32.14), Aramaic (*ḥamrā*), and classical Arabic (*ḫamr*). In the NIN.DINGIR festival, the B-text of line 38 provides a gloss with the idiom for filling cups: *ka-sà-ti* KAŠ.MEŠ.GEŠTIN : *ḫa-am-*[*ra*...]. This idiom consistently includes *mullû* and the double accusative with cups and beverage, enabling us to complete the text of 370.29-30 in the *maš'artu* installation: [...*ka-sà-ti* KAŠ.MEŠ.GEŠTIN] : *ḫa-am-ra ú-*[*m*]*a-al-lu-ú*, or something very close to this. KAŠ.ŠE then distinguishes a barley-beer, which may likewise have a local Semitic name. Note that *ḫamru* appears to be a generic term for "wine" at Emar, not a single stage in the fermentation process.[238] KAŠ.GEŠTIN is known in some Hittite texts, where the term occurs alongside regular wine.[239]

A variety of vessels is used to serve the wine and beer of the Emar NIN.DINGIR installation. The most frequent is the *ḫizzibu*,[240] which may hold either wine (369.4, 27, 72) or barley-beer (lines 14, 19, 47, 55). Like the *naptanu*-bread, the *ḫizzibu*-vessel measures one meal-serving for human participants in the feasts (see lines 14, 54-55). In inventories, the *ḫizzibu* is associated with the *ḫubu*-vessel (*passim*, in texts 274, 305, 307, 363, and 364), and the two containers are found together in ritual texts that are no more than lists of materials for offering, 462.30; 465.3; 466.5; cf. 484.4. Otherwise, the

---

236 Arnaud takes KAŠ.GEŠTIN as *karānu* in his "Religion assyro-babylonienne," *AEPHER* 89 (1980-1981) 306.

237 The Baal Cycle, KTU 1.3 I:16; and the ritual with the birth of the gods Šaḥar and Šalim, KTU 1.23:6.

238 This is suggested for *ḥemer* by Koehler and Baumgartner, "(noch garender) Wein." Cutler and MacDonald, *UF* 14 38, likewise suggest that *ḫmr yn* in KTU 1.23 may indicate different degrees of maturity in wines. The context demands wine that is difficult to obtain; perhaps *ḫmr* is wine from inland regions. A shortage would be severe indeed if one could get neither the local product nor wine from the neighbors to the east.

239 See Erich Neu, StBoT 25, text 12, Rs III.17', text 31, Rs III.11', etc., measured with the *ḫuppar*. Singer, *KI.LAM* I, 157 and n.25, prefers the interpretation that this is some second type of wine to the translation "beer (or) wine," and the Emar occurrence should support his view. Following G. Steiner, he suggests this is inferior or young wine.

240 The word is always spelled *ḫi-zi-bu*, except in the inventory text 274, *passim*, *ḫi-iz-zi-bu*; it occurs only once with the determinative DUG, in the *kissu*, 388.52. Dietrich, *UF* 21 78, reads *ḫisipu* and translates "Schöpfbecher." Dietrich and Loretz, "Die ugaritischen Gefässbezeichnungen *ridn* und *kw*," *UF* 19 (1987) 31 n.25, compare Ugaritic *ḥsp* ("to pour") and Akkadian *ḫassāpu* (an unidentified implement). The relation to *ḥsp* is attractive, but there is scant evidence to define *ḫassāpu* as a vessel.

ḫubu is only mentioned in the NIN.DINGIR festival as the measure for wine in the priestess' annual ration, 369.87, and in the *maš'artu* installation holding wine (for some offering?), 370.71. By contrast, the *ḫizzibu* is a regular feature of Emar ritual, though it is missing from the *zukru* festival and annual cycle Emar 446, along with the rites for the Hittite gods. The *ḫubu*-vessel at Emar is probably related to Akkadian *ḫābû* (see *CAD*, *AHw*, a storage jug), though the form with the "*u*" root vowel is unique. There is no Akkadian parallel for the *ḫizzibu*.

The logogram DUG is used to describe a vessel holding barley-beer (369.18, 51, 56, 83) -- never wine, in the NIN.DINGIR festival. The sign would normally indicate Akkadian *karpatu*, but this is not proved at Emar by any syllabic spelling, and it could stand for a local term. Three times the DUG is paired with the ^{dug}*maḫḫaru*, which twice contains more barley-beer (lines 18, 57) and once, wine (line 50). Neither vessel is associated with the offering-presentation-feasting sequences (*naqû*-to-*akālu*/*šatû*), nor the division among the gods (*naqû-zâzu*), which use the *ḫizzibu*, along with the serving cups that are filled (*mullû*, with *kāsu* and *tašītu*). The DUG and *maḫḫaru*-vessels appear in portions set on tables (lines 18, 56-57) and with offerings to ^{d}IM during the seven-day period (line 51). Perhaps DUG is generic "pot," as is *karpatu*, since it appears to substitute for *ḫizzibu* in the administrative version of the seven-day feasting portions (line 83, cf. 55).

The DUG quite consistently holds barley-beer in Emar ritual,[241] in texts from the *kissu* and installation festival family, except the offering cycle, 460. We find KAŠ alone (*šikaru*?) for the beverage in 371.8; 393.4, 5, 7, 18, 28; and 394.19, all in the same group as those with barley-beer, and the same drink may be intended. Plural "pots" are mentioned in the *zukru* (373.181) and the broken 394.41, with no liquid, and the only other DUG in the *zukru* contains NINDA.GUR$_4$.RA (373.33). The only other example of this vessel outside the "festival" family breaks the pattern by containing wine (473.20, rites for the Hittite gods).

The *maḫḫaru*-vessel is rarer, occurring in the following scattered texts: the Dagan *kissu*, 385.17 (text A) and lines 17 and 24 of text E; 393.3, 19; the Abû offerings, 452.43 and 49 (repeated with both wine and barley-beer); and 460.5. There is no other Akkadian vessel *maḫḫaru*, though *ma*/*i*/*uḫḫuru*

---

241 370.15, 24; 385.17, 25; 387.2, 16, 21; 388.67; 394.28, 41; 396.12; 430.3; 460.2, 7, and *passim*.

means "offering" in Babylonian dialects.[242] The verb *maḫāru* can mean "to collect a liquid in a container" (*CAD* s.v. *maḫāru* 1d, medical and ritual texts).

The *qu'û*(^dug^*qú-'u-ú*)-vessel contains wine (369.4) and malt-beer (KAŠ.Ú.SA/*billatu*, see line 89; see below) in the NIN.DINGIR festival, and otherwise appears only in a list of ^dug^*qú-'u-ú* for soldiers (306.2, 11, 15, 17; line 12, ^dug^*qú-a-ta*). The vessel should be the same as the Akkadian vessel and measurement, the *qû* (see *CAD* s.v. *qû* B, *AHw* s.v. *qû(m)* II), which is usually spelled with the KU/*qú*-sign.[243] Emar's version is set apart by the *aleph* and the DUG determinative.

Two more vessels are specially associated with the verb *mullû*, "to fill": *kāsu*, "cup" (369.12, 27, (32), 38, 67), and *tašītu*, "goblet" (line 59A). These are consistently plural in the ritual idiom of both the NIN.DINGIR installation and other Emar ritual; compare *kāsu*, 370.47, 50, 53, 62, cf. 31?; 385.32 (^dug^GÚ.ZI *ša* DINGIR.MEŠ); *tašītu*, 446.97 (with wine); 463.7 (no object). Only the rites for Hittite gods use *kāsu* (GÚ.ZI), "cup," outside the formula with *mullû*, in lists of offerings, Emar 471 and 472, *passim*, and 477.7. Note the form *ta-ši-ti* in the small fragment 488.1 and the phrase 3 *ḫi-zi-bu a-na ta-ši-ia-ti*, "three *ḫizzibu*'s for the goblets" (463.13). Presumably the contents of the *ḫizzibu*-vessels are transferred to the more formal *tašiātu*. The royal votive offerings of text 42 are gold cups (GAL/*kāsu*(?))[244] weighing thirty shekels each (42.3, 17, 21), and the first may also be called a *ta-ši-i*?-[*ta*?], which might mean the *tašītu* is a fancy item. No other *tašītu* is known in Akkadian, though *kāsu* is a common term.

Oils

Oils are not a prominent part of NIN.DINGIR festival offerings.[245] Cedar oil (Ì.GIŠ (^giš^)ERIN.NA/*šaman erēni*) is among the materials for

---

242 OB?, NB, SB; see *AHw* s.v. *miḫḫuru(m)*, and *CAD*, with each vowel.

243 Dietrich and Loretz, *UF* 19 29-31, equate the Emar vessel with Ugaritic *kw* and *kwt*, along with OA KU-*a-tim* (MLVS 2:42). The common Akkadian vessel nevertheless should be the best equivalent.

244 For GAL as *kāsu* see the *CAD* s.v. *kāsu* 1b and the comment at the end of the article. In the OB period and earlier, GAL and *ka-sum* appear side by side and appear to represent separate items. Texts from Mari, Alalaḫ, Qatna and Nuzi mention GAL-vessels that are decorated, and these might not be read *kāsu*. Perhaps the Emar GAL belongs in this category as well.

245 It is very common in Ugaritic rituals; see de Tarragon, *Le culte*, 43-44 (above). Charpin has recently published a study of oil rations at Mari, many of which are for gods; see "Nouveaux documents du bureau de l'huile à l'époque assyrienne," *M.A.R.I.* 3 (1984) 83-84.

distribution to the gods (369.19), and fine oil alone (Ì.DU$_{10}$.GA/*šamnu ṭābu*)[246] is once offered to dIM (lines 42-43). The latter is otherwise used only for anointing (lines 3, 20), and the offering to dIM is made after the priestess is adorned with the ornaments of her new office, during the ceremony of her enthronement. One wonders whether this is the same oil that was used for her anointing. The oil is taken (*leqû*, lines 4, 20) from the palace and the temple of dNIN.KUR, but unlike the lots(?) and the red wool garment, but it is never returned. It is noteworthy that the lúḪAL receives a payment after the oil is offered (line 43), since he is also the anointer (lines 20-21, cf. the payment after anointing in line 5). Plain "oil" (Ì.GIŠ/*šamnu*) is offered to Šaḫru along with a sheep and other items after the NIN.DINGIR's death (line 92), and the priestess receives two different measures of oil in her annual allotment (line 86, two dug*ḫi-it-tá*[247] and one dug*za-du*).

In the *maš'artu* installation, a kid and cedar oil (Ì.GIŠ gišERIN.N[A]) are offered before (*ana pānī*, in the break?) the *sikkānu* on the roof of the priestess' residence during the night, 370.42, and the oil appears among the third day offerings of the cycle for the month of Abû, 452.4 (Ì.GIŠ ERIN.NA). "Fine oil" is not much more common. Beyond the NIN.DINGIR festival, it occurs only in a few lists of offerings, 459.1; 460.4, 31; 523.3. Both are known Akkadian commodities, cedar oil in Babylon and Mari (*AHw* s.v. *erēnu(m)* I 5a) and fine oil throughout Mesopotamia, though with greatest frequency in peripheral texts during the late second millennium (*AHw* s.v. *šamnu(m)* 3c, Nuzi, Alalaḫ, and Amarna). Plain oil is found throughout Emar ritual, missing only from the *zukru* and annual cycle (373 and 446) among the major rites.

The *zadu*-vessel is new to Akkadian texts, and is used only for oil at Emar.[248] It must be a small juglet. No *ḫittu*-vessel is found in the rest of the Emar texts, but it should be related to the Akkadian *ḫuttu*, a storage jar known in the Babylonian dialects from the Middle period on, and which may contain oil, according to an Amarna letter from Egypt, EA 14 iii:34.[249]

---

246 See the note to the translation for line 3; this "oil" may not actually contain oil.

247 Note *AHw* s.v. *ḫittu* III, *ḫattu* II, "ein Bierkrug" in jB. The Emar version is presumably smaller.

248 In the ritual texts, see 369.86, 92; 370.19, 42, cf. 97; 388.15; 452.2, 7, 37; cf. 463.29 (dugḪA *za-du*). See also various lists from temple M$_1$, 274.16, 18, 21; 303.5; 321.3, 6, 20. The term could conceivably be related to West Semitic *ṣāʿtu*, "basin"? See Huehnergard, *Ugaritic Vocabulary*, 170, for Ugaritic *ṣāʿu*.

249 Or compare *ḫindu*/*ḫiddu*, "bead" -- perhaps referring to a decoration (Huehnergard, personal communication).

Other offerings

Most of the NIN.DINGIR festival offerings fall into the classes described above: animals and their meat, bread, drink, and oil. However, there are a few items which do not and which occur just once each in festival offering lists. These include fruit, GURUN/*inbu*; barley or flour from barley, ŠE/*'û*[250] or ZÌ.ŠE/*tappinnu*(?); *zirtu*-wool, ^{síg}*zi-ir-tu*$_4$; and some unknown item(s) in line 92.

Fruit is last in the division of offerings for the gods in 369.19 and occurs in the month of Abû rites several times, usually last in offering lists (452.6, 40, 41, and 50; not last in line 45). The general term for fruit, *inbu*, is a Babylonian word (see *AHw* s.v. *inbu(m)* 1; *CAD* s.v. *inbu* 1), and *inbu* is included in Mesopotamian ritual offerings (*CAD* s.v. *inbu* 1b). The reading *inbu* for GURUN is attested in the Emar ritual 460.3, NINDA UD.DU *qa-du in-bi-šu-nu*, mentioned above in the discussion of breads.

During the NIN.DINGIR's installation, the measure ^{giš}PA/*parīsu* is used only with barley (ŠE, line 85, (twice)) and barley flour (ZÌ.ŠE, line 53), as part of her allotments.[251] The appearance in line 27 is unusual, since barley is not a common offering material in Emar ritual and is not otherwise offered by *parīsu*-measure.[252] None of these is found in the family of installation and *kissu* festivals. On the other hand, ZÌ.ŠE is more widespread, occurring frequently in the Abû cycle (452.16 and *passim*), in the rites for the Hittite gods (471.5 and *passim*), in various offering cycles (461.1, 5, 10; 462.18; 463.23, 28; 465.5), as well as in the ritual fragments, 432.5; 437.6, and 438.3. It is possible that Emar scribes do not intend *tappinnu* by ZÌ.ŠE, but separate terms for flour and barley. The parallel occurrence of ZÌ.ŠE and ŠE in provisions for the NIN.DINGIR (369.53, 85) suggests that the *parīsu*-measures of ZÌ.ŠE (line 53) are specifically barley-flour, not an unknown type of meal (*AHw* s.v. *tappinnu(m)*, "ein Mehlart"). Moreover, the alternate form

---

[250] Antoine Cavigneaux, *N.A.B.U.* 1989, 33 (no. 52), proposes that the Akkadian word for barley can now be identified as *'ûm/'âm/'îm*, based on various lexical texts, including several from Emar. Compare Emar 537(Sa Syllabaire).710, ŠE = *e-im*; 541(Ḫḫ. I).238, še ù maš-bi = *e-ú ù ṣi-bat-š[u]*; 542(Ḫḫ. II).92ff, še-ur$_5$-ra = *e-ia ḫu-bu-ul-li*, etc. Cavigneaux suggests a possible etymology in the root ḤY, "to live."

[251] The PA/*parīsu* is the main dry measure in the OB period at Alalaḫ, according to Wiseman, *The Alalakh Tablets*, 14. He says that the QA is used in the MB/level IV material. In Hittite texts, the PARĪSU may equal six BÁN; Hoffner, *Alimenta*, 65-66, and Vladimir Souçek, "Die hethitischen Feldertexte," *ArOr* 27 (1959) 387.

[252] 452.4, no measure, cf. line 3; 461.7, BÁN/*sūtu* as measure; 472.21, ^{dug}BUR.ZI/*pursītu* as measure.

ZÌ.DA ŠE would be an unusual spelling of *tappinnu*, and looks more like two separate words.[253]

Barley itself is a staple for all Emar residents, and the amount of individual allotments varies widely, presumably according to social standing (see the lists 279 and 319).[254] The largest amount in Emar 279 is thirty *parīsu* (lines 1, 3), the annual allotment for the NIN.DINGIR in a good year (369.85),[255] and the smallest is only two (279.29, 45). Forty *parīsu* of barley are part of the entourage and property that accompany a queen (SAL.LUGAL) who is transferred from the land of Qadeš (KUR *Ki-zu*) to the town of Šatappi (40 PA ŠE, 361.5). This may be her annual allotment. One Emar lawsuit lists three hundred *parīsu* of barley among the property belonging to one person's estate (33.6). Note that the term ŠE.BA/*ipru* for the "barley allotment" of the NIN.DINGIR (369.85C) is unique at Emar. It does appear widely in Akkadian texts from the Old Akkadian through late Babylonian periods, including documents from the west, Alalaḫ, Mari, Nuzi, and Amarna (see *AHw* s.v. *ipru(m)* 3, 4; *CAD* s.v. *ipru* 1d, e, g). However, the previously attested *ipru* seems to be used for lower level workers, not officials and priests.

On the last day of the festival, the table of Hulelu is set with bread, wine, and ^{síg}*zi-ir-tu*$_4$, some form of woolen cloth (line 72A and C).[256] During the rites on the last night of the *maš'artu*'s installation, the priestess places a wool *zirtu* (^{síg}*zi-ir-ta*, 370.87) on the head of Aštart (from line 84?).[257] This item from the Emar installations is otherwise unknown in Akkadian literature, though it may be related to the adjective *zīru*, "twisted" (see *AHw* s.v. *zīru* II, *CAD* s.v. *zēru* adj.). One reference is found in an Amarna letter of Rib-Addi, of some leather container (EA 120:4, 7, in *CAD* s.v. *zēru* adj.), and there is

---

253 388.7 and 442.5; see ZÌ.DA alone, 387.6, 17. Hoffner, *Alimenta*, 65-66, records the term ZÌ.DA ZÍZ, "wheat flour." ZÍZ is wheat in Hatti, as opposed to emmer (*kunāšu*) in Mesopotamia. In Mesopotamia wheat is described by the primarily Babylonian term *kibtu* and by the Old Assyrian *aršātum*.

254 "Barley was the most common cereal grown in antiquity and was normally cheaper than wheat." Hoffner, *Alimenta*, 66-67.

255 The NIN.DINGIR is to receive 30 *parīsu* of barley in a good year, but only 15 in a bad year. The fact that a special amount for bad years is institutionalized in the written ritual might indicate that Emar faced recurrent agricultural setbacks at the time when the ritual was recorded.

256 Text D has ^{síg}*za-zi-tu*$_4$, perhaps with similar meaning. See the text notes.

257 SÍG is based on collation; Arnaud reads TÚG, though his copy shows the long lower horizontal of SÍG.

some garment from Elam and Mari, *zīru*, with feminine plural *zīrātu* (*CAD* s.v. *zīru* B s.).

Allotments

The NIN.DINGIR's allotment

Some of the items discussed above are not strictly offerings to the gods in the NIN.DINGIR festival or the rest of Emar ritual. On the other hand, most of the materials given to the NIN.DINGIR in her rations (with *nadānu*, lines 86-90, cf. 53-54) never appear in installation offerings. These include wool (SÍG/*šīpātu*, 369.86), aromatics (GIŠ.ŠIM and ŠIM/*riqqu*, lines 86 and 88), grapes (GEŠTIN/*karānu*, line 87), apples (GIŠ.ḪAŠḪUR/*ḫašḫūru*, line 87),[258] apricots(?) (GIŠ.ḪAŠḪUR.KUR.RA/*armannu*, line 88),[259] milk (GA.MEŠ/*šizbu*, line 88), soured milk (GA.ḪAB/*kisimmu*, line 88), emmer (ZÍZ/*kunāšu*, line 88), malt-beer (KAŠ.Ú.SA/*billatu*, lines 53 and 89),[260] sandals (kušE.SIR/*šēnu*, line 89), boots (kušŠUḪUB/*šuḫuppatu*, line 89), gazelles (MAŠ.DÀ/*ṣabītu*, line 89), fish (KU$_6$/*nūnu*, line 90),[261] and doves (TU.MUŠEN/*wattu*(?), line 90C, or simply "birds" in A).[262]

None of the above materials is unique to Emar, and the NIN.DINGIR's annual allotment exhibits a customary diet and clothing shared by much of the ancient Near East. The use of logographic spellings throughout the list makes it difficult to tell whether the Akkadian words are in fact the correct readings.

---

258 I.J. Gelb prefers "apricot" for *ḫašḫūru* because it is the more common Akkadian term and more commonly cultivated in modern Iraq; "Sumerian and Akkadian words for 'string of fruit'," in G. van Driel et al, eds., *Zikir Šumim: Assyriological Studies Presented to F.R. Kraus on the Occasion of his Seventieth Birthday*, Leiden: E.J. Brill, 1982, 78-79, 81.

259 The Hittite fruit lists, 1328/2 ii 7f and Bo 2687 include grapes (GIŠGEŠTIN), "apples" (GIŠḪAŠḪUR), and "mountain apples" (GIŠḪAŠḪUR.KUR.RA). The "apple" is listed as one of the principal trees of the region, according to Hoffner, *Alimenta*, 17, 113-115 (the translations are Hoffner's). Gelb's argument would presumably apply to Asia Minor as well as Mesopotamia.

260 Dietrich, *UF* 21 83, translates *billatu* as "Normalbier." The fact that this is not used in the ritual proper shows that KAŠ.ŠE should be the good beer, for special occasions, and KAŠ.Ú.SA is for everyday consumption.

261 De Tarragon, *Le culte*, 35, observes that offering fish is rare in the Ugarit rituals, a surprising trait for a coastal town. The only examples he finds are KTU 1.106:22 and UT 2004.12. Emar would have had a ready supply from the Euphrates, but fish are lacking from the ritual offering materials there as well. (We should keep in mind that this is an allotment for a priestess.)

262 Emar lexical text 555.71 (text F, Msk 74158r) includes a gloss for the Akkadian *šummatu*: MIN : *šu-um-ma-tu*$_4$: *wa-at-tu*$_4$. Thus *wattu* (from **wantu*?) should be the local term for "pigeon." The Hebrew *yônâ* is remarkably similar, though they cannot be derived from the same root; *yônâ* should come from **yawn-at*, where Emar *wattu* would not derive from a middle-weak root.

Most of the Akkadian terms are both Babylonian and Assyrian, except *billatu* and the relatively rare *armannu* and *kisimmu*, which are only found in Babylonian dialects (see the *AHw* and *CAD* entries). The Akkadian words for wool, aromatics, apples, milk, emmer, boots, gazelle, fish, and dove are attested in various peripheral Akkadian dialects during the second millennium. Malt-beer (*billatu*) is found at Mari. As a whole, the NIN.DINGIR allotment fits comfortably into attested Akkadian terminology from the Western periphery in the late second millennium.

Within Emar ritual, the cycle for the month of Abû is the only rite that includes most of the materials in the NIN.DINGIR's annual allotment. There, doves (452.1 and *passim*), aromatics (line 27), emmer (line 29), gazelles (line 44; meat, lines 50, 51), apricots(?) and soured milk (line 45), and fish (UZU KU_6, line 51) appear in offerings, unlike the installation festival. Apricot trees(?), GIŠ.ḪAŠḪUR.KUR.RA, appear in a difficult context as part of someone's inheritance-share in the legal text, 116.3. The apricots and fish do not otherwise occur in Emar ritual, and the malt-beer, apples, and she-ass hides are not found at all beyond the one installation allotment. The other items are scattered through Emar ritual (and later?).

Of the containers and measures, the *ḫittu*, *zadu*, *ḫubu*, and *qu'û*-vessels have been discussed above. The unnamed units with the wool (six hundred) and aromatics (four hundred) are probably shekels. This seems to be a large allotment. The word for "pair," *tāpalu*, is only Babylonian, and the general use for identifying two objects is a feature of the peripheral dialects.[263] All the fruit in the priestess' ration is counted by "rack," *kudurru*,[264] 369.87-88. This is usually a reed basket (see (*CAD* s.v. *kudurru* B 1), only made of wood at Nuzi (*CAD* s.v. *kudurru* B 2), where it is used to carry hay (*AHw* s.v. *kudurru* I 1). The Emar item is unique in being made of wood but used to hold fruit (thus, it may be smaller than the Nuzi *kudurru*). In the *kissu* for Išḫara and ᵈNIN.URTA, a *kudurru*[265] is used to carry loaves of bread for offerings.

Assigned animal parts

Two NIN.DINGIR festival events involve assignment of meats from a slaughtered animal to human participants in the ritual, and the parts are distinct from meat offered to the gods, on the whole. These events are the setting of

---

263 *AHw* s.v. *tāpalu(m)* 1, Alalaḫ, Boghazkoy, Amarna, Ugarit, Nuzi, as well as Mari.
264 The Babylonian spelling, vs. *kadurru*; see the dictionaries.
265 Without the GIŠ determinative for wood, 387.15 cf. 14, of text F; 15 and 16 of text J.

tables for Emar dignitaries for the seven-day period (369.55-58) and the slaughter and division of an ox after the festival is over (lines 77-80). The division of portions between the [lú]ḪAL and the singers (lines 80-83) repeat some of the terms found in the latter event.

Tables are set for important Emar officials in the NIN.DINGIR's residence at the temple of [d]IM (see above) on each of the first full days of the installation (369.15, 39), and for the seven days which fall between the enthronement of the new priestess and the final day, when she departs her father's house (line 56, without *šakānu*). Description of the week-long event ends with a list of the cuts of meat assigned to each player. These are from the ox and sheep mentioned in line 56 (UZU G[UD] UZU UDU); it is not clear when these were slaughtered. The seven dried fruit breads, seven pots (DUG) and seven(!) *maḫḫaru*-vessels are the allotment for each participant for the seven days (*ša* U_4.7.KÁM, line 57). The same portion is given to each person on the day of hair preparation ("one each," 1 TA.ÀM, with the verb *leqû*, line 18). In that case, there is also meat from a sheep (UZU UDU, line 17), presumably with the same assignments as in lines 57-58. It appears that the sheep is the one slaughtered and cooked by the *bēl bīti* (lines 14-15), and perhaps a similar role is left unmentioned in the instruction for the seven-day period.

The first table and portion is the *naglabu*, "haunch," for the previous NIN.DINGIR. When tables are set up for the same dignitaries in the *maš'artu* installation (370.33-37, also for seven days), the same cut of meat is assigned to "the NIN.DINGIR of [d]IM" (line 35, cf. 33): *na-ag-la-ab* UDU.[266] In the fragment of the annual cycle 447.4, the same cut ([uzu]*na*]-*ag-la-bu*) seems to be given to the *nu-mi*[-??], after the king gets the [uzu]*ge-eš-šu* (line 3). This is likely some unknown player. One possibility is the chief scribe (GAL [lú]DUB.ŠAR), who gets the *na-ag-la-*[*ba*] in the festival 394.43. However, the scribe is last in a trio with the king and the [lú]ḪAL (394.40, 42-43), and the unknown player of 447.4 precedes the diviner ([[lú]MÁ]Š.ŠU.GÍD.GÍD). The *naglabu* is part of meat allotments for a temple in the Middle Assyrian ritual, Ebeling Parfumrez.pl.35.4 (see *CAD* s.v. *naglabu* A e), and one Neo-Assyrian text, in both of which the word is spelled UZU.MAŠ.$SILA_4$. The only dictionary example with the syllabic spelling for the cut of meat is from Hittite ritual (UZU *NA-AG-LA-BU*, an "Akkadogram," KUB 10 62 r.v4).

---

266 This reading is based on collation. Arnaud's copy shows *na-ag-la-ab* KU, but a third vertical is visible.

The NIN.DINGIR of Dagan, Lord of Šumi, takes the second place and portion in the NIN.DINGIR installation (369.55, 57). Her cut of meat is the *kabbartu*, uzu*ka-bar-tu*$_4$, line 57, and the same player can be filled in for the *maš'artu* installation, from the parallel: uzu*kab-bar-ta a-na* [NIN.DINGIR dKUR EN *Šu-mi*], 370.35 (also in line 33). One uzu*ka-bar-t*[*u*$_4$] goes to an unknown recipient in the ritual for the d*Ar-ú-ri* (see 393.1, 3, 6, 8, 18), line 20, cf. 14; there is no hint of any NIN.DINGIR in the text. The annual cycle 446.34 provides more certain evidence of another player getting this cut of meat, though again the text is broken: *kab-bar-tu*$_4$ *a-na* LÚ.GAL [...]. This LÚ.GAL also appears at the end of the *maš'artu* installation (370.115), broken again. Arnaud suggests for the latter that this is the chief scribe, elsewhere GAL DUB.ŠAR.MEŠ, *rab ṭupšarrī*, 385.25, cf. 394.40, 43. Another option might be LÚ.GAL [uru*E-mar*], from the sanctification day of the *maš'artu* [L]Ú.MEŠ GAL uru*E-mar*, 370.19. In the NIN.DINGIR festival, the plural marker MEŠ is sometimes dropped from the singers' title (369.73, 74, 81). The Akkadian *kabbartu* is only Babylonian, and designates some part of the foot, usually of humans.[267] As a cut of meat, the "hock" (Arnaud, "jarret"), the *kabbartu* is completely new.

In the NIN.DINGIR festival, the *maš'artu* takes the third table with the *silqu*, "boiled meat" (369.55, 58). The reading [uzu*sí*]*l-qu* is somewhat difficult in line 58 (see the text notes), but comparison with the *maš'artu*'s own installation confirms it. There, the previous priestess (f*maš-ar-ti ma-*[*ḫi-ri-ti*], vs. Arnaud, 370.36) follows the king of Emar, in the last position of four, but she receives the same cut of meat, uzu[*s*]*íl-qu*. The noun *silqu* is unexpected for two reasons. First, *silqu* as (boiled) meat is primarily an Assyrian ritual element (see *CAD* s.v. *silqu* A 2a; *AHw* s.v. *silqu(m)* I 2b), and the Emar NIN.DINGIR festival does not generally make use of Assyrian terminology (see more, below). Further, our context calls for a specific part of the slaughtered animal, not a description of the way the meat is prepared. In spite of these difficulties, I have discovered no better reading, and the Emar word could reflect a particular local use -- not an unusual situation in our text.

The few Babylonian instances of *silqu* as meat do include a helpful reference. The late ritual text, BBR No. 1-20:52, 109 (cf. BMS 40:10), lists the *silqu* with other specific meat-parts (*imitta*, *ḫinša*, *šumê*, not found at Emar; see *CAD* s.v. *silqu* A 2a). Another interesting fact is that the single use

---

267 See *CAD* s.v. *kabbartu*; *AHw* s.v. *kabartu* 2, gives one example with an animal.

of *salāqu*, "to boil," listed in the *CAD* (s.v. *salāqu* A) is from the Mari ritual, CRRA 26.142 i 11, with the object *šīrum*, meat. At Emar, *silqu* could therefore be a special part of the animal which is boiled.

There are two versions of the dignitary list for the NIN.DINGIR festival. The more common one (texts B, C, D, E) has four officials, the three priestesses and "the king of the land," LUGAL KUR, while text A specifies the king of Emar and adds the king of Šatappi (see above). Even in the A text, both kings really occupy the same ritual position, though there is a fifth table (369.55 and 58; see lines 15, 17, 39). This is shown by their meat portion, the kidneys, ^{uzu}ELLÁG/Akkadian *kalītu* (line 58). The kidneys are consistently the king's portion in Emar ritual. After the NIN.DINGIR is installed, the king's representative receives the ^{uzu}ELLÁG from the slaughtered ox, and the ritual for cattle, 394.42, once again assigns the kidneys to the king. In the *maš'artu* sequence, the king comes third, before the *maš'artu*, and his portion is lost in the break, but the pattern established so far allows us to restore the text with confidence, [^{uzu}ELLÁG] LUGAL KUR TI-*qé*, "the king of the land will get [the kidneys]," 370.35-36. Also restore [LUGAL KUR] to the opening list at the beginning of line 34.

The ritual fragment 406 provides further information about the royal portion. Although there is little to each line, the first part of the fragment involves a list of meats and officials. Line 406.1 mentions some meat (UZU), and the next line reads [...] ^{uzu}ELLÁG-*šu* 2?[...], followed by a line with something "of the battle," and lines with the diviner ([^{lú}MÁŠ(?)].ŠU.GÍD.GÍD), the $^{f.meš}$*mu-na-bi-ia-ti*, and the scribe. If the number "two" is accurate, the king may still be the recipient, via royal representatives, LÚ LUGAL KUR, as in 369.79 and 399.4 (two!). This would suit the place of ^{uzu}EllÁG-*šu* near the top of the list. When the royal portion is spelled syllabically in Emar ritual, it is ^{uzu}*ge-eš-šu* (447.3; cf. ^{uzu}*ge*$_5$-*eš-ša*, 388.62), and it is more likely that -*šu* in 406.2 is a phonetic complement than a pronominal suffix. Thus, we should read ELLÁG/*geššu*, a local term for "kidney," in the NIN.DINGIR installation, 369.58. Akkadian *kalītu* is a cut of meat in first-millennium Babylonian and Assyrian ritual (see *CAD* s.v. *kalītu* 2e; *AHw* s.v. *kalītu(m)* 2b), but it does not seem to be associated with kings. Note that Yahweh receives the kidneys in the biblical "peace offering" of Lev 3.4, 10, 15, etc.

As just observed, the king also receives the ELLÁG/*geššu* in the second main division of meat portions to human participants during the NIN.DINGIR festival, when the ox from the last procession is slaughtered by the men of the *qidašu* (369.77-80). Division of this ox is described using a repetitive format: the special meat portion "and his share" (*ù* ḪA.LA-*šu*; with additional meat added for the lúḪAL, line 78), followed by the recipient and the verb TI-*qé*, *ilaqqe*, "he will get." This formula is repeated for the royal representative (LÚ LUGAL KUR, line 77), the lúḪAL (line 78), and the singers (line 79), the three groups who apparently make up the LÚ.MEŠ *ša qí-da-ši* in the NIN.DINGIR festival. The term ḪA.LA-*šu*/*zittašu*, "his share," is the legal share of each heir in a will (see Emar 15.28; 34.16; 40.5, 7; 69.11; etc), and here it probably refers to a regular amount of the remaining meat which each of the three recipients get in addition to the special portion.

The lúḪAL receives several parts of the slaughtered ox, but he has a special portion which is not a known Akkadian word, the uzu*ḫaṣītu* (369.78).[268] Apparently he gets this portion of all the oxen and sheep sacrificed during the festival (line 83C), and there are two more instances of the *ḫaṣītu* which probably are associated with the lúḪAL. The ritual for cattle, 394.26-44, ends with division of meat portions to the king, the lúḪAL, and the chief scribe, and the lúḪAL's cut appears to be the *ḫa-*[*ṣ*]*i-ti*.[269] The same three officials are found at the end of the *kissu* for Ea, also (386.22), and the last line seems to end, [*ḫ*]*a-ṣi-ti* GAL DUB.ŠAR, as if this portion belongs to the chief scribe. However, this part of the Ea *kissu* is reconstructed from two fragments (left, Msk 74286b; right, Msk 74303i, both for text F), and the alignment of the two sides can be determined by comparison with 394.40-44, with knowledge of normal ritual idiom at Emar. Arnaud's text makes the final line of each side match, but the last line of the left side is the true end of the ritual:

386.18 gišBAN[ŠUR...] GAR-*nu* 7 nindanap-ta-ni
19 7 NINDA UD.DU [7 NINDA UD.DU GUR]UN *ana* dKUR GAR-*nu* GAL KÙ.BABBAR.MEŠ
20 KAŠ.GEŠTIN KAŠ.[ŠE...lú.meš*šar-ru n*]*a-di-nu qí-da-ši*
21 *ina* É dKUR [KÚ NAG-*u*... *i-na* KÁ] gišBANŠUR-*šu-nu* TI-*u*
22 *ù i-na gá*[*b-bi* EZEN.MEŠ *an-na-ti*] LUGAL KUR lúḪAL GAL DUB.ŠAR.MEŠ
23 *iš-tu* ninda*ḫu-*[*ki* DUG KAŠ.ŠE *ú-qa-d*]*a-šu-nu-ti*[270] *gáb-ba*

[268] Perhaps compare the Hebrew *ḥăṣôt* and *ḥăṣî*, "half"; E. Lipiński, personal communication.
[269] Line 43, not *ḫa-*[*kur-r*]*a-ti*, as Arnaud.
[270] I do not add -<*šu*>- for the third radical of the root *qdš* because this spelling is used in every instance of this idiom (see below, The *qaddušu*-Ceremony).

24 GUD.ḪI.A LUGAL K[UR ^{uzu}ELLÁG ^{lú}ḪAL *ḫ*]*a-ṣi-ti* GAL DUB.ŠAR

25 UZU.MÁŠ.SILA$_4$ T[I-*qé*]

First, observe that the meat-portion comes after the recipient, not before, as in other ritual texts. Moreover, the similarity between this text and the end of 394, even with the phrase EZEN.MEŠ *an-na-ti*(?), and the fact that the left side is part of the multiple *kissu* text, Msk 74286b, mean that text 394 is closely related to the *kissu* feasts. It may even be one of them, and 394.39, "in all these festivals," may refer to the *kissu* festivals particularly, and the group is larger than previously apparent. Note the feminine plural with EZEN/*isinnu* (see *AHw* s.v. *isinnu(m)*). Along with the further evidence for the ^{lú}ḪAL receiving the *ḫaṣītu*-portion, we have here a logographic spelling of the *naglabu* (see above), taken by the chief scribe: UZU.MÁŠ.SILA$_4$, usually with MAŠ$_1$ (see the dictionaries).

In the division of the slaughtered ox, the ^{lú}ḪAL is the only one to receive more than just his special cut of meat and "his share." He also gets the head and the heart, parts that otherwise are part of offerings to gods (see above), as well as the fat and the hide. Evidence for the fat in other Emar ritual does not offer a consistent picture. The men of the *qidašu* eat the fat of an ox (Ì.UDU GUD) along with half the intestines, at the end of the *kissu*, 388.64. The fat and the head appear to be part of an offering in the *maš'artu* festival, 370.13. Two other occurrences are in broken texts that do not show who is the recipient, or even whether the fat is part of offerings or allotments, 408.4 and 472.10. Hides are largely the allotment for the ^{lú}ḪAL, however. He receives another ox-hide in the NIN.DINGIR installation (369.82), and he shares all the festival's sheepskins with the singers (lines 81-82). During the annual offering cycle, text 446, the ^{lú}ḪAL repeatedly gets the hides of offered animals, lines 27, 44, 80-81, and 101. The text for all the *kissu* rites includes three hides which may go to the ^{lú}ḪAL (388.19-20), and the first ritual of text 394 (lines 1-25) appears to repeat the division between the ^{lú}ḪAL and the singers found in the NIN.DINGIR festival (394.23; cf. 369.81-82).

The third special portion of the NIN.DINGIR installation ox-division belongs to the singers. They receive the lungs (^{uzu}MUR/*ḫašû*) which were part of the daily offering for the seven-day period, with the heart of a sheep (369.79; cf. line 50). We are told that the singers receive all the lungs from sheep offered throughout the festival (lines 83C), and perhaps the single inclusion of sheep lungs in an offering list (line 50) displays the ultimate human receipt of many offerings more transparently than usual. The same offering list is the only one to identify the recipient of offering (verb, *naqû*) as anything but a god: *a-na* É ^{d}IM, "to the *temple* of ^{d}IM." It is the singers who get the lungs in text 394.25, while the ^{lú}ḪAL is given the odd ^{uzu}*za-az-ia-ti*.MEŠ, not the *ḫaṣītu* (line 24). One more mention of the lungs is found in the broken 412.3.

The last meat portion involved in the division of the ox after the NIN.DINGIR festival is the intestines (*irrū*), which are to be eaten by all the men of the *qidašu* (369.79-80). In the *kissu*, 388.63-65, the intestines receive slightly different treatment. The ox-fat is eaten with half the intestines by the men of the *qidašu*, and the other half is taken by the king, with the head and kidneys (see above).

3. The Hospitality of the Storm God's House

When evaluating the description of a single offering it is natural to look for the human giver and the divine recipient, and other scenarios are unexpected. In the great sacrifices of the shaving and enthronement days, however, the offering of the ox and the sheep is described in two stages (lines 11, 32A, B(31-36)h, 37). First the animals are ritually slaughtered (*naqû*), and then their meat is set out as an offering (*šakānu*). On the enthronement day, the offering appears to follow an expected pattern: the meat is offered to ^{d}IM, as the sacrifice seems to have been made for him.[271] ^{d}IM likewise receives the offerings of breads and drink that follow (line 37). The great sacrifice of the shaving day does not display this straightforward pattern, however, and the variation provides opportunity for further insight into the possibilities inherent in the occasion.

The offering of this first great sacrifice has two divine points of reference. The slaughter itself is carried out before ^{d}IM (line 11), as expected after arrival at his temple and performance of the *kubadu* before him. Then, the meat from the animals is given not to ^{d}IM but to "the gods," and the gods receive the rest of the food offerings as well (lines 11-12). Having sacrificed the ox and the sheep before (*ana pānī*) the storm god, the officiants proceed to

---

271 Caution is necessary because ^{d}[IM] is restored in line 32A, but the pattern of lines 9-11 shows arrival at his temple, with *kubadu* and sacrifice performed before him. The parallel pattern and subsequent offering of meat makes any other restoration in line 32A unlikely.

give all the offerings to others. This phenomenon might be explained as the hospitality of ᵈIM's house. On this first full day of the installation festival, with the first arrival at ᵈIM's temple, the storm god receives and approves the sacrifice before playing host to the gods of Emar, and through them the whole city.

In the first great sacrifice of the NIN.DINGIR installation, the powerful force of hospitality operates in a complex communion that unites the people and gods of Emar in the business of the festival. The hospitality begins with the humans making the offerings. Around the world, the opening of family and home in a shared meal makes a powerful welcome to an outsider. Eating together lowers the barriers which separate those who move in different spheres, but at the same time the guest is invited into the cares of that community and takes on a responsibility for interest in its welfare. The age-old Near Eastern custom of the offering with ensuing feast is a true communion, which invites the gods to concern for the well-being of the offerers. In the Emar sacrifice and feast, both ᵈIM and the gods of Emar are joined in the hospitality of the people of Emar. At the same time, the tables for the major regional priestesses and the king(s) welcome the peers of the NIN.DINGIR into her home and make her significance city-wide. Finally, ᵈIM brings the divine community into his house, has his servants kill the fatted calf, and the gods of Emar are treated to a fabulous banquet at his expense. The image of the storm god as host powerfully pushes the scope of the festival beyond the immediate interests of the god and his cult. Installation of a new NIN.DINGIR for ᵈIM is to be the affair of the whole city, and the first great offering of the installation festival is staged to accomplish this.

E. SPECIAL FESTIVAL RITES

The remaining events of the NIN.DINGIR festival primarily consist of actions that are specially characteristic of Emar ritual, or that are uniquely part of the installation process. These are divided into two groups: ceremonies that are found only at Emar, but are used beyond the narrow scope of installation rites; and events that are specifically part of the NIN.DINGIR's installation into priestly office, the ceremonies which move her from the world of the citizen, in her father's house, to the world of service to the storm god dIM, in his house. The first group is treated under the heading, "Special Festival Rites," and the second under "The NIN.DINGIR's Progress."

1. The Sanctification Ceremony, the qaddušu

One of the most prominent features of Emar festivals is the "day of sanctification,"[272] *ūmi qadduši*, which marks the opening of the festival. This commencement may be described with or without the mention of a "day" (*ūmu*), with no apparent distinction. Compare the following:

370.2, [*i-na* u_4-*m*]*i qa-ad-du-ši*, for the first day of the *maš'artu* installation.[273]

385.3, *i-na* u_4-*mi qa-ad-du-ši ša* ŠIM, "on the sanctification day of the aromatics," for the first day of Dagan's *kissu*, after the heading.

385.28-29, *i-na* u_4-*mi qa-ad-du-ši ša* ezen*ki-is-sí ša* dEREŠ.KI.GAL, "on the sanctification day of the *kissu* festival of dEREŠ.KI.GAL," for the first day, serving as the text's heading.

387.1, *i-na* ([u_4-*m*]*i*, text J) *qa-du-ši ša* ezenLA (LA, only J), where ezenLA replaces *kissu ša* DN, for the festival of Išḫara and dNIN.URTA. The LA-logogram normally stands for *lalû*, "abundance."[274]

388.1, *i-na* u_4-*mi ša qa-du-ši ša* ezen.meš*ki-is-sí*, for the opening of the text for all *kissu* festivals, or the *kissu*'s as a group.

394.26, *i-na qa-ad-du-ši ša ḫe-en-pa* GUD.MEŠ, "at the sanctification of the *ḫenpa* of the oxen," for the heading and first day of the ritual (394.26-44).

---

272 As noted in the translation that precedes the commentary, I have chosen to translate the verb *qaddušu* with the archaic English "to sanctify" instead of "to consecrate," which carries the sense of purification for entry into the sphere of deity. When found with the gods as object, the verb appears to mean "to treat as holy" as well as "to make holy," and I have chosen the English "to sanctify" as a single verb that can encompass both meanings, though the first definition belongs to older English. Two examples are preserved in the King James Version of the Bible: Deut 32.51, "because ye sanctified (Piel, *qādaš*) me (YHWH) not in the midst of the children of Israel," and 1 Peter 3.15, "sanctify (*hagiazō*) the Lord God in your hearts." Because this translation derives from the Latin *sanctus*, "sacred," it can express succinctly both meanings of the verb *qaddušu*, "to make sacred" and "to treat as sacred." Another possible translation would be "to worship," with the associated noun, "worship." Any English translation will require comment.

273 Collation shows room for *i-na*, instead of simple AŠ (*ina*).

274 See *CAD* and *AHw* s.v. *lalû*(*m*).

460.5-6, *i-na* u_4*-mi ša qa-du-ši* ᵈINANNA *ta-ḫa-zi*, for the first set in a cycle of gifts to both humans and gods, associated with *Aštartu tāḫāzi*.

The NIN.DINGIR installation has the most complex use of sanctification ceremonies at Emar in that there are two of them, one introducing the day of shaving and one the enthronement day:

369.6, *i-na qa-du-ši ša gal-lu-bi*, at the end of the description of selection but before the *gallubu* begins (line 7).

369.22, *i-na* u_4*-mi qa-du-ši ša ma-al-lu-ki*, introducing the section, lines 22-28, before the *malluku* begins (line 29); text B has ⌜*i*⌝*-na* u_4*-mi qa-ad-du*<*-ši*> *ša m*[*a-al-lu-ki*].

The inclusion of two sanctification ceremonies in the NIN.DINGIR festival at parallel points in the installation's structure shows that the "sanctification" is likely a complex ritual in itself which is summarized by the clause, DINGIR.MEŠ ᵘʳᵘ*E-mar gáb-bá iš-tu* NINDA.MEŠ KAŠ.MEŠ *ú-qa-da-šu* (lines 6 and 22). On the first day, this action represents the whole, whereas the second sanctification goes on to include setting of tables for gods and further offerings. The fact that the festival has two *qaddušu* rites also appears to reflect a conception of the entire installation in two parts. The second rite, introduced in lines 22-28, serves the rest of the festival -- the enthronement day and the seven-day celebration which follows. This scope is expressed in the fact that ᵈNIN.KUR is laid down at this time in preparation for her seven-day stay at the father's house, and in the instructions for some seven-day offering (line 26B?). The separate *qaddušu* for the shaving day adds to the impression that the shaving and first great sacrifice at one level constitute a separate festival.

Variations of the above sentence with the verb *qadāšu* are associated with some of the other sanctification days:

385.3-4, IGI ᵍⁱˢBANŠUR.MEŠ DINGIR.MEŠ *ša* URU *iš-tu* NINDA.MEŠ KAŠ.MEŠ *ú-qa-ad-da-šu*, "before the tables they will sanctify the gods of the city with bread and beer," and table-setting for the gods follows (lines 7-9).

385.28-29, *u* ᵈEREŠ.KI.GAL *iš-tu* ⁿⁱⁿᵈᵃ*ḫu-uk-ki* NINDA UD.DU GURUN DUG KAŠ.ŠE.MEŠ *ú-qa-ad-da-šu*, this time giving specific types of bread and beer (following texts A, H, especially).

387.2(F), *iš-tu* ^{ninda}*ḫu-uk-ki* NINDA UD.DU GUR[UN] DUG KAŠ.ŠE *ú-qa-da-šu*, probably with divine objects Išḫara and ^{d}NIN.URTA, not repeated as ^{d}EREŠ.KI.GAL was in 385.29; text J reads, 1 ^{ninda}*ḫu-uk-ku* [1 DU]G KAŠ.ŠE.MEŠ 1 NINDA UD.DU *a-na qa-du-ši*, using the infinitive.

388.5, DINGIR.MEŠ *ša* ^{uru}*Ša-tap-pí* (*iš-tu*, text J) NINDA.MEŠ *u* KAŠ.MEŠ *ú-qa-da-šu*, mentioning four tables in line 4.

394.27-28, ^{d}KUR *iš-tu* ^{ninda}*ḫu-ki* NINDA UD.DU GURUN DUG KAŠ.ŠE *ú-qa-da-šu*.

A subset of these texts also includes a sanctification statement at the end of the rituals, each belonging to the *kissu* sphere and involving the same ritual players:

385.25-26(A), LUGAL KUR ^{lú}ḪAL *u* GAL DUB.ŠAR.MEŠ *iš-tu* ^{ninda}*ḫu-uk-ki u* DUG KAŠ.ŠE *ú-qa-ad-da-šu-nu-ti*;

394.40-41, LUGAL KUR ^{lú}ḪAL ^{lú}DUB.ŠAR *iš-tu* [^{ninda}]*ḫu-ki* DUG KAŠ.ŠE *ú-qa-da-šu-nu-ti*;

cf. 386.22-23, [L]UGAL KUR ^{lú}ḪAL GAL DUB.ŠAR.MEŠ *iš-tu* ^{ninda}*ḫu-*[*ki* DUG KAŠ.ŠE *ú-qa-d*]*a-šu-nu-ti*.

All add the 3mp pronominal suffix, *-šunūti*, omitting the "*-šu-*" sign for the third radical in *qdš*, and replace the gods with the three human officials. The consistent use of the suffix, which never appears when gods are the object, indicates that in this case the first element of the sentence should be the subject. Thus, we have the same action as the one mentioned at the opening, but set within an administrative section at the end: "The king of the land, the ^{lú}ḪAL, and the chief scribe will sanctify them (the gods) with *ḫukku*-bread and barley-beer." If the humans were the ones sanctified, we should not find the use of the suffix *-šunūti* restricted to this setting.[275]

One bit of evidence which might suggest that this sanctification can be performed equally for gods and humans is found in the cycle of offerings for the *ša-aṭ*(?)*-ra-ḫi* rites of *Aštartu tāḫāzi*, Emar 460. In this text, the first set of offerings is summarized by the words, *a-na u*?*-nu-*tu_4 *i-na* u_4*-mi ša qa-du-ši* ^{d}INANNA *ta-ḫa-zi*, where the leading phrase seems to be a confused version

275 One alternative reading might be *uqaddaš-šunūti*, with a 3ms subject and *-šš-* for the normative *-ss-*. However, a singular subject without a definite referent is unlikely in Emar ritual.

of *annûtu* or *unūtū annûtu*; "these things(?) (are) on the sanctification day of *Aštartu tāḫāzi*" (lines 5-6). The second set consists of a short list of offerings and the summary, *qa-du-šu ša* ^{lú}SANGA *ša* INANNA *ta-ḫa-zi*, which again has an equivalent grammatical structure that might reflect interchange of divine and human recipients of sanctification offerings (line 9). However, the wording may represent a sanctification offering made *by* the priest of Aštart on that day. Some uncertainty remains, but the simplest explanation of the Emar use of *qadāšu* identifies a single ritual action, sanctification of the gods with festival-commencement offerings.

The usual idiom of sanctification makes the gods the direct object of the verb *qadāšu* (D), but a variant may show grammatically what context already suggests, that offering to the gods is in view. Text D of the Dagan *kissu* festival diverges from A at the point where the sanctification is described. It mentions different breads (385.5, [ ] x TUR 1 NINDA.[GUR$_4$.R]A TUR ^{ninda}*ḫu-la-šu* TUR, "small" breads) and then places the gods in the normal position for the indirect object, with *ana*, directly before the verb: [*a-*]*na* DINGIR.MEŠ *ša* URU *ú-qa-da-šu*, "[...one] small [... -bread], one small *kerṣu*-bread, a small *ḫulašu*-bread, [...], they will sanctify to the gods of the city" (lines 5-6).

We have no text for the sanctification day of the *zukru* festival, though reference is made to it in later parts of the festival. In 373.198, the instructions require that rites be performed at the great gate of the center (-city) "just as for ('of') the sanctification day."[276] This closes the events of the principal day of the *zukru* (day 15; see below, chapter IV). Though we have a text for a beginning of the *zukru* (375), it is not certain that this version can be read together smoothly with the larger text 373 (see chapter IV). We join the action of the *zukru* in some period of preparation that ends with the 24th and 25th days of an unknown month (373.7, 14). At the end of this preparatory stage of the festival, the text offers a total of calves and sheep, which is identified as ŠU.NIGÍN 4 AMAR 40 UDU.ḪI.A *qa-du-ši*, "Total: four calves (and) forty sheep of the sanctification" (373.31).[277] One other occurrence of *qadāšu* would be unique if the reading is correct: at the end of the *zukru* it is

---

[276] The text: *i-na* KÁ.GAL *ša qa-ab-li pár-ṣi ki-i ša* u_4*-mi qa-du-ši-ma* DÙ-*šú* (not -*ši*; collated).
[277] Or translate, "Total *of* four calves (and) forty sheep of the sanctification."

stated, [...]⌈^{ezen}*zu-uk*⌉*-ra ú-qa-*[*ad-da-šu*], "they will sanctify the *zukru* festival" (373.210).[278]

What is the significance of the Emar *qaddušu*? In Mesopotamian Akkadian the D conjugation of *qadāšu* means "to purify" (*AHw* s.v. *qadāšu(m)* D, 2 "kultisch"; *CAD* s.v. *qadāšu* 3) or "to consecrate" or "dedicate" *to* the gods (*CAD* s.v. *qadāšu* 4). The latter falls in the class of offering, and indicates a gift to the gods, whereas the former refers to cleansing so as to be ready for divine use, whether persons (*CAD* s.v. *qadāšu* 3a), buildings or images (3b), or appurtenances for ritual (3c). One does not "consecrate" gods because they are already sacred. Emar's *qaddušu* appears to mean "to treat as sacred" by means of concrete offerings. This special "sanctification" offering (see above) apparently makes the festival holy by giving cult to the gods as holy.[279] For a similar meaning with the D conjugation of a denominative verb, compare Akkadian *kubbutu* when addressed to gods or to parents (*CAD* s.v. *kabātu* 6a,b). Here, we would translate "to treat as important" rather than "to make important."

2. The kubadu, Presentation of the Sacrifice

Just as the shaving day and the enthronement day are preceded by sanctification ceremonies, these two days include the only *kubadu* ceremonies of the NIN.DINGIR festival. Whereas the *qaddušu* represents a specific Emar use of Akkadian terminology which does not fit the normal Mesopotamian range of meaning for the verb *qadāšu*, the *kubadu* is not a known Akkadian word. The term is shown to be derived from the root *kbd* ("to be heavy, important") by use with the cognate verb *ú-ka-ba-du* in Emar 446.56 and 96 (cf. 448.16 and 449.4). Each of the first two full days of the NIN.DINGIR installation begins with a procession to ^{d}IM's temple, followed by performance of the *kubadu*. On the first day, only the shaving of the priestess intervenes (369.8-9). This *kubadu* is defined by three clauses:

-- they perform (*epēšu*) the *kubadu* "before" ^{d}IM, lines 9 and 30;

---

[278] This reading is based on collation.

[279] Note the Alalah̬ text in *CAD* s.v. *qadāšu* 4: one sheep <<DIŠ>> *inūma* DN *ú-qa-ad-di-iš*, *CAD*, "he consecrated at the time of (the festival of) DN"; but at face value, the text appears to say, "when he sanctified DN" (346.5, OB).

-- the father (line 10) or the priestess (line 31A, cf. B(31-36)e) performs some central action that involves lifting up (*našû*) the divine weapon (*kakki ili*);
-- they complete (*gamāru*, D) the *kubadu*, lines 10 and 31A.

The *kubadu* ceremony of the NIN.DINGIR festival is an unusual element in that it is a rite not found in the *maš'artu* installation or *kissu* feasts, but prominent in rituals that have less in common with the NIN.DINGIR event. These are the *zukru* festival,[280] the annual offering cycles,[281] the month of Abû cycle,[282] and the door rites (463.4). Although it has the *kubadu* in common with these more distant ritual kin, the NIN.DINGIR festival version is distinct from the others. Where there is any detail given, the other *kubadu* ceremonies refer only to making offerings,[283] but the NIN.DINGIR *kubadu* makes no direct mention of offerings, and the central act has to do with bearing the divine weapon (see below). In fact the unusual detail of the descriptions in the installation text can obscure the context which shows the relation to offering. When the *kubadu* is examined in its position between the sacrificial procession and the great sacrifice and feast, it becomes evident that the *kubadu* functions as a rite of preparation for sacrifice.

In the NIN.DINGIR installation, the first clause simply declares the performance of the *kubadu*, thus placing it at the temple of ᵈIM after the arrival of the procession. The *kubadu* is to be the "great" (GAL) variety (see below), and it is to occur "before" ᵈIM (369.9). Both texts A and B for the enthronement day specify that the new priestess only enters the temple immediately before the sacrifice (lines 32A, B(31-36)h), and so her role in the *kubadu* should place it outside the main sanctuary. Perhaps ᵈIM's statue is in the temple courtyard for this part of the festival, or even in the gate (cf. line 9, *ana pî bāb(i) tarbāṣi*). Unlike the *zukru* instructions, there is very little mention of moving statuary in the NIN.DINGIR festival text (only the *sikkānu* of Hebat, lines 35-36). Wherever the absolute location, the *kubadu* occurs at the place of the sacrifice, before ᵈIM (so, line 11).

Use of the verb *epēšu*, "to perform" (a rite), is found throughout the Emar texts, with the following objects: rites, generally (*parṣu*), 373.198, 209;

---

280 373.33-35, 59-60, 171, and 177-178.
281 446.55-56, 95-96; 448(A)15, 16; 449.4, 5, 7.
282 452.14, 34-35, 45-46.
283 373.33-35, 59-60; 452.34-35, 45-46.

the *zukru*, 373.36; the *kissu*, 385.2; the *imištu* of the king, 392.2; and a song (*zimaru*), 452.48. This use is well-known to Akkadian (see *AHw* s.v. *epēšu(m)* G5g, Tempelkulte). The verb *epēšu* is found with the *kubadu* in the *zukru* festival (373.34, 59, 171, 178) and the Abû cycle (452.35; cf. 26?, [...] *ep-pa-šu*, and possibly 14, in the break?) The latter makes the offering aspect explicit in one instance by using the verb *naqû* (452.46), and the verb *zâzu* (D) might be used for performing the *kubadu* in 463.4. A family of texts for annual offering cycles uses the verb *kabādu* (D), 446.56, 96; 448(A).16; 449.4.

Only the NIN.DINGIR festival *kubadu* is focused on bearing the divine weapon, and the action appears nowhere else in Emar ritual. The verb *našû* can bear several meanings that might make sense in our context: it can mean "to lift something up during a ritual" (*CAD* s.v. *našû* A 1a2'), "to brandish a weapon, a torch, a signal" (*CAD* A 1b), simply "to carry" (*CAD* A 2a2'a', with examples during ritual), or "to wear or carry a symbol, weapon, or tool in exercise of one's function or duty, or as a sign of office or status" (*CAD* A 2c). The first and third definitions ("to lift up", and "to carry") seem to fit our context best, being more general. It is unlikely that both the priestess and her father wear the divine weapon as a symbol of office, and there is no sign that the weapon is brandished as if for use. Two Emar legal texts use a similar idiom to describe taking on the bond of service to the king. In one, the king's brothers are "those who bear the bronze spear before the king," *ša* ZAG ZABAR *a-na muḫ-ḫi* LUGAL-*ri na-šu* (17.5; or, "whose spears are borne..."). In the other, the sons of a certain Kitta are enjoined to take their rights to their father's house, and to "bear the weapon of the king...," ^{giš}TUKUL *ša* LUGAL *kir-kir-da-na li-iš-šu-ú* (18.19-20).[284] Three further texts published by Arnaud and Tsukimoto define service to private individuals with the idiom ^{giš}TUKUL ... *našû*, "to bear the weapon."[285] Possibly the NIN.DINGIR's father bears the divine weapon on behalf of the priestess on

[284] The word *kir-kir-da-na* is unknown. Arnaud suggests that it is a gloss on "weapon," perhaps related to the Hurrian word *karkarni* (note on 18.19). Durand, *RA* 83 177, reads *kir-kir-ra*!-*na*, and compares this Hurrian word for "bronze" to the ZAG ZABAR of Emar 17.5, above. Alternatively, the word may mean "in perpetuity" or the like (P. Steinkeller, personal communication).

[285] D. Arnaud, *AuOr* 5 233, No. 13 (ME 121), lines 12-14 (in an adoption); A. Tsukimoto, "Eine neue Urkunde des Tili-Šarruma, Sohn des Königs von Karkamiš," *ASJ* 6 (1984) 66-68, HCCT-E 5:4-5; HCCT-E 16:11.

the shaving day, when she still belongs to his household, and the central act of the *kubadu* signifies her entrance into the storm god's service. Just as the king's soldiers will thenceforth bear a weapon on his behalf, the priestess will always bear the divine weapon in the rites that call for its use. This aspect of the *kubadu* is mentioned in the NIN.DINGIR festival because it becomes part of her initiation, including the contrast between the shaving and enthronement days.

The divine weapon is an important part of the whole NIN.DINGIR festival, not just the *kubadu*. Its significance must be related to the fact that it always stays with the priestess, even when someone nearby has care of it. A natural corollary to the rule of proximity to the priestess is that the weapon is found in each festival procession, following the NIN.DINGIR (369.45, 63; cf. lines 7 and 29, "the divine weapon and the NIN.DINGIR"). The priestess' father holds the weapon during the first of the two *kubadu* ceremonies (lines 10 and 31A), and the goddess ᵈNIN.KUR wears it during the seven-day period at the father's house (line 46, see below).

In the NIN.DINGIR installation, the most frequent form of the term is ᵍⁱˢTUKUL DINGIR.MEŠ (text A, lines 7, 10, 29, 31, 33, 45, 63; text B, lines 29 and (31-36)e; text C, lines 7 and 10). Line 46 of text A has the variant ᵍⁱˢTUKUL DINGIR-*lì*. The signs ᵍⁱˢTUKUL.DINGIR can form a logogram for the noun *miṭṭu*, "mace," but if the spelling in line 46A does not eliminate that interpretation of the Emar signs, two ritual fragments use one that does: ᵍⁱˢTUKUL *ša* DINGIR-*lì* (420.1, 5, cf. 6 without *ša*; 422.11).[286] The compound term is also suggested by the alternate form *ḫa-ṣi-in-nu* (*ša*) DINGIR.MEŠ, in lines 45, 46, and 63 of text B, and line 63 of text D. If we are to understand the *kakki ili* to be a symbol of the NIN.DINGIR's office, it is not exclusively so. Neither of the above fragments mentions the NIN.DINGIR, and the first text might associate the weapon with the king (420.4, 7). Moreover, the *ḫa-ṣi-(in-)nu ša* DINGIR is a regular participant in the rites for the annual cycle (446.15, 40, 43, 87, 100, 102; 447.14), and though the NIN.DINGIR has no role, the divine axe once again appears at the end of ritual processions.[287] During the month of the god Halma, the axe takes up residence (*uššab*, 446.100) in Dagan's temple, with the god and a sheep

---

286 Dietrich, *UF* 21 63 and n.43, interprets the signs as *miṭṭu* and translates "Götterembleme."

287 446.43, 87, 102; 447.14; all "after"/*arki* other participants; cf. 446.15, 40.

(see line 99). It appears that the divine weapon is not the particular symbol of the NIN.DINGIR or the storm god, but in more than one Emar ritual it accompanies the players through their appointed rounds. However, the weapon *is* specially associated with the NIN.DINGIR for her installation and carrying it seems to serve as one mark of her office. Perhaps it is best to guess that there is more than one divine weapon, and the scribes do not deem it necessary to identify the particular symbol required, since it would be obvious to those involved.

The last element in the NIN.DINGIR installation *kubadu* refers to its completion (*gamāru*, D), set into a circumstantial clause with the conjunction *kīmê*, "after." This clause creates a direct link between the *kubadu* and what follows. The simplest sequence is found in lines 10-11C: "When they finish the great *kubadu*, they will sacrifice the one ox and the six sheep before ᵈIM." In text A, a payment to the diviner is inserted between the *kubadu* and the sacrifice, but that may represent an administrative note rather than a ritual pause. On the enthronement day, the sequence is expanded to include some purification rite, followed by the entry of the priestess into ᵈIM's temple and then the sacrifice (lines 31-32A, B(31-36)g-h). On the last day of the cycle for the month of Abû, they purify the city (URU.KI *ú-kap-pa-ru*, 452.53) before offering (*naqû*) barley flour, some drink, and sheep(?) to ᵈEN *Ak-ka*. In the NIN.DINGIR festival, the purification should prepare for the sacrifice, whether by cleansing the place, the people, or some unknown sacrificial implements. Despite the additions of the other examples, the simple connection between *kubadu* and sacrifice in lines 10-11C should indicate the essential nature of the *kubadu* as a presentation ceremony for the offering itself and the people who give it.

It is difficult to tell whether all the Emar *kubadu* rituals were distinct from the actual offering, which would follow. Often the ritual texts only supply detail when it represents a departure from normal procedure. For example the rites for the month of Abû describe two *kubadu*'s simply as lists of materials for offering (Emar 452.34-35, 43-46), and the second even uses the verb *naqû*. There is no way to tell, however, whether a distinct offering is assumed and the whole is referred to by the *kubadu* because the offering specially requires the preparatory ritual. Several *kubadu* rites are mentioned without indication that offering is involved at all: compare 373.171-172, 176-

178; 446.55-56, 95-96.[288] The *kubadu* ceremonies of the *zukru* festival offering section (373.33-35, 59-61) separate performance of a *kubadu* from burning the offerings (verb, *qalû*). In lines 33-35 a ewe, bread, and drink are present for the *kubadu* (in *casus pendans*), but only "that ewe" (UDU.U_8 *ša-a-ši*) is said to be burnt. The second text describes the same scenario, but a ewe, drink, and bread are only introduced after the *kubadu*, when all are burned. These *zukru* examples may then distinguish a separate preparatory rite, with the offering itself contained in the verb *qalû*.

The *kubadu* ceremonies of the NIN.DINGIR installation may take place in the gate of the ᵈIM temple on both days. The first is performed immediately after they shave the priestess "at the opening of the courtyard gate" (line 9), and the priestess carries the divine weapon for the *kubadu* on the enthronement day before she is allowed into the temple (see above). The *zukru* rites before the burning take place "before the great gate of the (city-?) center," *a-na pa-ni* KÁ.GAL *ša qa-ab-li* (373.33-34, cf. 59), and another one "at the gate of the stelae," *i-na* KÁ $^{na4.meš}$*si-ka-na-ti* (373.177), outside the city (see lines 176, 186, 193). The broken text of 449.5, [*ku*?]-*ba-de*$_4$ *bi-ri-it* [...] suggests the same location, and line 4, KÁ.GAL.ḪI.A recalls the *zukru*'s central gate, but neither is certain. On the twenty-fifth day of the month of Abû, "the gate of the tomb," (*i-na*) KÁ KI.MAḪ, serves as the *kubadu* setting. The rest of this section, describing rites for days 25 through 27, involves specific Emar sites, so this "tomb" should be a single spot, possibly the royal tomb or a burial place for the most influential Emar citizens.[289] In contrast to all these gates, one of the *kubadu* ceremonies in the annual cycle simply takes place "in Dagan's temple," *i-na* É ᵈDa-gan (446.96), and the second *kubadu* in Emar 452 occurs before the *a-bi-i* of the same temple (lines 43-46).

The ceremonies during the NIN.DINGIR festival are the *kubadu rabû* (GAL), 369.10 and 30, as are the *kubadu* at the tomb in the Abû cycle (452.35, GAL) and the one in the rites for doors (463.4, *ra-ba-a*). There is

---

288 Emar 446.55-56 is imbedded in an extremely obscure section of the text. Line 54 mentions a sacrifice (verb *ṭabāḫu*) for Dagan in a confused context. The next lines specify a particular sort of *kubadu*, *a-na* x MA *da-ri-ia u a-na da-na*-x[(?)], which I cannot translate. This may qualify the execution of the *kubadu* for the stated sacrifice rather than introduce a new element in the ritual sequence.

289 This placement of a *kubadu* at an important Emar burial site does not necessarily restrict the ceremony to the context of mourning and ritual for the dead. Most other instances show no sign of involvement with this realm.

also the *kubadu* TUR (*ṣeḫru*), 373.59, 171, 177; 452.14?, 45. In the cycle for the month of Abû, both GAL (lines 34-35) and TUR (lines 44-45) versions include lists of offerings, with the TUR-list longer than the GAL-list. We should not rule out that the adjectives simply reflect the significance of the offering, expressed by size. The one point of overlap between the lists is sheep, and the "great" *kubadu* includes two, versus one in the "lesser." Aside from the question of the offerings' size, the "great" *kubadu* should provide the greater honor. This would be appropriate to the great event for ᵈIM, and the great *kubadu* in Emar 452 takes place at the grave, which may be the most important sacred site of that ritual cycle.

Note that the "*kubati*" appears in the Hittite letters from Emar, which record oracles conducted at the city. One of these deals with a fraud which is said to have involved the *kubati*, and two sheep are required as reparation. Such a penalty would be appropriate for theft of offering materials.[290]

The noun *kubadu* is not known in Akkadian, though the root *kbd/t* is common in ancient Semitic languages of both east and west. In Akkadian, the character of the dental is not always made clear by the spelling, but the "*d*" generally belongs to the dialects of Mari, Boghazkoy, Amarna, and Ugarit, as well as Old Assyrian.[291] The word *kubadu* should have something to do with the derivative meaning, "honor" (from the root, "to be heavy").[292] Emar attests a similar but separate word in legal documents, the *kubuddā'u*, which defines some part of heritable property.[293]

---

290 See E. Laroche, in *Le Moyen Euphrate*, 241; Msk 73.107+127, a royal letter sent to the Hittite officer, Alziyamuwa.

291 Compare the dictionary articles on *kabātu*, *kabtu*, *kubbutu*, and *kubtu*. The *quttalu* form is the D infinitive at Ugarit (Huehnergard, personal communication), but we do not find **ku-ub-ba-du/di* at Emar, and the D infinitive is usually *qattulu* at Emar. Most of the evidence for this comes from Emar 369 itself: *i-na q*[*a-ad*(?)-*du*]-*ši ša gal-lu-bi*, line 6; *gal-lu-bu ša* NIN.DINGIR, line 7; *i-na qa-dú-ši ša ma-al-lu-ki*, line 22; and *ma-al-lu-ku ša* NIN.DINGIR, line 29. The words *qaddušu*, *gallubu*, and *malluku* are D infinitives (or infinitival nouns).

292 John Huehnergard translates **kubuddatu* at Ugarit as "honorary gift"; see *Ugaritic Vocabulary*, 135, KBD-b; the form is the plural *ku-bu-da-ti*, in PRU 3 98f:6-8. Sivan, *Grammatical Analysis and Glossary*, 238, translates "thing of value, honorary gift." The Ugaritic term *kbd* appears frequently in administrative lists with the apparent meaning "in tutto," without limitation to cultic contexts. See Mario Liverani, "*Kbd* nei testi amministrativi ugaritici," *UF* 2 (1970) 89-108; cf. G. del Olmo Lete, "Catalogo de los festivales regios des Ugarit (KTU 1.91)" *UF* 19 (1987) 11-12.

293 See Emar 112.11, 14; 198.5; *AuOr* 5 236, no.15 (ME 124), lines 13, 25; and J.-M. Durand and F. Joannes, "*kubuddâ'u* à Mari et Emar," *N.A.B.U.* 1990, 53-54 (no.70). Durand and Joannes argue against Arnaud that the word does not refer to a "dowry" only.

In sum, the *kubadu* is performed prior to making an offering in order to honor the god before killing the animal or handing over the gift. The offerers would honor the god by submitting themselves and their offerings before daring to assume either would be acceptable.

3. ^{d}NIN.KUR's Role

The goddess ^{d}NIN.KUR is closely identified with the NIN.DINGIR priestess through her installation. Oil for her anointing comes from ^{d}NIN.KUR's temple, along with the palace (lines 4, 20). Then, as part of the *qaddušu*-preparation for the enthronement and ensuing celebration, ^{d}NIN.KUR enters the house of the NIN.DINGIR's father, where she is laid down (*niālu* Š, 369.22-23) and clothed with a red wool garment (*ana muḫḫi...šakānu*, line 23). In the evening of the enthronement day, after the priestess returns home from ^{d}IM's temple in procession with the divine weapon (line 45), the weapon is put on ^{d}NIN.KUR as well (again, *ana muḫḫi...šakānu*, line 46). The goddess wears the weapon for the seven days of celebration while feasts are held in the *bīt* NIN.DINGIR at ^{d}IM's temple, and the priestess stays with ^{d}NIN.KUR. Finally, ^{d}NIN.KUR's departure from the father's house when she is raised up (*tebû*, Š, line 60) signals the end of the NIN.DINGIR's stay there as well, and the divine weapon accompanies the priestess back to ^{d}IM's temple in the last procession (lines 63-64).

Among the above aspects of ^{d}NIN.KUR's role, lying down in the father's house and rising from it constitute the crucial framework, and this is the one feature that appears elsewhere in Emar ritual. The practice of moving ^{d}NIN.KUR into some ritual location does not turn out to be a trait of the installations in particular. ^{d}NIN.KUR does not even appear in the *maš'artu* installation (Emar 370), and she is laid down in two rituals from the *kissu* set that have no apparent connection with installation of any kind. These two rituals are Emar 385.1-26 and Emar 388, the rites that form an envelope for the *kissu* set. Emar 385.1-26 is called "the *kissu* festival of Šatappi" (line 1), though the next line declares that this *kissu* is performed for Dagan. In the *kissu* rituals directed at other specific deities, Dagan's temple is the sacred site that unites them all: ^{d}EREŠ.KI.GAL, feasting "in his temple," *i-na* É-*šú*, 385.38; Ea, feasting "in the temple of Dagan," *ina* É ^{d}KUR, 386.20; and Išḫara and ^{d}NIN.URTA, the gods themselves doing something in Dagan's temple, *ina* É ^{d}KUR *ú*-[...], 387.25, text F. On the sanctification day of the *kissu* of Šatappi, ᵈNIN.KUR is laid down in Dagan's temple, the common center of the *kissu* set (*niālu* Š, 385.5). As in the NIN.DINGIR installation, she is raised (*tebû* Š, line 21) on the last day of the festival, and her departure sets in motion the concluding events of the ritual.

Emar 388 is directed toward all the *kissu* rituals, either in their individual performance or somehow collectively. It begins, "on the day of sanctification of the *kissu* festivals...," *i-na* u_4*-mi ša qa-du-ši ša* ᵉᶻᵉⁿ·ᵐᵉˢ̌*ki-is-sí* (line 1). In the first stated action, ᵈNIN.KUR is laid down in the place (É) of the *bēl bīti*, the ritual supplier of the NIN.DINGIR installation and apparently of the *kissu*'s as well (line 1-2, *niālu* Š). Unfortunately, Emar 388 is damaged so severely that it is difficult to get a sense of the whole ritual, but the first section shows a continued interest in the *bēl bīti* (lines 10, 18) and affairs of food preparation. Her rising is lost.

ᵈNIN.KUR's visits to the NIN.DINGIR's family home, Dagan's temple, and the place of the *kissu* festival *bēl bīti*, make a unique and remarkable part of Emar ritual. No other deity enters another temple, never mind what would seem to be the profane territory of a private household -- the father's house, and perhaps also the place of the *bēl bīti* (see above).[294] What can be the significance of her lying down in and rising from these diverse locations? While the nuances may vary, the paired actions should display fundamentally the same function in all three instances. In the context of the NIN.DINGIR installation, it is tempting to interpret her actions as symbolic death and rising, either as a pattern for the transition from old to new in the office, mourning the previous priestess, or as a picture of the new NIN.DINGIR's own death in her rite of passage.[295] Alternatively, lying down could simply indicate taking up residence as a house-guest. The *ḫamša'u*-men lie down in the *maš'artu*'s temple residence for the seven days of her installation, *it-*[*t*]*a-lu* (*i/utūlu*, 370.31). In this view the significance of the stay would be derived more directly from each context.

---

294 The person who plays this role may be either a man or a woman, as seen in the fragment Emar 410.6, where ᵈNIN.KUR is laid down in the residence of the *bēlet bīti*, [*i-na* É GA]ŠAN É-*ti* ᵈNIN.KUR *uš-na-*[*al-lu*].

295 The dying-and-rising of ᵈNIN.KUR is suggested by Arnaud, *Bulletin de la Société Ernest Renan* 1979, 118. Mary Douglas, *Purity and Danger: An Analysis of Concepts of Pollution and Taboo*, New York: Frederick A. Praeger, 1966, 96, observes that initiation rites often use the symbol of death and rebirth: "the initiates die to their old life and are reborn to the new."

In all three examples of this rite, ^{d}NIN.KUR is laid down during the *qaddušu* ceremonies, and her stay is associated with two other rituals: the setting of four tables for the gods and the cries of the *nugagtu* (see below). In Emar 388.1-4, ^{d}NIN.KUR is laid down in the place of the *bēl bīti* and she plays host to a sacrifice for the gods.[296] The *nugagtu* gives her cry, and four tables are set before the gods.[297] In the *kissu* of Šatappi the same cluster of rites is placed at the end of the description of the sanctification day (385.5-9). ^{d}NIN.KUR is laid down in Dagan's temple, and she herself receives the same sacrifice of one ox and one sheep. The *nugagtu* gives her cry after the sacrifice but before the meat is placed before ^{d}NIN.KUR, and then four tables are set, one table for Dagan, one for Išḫara and ^{d}NIN.URTA, and two "on the ground" for Alal and Amaza, underworld deities (cf. DINGIR.MEŠ KI.TA, 369.24-25). In the NIN.DINGIR installation, ^{d}NIN.KUR is laid down only at the second *qaddušu*, for the enthronement, and four tables are set for the gods, one each for ^{d}IM and another deity (Hebat?), and two "on the ground" for the underworld gods (369.23-25). The cry of the *nugagtu* is not mentioned until line 48, when the divine weapon is placed on ^{d}NIN.KUR.

Finally, if the *kissu* rituals are indeed "throne" festivals for the gods (see below), ^{d}NIN.KUR is always laid down in preparation for an enthronement. If the *nugagtu*'s cry is a lament (see below), and the special consideration for underworld gods in the table offerings reflects attention to death, the image of ^{d}NIN.KUR dying and rising seems plausible for the *kissu* festivals as well as the installation. The symbolic death would not then be confined narrowly to human initiation but might belong to the wider realm of all enthronement, when perhaps the powers of life are renewed against the pull of death.

Within the larger framework of ^{d}NIN.KUR's lying down and rising, the NIN.DINGIR installation provides two more details. When the goddess is laid down, she is clothed with a red wool garment from her own temple (see lines 23 and 60), and ^{d}NIN.KUR wears the divine weapon for seven days at the father's house (line 46).

Only the two installations mention the red wool garment at Emar (369.23, 60; 370.17), though the context is not the same. The *maš'artu* installation instance occurs during the night after the consecration day (the

---

296 The sacrifice is to (*ana*) ^{d}NIN.KUR, but the meat is given to the gods (see above).
297 The table setting is qualified by the phrase *ki-i* ^{níg}PEŠ.KU, which remains obscure (possibly, "as an inheritance"??).

first), in a ritual with a bed and chair that recalls the final day of the NIN.DINGIR festival (369.70-71). An *i'lu*-vestment (^{túg}GUZ.ZA) and the red wool garment are perhaps spread out on the bed, *i-na* ŠÀ-*šu* [...], following 369.71, where the Akkadian garment is laid out thus. In the NIN.DINGIR festival, the red wool garment belongs to ^{d}NIN.KUR, and it is returned to her temple with the goddess herself.[298]

We expect the garment, ^{túg}ḪÉ.ME.DA, to be read *tabarru*, as opposed to *nabāsu*, both "red wool."[299] Both nouns occur in peripheral Akkadian texts of the late second millennium, but the Hurrian loanword *tabarru* is particularly widespread for that period, appearing at Nuzi, Amarna, Ugarit, and Alalaḫ, as well as in Assyrian and Babylonian texts (*AHw* s.v. *tabarru* 1, 2, and 3). The editors of *CAD* (*nabāsu*, final note) follow Landsberger and Ungnad in concluding that the logogram ^{síg}ḪÉ.ME.DA has the reading *tabarru* from the MB period on, though von Soden is less sure (see *AHw* s.v. *tabarru* 4). The lexical text Emar 556.19 (Ḫḫ., B: Msk 74190j) offers the equation, síg-gan(ḫé)-me-da : *na-ba-su* : *i-ki-ṭu*. Apparently, the Akkadian *nabāsu* survives in MB lexical contexts, and the Emar reading should be indicated by the gloss, *ikiṭu*.

The material of ^{d}NIN.KUR's garment is the same as the red wool of the headdress that is put on the NIN.DINGIR at her enthronement (369.42). It might be tempting to connect the color red with death or mourning, but the headdress of the priestess should be part of her permanent regalia, and perhaps the color simply pertains to her honor or stature. The fact that ^{d}NIN.KUR specially wears the same color for her stay with the priestess may be related to her other service, wearing the divine weapon for the same period. Perhaps ^{d}NIN.KUR becomes a substitute for the priestess during this time when she may not yet take on the responsibilities of her office. This would make sense in connection with a death and rebirth image for this transitional stage.

---

298 It is interesting that the excavators found two fragments of female figurines in chantier D which were covered with red paint; J. Margueron, "Rapport préliminaire sur les 3e, 4e, 5e et 6e campagnes de fouilles à Meskéné-Emar," *AAAS* 32 (1982) 235. This paint recalls the red garments of the installation festivals.

299 See *AHw* s.v. *tabarru*; *AHw* s.v. *nabāsu(m)*; *CAD* s.v. *nabāsu*. Moran reads *tabarru* for ^{síg}ḪÉ.ME.TA in the Amarna letters; see EA 22, note 11. The color red is indicated by comparison with blood; e.g., *damēšunu kīma na-pa-si šadû lū aṣrup*, "with their blood I dyed the mountain as red as dyed wool" (AKA 272 i 53, in *CAD* s.v. *nabāsu* a).

4. The nugagtu's Cries

On the enthronement day ("the third day," *i-na* 3 *u*$_4$*-mi*) of the NIN.DINGIR installation, a personage found only in Emar festivals gives forth ritual cries, ^{f}*nu-gag*^{ag}*-tu*$_4$ BÚN SUM (*killa inandin*), 369.48. The title *nugagtu* is discussed above (see human participants); this female ritual player has no function other than to give her wailing. She appears on the sanctification day of the *maš'artu* installation (^{f}*nu-ga*$_5$*-ag-tu*$_4$, 370.14; not in line 3, vs. Arnaud),[300] on the first day of some broken ritual instruction (^{f}*nu-ga*$_5$*-ag-*[*tu*$_4$], 421.4; cf. *i-na* U$_4$.2.KÁM of line 5, after a section divider), and ^{f}*nu-*[...] in 393.26 may begin her title. However, the only texts which witness the *nugagtu* in an intelligible context are the same ones that mention ^{d}NIN.KUR (see above).

The logogram BÚN is a new spelling for *killu,* only illuminated by the syllabic spelling in 388.4, *ki-il-la-ši.* The Akkadian noun *ikkillu/killu* refers to loud wailing, and in particular to the ritual wailing at death (see *AHw* s.v. *ikkillu(m)* 1, *CAD* s.v. *ikkillu* b). It appears that the Emar *nugagtu* is a lamentation priestess who performs this ritual wailing in mourning for ^{d}NIN.KUR's symbolic death. In the NIN.DINGIR installation this becomes part of the imagery for the transitional period after the death of the previous priestess and before the new priestess fully takes on the office.

F. THE NIN.DINGIR'S PROGRESS

The remaining ritual actions in the NIN.DINGIR festival are those which pertain directly to her installation as high priestess, and which move her through the ceremony from her place in her father's house as a daughter of a prominent Emar citizen to a new role as head of ^{d}IM's household. These actions are clustered about key festival events: selection and anointing of the priestess, shaving for purification, enthronement with the accompanying homage and decoration, presentation of figurines to ^{d}IM and Hebat, and all the

---

300 Instead of BÚN, which is not otherwise found with the verb *(w)aṣû,* perhaps read [^{d}*Iš*$_8$*-tár*] MÈ(?) *ú-še-ṣu-ni* [ ], "they will bring out Aštart of the battle(?)," cf. 370.20.

events which mark the final day. Mention of her death at the end of the administrative section is treated here as well.

1. Selection and Anointing

Emar's two installation festivals give us a unique look at the whole process by which temple officials were put in office. Besides coronation rites for kings, we have very little information about ancient Mesopotamian practice, in spite of the vast numbers of Akkadian and Sumerian texts. One of the most interesting aspects of the installation of priestly personnel is the selection itself, and the A-text of the NIN.DINGIR festival provides a single brief account for the particular case of one priestess. Unfortunately, the beginnings of the *maš'artu* text and the other NIN.DINGIR texts are lost.

The general term for initiating the installation of the NIN.DINGIR is the verb *našû*, "to elevate," which has this sense only in this one Emar occurrence. However, the use of *našû* for elevating or dedicating someone to sacred office is known in Old Babylonian texts (including Mari), Middle Assyrian law, and later Babylonian writings.[301] In the earlier texts there is a notable association of the formula with dedications to Adad: Grant Smith College 260:4 (OB), a *qadištum*-priestess to Adad; ARM 8 28:18 (Mari), a daughter as some priestess to ^{d}IM *ša App*[*an*]; and KAJ 179:4 (MA), a priestess to Adad. The usual pattern involves a father dedicating a daughter; although the father's role in the NIN.DINGIR installation reflects this responsibility, the subject of *našû* here is not the father, but the "sons of Emar." Only the *kissu* for Dagan begins similarly (385.2, text A): *e-nu-ma* LÚ(.MEŠ, text D) DUMU.MEŠ ^{uru}*Ša-tap-pí* ^{ezen}*ki-is-sà a-na* ^{d}KUR *ep-pa-aš* (*ep-pa-šu*, text D), "when the man/men of the sons of Šatappi perform(s) the *kissu* for Dagan..." It is interesting that while the NIN.DINGIR installation is identified as a "festival" (EZEN, 369.48), the term is not part of the introduction to the text. One Emar letter includes a complaint that someone has failed to install (*šakānu*, 268.9-10, 15, 18, 24) a man as a priest (*a-na* ^{lú}SANGA, line 14; *a-na* ^{lú}SANGA-*ut-ti ša* ^{d}NIN.KUR, lines 7-9, 22-23).

---

301 See *CAD* s.v. *našû* A 1c, especially 1', "with the position specified"; *AHw* s.v. *našû(m)* II GI5c, especially *alpha*, "im Kult."

The priestess is elevated by "the sons of Emar," and "the daughter of any son of Emar"[302] may be selected. This is a remarkable qualification, and the explicit declaration may constitute a deliberate response to claims on the office by royalty or other powerful citizens. Any candidate would still come from a leading Emar family, as seen by the wealth required for the family gifts prescribed at the enthronement (lines 40-41, 45). However, the inclusion of such a clause seems to reflect an underlying antipathy to royal domination in religious affairs.

The selection of the NIN.DINGIR consists of two rites, identification by means of the *purû* and anointing by pouring oil on her head. The candidate for NIN.DINGIR is "identified" (*tarāṣu*, N)[303] by ᵈIM himself by *purû*, surely some means of divination. The choice of the verb *ṣabātu* for "holding" the *purû* may not explain the manner of its use, since the verb often describes the handling of tools or implements according to their normal function. Examples listed in the *CAD* (s.v. *ṣabātu* 3j) involve balances, a hoe, a stylus, reins, a bow, a plow, etc. All of these are held with the hands, however, and the *purû*-divination should likewise involve holding or handling some implement; "lots" would make sense with this verb. Akkadian *pūru* can refer to a bowl (*AHw* s.v. *pūru* I)[304] or to a lot (*pūru(m)* II), both of which could conceivably fit the divination context. Until the late period, *pūru* as "lot" occurs only in Assyria and at Nuzi, and the verbs which express use of the lot are characteristically Assyrian, *karāru* and *ṣalā'u* (see Müller, MVAG 41/III), "to cast." No other texts combine *pūru* and *ṣabātu*, which together form an idiom not attested in Mesopotamian divination.

Although in Mesopotamia the use of a bowl would suggest divination by pouring oil on water (lecanomancy), classical Greek tradition of the oracle at

---

302 See the notes to the translation on the indefinite pronoun *ayyimmê*. The masculine pronoun should modify the masculine DUMU "son," though it precedes it; for other examples of this word order, see BoSt 8 102f:37, 45; *AASOR* 16 91:10; and EA 27:35, in *AHw* s.v. *ajjummē* (cf. *CAD* s.v. *ajumma*).

303 The basic meaning of *tarāṣu* is "to stretch out," often of limbs (*AHw* s.v. *tarāṣu(m)* I G1) or other parts of the body (G2) when people are concerned. The Emar use is unusual in that it lacks any such referent for *tarāṣu*; it is the priestess herself who is "stretched out." In the Code of Hammurabi "to stretch out the finger (*ubānum*)" means "to point out" or "to identify" (CH law 127, Š conjugation), and the passive is "to be pointed out/identified" (CH law 132, N). I have translated *tarāṣu* as "to identify" in the NIN.DINGIR installation, with reference to these examples. This interpretation of *tarāṣu* was suggested to me by P. Steinkeller, personal communication.

304 This word is attested in Mesopotamian MA and MB texts as well as at Boghazkoy.

Delphi may involve a shallow bowl which holds lots, echoing both possible meanings of Akkadian *pūru*.[305] A text for the tariff of Sciathus mentions a decision by two beans, and the Greek verb that describes the Pythia's oracular answer at Delphi is *anhairein*, "to pick up." The Greek lot then may involve beans of two colors picked from a bowl.[306] A reference in Cleisthenes from the end of the sixth century B.C.E. describes selection of ten heroes from a list of one hundred.[307] These examples from the later Mediterranean world do not resolve the problem of what exactly is performed in the Emar festival, but they do provide one possible scenario.

Sollberger says that OB year names show that EN-priestesses were designated by extispicy,[308] but no animal appears to be involved in the selection of the Emar NIN.DINGIR.

Once the chosen candidate has been selected by ᵈIM, she may be anointed by having fine oil placed (*šakānu*) on her head, 369.4. Then, at the end of the shaving day, she is anointed again before she returns to her father's house by oil poured on her head (*tabāku*, lines 20-21). The verb *tabāku* (line 21) is a common word for pouring oil on the head (see *AHw* s.v. *tabāku(m)* G4, especially c; *CAD* s.v. *qaqqadu* 1a4'), in contrast to *pašāšu*, which more often is applied to rubbing oil on the body or on objects (*AHw* s.v. *pašāšu(m)*). The verb *šakānu* is unusual, and I have observed only one instance with anointing the head, in EA 51:6. During the late second millennium, the practice of anointing seems to be characteristic of Assyria and the periphery, and is not attested in Babylon.

There are no other examples of anointing people in the Emar Akkadian texts, but a rite performed at closure of a sale includes anointing a table: "they

---

305 On the Greek evidence, see J.S. Morrison, "The classical world," in Michael Loewe and Carmen Blacker eds., *Oracles and Divination*, Boulder, CO: Shambhala, 1981, 98-100 and Pl. 8. A vase painting shows the Pythia of Delphi seated, "gazing at a flat dish which she holds in her left hand," with a man facing her, presumably the enquirer.

306 See H.W. Parke, *Greek Oracles*, London: Hutchinson University Library, 1967, 85-86 and n.22; cf. Morrison, in *Oracles and Divination*, 98-100.

307 Parke, *Greek Oracles*, 86.

308 See E. Sollberger, "The temple in Babylonia," in RAI 20, 34 and n.13: maš-e ì-pà, "the (omen-)kid chose."

received the silver; their heart is satisfied; *ḫukku*-bread is broken, the table is anointed with oil."[309]

Anointing is widely understood as a rite of purification. Thorkild Jacobsen has interpreted the Sumerian GUDU-sign as UḪ(louse)+IŠIB(anointed, Akkadian *pašīšu*), so that anointing originated in Mesopotamia quite literally as a cleansing.[310] If this model is correct, the practice of anointing pillars or stones, which so precisely parallels the pouring of oil on the priestess in the NIN.DINGIR installation (line 35A, cf. B(31-36)b-c), should ultimately be in imitation of human anointing. Walter Burkert proposes an interesting alternative in the context of Greek ritual, which likewise attests anointing of stones. Such libations had been understood as offerings, but Burkert argues that the oil is more likely put on the stones simply to mark them. The stones are thus distinguished as sacred territory.[311] If the practice of anointing stones has an independent origin, cleansing from lice makes less sense than marking to set apart as sacred, and human anointing likewise could have originated in marking rather than purification. Once the two practices are established, the alternative interpretations may be indistinguishable, since both prepare for entry into service in the divine sphere.

The NIN.DINGIR is anointed twice during the installation, and I am aware of no other instance of such repetition of the rite. When the priestess is selected anointing is the rite that first marks her as ^{d}IM's. Perhaps the second anointing, before she returns to her father's house after the shaving day, renews this identification, since she is now effectively on loan back to her father. It is possible that the shaving itself makes necessary the repetition, if her anointed hair has been removed. Finally, the fact of two anointings further emphasizes the separation of the shaving day as a ritual event unto itself, as discussed above.

---

309 ^{ninda}*ḫu-ku ka-si*$_{17}$*-ip* ^{giš}BANŠUR Ì.GIŠ *pa-ši-iš*, 20.16-19; see also 109.17-18; 110.23-24, and more. The reading *si*$_{17}$ for ŠI reflects the occasional confusion of sibilants at Emar. The first idioms tend to alternate 3ms and 3mp reference to the seller (and his relatives). The new texts from Mumbaqat/Ekalte now attest the same idiom, with the same spelling of *kasip* with *š*: MBQ-T 21:15-16, ^{ninda}*ḫu-un-gu ka-ši-ip* ^{giš}BANŠUR Ì.GIŠ *pa-ši-iš*; MBQ-T 35:19-20, ^{ninda}*ḫu-gu ka-šip* ^{giš}BANŠUR GIŠ.Ì *pa-ši-iš*, in W. Mayer, *MDOG* 122 55, 60.

310 T. Jacobsen, W.L. Moran ed., *Toward the Image of Tammuz and Other Essays on Mesopotamian History and Culture*, Cambridge: Harvard University Press, 1970, n.11, pp. 325-326.

311 See Burkert, *Structure and History*, 41-43.

The meaning and origin of the practice of anointing have been thoroughly discussed by biblical scholars because the rite is so prominent in accounts of selecting both kings and priests. Martin Noth and Roland de Vaux, two leading students of Israelite religious practices, consider that priests were not anointed among the Jews until after the Exile,[312] since the biblical tradition is largely confined to the priestly materials of the Pentateuch, and we do not have evidence for earlier anointing of priests elsewhere in the ancient Near East.[313] Thus, while anointing is quite frequently mentioned in Akkadian writings, this Emar festival provides the first known instance of anointing a priest.

It should be observed that anointing by pouring oil on the head is also part of wedding ritual in Middle Assyrian law[314] and in diplomatic correspondence from the late second millennium B.C.E.[315] However, women of this period may be anointed for other purposes as well. One legal document from Ugarit records anointing specifically linked to an act of manumission from status as a prostitute (^{sal}KID.KAR/*ḫarimūtu*): *aštapak šamna ana qaqqadīša u uzakkīša*, "I poured oil on her head and so freed her."[316] Pardee finds that the anointing of a woman in the Ugaritic letter RS 34 124:26'-29' at least leaves in doubt whether any marriage is involved and appears to be

312 Martin Noth, *The Laws in the Pentateuch and Other Essays*, Philadelphia: Fortress Press, 1967, 237-238; Roland de Vaux, *Ancient Israel: Its Life and Institutions*, New York: McGraw-Hill, 1961, 105, 347.

313 De Vaux argues this on page 105, whereas Noth bases his case on internal biblical evidence primarily and says that anointing priests is known in Hatti (page 239 n.29). One Mesopotamian temple official that must be accounted for is the $GUDU_4$/*pašīšu*, whose title is derived from *pašāšu*, "to anoint." The name means "anointed," and the etymolological association of the Sumerian title with lice suggests the head, but this may alternatively refer to rubbing oil on the body rather than pouring/placing oil on the head. The verb *pašāšu* most often describes the former, though the latter is attested (for *pašāšu* with *qaqqadu*, see *AHw* s.v. *pašāšu(m)* G1a). Renger, *ZA* 59 143, notes that the form *pašīšum* is made certain by the writing *pa-ši-i-šu* in *RA* 17 196.

314 See *CAD* s.v. *qaqqadu* 1a4' and H.W.F. Saggs, *The Might that was Assyria*, London: Sidgwick and Jackson, 1984, 142.

315 Ernst Kutsch, *Salbung als Rechtsakt im Alten Testament und im Alten Orient*, Berlin: Verlag Alfred Topelmann, 1963, 27-29, lists the Amarna letters EA 29:22f (Tušratta of Mitanni to Amenophis IV) and EA 31:11-14 (Amenophis III to Tarḫundaraba of Arzawa), as well as two letters to Ramses II from Puduḫepa, queen of Hatti (see KUB III 63 Vs 2.15f). See also Artzi, "Political Marriages," 26, and Moran, EA 11, note 7.

316 PRU 3 110:8 (= RS 8.208:8, *Syria* 18 253-254); see Kutsch, *Salbung*, 16-17.

associated with atonement for some wrong.[317] Anointing by pouring oil on the head also accompanies the confirmation of various binding contracts.[318]

The Bible records the anointing of several Israelite rulers,[319] but this practice is not much better attested outside of the Bible than the anointing of priests. A New Kingdom Hittite prayer to the storm god of Nerik mentions that king Tudḫaliya is anointed, but this is "for the priesthood" at the provincial cities of Hakmiš and Nerik, and is not clearly associated with installation as king.[320] The Amarna letter EA 51:6-9 from Adad-nirari of Assyria mentions the anointing of a local official named Taku as king of Nuḫašše, a region in northern Syria that is not far from Emar, and EA 34:50ff speaks of oil sent by the king of Alašiya (Cyprus) to the king of Egypt which is to be poured on the head of the Egyptian king, "puisque [*inūma*] tu t'es assis sur ton trône royal."[321] The last example may reflect Cypriote rather than Egyptian practice.

The anointing of the NIN.DINGIR at Emar sets her apart for a new status as priestess and for entry into the service of [d]IM. There should be no barrier to considering the rite as a new example of anointing in ritual for the installation of priests.[322]

---

317 Dennis Pardee, "A new Ugaritic letter," *BiOr* 34 (1977) 4, 17-18. Pardee says that anointing is essentially a purification rite used to prepare for change in status where ritual purity is a safeguard against disaster. Applied to kings and priests, it prepares them to pass into the semi-divine sphere.

318 Kutsch, *Salbung*, 17-18; the buyer and seller are frequently anointed in OB period records for the sale of land or slaves. See also Tryggve Mettinger, *King and Messiah: The Civil and Sacral Legitimation of the Israelite Kings*, Lund: C.W.K. Gleerup, 1976, 228, and examples in the *CAD* entry for *qaqqadu*, 1a4'.

319 For example Saul as *nāgîd*/commander (1 Sam 10.1) and David as *melek*/king (1 Sam 16.13, cf. v 1); see Kutsch, *Salbung*, 52ff., for a full treatment.

320 KUB XXXVI 90, pp. 15-18; see Kutsch, *Salbung*, 36-37; Johannes Friedrich, "Ein Sonderfall partitiver Apposition beim hethitischen Personal Pronomen," *AfO* 18 (1957/8) 127. Perhaps this instance should be accounted as evidence for anointing priests rather than kings, since the act seems to install the king as priest of the cults at these cities.

321 See Kutsch, *Salbung*, 34-35, 41-42; the translation is from Moran, *El-Amarna*, 199.

322 The biblical testimony to anointing Israelite priests should be re-evaluated. Emar's NIN.DINGIR of [d]IM is a person delivered into service of a god and the Israelite record of anointing priests may derive from this ancient legal tradition applied to divine service, and may not be a late application of defunct royal tradition to post-exilic high priests. One remarkable link between Emar practice and biblical tradition is found in the anointing of stelae. On the enthronement day, the NIN.DINGIR pours oil on the "head" (top) of the *sikkānu* of the goddess Hebat (369.35), and Jacob does the same to a *maṣṣēbâ*, or "standing stone," for El at Bethel in Gen 28.18 (cf. 31.13; 35.14).

Jacob anoints the *maṣṣēbâ* at Bethel to consecrate it for use at this shrine, and the NIN.DINGIR may anoint the *sikkānu* of Hebat with similar purpose. It seems likely that she dedicates a *new* stone to enter the household of [d]IM in the *bīt* Gadda, just as she is about to enter the household of [d]IM as his priestess. The NIN.DINGIR thus dedicates the stone by the rite of anointing just as she was dedicated earlier in the ritual.

2. Shaving

The first full day of the NIN.DINGIR festival, after the confirmation and anointing, is identified as the *gallubu* of the priestess (369.7, 39; cf. line 6, its sanctification ceremony). The action itself takes place immediately on arrival at ᵈIM's temple, after the first procession (lines 8-9), "at the opening of the gate of the courtyard," *a-na pí-i* KÁ *ta-ar-ba-ṣi*. Although this represents the sole mention of the shaving, the fact that the entire day is identified by the shaving rite demonstrates that the great procession, sacrifice, and feast all serve to support and celebrate this one stage in the NIN.DINGIR's progress.

What rite does the verb *gallubu* indicate? The basic meaning of Akkadian *gullubu* is "to shave" (*CAD* s.v. *gullubu* 1; *AHw* s.v. *gullubu(m)* II 1). When referring to humans, the shaving may be to remove half the hair as punishment (*muttata gullubu*, *CAD* 1a1', *AHw* II 1a), to leave an *abbuttu*-lock characteristic of slaves, or to remove it (*CAD* 1a2', 3'; *AHw* II 1b, c), or for other purposes (see *CAD* 1b; *AHw* II 1d, e). The verb *gullubu* also means "to consecrate a priest or a craftsman connected with the temple (by shaving the hair of his head and body)" (*CAD* 2, cf. *AHw* II 2), and the Emar instance must be related to this use, though the Mesopotamian examples come only from the first millennium. This consecration is literally a matter of shaving, not just dressing the hair,[323] and the purpose seems to have been cleansing,[324] just as with the anointing.

Our modern bias may make it difficult to imagine this shaving for a female priestess, but in fact none of the dictionary examples involve women, and we have no evidence of such shaving for women. No detail is provided in the NIN.DINGIR installation, though the Akkadian idiom usually mentions the part of the body shaved -- hair, head, beard, etc. It is not apparent whether just the head or the whole body is involved. Two options are most likely:

---

[323] Neither Arnaud nor Dietrich comment on the precise meaning of *gallubu* in the installation, but both envision cutting of head hair only. Arnaud translates the infinitive noun as "coiffure" and Dietrich, *UF* 21 78, "Tonsur" (stronger?). Dietrich translates the verb, "(am Haupthaar) scheren" (p.79).

[324] In cultic contexts, shaving is attested "in connection with services performed in sanctuaries, mostly cleaning duties"; *CAD* s.v. *gallābu*, "barber," end comment; compare *gallābūtu* 2, "to submit to a cleansing of the body by the *gallābu*."

either the priestess is actually shaved (partly or completely) for ritual cleansing, or some part of her hair is shaved or cut to produce a hair-dressing that is symbolic of her office.[325]

Whatever the exact treatment of the NIN.DINGIR's hair, the shaving is a rite of submission. The Akkadian *gullubu* is performed for two primary categories, temple personnel and slaves. Both groups face entry into service. When the act is performed by another person bearing a knife or other sharp instrument it carries at least symbolic danger and humbles the object. Burkert comments on Greek votive offerings that involved cutting and dedicating one's own hair to some deity: "By dedicating his hair, a man surrenders a part of himself to a higher power."[326]

In Arnold van Gennep's scheme of "rites of passage," major life-changes are marked in many societies by transitional rituals that may be divided into three categories: rites of separation from the old life and world, of transition, and of incorporation into the new situation.[327] According to van Gennep, the cutting of hair is intrinsically a rite of separation; the original hair identifies the person with family, sex, and class. Likewise a haircut can mark incorporation into a new group or stage of life, if that style is permanent.[328] The shaving of the NIN.DINGIR may thus mark the passage of the priestess both out of her identity with her family and into the service of ᵈIM. The symbolic submission is also characteristic of the transitional ("liminal") period between departure from the old life and entry into the new.[329] Finally, rites of passage are typically given a concrete spacial expression by placement at physical thresholds, especially doors, which represent the boundary between the two worlds.[330] The NIN.DINGIR is shaved "at the opening of the gate of the courtyard" at ᵈIM's temple, on her first arrival there with the sacrificial procession (so the verb *kašādu*, line 8). The gate is the threshold to the new world of the NIN.DINGIR, as well as the point of submission to the authority

---

325 The *kezertu* ("prostitute") is identified by a special hair-style, and the verb *kezēru* means, "to furnish with the hair-style of a *kezertu*"; compare the *CAD*, "to curl the hair," and the *AHw*, "mit einer bestimmten Haartracht (Zopf?) versehen."
326 Burkert, *Greek Religion*, 71.
327 Arnold van Gennep, M.B. Vizedom and G.L. Caffee trs., *The Rites of Passage*, Chicago: Univ. of Chicago Press, 1960, 11.
328 *Ibid*, 53-55, 166-167.
329 See Victor Turner, *The Ritual Process: Structure and Anti-Structure*, Chicago: Aldine Publishing Co., 1969, 95-96, 100, 102.
330 Van Gennep, *Rites of Passage*, 19-20.

of the ᵈIM's domain. In the Mesopotamian tale of Ištar's Descent, it is at the gate to the underworld that the goddess sheds her clothing and with it her power to act against the rule of the realm.[331]

The shaving ritual is therefore a rite of separation from the old life of the NIN.DINGIR, with corresponding emphasis on her submission as she enters the service and domain of the storm god. Only once she has bowed to this rite may she be raised high in enthronement.

3. Enthronement

"The installation of the NIN.DINGIR is on the next day" (line 29). This "installation" (*malluku*) probably encompasses both the enthronement of the priestess and the seven days of feasting which that event initiates, since the sanctification of the *malluku* in lines 22-28 prepares for all seven days of ᵈNIN.KUR's stay at the father's house (see above). The term *malluku* only appears as an infinitival noun at Emar, and only in the festivals to put in office the NIN.DINGIR and the *maš'artu*.[332] Akkadian use of the verb *malāku* for "to rule" is only found at Ugarit,[333] reflecting the West Semitic *mlk*. The D conjugation at Emar must derive from the same root and mean "to make rule" or "to put into office." Therefore, I have used the English term "installation."

The installation of the NIN.DINGIR begins with a great procession and sacrifice following the model of the shaving day event (lines 29-39), and the rites that center on the priestess do not begin until the evening (*ana pānī nubatti*, line 40). In the evening, the NIN.DINGIR is set on her throne, given a table, and adorned with various ornaments (lines 40-42), before receiving gifts from her brothers and the elders of Emar and returning in procession to her father's house (lines 43-45). The rites surrounding her enthronement endow the new priestess with the essential accountrements of the NIN.DINGIR's office, and in receiving them she enters into her new identity. Each part of the evening ceremony constitutes a ritual identification with the NIN.DINGIR office, thus a rite of incorporation (van Gennep).

---

331 See the Descent of Ištar, lines 42-62, Akkadian version.

332 The *maš'artu* installation *malluku* likewise covers seven days; 370.20, 41, and see below. Note also *ma-lu-ki* in the tiny fragment 407.1.

333 *CAD* s.v. *malāku* B; *AHw* s.v. *malāku* III; only the G conjugation. See also Huehnergard *Ugaritic Vocabulary*, 147, MLK a, PRU 3 134f:15-16.

Before all else, "they seat the NIN.DINGIR on her throne" (line 40). Enthronement is the central, definitive act of both installation festivals. This is seen in the way the *maš'artu* festival is summarized at the head of its administrative section: *ki-i* ᶠ*maš-ar-tu₄ i-na* ^giš^GU.ZA-*ša uš-š*[*ab*], "when the *maš'artu* sits on her throne...," 370.108. A similar summary begins a parallel part of the NIN.DINGIR administrative section: *ki-i* NIN.DINGIR *i-na šu-kúl-ti-ša uš-šab*, "when the NIN.DINGIR is enthroned at her feast," 369.84 (see discussion of *šūkultu*, above). The statement harks back to the same temporal clause in the body of the text, line 51, where it defines the setting for the presentation of figurines (see below). This event is actually an independent part of the instructions that follow the enthronement of the NIN.DINGIR. Daily offerings are provided for ᵈIM and Hebat for seven days (lines 49-51a), figurines are presented to them "when the NIN.DINGIR is enthroned at her feast," with an offering to Šaḫru (lines 51b-52), and there is a banquet in the ᵈIM temple residence of the NIN.DINGIR (lines 53-58). The priestess is not at the banquet, and *šūkultu* cannot refer to the feast at the *bīt* NIN.DINGIR (line 53). Rather, the temporal clauses refer to the enthronement of line 40 (cf. 370.108, "on her throne"), and *šūkultu* is either a general term for "feast/festival" or, more likely, the word for the meal she is served on a new table immediately after her enthronement (lines 40-41, though she is not said to eat).

Whereas the table given next is new (line 40), and on the final day she receives a bed, a chair, and a footstool for her residence (line 70), the chair on which she is seated is simply "her throne." This may reflect the fact that the throne belongs to the office rather than the individual holder, and in sitting on it, she takes on the entire role, with the attendant duties and honor.

After the NIN.DINGIR is seated on her throne, she is given a new table from her father's house. In the installation festival, tables are never set for groups, whether divine or human. Only the city dignitaries receive tables for their portions from the various feasts: the two NIN.DINGIR's, the *maš'artu*, and the king(s). Perhaps this new table, with its portion of bread, places the new priestess in the elite group of her peers. It is possible that the table of the previous NIN.DINGIR (lines 16, 55) is still being used in the *bīt* NIN.DINGIR until the end of the seven-day feast. The "new" furniture is unique in Emar ritual, though a ^lú^ḪAL is responsible for a list of valuables (for ritual?!) which are called *ú-nu-tu-ú an-nu-tu*$_4$ GIBIL, "these new items" (285.16-17),[334] including bronze utensils and ornaments, bows and arrowheads, gold and silver, and clothing.

Ritual officials clothe the NIN.DINGIR with three decorations. They place gold earrings in her ears, place a gold band on her right wrist ("hand"), and wrap her head with a red wool headdress (369.41-42). The verbs are *šakānu* and *rakāsu*, and none of the actions has an Emar parallel. NÍG.GEŠTUG means "earring" in Sumerian, and perhaps the reading here is *a/inṣabtu*, "earring." The noun *iqqu* appears to be a local form of *unqu*, "ring" (see *AHw* s.v. *unqu(m)*), a common term in second-millennium peripheral texts.[335] It is not certain whether the term denotes a bracelet outside Emar. A silver ring (ŠU.GUR) is placed in the water that washes the NIN.DINGIR's feet on the final day, to be given to her sister (line 75), and one temple inventory includes a "silver ring of the *zābiḫu*-priest," *iq-qu* KÙ.BABBAR *ša* [lú]*za-bi-ḫi*, 282.13.[336] The right hand is the active hand which greets, holds weapons, and carries burdens (see *CAD* s.v. *imittu* A 2), as well as the hand that bears the identifying mark of slaves (see *CAD* s.v. *qātu* 1c). The "headdress" of the NIN.DINGIR is a [túg]BAR.SIG/*paršīgu*, a Babylonian term with strong northern attestation (Nuzi, Boghazkoy, and Alalaḫ; see *AHw* s.v. *parš/sīgu(m)*). It is made of "red wool" ([síg]ḪÉ.ME.DA), the material for [d]NIN.KUR's garment. This occurrence in the priestess' enthronement decoration gives the material a particular association with the NIN.DINGIR office (see above, [d]NIN.KUR's Role).

The OB (level VII) Alalaḫ tablet AT 411 lists gifts received by the governor's daughter at her marriage, and these include earrings (*in-ṣa-ba-at*, line 4), a gold *tudittu*-pin (line 8), and a headdress ([túg]BAR.SI[ig], *paršīgu*, line 10).[337] However, these might simply represent typical female finery appropriate to any woman who is beginning life in a new household. In the

---

334 The word order is unusual; we expect the demonstrative to come last.
335 Note, for instance, the Qatna inventories, I:296, in Bottéro, *RA* 43 15. This identification of *iqqu* was suggested to me by W.L. Moran (personal communication), and Dietrich, *UF* 21 82 n.77 makes the same equation. Durand, *RA* 84 54, observes that *unqum* is known at Mari.
336 ŠU.GUR is the equivalent of Akkadian *unqu* and is presumably to be read *iqqu* in this context. However, the equivalence is not proven.
337 I am extremely grateful for the assistance of Professors Manfried Dietrich and Oswald Loretz, who generously shared their new copy of this text, based on a collation of the original.

ancient world, this would normally occur at marriage and with entry into cultic service.

Most likely, the earrings, the bracelet, and the red wool headdress are the official, identifying adornment of the storm god's NIN.DINGIR. No garment is included, and the three ornaments are all visible no matter what else is worn, so that different garments could be worn for different occasions without covering them.

After the NIN.DINGIR has been provided with these official ornaments for her person, she is borne back to her father's house. Imbedded in the description of the procession is an encounter with the elders of Emar, who bow down at her feet as to a superior (369.44). The verb is *maqātu* (G) in text A, *šukênu* in B, both of which appear in the formulaic submissions found in the greetings of Emar letters written to superiors.[338] The tribute of the elders is twofold, with both ritual submission and a concrete gift (see *qiāšu*, above). Emar's elders recognize the NIN.DINGIR's legitimate holding of the office on behalf of the political leadership. The king's absence is striking and shows that the roots of the festival predate that institution's arrival at Emar.

4. Figurines for ᵈIM and Hebat

When the NIN.DINGIR has been enthroned, she presents two gold figurines(?) to ᵈIM and Hebat (369.51-52). The setting of this event is not certain, because the instruction comes after she has returned to her father's house, but it could refer to the time right after her enthronement, when she is still at ᵈIM's temple. Attention to ᵈIM and Hebat together is probably necessary because the NIN.DINGIR is going to be a human counterpart to Hebat, a human wife for ᵈIM. The gift of figurines stands out from usual offerings by virtue of both the verb and its object. In Emar ritual, offerings regularly consist of provisions for "the care and feeding of the gods," and the

[338] Compare *maqātu*, 258.5; 260.5; 261.6; 263.6; 264.6; 267.7; 269.4; 270.7; Arnaud, *AuOr* 2 179-188, text 1.5-6, text 3.5-7; and *šukênu*, 265.7; 266.23. Only one ritual text uses the formula: the *maš'artu* prostrates herself (*tu-uš-ḫé-ḫa-an*) before Ea before addressing him in his temple, following the same protocol found in the letters (370.83). The form *šuḫeḫunu* occurs only in the periphery, at Amarna, Ras Shamra (not texts written at Ugarit proper), Boghazkoy, and Nuzi (see *AHw* s.v. *šukênu(m)* 2c-f). One Emar letter uses the verb *qarāru* (N), "to roll over" (266.4-5; see *AHw* s.v. *q/garāru(m)* N1a; *CAD* s.v. *garāru* A 3a1').

presentation of figurines is unique. The verb *elû* (Š) can mean "to consecrate to a god,"[339] though this is the only Emar occurrence.[340]

Figurines are likewise found only here in Emar ritual, but they appear in two temple inventories, among items which are stored "on" (*ina libbi-*, the preposition used with things placed on tables) a *mar-šu*$_{14}$(ŠUM) KÙ.BABBAR, some silver furnishing. Most of the items are made of gold, silver, and precious stones, and include many unfamiliar terms. Among the gold treasures are the *tar-ra-wa-nu* (43.8), the *ki-pu-na-nu* (43.9), the *si-la-ru* (43.10), and the *ku-pí-ia-nu* (282.8, cf. 3), of which only the *sillaru* is attested elsewhere (Qatna alone; see *CAD* s.v. *sillaru*). Perhaps our figurines have some unknown name. The sign in 369.51 is itself a problem, ending with vertical wedges not proper to the ALAM sign (see Labat, No. 358, MB version).[341] In the inventory for ᵈINANNA, the gold figurine is written ALAM KÙ.GI (*ṣalam ḫurāṣi*), with a more familiar ALAM-sign and no divine determinative, 43.8, cf. 7, 14, also with the same ALAM. However, the gold figures in the inventory 282.2, 8 are written with the odd sign from 369.51 and are likewise preceded by the divine determinative. If ALAM/*ṣalmu* is not intended, the sign should at least indicate some related term that might refer more narrowly to a divine image. The *ṣalmu* as a figurine made of precious metal or stone is specifically a western phenomenon (Qatna and Amarna, especially in texts of Tušratta; see *CAD* s.v. *ṣalmu* s. a3', *AHw* s.v. *ṣalmu(m)* II 4a). These are spelled with the logogram ALAM, which might have another reading, even without the strange sign and divine determinative.

It seems likely that the two figurines would be images representing ᵈIM and Hebat.

5. The Final Day

On the last day of the festival, probably the seventh day of the *malluku* feast, the NIN.DINGIR leaves her family home for the last time and is moved into the *bīt* NIN.DINGIR at the temple of ᵈIM. At one level, this is the

---

339 See *AHw* s.v. *elû(m)* IV Š2h, including Alalaḫ and Middle Assyrian ritual; *CAD* s.v. *elû* 9c.

340 In the *zukru*, 373.58, this is a procession verb, "to bring up" -- to the city.

341 One example of a comparable sign appears at Ugarit in the list of personnel, PRU 6 93:22, ˡúALAM.ZÚ (see Huehnergard, *Akkadian of Ugarit*, 388; cf. *CAD* s.v. *aluzinnu* 1 "(a profession)"). This might confirm the reading ALAM for the unusual sign at Emar.

culmination of the long transition process and indeed a high point of the festival, but at another, the final day constitutes a kind of dénouement. The offerings of the final day are less elaborate than those of the shaving and enthronement days. The last day has no special *qaddušu* ceremony, since it properly belongs to the seven-day *malluku*. There is a grand procession, with an ox, seven sheep, and three lambs, but only the lambs are actually sacrificed, only one to ^{d}IM. Without the great sacrifice, no *kubadu* need be mentioned.

The business of the final day is to settle the NIN.DINGIR in her new home in the household of ^{d}IM. The priestess is the human consort of the storm god, the counterpart of Hebat, and the final day's move to the temple occasions comparison with a bride's departure from home for the house of her husband. Because so little is known about ancient wedding rites, it is difficult to be sure what does or does not belong to a marriage theme, but it is conceivable that many of the rites recorded in 369.60-75 reflect north Syrian wedding custom.[342]

The events of the final day fall into two groups. The festival ends with a cluster of events which take place in ^{d}IM's temple in the evening (lines 69-75; cf. *ana pānī nubatti*, line 63), but the rites that are explicitly those for a bride occur earlier in the day, after the goddess ^{d}NIN.KUR is raised and presumably leaves the father's house (lines 60-62). It is the NIN.DINGIR's own departure from her family home that is compared to a bride leaving home. Two events accompany her exit: they cover her head with a colorful sash "as a bride" (*ki-i* É.GI$_4$.A, line 61), and her two female companions embrace her "as a bride" (*ki-i-ma ka-al-la-ti*, line 62).[343]

Gods' faces (*pānū*) are covered (*katāmu*, D; the same verb as with the NIN.DINGIR) for travel in various *zukru* festival processions,[344] and

---

342 Arnaud, *AEPHER* 84 224, remarks that this is from the "déroulement d'un mariage ordinaire."

343 When Zimri-Lim, the king of Mari, marries Šibtu of Halab, he sends envoys to get her, and they put a veil on her head; F. Abdallah, "La femme dans le royaume d'Alep au XVIIIe siècle av. J.-C.," in Durand ed., *La Femme dans le Proche-Orient antique*, 14. This act is then part of the Syrian ceremony associated with marriage. Abdallah says that wedded women of the Mari texts continue to wear this veil, while M. Tsevat finds that in the Hittite Laws (par. 197-198) veiling was not for married women generally, but was reserved for the wedding day; see "The husband veils a wife (Hittite Laws, 197-98)," *JCS* 27 (1975) 237-238. The Middle Assyrian laws show that veiling was the main feature of the ceremony by which a man could promote his concubine to the rank of wife, and married women were veiled in public. See Saggs, *The Might that was Assyria*, 140-141.

344 373.15, 178, 181, 187, 194, 197, 203, (209).

correspondingly uncovered (*petû*, line 207, cf. 177) for certain rituals. It is possible that the NIN.DINGIR's head is likewise covered for travel, so the populace cannot see her face, but then it is strange that the idiom uses "head" (*qaqqadu*) instead of "face" (*pānū*). Akkadian *katāmu* (D) may mean "to veil,"[345] but not with object "head." The same covering with a sash appears in a broken section of the *kissu* festival, 388.32, túgÍB.LÁ *ú-kat-*[*ta-mu*], but we do not know what is covered, and the "sash" (túgÍB.LÁ/*nēbeḫu*) is not "multicolored" (*birmu*). These terms are not found in other Emar ritual, but the temple inventory inspected by the diviner includes seven túgÍB.LÁ GÙN.A, *nēbeḫū birmūtu*, and six TÚG.HI.A GÙN.A, *ṣubātu*(?) *birmūtu*, 285.13-14. Both *nēbeḫu* and *birmu* are common late second-millennium Akkadian terms, though the combination may be a new one. Note that a table is covered (*kuttumu*) with garments for the seven days of the *maš'artu* installation, 370.28.

After the NIN.DINGIR's head is covered, her two companions (*tappūtāši*, dual) embrace her (*epēqu*, G). The verb *epēqu* is only attested in one Old Babylonian and one Neo-Babylonian lexical text (*AHw* s.v. *epēqu(m)* G2), but the Emar text seems to offer a context that confirms the meaning "to embrace." It bears a strong West Semitic color, from comparison with Ugaritic *ḥbq* and Hebrew *ḥābaq*, "to embrace."[346] The noun *tappātu* occurs at Mari and Amarna (see *AHw* s.v. *tappātu(m)*); the *u*-vowel in the NIN.DINGIR text is unexpected.

Both of the rituals that have the priestess act "as a bride" are rites of separation. Veiling separates the NIN.DINGIR from her old surroundings, since "seeing is itself a form of contact."[347] The two companions of the priestess should represent her girlhood companions, like modern bridesmaids, and when she embraces them she bids farewell to her old life. In both acts, the departure of the NIN.DINGIR to serve dIM is equated with a bride's departure.

---

345 The face; one example, in Erra p.19 II iv 14 (see *CAD* s.v. *katāmu* 5b, *AHw* s.v. *katāmu(m)* D5b).

346 In Ugaritic poetry, see the Baal Cycle (KTU 1.4 IV 13, *qdš w'amrr* embraces Athirat to lift her on a donkey), and for embracing in conjugal love, the 'Aqhat legend (KTU 1.17 I 41, 19 II 63, 70) and KTU 1.23:51. See *BDB* for the biblical examples of embracing in greeting or blessing.

347 Van Gennep, *Rites of Passage*, 168. This interpretation assumes that this is a veiling that covers the eyes. Karel van der Toorn, "The significance of the veil in the ancient Near East," 1991 Society of Biblical Literature Annual Meetings, Kansas City, suggests that this is not so.

At the end of the NIN.DINGIR festival, preparations are made for the priestess' first night in her new residence. These begin with gifts from the elders of a fine garment, a bed, a chair, and a footstool (369.69-70, see discussion above). Then, an "Akkadian blanket"[348] (TÚG.GAR URI/*ṣubātu akkadû*) of the *bīt urši* (see above) is spread out on the bed, 369.70-71. It is interesting that the adjective "Akkadian" is not a peripheral term for Mesopotamian goods but rather belongs to Babylonian and Assyrian vocabulary (see *CAD* s.v. *akkadû* b; *AHw* s.v. *akkadû(m)* 2, 3). The blanket is surely a fancy import, perhaps from Assyria (see *AHw* 3, MA and OA examples).[349]

Preparation of the NIN.DINGIR's chamber also involves an elaborate table rite. "The table of Hulelu" is set "at the gate of(?) its (the bed's)[350] head," *a-na* KÁ *re-ši-ša*. Food, drink, and *zirtu*-wool are put on it, and the singers perform rites for that table, which apparently include an address to Hulelu in song, 369.71-74. All but the singing itself has already been treated above, under The Materials (chapter III). Similar song occurs in the *maš'artu* installation and Dagan's *kissu*, always performed by the singers (*zammārū*), with divine names as the objects of the verb *zamāru* (G): 370.43, the gods and goddesses, DINGIR.MEŠ *u* ^{d}*Iš*$_{8}$*-tár*.MEŠ*-ti*; 385.23, ^{d}*Šu-wa-la* and ^{d}U.GUR (see above, The "ritual portion(?)"). This Emar form of the idiom with *zamāru* is unique, though the verb is found with the object *zamār* DN, "the song of DN," in second-millennium texts including Mari ritual (RA 35 3 iii 14) and Hittite (KBo 1.11r.14; ritual?); see *CAD* s.v. *zamāru* A 1a, *AHw* s.v. *zamāru(m)* II G1. Emar 452.48 uses a different idiom, *epēšu* with "a song of the gods," *zi-ma-ra* DINGIR.MEŠ, which reflects the absence of the *zammārū* as subject.

Once the NIN.DINGIR's bed is prepared, she herself is readied for her first night in her new residence by the washing of her feet (verb *mesû*, G), 369.74. This very personal rite is performed by her sister (NIN-*ši*), who receives a silver ring which is placed in the water "which washed her feet," line 75. The second occurrence of *mesû* is a pluralic D, *ú-ma-as-su-u*. Although washing the feet is common in Mesopotamia (see *CAD* s.v. *mesû*

348 In this context, the *ṣubātu* (usually "garment") serves as a spread or blanket for the bed; see *CAD* s.v. *eršu* 1a4'.
349 "Hittite" and "Assyrian" weapons are mentioned in the Emar legal text 33.10.
350 See the note to the translation of line 72, above.

1a2', *AHw* s.v. *mesû(m)* G 1b), the particular combination of water (*mû*) and the verb *mesû* in 369.74 is not attested in the dictionaries (see *CAD* s.v. *mû* A 1c). The usual verb for washing with water is *ramāku*. This is a cleansing ceremony, and washing the feet is appropriately the last thing done before getting in bed.

The instructions for the NIN.DINGIR festival end with the priestess climbing onto her bed (*elû*, G) and lying down (*i/utūlu(m)*; see *AHw*, "liegen, schlafen"), 369.75. No other Emar text includes this action, though the *ḫamša'u*-men lie down in the *maš'artu*'s residence for the seven days of her installation, *it*-[*t*]*a-lu*, 370.31. This parallel shows that the verb *itūlu* is not conclusively part of marriage imagery in Emar ritual; a sexual overtone in the *maš'artu* ritual is unlikely. Sacred prostitutes are never mentioned in Emar ritual, and we have to read much into the *maš'artu* context to find such activity. In the case of the *ḫamša'u*-men, the lying down refers to taking up residence in the *bīt maš'arti*, without indicating any connection with sex or marriage. We should not look for a sexual overtone in the action of the NIN.DINGIR; rather, her lying down is the final severance from the house of her father, as she begins life in her new home. Thus, we do best to decline the temptation to look for a partner for the bed, because her installation is complete in her lying down alone. The NIN.DINGIR ritual does not pull the blind just before the climax of the event; rather, this *is* the climax -- the end of the NIN.DINGIR's progress.[351]

With the appearance of the bed, we are once more required to ask whether this ritual is in any way a part of a "sacred marriage" cult for the earth's fertility. We have a high priestess who is made the human head of ^{d}IM's household in a rite that includes wedding imagery. This should be a key part of the cult which is meant to ensure the continuing favor of the storm god. ^{d}IM is to bring rains when they are needed so that crops will grow, and the storms must not be so violent that they destroy the very life the rains bring forth, either directly or by floods. However, while any cult for the storm god will include an orientation toward fertility, we have no evidence that the NIN.DINGIR's installation involves the sexual aspects usually associated with "sacred marriage," even though the NIN.DINGIR is the human consort of the god. The last act of the ritual gives no indication of actual or symbolic consummation to follow.

---

351 Contrast Douglas Frayne, *BiOr* 42 (1985) 21.

It might be useful to distinguish sacred marriage from divine marriage in Mesopotamian ritual. If "sacred marriage" is to describe the Sumerian rites for Inanna and Dumuzi, where human sacred personnel play out the consummation of the union of the gods, then "divine marriage" may define the rites where a marriage between the gods is celebrated with no hint of human stand-ins for the divine roles.[352] The human conjugal act is strongly evidenced in what Jacobsen calls the "Iddin-Dagan Text" of the Inanna-Dumuzi myth, where Iddin-Dagan explicitly takes the role of Dumuzi (so, "sacred marriage"?).[353] On the other hand, the second- and first-millennium evidence examined by Matsushima does not display this human act and should be classified separately (so perhaps, "divine marriage"?).[354] The Emar festival for the NIN.DINGIR does not match either Mesopotamian type, and it is best defined as the installation of the storm god's high priestess, which includes some marriage aspects because of the nature of the office. Many elements of the festival may not derive from the context of marriage, and the overall interpretive model should not serve to force the whole event into that context.

The rites of the final day have as their goal to set up house for the NIN.DINGIR, whether as a new bride or like any young woman leaving home for sacred service. She is given the bed, chair, and stool that will constitute the basic furnishings of the *bīt* NIN.DINGIR, which is likely a single room in the temple complex. The bed is made, whether with a blanket or hangings (as Durand). Hulelu and her table are difficult to place, since we do not know the character of the goddess. Perhaps she is a household goddess, a lesser

---

352 Frayne, *BiOr* 42 6, specifies that sacred marriage rites promote fertility by a sympathetic sexual act, but he observes that the texts after the Sumerian period have "no direct human participants" (page 12, cf. Jean Bottéro in S.N. Kramer, Bottéro ed., *Le Mariage Sacré*, Paris: Berg International Editeurs, 1983, 205). Neither Frayne nor Bottéro distinguish the later texts with a second title, though the initial definition of a sexual sacred marriage calls for some separation of categories.

353 T. Jacobsen, *The Treasures of Darkness: A History of Mesopotamian Religion*, New Haven: Yale University Press, 1976, 37-39. Frayne, *BiOr* 42 7-8, includes also Enmerkar and Ensuḫkešdaanna, the "Herder Wedding Text" (Jacobsen's title), Šulgi X, but concludes that the Iddin-Dagan text "is undoubtedly the most explicit statement of what was involved in the Sacred Marriage Ritual." For further treatment of the Sumerian sacred marriage texts, see Kramer, *Le Mariage Sacré*, chapter 2, or the more accessible English edition, *The Sacred Marriage Rite*, Bloomington: Indiana University Press, 1969, chapter 3; J. Renger, "Heilige Hochzeit. A. Philologisch," *RlA* 4 (1972-1975) 251-259.

354 Eiko Matsushima, "Recueil de Travaux de l'U.A. 1072 du CNRS (France)," 1985, 92-113; "Le lit de Šamaš et le rituel du mariage à l'Ebabbar," *ASJ* 7 (1985) 129-137; "Le rituel hiérogamique de Nabû," *ASJ* 9 (1987) 131-175; "Les rituels du mariage divin dans les documents accadiens," *ASJ* 10 (1988) 95-128.

member of dIM's divine circle. The problem will have to await emergence of further evidence. Her favor is courted, apparently for assistance in the satisfactory conclusion of the move into the NIN.DINGIR residence.[355] Finally, the sister of the priestess washes her feet to prepare her for bed.

The rites for the last day include nothing that is evidently erotic, such as a special garment to wear to bed or perfumes to please a bridegroom.[356] Rather, the rites seem to deal with the reality of changing homes. They are centered on the room with the bed not because the groom is to come there but because this will be the personal domain of the priestess.

G. THE INSTALLATION IN THE LIFE OF EMAR

The installation of the NIN.DINGIR plays a prominent role in the maintenance of life at Emar. It is intended to repair the breach in the fragile order of the world that is created by the death of the storm god's high priestess. To this end, the festival methodically reaches beyond the immediate sphere of dIM's cult to include the whole Emar community. The community displayed in the festival is not the palace-centered city-state so well-known across the ancient Near East in the second millennium, and evidence points to a society with stronger influence from the institutions of village and clan. Discussion of these characteristics of the festival will conclude the commentary on the installation itself.

1. Repairing the Breach: The Effect of the Ritual

For life at Emar to prosper, peaceful and profitable relations had to be maintained not only within the larger human community but also with the realm of the gods, whose activities lay behind the experiences of day to day existence. The NIN.DINGIR would have been the key figure in the relationship between the storm god and the city of Emar. Therefore, when the

355 If Hulelu were demonstrated to be a sex goddess, the sacred marriage alternative for the final day would be more attractive.

356 For instance, in the Iddin-Dagan text in *Treasures of Darkness*, 38, Inanna prepares for consummation of the sacred marriage by bathing her loins, rubbing herself with soap, and sprinkling the floor with cedar perfume (following Jacobsen).

priestess died a breach was opened in the city's divine relations which had to be repaired with care. The very occasion of the festival was not then the calendar, whose rites provided a kind of preventive maintenance in these relations, but rather a crisis.

In this context, the installation festival has two principal goals: to move a young woman from her profane world into the sacred office and household of dIM, and to deal with the intrusion of death into the affairs of the god's house.

The movement of the new priestess is effected by rites of sacralization and by gradual introduction into her new role and residence. The sacralization rituals include the anointings and the shaving, which prepare the NIN.DINGIR for entry into the sacred realm by marking and/or purification. She is introduced to her role by increased participation in the offering ceremonies and by the enthronement rites of the third day. On the enthronement day the priestess anoints the *sikkānu* of Hebat and is allowed to hold the divine weapon in the second *kubadu*, and on the final day she takes over responsibility for the offerings at the *bīt tukli* and the temples of dNIN.KUR and dIM. The enthronement itself invests the NIN.DINGIR with the formal trappings of her office. These rites are all given a spacial component by the processions which conduct the priestess between her father's house and dIM's temple, the poles of her old and new existence. Three processions to the temple make forays into the sacred realm of dIM, advancing the priestess further each time but retreating to the father's house each night until the final day. The shaving day brings the NIN.DINGIR only to the courtyard gate of the temple, and she is led into the temple proper on the next day, for her enthronement. The last day of the festival and its procession finally bring the priestess to her own temple residence, where she will remain as mistress of the storm god's house. This day's ritual governs her final departure from her childhood home and establishment in a new one.

The start and finish of the NIN.DINGIR installation are defined by this process and no other, and the movement of the new priestess is the dominant order of business. Nevertheless, there seems to be an undercurrent running through the festival that responds to the intrusion of death into dIM's house. If the absence of placement in the annual calendar really indicates that the NIN.DINGIR holds the office for her lifetime, then the installation process begins with a death. When the priestess dies in the temple, several considerations are introduced into the ritual situation.[357]

As with any dead person, she must be honored and cared for so she will have no reason to disturb the institution she leaves. Even if her family takes responsibility for her continuing care, along with her personal property (cf. line 94), some immediate gesture would surely fall to the temple. With the death of the previous NIN.DINGIR, a brief period transpires during which the storm god has no priestess, since the new candidate cannot be readied instantly. The festival might need to make some accomodation. Then, the residence of the NIN.DINGIR still belongs to the dead and must be prepared to change hands.

Several elements of the NIN.DINGIR installation may reflect this undercurrent in the festival. First, the table in the *bīt* NIN.DINGIR for "the previous NIN.DINGIR" (lines 16, 55) would represent direct references. She is given this table for the feasts of the great sacrifices on the shaving and enthronement days, as well as for the seven days before the new priestess moves in. The new priestess does not set foot in the *bīt* NIN.DINGIR until the final procession brings her there. Perhaps the former priestess is considered resident through the period of the festival, thus both honoring the dead and providing a transitional office-holder. On the day of enthronement the residence is called the *bīt BuKKi*, which could be "the house of mourning" (line 39; from the verb *bakû*, "to weep, mourn").[358]

The role of ^{d}NIN.KUR seems to give particular consideration to death and the underworld. When she is laid down in the father's house, she joins in the death transition which the office undergoes and wears the divine weapon on the new NIN.DINGIR's behalf while the new priestess spends her last days in (and so mourns?) her old surroundings. At the same time, four tables are set out for the gods, two of which are reserved for "the underworld gods" (lines 24-25). In her lying down and rising ^{d}NIN.KUR seems to link the worlds of the living and the dead, just as the tables join the gods of the two realms. The *nugagtu* gives her cries on the day when ^{d}NIN.KUR is laid down (line 48; 385.5-6; 388.2-3), lamenting the dead: perhaps the goddess, the old

357 This aspect of the ritual was observed independently by W.L. Moran and P. Steinkeller (personal communications).

358 The final long vowel may not be marked. Compare the Emar *kissu*, the form of which is discussed below, "The *kissu* as 'throne'."

priestess, and even the symbolic death in the passage of the new NIN.DINGIR. The seven-day unit can be associated with mourning as well as celebration, and these aspects may overlap in the NIN.DINGIR installation. Gilgamesh mourns his friend Enkidu for seven days and seven nights in the OB Gilgamesh Epic (X ii:8).

2. Uniting the Community: A Rite for all Emar

All the ritual texts from Emar were found in the archive of a temple which was supervised by a diviner who bore the title, "^{lú}ḪAL of the gods of Emar" (see above, The diviner). The installation festival for the NIN.DINGIR of ^{d}IM is one of the most important events recorded in the archive, judging by the length and size of the tablets, along with the number of copies. We cannot automatically assume, however, that the festival was therefore important for the whole city. The diviner's archive need not represent every Emar consitituency, and the festival itself pertains to the cult of one deity. Although external corroboration would be required to produce a more definitive judgment, many aspects of the text itself indicate that the festival was intended to involve many segments of the Emar community and certainly to reach beyond the immediate circle of ^{d}IM and his temple. This wider intent can be observed in the involvement of all the gods of Emar and in the network of human players included in the ritual.

The reach of the NIN.DINGIR installation is seen first by the inclusion of multiple cults in the ceremonies. ^{d}NIN.URTA, the city-god of Emar (see below), provides the instruments for confirmation of the new candidate (lines 2-3). ^{d}NIN.KUR, a major Emar goddess, plays an active part in the transitional aspect of the festival, and provides oil for anointing the priestess (lines 3-4, cf. 20). Adammatera and the *bīt tukli* storehouse receive attention in two procession stops. While such participation brings a selection of outside deities into ^{d}IM's affairs, the city-wide scope of the ritual is best seen in the offerings to "all the gods of Emar." This phrase is used both for the sanctification of all the gods with bread and beer (lines 6, 22) and for the offerings by distribution (*zâzu*, 19, (39), 48, cf. 83C) to all the gods of Emar. As argued above, the phrase "all the gods of Emar" is not used loosely, but rather is applied especially to offerings distributed to each Emar deity, as represented in the lengthy list of the *zukru* festival (373.66-167). The phrase appears only in the two installations, the *zukru* (most frequently), and Emar

446, the rites for the annual calendar. Such offerings involve a large and expensive outlay of foodstuffs, judging by the *zukru* god-list, and this would be undertaken only for rites that are intended to serve the whole city. Various offerings to "the gods" in the temples of ^{d}IM and ^{d}NIN.KUR do not likely require such literal distribution, but they likewise give attention to the whole divine community.

The NIN.DINGIR installation likewise reaches beyond the confines of ^{d}IM's temple at the human level. The city leadership demonstrates their approval through gifts (lines 44, 69-70) and by bowing before the priestess at her enthronement (line 44). Their influence may also be felt in the confirmation rites of the *purû*, since ^{d}NIN.URTA is specially associated with the elders in economic texts (see below). The setting of tables for local dignitaries places the NIN.DINGIR of ^{d}IM among a group of peers that includes the NIN.DINGIR of Dagan at Šumi, the *maš'artu* of Aštart, and the kings of Emar and Šatappi (only text A). Ritual leadership by the men of the *qidašu* (including ^{lú}ḪAL and singers) reflects a larger religious circle than ^{d}IM's cult, though not necessarily the only power in Emar ritual. Provision for the festival comes through the *bīt tukli*/*bīt ili*, the *ḫamša'u*-men, and the *bēl bīti*. The *bīt tukli* supplies various Emar rituals from different religious spheres.

The processions of the NIN.DINGIR installation are a concrete expression of the festival's reach into the larger community. Temple ritual is focused on enclosed places and plays to a limited audience. By contrast, processions are the most public of festival events. Even if the populace is not specially gathered for the occasion, the simple departure from the sacred domain of the temples into streets, the domain of everyday life and traffic, involves the city at large in the religious event of the temple institutions. Processions proclaim a relevance and perhaps an authority of affairs from the sacred sphere in the affairs of the profane world. The sacred is literally brought into the profane -- officials, divine statues and ritual paraphernalia, and animals for offering, all venture into the streets. In moving out from the temple, procession invades the world of the community, and it returns not in retreat but in conquest. Symbolically, the people and their needs are brought into the sacred center, even as physically they must be excluded, represented by those prepared.

Altogether, these diverse characteristics of the NIN.DINGIR installation display an effort to make the festival reach all Emar, even if we cannot determine the degree of success. The storm god was one of the dominant Emar deities, the maintenance of his cult was to be the concern of the whole city, and all Emar would benefit from his favor.

3. Beyond the City-State: Cultural Characteristics

I stated above that the circle of "the lúḪAL of the gods of Emar" might not have been the only religious power in the city. One of the economic texts published by Tsukimoto (HCCT-E 10) deals in part with a royal reward for Mašruḫe, "the diviner of the king and of the city."[359] Mašruḫe is not part of the family of *Zū-Baʿla*, the patriarch of the diviner clan of the temple M_1 archive. The contrast between Mašruḫe and *Zū-Baʿla* reflects a larger tension in 13th-century Emar society between the new regime of kings and a pre-monarchic era. J.-M. Durand concludes from the Mari records that several centuries earlier, during the OB period, Emar (Imar) was autonomous but did not yet have a king.[360]

The archive of the temple M_1 diviner preserves ritual that acknowledges the presence of a king in Emar but originates in the time before kings. Several features of the NIN.DINGIR installation place it in this group. Foremost among these is the secondary position of the king and the palace, in contrast to the role of the elders noted above. Approval from the city leadership comes from the elders, not the king. The NIN.DINGIR festival is initiated by "the sons of Emar" (line 1), and it is stated emphatically that "the daughter of any son of Emar" may be selected. Domination from the palace is at least theoretically excluded. Finally, the tradition of ritual supply via the *bēl bīti*, or household head, appears to derive from life organized by family units (so clan, tribe) rather than the palace center of the city-state.

The Emar society reflected in the NIN.DINGIR installation is not the centralized urban society that is most commonly reflected in ancient Near

359 See above, The diviner, and Tsukimoto, *ASJ* 12 (1990) 190, Text 7, lines rev. 29-37.
360 Durand, *RA* 83 170 n.23. See Durand, "La cité-état d'Imâr à l'époque des rois de Mari," *M.A.R.I.* 6 (1990) 55-61, on the various political officials known at Imar from the OB period Mari archives. A. Archi, "Imâr au IIIeme millénaire d'après les archives d'Ebla," *M.A.R.I.* 6 24, finds the names of four Imar "kings" (EN) from an even earlier period, though the specific meaning of the Ebla EN must be accounted for. Piotr Michalowski, "Third millennium contacts: observations on the relationships between Mari and Ebla," *JAOS* 105 (1985) 294 n.7, wonders whether EN "was a polysemic word and that one of a number of en's may have been the highest ruler of the city." The last reference was brought to my attention by Mark Smith.

Eastern cuneiform archives, nor does it represent a tribal-nomadic culture that might be understood as a polar opposite. In the ritual texts we are shown life in a smaller Syrian city that exhibits traits from varied influences, in a region where tribal and urban cultures may have interacted without the complete dominance of either. The Emar rituals contribute a new perspective to our understanding of religious practices in this intermediate realm.

IV. THE EMAR FESTIVAL TRADITION: PATTERNS AND DEVELOPMENT

A. INTRODUCTION

Although the texts of the Emar diviner's archive were badly broken,[1] they included a wide variety of ritual material, bearing witness to several facets of a complex religious practice at Emar. Close examination of the Emar ritual texts shows that neither the pantheon nor the ritual terminology is constant from one text or group to another, and these divergences provide many clues to the development of the Emar cult. In spite of the fact that all the material is from one archive in the 13th century, it is possible to draw tentative conclusions about earlier and later features, and the variety itself reflects the multiple contexts in which Emar ritual came into being.

The focus of our interest is the complex of features that sets apart the "festivals" (EZEN) at Emar, and the relationships between the festivals. This group includes many of the longest texts as well as the rituals found in multiple copies (or fragments from separate copies, at least). They are the texts that seem to make up the core of a deeply rooted local religious practice at Emar. The major events are the NIN.DINGIR and *maš'artu* installations (369 and 370), the *zukru* festival (373 and 375), and the set of *kissu* festivals (385-388).

The purpose of this section is to examine some wider issues in Emar religion in the context of this festival tradition at Emar. For each major event

[1] See Margueron, *CRAIBL* 1975, 209; "Quatre campagnes de fouilles à Emar (1972-1974): un bilan provisoire," *Syria* 52 (1975) 55, 65-66; texts of temple M_1 in Arnaud, Emar VI.3, nos. 137-535.

-- the installations, the *zukru*, and the *kissu*'s -- we will deal with the basic character of the ritual itself, the points of comparison and contrast found in the language, and issues that arise through evaluation of the core pantheons of each festival. Considerable space will be devoted to the distinct patterns that emerge within the Emar pantheon, and it has seemed best to discuss these within the framework of the festivals themselves because their identification originally arose through study of the festivals, and the festivals are best understood in the context of these patterns.

Examination of the major festivals at Emar helps to place the NIN.DINGIR installation in its larger setting, in its relationships to the larger world of the Emar cult. This portion of the study involves casting a wider net, with what is necessarily a more diffuse effect. Treatment of detail becomes somewhat less precise and more selective. Nevertheless, the issues raised by the broader look at Emar religion are provocative, and they are important to on-going study of ancient Syrian religion. The discussion which follows is not offered as a definitive statement, but rather is intended to introduce a body of data and interpretation that will contribute to continuing work on an intriguing site.

1. Classification of The Emar Rituals

The texts from the diviner's archive at Emar were so severely damaged by the 12th-century destruction and later disturbance that it is difficult to make a reliable catalog of the rituals found in it. In particular, it is quite likely that there are rituals and ritual types yet unidentified because of their fragmented state. The following is a survey intended to underline the major divisions, not to classify each ritual tablet precisely. My organization is not precisely that of Arnaud,[2] but it is in agreement in the main outline:

Arnaud, Emar VI.3:

- 369, intronisation et mariage de la prêtresse-*entu*
- 370-372, intronisation de la prêtresse-*maš'artu*
- 373-377, la fête-*zukru*
- 378-384, les listes sacrificielles
- 385-391, les rituels des fêtes-*kissu*

[2] See Emar VI.3, table des matières, p. 5.

392-394, rituels divers
395-445, (fragments)
446-451, les *ordo* liturgiques annuels
452-459, les *ordo* liturgiques mensuels
460-470, les *ordo* récapitulatifs
471-490, les rituels anatoliens
491-535, (fragments)

Alternative arrangement:

1. The festivals (EZEN): 369, 370, 373, 385-388, 394 (fragments not included).
2. Calendar ritual.
   a. Annual cycle: 446 and fragments 447, 448.
   b. Monthly cycle: 452 (ritual for the dead?), 463?
3. Offering lists: 379-382, cf. 378, 383; 461 and 462?, cf. 460. Properly include the festival lists, 373.10-12, 66-167; cf. the cycle of 370.45-54, 60-68.
4. Rites for the gods of Hatti: 471-473 are largest.

The festivals

The Emar scribes used the Sumerogram EZEN (Akkadian *isinnu*, but unknown reading at Emar) as an identifying term in a group of ritual texts that appears to display the least evidence of foreign influence of the Emar rituals. These include the NIN.DINGIR and *maš'artu*-priestess installations,[3] the set of *kissu* festivals,[4] and the pair of rituals 394.1-25 and 26-44.[5] Although the *zukru* festival (373) lacks many of the traits that link the other texts (see below), it is also called EZEN.[6] The broken texts 392 and 393 display similarities in language and form, though the term EZEN does not appear.

"Festival" is only one possible translation of Emar EZEN, which might also be rendered "feast" or "celebration" or the like. The English "festival" need not imply a tie to the calendar (see above), and it is difficult to find another word that properly communicates the reality of a coherent religious

---

[3] 369 and 370, see 369.48 and 370.41.
[4] 385-388, see 385.1, 27; 387.1; 388.1; 370.113; cf. 386.1.
[5] EZEN.MEŠ *an-na-ti*, 394.39, refers to a group of unknown extent.
[6] 373.36, 40, 65, 174; cf. 210; 375.1.

celebration that covers several days and centers around a specific occasion.[7] Whatever the English translation, the Emar term EZEN represents a valuable key for identifying a group of rites that were associated in the minds of the scribes who recorded their instructions.

Calendar ritual

Daniel Arnaud classifies a large portion of Emar ritual as "*ordo*," highly repetitive rites ordered either by the calendar or by recipients of gifts. These are generally outside the scope of this study, but it should be noted that they are a complex group not at all cut out of the same mold. Two rituals are conducted according to a cycle of months: the "annual *ordo*" 446 and the *zukru*, which operates on a seven-year cycle (373.174) and specifies rites for the months of Zarati (375.3) and Niqali (373.185), but centers on a seven-day period (373.65; cf. 202, read *i-na* U_4.7.KÁM, "on the 7th day") beginning on the 14th and 15th days of the first month, ^iti^SAG.MU (373.36, 175, 191). Text 446 apparently begins with the first month, though the first lines are too broken to be sure. Five other months are involved: those of ^d^NIN.KUR.RA (446.58), ^d^*An-na* (line 77), ^d^*A-dama* (82), *Mar-za-ḫa-ni* (85) and ^d^*Ḫal-ma* (95). Arnaud finds that this tablet is the work of a poor scribe, who was forced to make smaller and smaller descriptions of each month as he progressed through the year.[8] However, this cannot be assumed out of hand. Very likely the first month is given lengthy attention because it is the New Year, as in the *zukru*. Even text 446 may thus make no systematic attempt to cover the entire calendar by months.

The monthly rituals are also difficult. Only one text moves through a month's rites according to the sequence of days: Emar 452 is no simple monthly cycle, however. It is a ritual for the month of Abû which is part of a cult of dead ancestors (see appendix). One "recapitulative" *ordo*, 463, may move through a month, since it mentions a 16th and 20th day (463.19, 26), but no specific month is mentioned, and these two days do not constitute a calendar.

---

[7] EZEN is the common Hittite denotation for "festivals"; see for example the glossary of Haas and Jakob-Rost, *AoF* 11 221. Lebrun, *Šamuḫa*, 44-45, observes that at Šamuḫa, EZEN marks ceremonies of official character which are linked to the calendar (perhaps versus Emar), while SISKUR marks simple offerings or *ad hoc* ceremonies.

[8] Arnaud, "Religion assyro-babylonienne," *AEPHER* 85 (1977-1978) 213. The tablet is indeed small for the amount of text squeezed onto it, and the script is difficult to read.

Although it remains uncertain whether any Emar ritual is intended to follow a monthly or annual cycle for its own sake, the connection to the calendar sets the group apart from the festivals, which are given no such definition. The *zukru* is the only exception, perhaps because its very function is to mark the New Year. Arnaud's fragments, 447-451 and 453-459, are placed in these groups because of the appearance of months or sequences of days that seem to belong to a calendar pattern.

Offering lists

Several texts from the diviner's archive are lists of deities, with and without an offering specified (379-382, vs. 378 and 383). These are not bound to specific dates and describe no actions -- they have no verbs. The "recapitulative" *ordo* rituals 460, 461, and 462 have the same traits, and might be better placed here than with the calendar rituals, though they offer more detail for the offering than the god-lists, and text 460 mainly involves gifts to city and cult officials. The long offering list of the *zukru* festival, 373.66-167, really belongs here as well. Its pantheon is not that of the active *zukru* -- ^{d}IM never appears outside of this offering list and the short version in lines 10-12 -- and the order of the gods is very like that of list 378. A similar pantheon, headed by Dagan/^{d}KUR and ^{d}IM, appears in the cycle of feast days in the *maš'artu* installation, 370.45-54, 60-68, with the same preparations and temple meal repeated for each day with a different god.

Rites for the gods of Hatti

The above heading belongs to text 471, and the ritual and pantheon which follow suit the title. Without clear Hurrian-Hittite parallels, it is premature to say these copy actual Hittite rituals,[9] but they are likely descriptions of observed Hittite practice, at least. The very fact that the copies of these were stored in temple M_1 with the rest of the Emar ritual might indicate that they were composed at Emar. Perhaps these texts were drawn up as a provision for the contingent of Hittites stationed at Emar.

[9] See Arnaud, "Religion assyro-babylonienne," *AEPHER* 92 (1983-1984) 235: the Akkadian appears to be a faithful (if servile) translation of the Hittite. Cf. Arnaud, in *Le Moyen Euphrate*, 252; in *Hethitica VIII*, 17. E. Laroche, "Observations sur le rituel anatolien provenant de Meskéné-Emar," in Fiorella Imparati ed., *Studi di Storia di filologia anatolica dedicati a Giovanni Pugliese Carratelli*, Firenze: Elite (edizioni librarie italine estere), 1988, 112 and n.6, calls them the work of a local Syrian/Semitic scribe translating imperial Hittite or Louvian texts. He does not suggest specific Hittite ritual comparisons.

2. Patterns of Festival Interrelationships

In spite of the fact that the 13th-century scribes of Emar classified several major rituals as EZEN/"festival," these religious celebrations show significant differences, as well as important points of contact. No two of the major events come from a single setting, and many questions arise regarding their interrelationships. Can we distinguish between earlier or later festivals? Do we find hints of development within individual festivals? Do the rituals share the same temple and city infrastructures? the same teams of personnel? Do they share the same procedures for offering, procession, and other basic ritual acts?

Two lines of evidence throw light on these and related problems: compared ritual language and terminology, and the pantheon. The words and larger language units which describe the events of the festivals signal associations and distinctions among the cults that operate behind each ritual. A discussion of each major festival below will move from patterns in the terminology to pantheon issues.

3. The Festival Pantheons

It will be observed below that the offering lists from Emar combine a wide range of deities and include all the major gods attested at Emar. The pantheons of the major festivals are fundamentally different from the pantheon of those lists, and when the festivals include offerings to listed deities, we find a contrast between the gods of the lists and the gods of the remaining ritual. This is strikingly visible in the *zukru* festival, with its great central list of gods receiving offerings (373.66-167, cf. the shorter version in lines 9-13): while ^{d}IM is second in the pantheon of the lists, and a major figure in Emar religion, he has no role whatsoever in the *zukru*. The reverse side of this remarkable situation is that Dagan/^{d}KUR, the head of the pantheon in the *zukru* offering lists, and the major player in all aspects of the festival, has no part in the installation festival for ^{d}IM's high priestess. His name is only mentioned once, when the local dignitaries are assigned tables for the seven-day feasting period: one is the NIN.DINGIR *ša* ^{d}KUR EN *Šu-ú-mi*, "the NIN.DINGIR of Dagan, lord of Šumi" (369.16, 55, 57). Moreover, no *kissu* festival is performed for the storm god, who only appears through his NIN.DINGIR in the *kissu* for

Dagan (385.16), and the *maš'artu* installation ignores Dagan, outside his place in the cycle of offerings.

The following chart displays the major and minor deities of each festival type. Different grounds are used for distinguishing the primary gods in each festival. Šaḫru, Hulelu, and Adammatera from the NIN.DINGIR installation are not found in any of the lists, and are certainly not major figures in any Emar sphere. Šamaš appears in the *maš'artu* installation only as the (literal) sun (370.18, 70), and Alal is not part of the ritual proper. His priest is among the recipients of payments at the end (line 110). Dagan and ^{d}NIN.URTA entirely dominate the action of the *zukru* festival, along with the *šaššabētu* of ^{d}NIN.URTA's temple (see especially line 23). Three palace deities, ^{d}NIN.É.GAL-*lì*, and ^{d}30 *u* ^{d}UTU *ša* É.GAL-*lì*, are brought out of the city to the gate of the *sikkānātu* both in the period before the *zukru* week (373.27-28) and during the *zukru* itself (lines 44-45).[10] They have no role beyond this presence at the offering, and do not appear in the description of general movements in lines 168-209. The god Šaggar is strictly associated with the 15th day of the month and its activities, and is not otherwise a major pantheon figure.[11] The principal deities of the *kissu* festival set are simply the gods who are honored with a *kissu* rite, plus ^{d}NIN.KUR, who plays a key role in initiating ^{d}KUR's festival (385.1-26) and the text for all the festivals (388).

---

10 Read line 44, [^{d}NIN.É.GA]L-*lì* ^{d}30 ⸢*u*⸣ ^{d}UTU *ša* É.GAL-*lì*, based on collation.

11 See lines 42, 176, 183, 192, 195, and cf. 196, NINDA(?).MEŠ *šag-ga-ru*. Arnaud (personal communication) wonders whether Šaggar might be the reading for ^{d}30, normally Sîn. Laroche, "Les hiéroglyphes de Meskéné-Emar et le style 'Syro-Hittite'," *Akkadica* 22 (1981) 12, no.46, found one personal name among the Emar seals that offers the equivalence, ^{md}30-*a-bi* = *Šà-ga+ra?-a-bu*. The equation Šaggar = ^{d}30 seems unlikely in the ritual texts, however. Šaggar of the 15th day is spelled syllabically several times in text 373 of the *zukru* festival, and Emar 375.4, the second *zukru* tablet, provides a logographic writing for the same day: *i-na* u_4*-mi* 15 ^{d}ḪAR-*ar*. It appears that ^{d}ḪAR-*ar* = Šaggar. M. Stol, *On Trees, Mountains, and Millstones in the Ancient Near East*, Leiden: Ex Oriente Lux, 1979, 75-76, has already observed the equation *sag-gar* = ^{d}ḪAR in CT 2945 ii:7, and he proposes that this Saggar is the deified mountain Djebel Sinjar. D. Soubeyran, "Une graphie atypique de Saggarātum?," *M.A.R.I.* 3 (1984) 276, finds the same equivalence at Mari (ARM XXIII 83) in the form ^{d}ḪAR-*a-tim*^{ki}, which he identifies as Saggaratum, a city on the Habur.

Festival Deities

Primary gods:

NIN.DINGIR(369)	*maš'artu*(370)	*zukru*(373)[12]	*kissu*(385-388)
ᵈIM	Aštartu	Dagan	Dagan
Hebat	Ea	ᵈNIN.URTA	ᵈNIN.KUR
ᵈNIN.KUR	ᵈIM		ᵈEREŠ.KI.GAL
ᵈNIN.URTA	ᵈNIN.URTA?		Ea
			Išḫara
			ᵈNIN.URTA

Secondary gods:

Adammatera	Alal	Bēlet-ekalli	Alal
Hulelu		Sîn *u* Šamaš *ša ekalli*	Amaza
Šaḫru			Udḫa
			Šuwala
			Ugur
			ᵈ*As-si-la* (*-il-la*)
			ᵈKUR EN *am-*[*qí*]

Our evaluation of the major Emar festivals will include further discussion of the differences between these pantheons and the possible implications for Emar

[12] Note that the fragments 375 and 376 definitely belong to the *zukru* festival. Text 375 is a version of the *zukru* festival's opening, but it has a number of features that are not found in 373, the principal text of the *zukru*. In contrast to 373 and the major festival texts, the high god is spelled ᵈ*Da-gan* (375.2, 3, 10, (17), 19), not ᵈKUR. ᵈNIN.URTA only appears identified with a *sikkānu*, the one instance of a named deity besides Hebat connected to this sacred object. Important new figures are introduced: ᵈNIN.KUR(.RA) in line 11 and the ᵈ*Ḫaṣṣinnu ša* DINGIR in lines 6, 12, and 22 (line 22, ᵈ*Ḫa-ṣí-nu ša* ᵈKASKAL(?)). These features suggest a relation to the annual calendar ritual 446, which also uses the spelling ᵈ*Da-gan*, and which is the only Emar ritual besides the NIN.DINGIR installation to involve the *ḫaṣṣinnu ša ili*, "the divine axe" (446.15, 40, 43, 87, 100, 102). Text 376 only mentions ᵈKUR (lines 2, 3). Fragments 374 and 377 may be part of the *zukru* festival milieu, but they do not seem to belong to the specific instruction-set found in 373. Some unfamiliar traits are the conditional sentences marked by *šumma* (374.7, 8), the mention of the ˡᵘ́·ᵐᵉˢ̌*nu-pu-ḫa-ni* (line 12), the plural with ventive, *-ūni-*, on *inaššûnima* (line 6), and the verbs *nabalkutu* and *ṣamādu* (377.2, 3).

religion generally. The principal deities of Emar can be divided into two distinct circles, which occupy distinct festival settings. The storm god ^{d}IM and his consorts are mainly confined to the installations: the NIN.DINGIR is devoted to ^{d}IM, with special attention given to his consort Hebat, while the *maš'artu* operates in the religious sphere of Ištar/Aštart, known to be Baal's consort in western Syrian traditions of this period. On the other hand, Dagan and ^{d}NIN.URTA dominate the action of the *zukru* festival, though neither plays a large part in the installations. None of the gods of ^{d}IM's circle is significantly involved in the *zukru*. Following this pattern in our remarks below, ^{d}IM's circle will be treated with the installation festivals, and Dagan, ^{d}NIN.URTA, and their possible consorts will be discussed with the *zukru* festival.

4. Emar Deities in Light of Known Syrian Pantheons

The site of Meskéné/Emar, situated in north central Syria during the 13th century B.C.E., fills an important gap in our knowledge of ancient Syria. However, it by no means enters a vacuum. The Emar material contributes to a growing body of information regarding this part of the Near East, and likewise needs to be examined in light of it. Besides purely archaeological data, we have a selection of written sources for Syrian religion that cover a wide span of time and geography. Ebla (late third and early second millennium), Mari (early second millennium), Alalaḫ (level VII, 17th century; level IV, 15th century)[13] and Ugarit (15th-13th centuries) provided archives of cuneiform texts from ancient Syria, and there are numerous scattered sources. The extensive finds from Boghazkoy/Hattuša, the capital of the Hittite empire, provide direct historical information about that people's Syrian contacts. Thirteenth-century Hittite religion had become an amalgam of elements from Hittite, Hurrian, and north Syrian cultures, and various Hattuša texts thus reflect aspects of Syrian religion. Many of the letters found at El Amarna in Egypt came from vassal states in Syria, and some offer clues to the local

---

13 See Horst Klengel, *Geschichte Syriens im 2. Jahrtausend v.u.Z.* I, Berlin: Akademie-Verlag, 1965, 6. More recently, M.-H. Carre Gates has argued from the evidence of imported pottery that Alalaḫ levels VI and V can be reliably dated from 1575-1460, placing the end of level VII in the early 16th century. See "Alalakh levels VI and V: a chronological reassessment," *Syro-Mesopotamian Studies* 4/2, 1981, 1.

pantheons. A few cuneiform tablets have turned up from the ancient central Syrian city of Qatna, and from Tell Hadidi/Azu on the Euphrates between Emar and Carchemish, more recently supplemented by a growing number of tablets from nearby Mumbaqat/Ekalte.[14] Texts from Hatti and Ugarit offer some second-millennium data on Carchemish, and archaeological excavations have produced some first-millennium inscriptions, though more sources from the Hittite period would be helpful.[15] Writings from the New Kingdom in Egypt show some contact with Syrian religion and provide a witness for late second-millennium patterns. The number of sources for greater Syria multiplies in the first millennium, but there is little from northern Syria specifically until the Roman period. Sites such as Dura Europas and Palmyra will doubtless assist our understanding of the earlier Emar religion and culture, but this study does not penetrate beyond *ad hoc* reference to the material from Palmyra.

Although the above resources are scattered, they go far toward building a frame of reference for Emar religion via their pantheons. One can glean information about the gods worshipped from even the sparsest textual finds, and although pantheon data are complex and full of ambiguities, they are at least relatively abundant. The most important sites are Ebla, Mari, Hattuša, and Ugarit. The last three give us a second-millennium ring surrounding Emar, with control points to the east, north, and west. Ebla is the nearest to Emar, and its archives have shown that a number of deities previously thought to be Hurrian are more likely native Syrian, since Ebla predates Hurrian influence in Syria.[16] Mari had close relations with the kingdom of Yamḫad, centered at Halab (Aleppo), northwest of Emar, and the chief Mari cult of Dagan was based at Terqa, between Emar and Mari along the Euphrates. Therefore the Mari archives offer some access to life in central north Syria, a few centuries before Late Bronze Age Emar.

Alalaḫ is a special case. By the late 18th century B.C.E., documents from the Mari palace show us a wreath of Hurrian city-states from north Syria

---

[14] On the evidence for the identification of Mumbaqat as Ekalte, see Mayer, *MDOG* 122 49-63.

[15] For the extant inscriptions, see J.D. Hawkins, "Karkamiš," in *RlA* 5 (1980) 426. Hittite sources show temples to [ ] and ^{d}KAL/Kurunta at the time of an invasion in 1352 B.C.E. (page 429), and excavations uncovered a first-millennium temple to the storm god and texts that call Kubaba the "Queen of Karkamiš" (page 443 and text A 23).

[16] See A. Archi, *AAAS* 29-30 (1979-1980) 171; G. Wilhelm, *Grundzüge*, 1982, 78.

across northern Mesopotamia, with its western end at Alalaḫ, near the northern extreme of the Orontes River.[17] Even in the level VII texts, before actual control by the Hurrian state of Mitanni,[18] half the Alalaḫ personal names are Hurrian.[19] The mix of Hurrian and West Semitic elements is not unique, but the Hurrian portion is stronger at Alalaḫ than at nearby Ugarit, and we have no archive of texts in the local dialect to help distinguish what belongs to a native West Semitic culture. We will consider the Alalaḫ texts where appropriate, but they raise as many questions as they answer, and require further study.

B. THE INSTALLATION FESTIVALS

1. The NIN.DINGIR Installation

Emar 369 is attested by two tablets that together form a nearly complete copy (above, text A), three more substantial fragments (texts B, C, and D) and a small splinter (text E). Arnaud finds that the number of duplicates, the length of the documents, and the care of composition show it to be the most important ritual at Emar,[20] though the *zukru* festival might compete. See chapter III for full commentary.

2. The maš'artu Installation

Emar 370 is the sister text to 369, found only in one long copy, over one hundred lines long (Msk 74303a). Though a break at one end of the tablet badly obscures the beginning and the end of the ritual, the middle is fairly complete.

The fragments Emar 371 and 372 do not belong to this festival. Text 371 includes the god Šaḫru (line 10, otherwise only in 369) and ^{d}NIN.KUR (line 11), who do not belong to the *maš'artu* installation. Both fragments mention the LÚ.MEŠ *ša qí-da-ši* (line 17, cf. 372.6, 10), who are not attested

---

17 See Wilhelm, *Grundzüge*, 17-18.
18 *Ibid*, 35: about 1470 B.C.E.
19 *Ibid*, 18.
20 Arnaud, *AEPHER* 84 223.

in text 370, and both may belong more to the sphere of the storm god's temple than to the realm of Ištar/Aštart.[21] Other traits[22] place the texts in close relation to the installations, and if there is a direct association, it is more likely with the NIN.DINGIR than the *maš'artu*.

Although the beginning of text 370 is broken, it is possible to follow the events of the *maš'artu* festival fairly closely. After the (opening) sanctification day (*qaddušu*), 370.2-19, there is a seven-day feast and cycle of offerings, 20-91.[23] Lines 20-40 describe provisions for all seven days and offerings for the first day (especially lines 39-40?). The second day of the cycle is indicated by the temporal phrase, [*i*]-*na* U_4.2.KÁM *ša* [ezen]*ma-al-lu-ki*, (line 41) versus [*i*]-*na* U_4.2.KÁM *ma-al-lu-ku* DN, (line 20), a verbless sentence like those in 369.7, 29.[24] Based on the pattern of the NIN.DINGIR installation and the literal sense of line 41, this should represent the second day of the seven-day *malluku*, so the third day of the whole festival.

The *maš'artu* installation places key ritual events at night (*mūšu*, vs. *nubattu*), underlining the necessity for darkness, and the priestess has some special connection to the military of Emar. The night-time rites begin with provision of furniture and special clothing for the *maš'artu* at the end of the first day, 370.16-18.[25] On the second day, when the cycle of feasts at various temples begins, a special set of rites is performed on the roof of the *maš'artu*'s house before the *sikkānu* (of Ištar/Aštart?) which has been brought there (see Chapter III, Hebat and her *sikkānu*). This introductory set is performed at night (*i-na mu-ši*, 370.42), and the first day's offering and feasting (for Dagan) begin "when day breaks," *kīma inammir* (370.45). The cycle continues through the seventh day (line 68), but lines 69-91 (at least) describe events that are to take place on that last day, beginning on the roof of the *maš'artu*'s house, where we left the *sikkānu* on the second day (370.69), with offerings made to Aštart at daybreak (*kî šamšu inappiḫ*, line 70). Action moves to the evening watch (*ana pānī nubatti*, line 76), but the focus of the final day's rites comes once again at night (lines 79 and 81). In Ea's temple, the *maš'artu*

---

[21] See [d]IM, 371.16; 372.4.
[22] E.g. meat GARZA, 371.12; the father's house, 372.5.
[23] At least seven days; the text is severely damaged here.
[24] Collation shows *-ki* in line 41, for the genitive, and *-ku* in line 20, not *-lu* for both as in Arnaud's copy.
[25] Cf. 369.69-71, on the last day of the NIN.DINGIR installation, in the evening -- *ana pānī nubatti*, line 62.

bows down before him and declares, "I will draw water for the bathing of Aštart, my mistress" (line 84) -- the only direct speech recorded in Emar ritual.

The events of this last night also involve the second distinctive *maš'artu* installation feature, a link to military matters. Unfortunately, much of the festival's end is broken, but we do find the statement, "(When) they go away on campaign, they will give her reverence...," *ina ḫarrāni ittalkūma ipallaḫūši* (370.88).[26] It is not clear whether this means Aštart or the *maš'artu*, but either way this gives a hint of the *maš'artu*'s function, as a priestess for battle-preparation and military success. Then, she (the *maš'artu* on behalf of the goddess?) is given a gift of silver, and the soldiers (LÚ.MEŠ *ta-ḫa-zi*) fall at her feet, *a-na* GÌR.MEŠ-*ša i-*[*ma-qu-tu*] (line 90, following 369.44). These soldiers are the major human players in the *maš'artu* festival. They are the ones who make the rounds on each feast day, eating and drinking in each temple (370.62, 65, 68, but also in the breaks of lines 47, 50, and 53, following the pattern repeated for each day), and they are found in the "courtyard" of the *maš'artu*'s house (*i-na* (not *ša*) TÙR *ša* É [f]*maš-*[*ar-ti*]) from the beginning (the meaning of *ina ūmi šâšu*?) of the rites there (line 32). "Soldiers" are listed as recipients of *qu'û*-jars in Emar 306, LÚ.MEŠ *ta-ḫa-zi* in line 1, LÚ.MEŠ *ša i-la-ti* ("men of the army," *illatu*) in line 19, but they appear in no ritual context besides the *maš'artu* installation.

3. The Language of the Installations

The distinction between the *zukru* and the other three major festivals is the most striking pattern among the Emar festivals (see below, The Language of the *zukru*), but a few others are worth noting. It should not be surprising that the two installations share further characteristics, since they celebrate similar occasions within one cultic tradition. Both use the term *malluku* to describe the putting-into-office proper (see the section III), and to sum up the event in terms of the new priestess taking her official seat *ina šūkultīši*, "at her feast" (369.84) or *ina* [giš]GU.ZA-*ša* (*kissîša*), "on her throne" (370.108). In each, the summary statement is followed by allotment of payments to ritual

[26] The second verb is normalized according to Arnaud's transliteration, *i-pala-ḫu-ši*, for the expected durative. Perhaps, however, the spelling should be *i-pal-ḫu-ši*, with the expected reading of the second sign, and the verb form is simply irregular.

personnel and rations to the priestess (369.84-90; 370.108-117), probably "for one year," *ša* (369.94), or *i-na* (370.117) MU.1.KÁM. Only the installations include the tables set for the same city dignitaries, interchanging the "previous NIN.DINGIR" and the "previous *maš'artu*" as appropriate (369.16, 55; 370.34). The same meat assignments are made, and the tables are set up in the respective residences of the priestesses, the *bīt* NIN.DINGIR (369.15, 53), and the *bīt maš'arti* (370.33). The cycle of offering and feasting in major Emar sanctuaries from the second to the seventh day of the *maš'artu* installation repeats the action sequence *naqû-šakānu*(meat)-*mullû-akālu/šatû* that is characteristic of the NIN.DINGIR festival (370.45-68; see above, for further discussion). Certain gifts to the two priestesses appear in no other ritual texts:

- the red wool garment, túgḪÉ.ME.DA/*ikiṭu*(?), 369.23, 60 (of dNIN.KUR); cf. sígḪÉ.ME.DA, 369.42 (of the NIN.DINGIR); 370.17;
- the bed and chair, 369.70; 370.16, 79;
- the *zirtu*-material, 369.73; 370.87;
- the *tudittu*-pin, 369.44; 370.105(?);
- gold, 369.41; 370.85.

Only the installations involve the "courtyard," *tarbāṣu*, the place where the NIN.DINGIR is shaved,[27] and a part of the *bīt maš'arti*.[28] The "father's house" (É *a-bi-ša*) appears only on the sanctification day of the *maš'artu* festival (370.8, 9) in our one broken tablet, but it is an important point of contact with the NIN.DINGIR event, where it is the counterpoint to the É NIN.DINGIR in the storm god's temple, her old home which she leaves for the new (see above). Finally, the city elders only appear in the two installation rituals, (369, above, and 370.18) and the lú.meš*ḫamša'ū* belong to this sphere (see above). The similarity of roles is especially striking for the periods of feasting at the *bīt* NIN.DINGIR (369.53-54) and the *bīt maš'arti* (370.30-31).

The likeness between certain installation elements can probably be explained by two primary factors. One is simply that both are priestess installations and it is natural that these are the events where the father's house

27 *a-na pí-i* KÁ *ša ta-ar-ba-ṣi*, "at the opening of the courtyard gate," 369.9.
28 *i-na* (not *ša*) TÙR *ša* É f*maš-*[*ar-ti*], "at the courtyard of the house of the *maš'artu*," 370.32.

is prominent, for instance. A second factor is the possible association between the Emar cults of Baal and Aštart (^{d}IM and ^{d}*Iš*$_8$-*tár*/^{d}INANNA). This latter point will receive considerable attention below, but we should observe here that the installation festivals do provide some indication of a connection. The parallel *bīt* NIN.DINGIR and *bīt maš'arti* hint that there may even be a shared architecture, perhaps echoed in the *tarbāṣu* as well. Often it is difficult to separate the operation of these two factors and after all, it may be no coincidence that the only two installation ceremonies found at Emar are for priestesses of Baal and Aštart.

Along with the similarities, we find important differences between the installations. The primary one may be the pantheons, which have little in common (see below), but even with a single flawed witness to the *maš'artu* festival, it is evident that it is no clone of the NIN.DINGIR feast. The centrality of the night (370.16, 42, and the climax, 81-99(?)) is entirely absent from the NIN.DINGIR ritual, as is the interest in battle which we see in the name ^{d}*Iš*$_8$-*tár* MÈ (*Aštartu tāḫāzi*, "Aštart of the battle," 370.20), and the place of "the men of the battle," LÚ.MEŠ *ta-ḫa-zi*, in the seven-day feasting period at the *bīt maš'arti* (370.32) and at the various sanctuaries (lines 62, 65, 68, but on the first three days also). These players, either actual soldiers or personnel responsible for the ritual aspects of warfare,[29] appear again on the last night of the festival, the climax, which is unfortunately broken. They may do obeisance before the *maš'artu*, like the elders before the NIN.DINGIR:

> LÚ.MEŠ *ta-ḫa-zi a-na* GÌR.MEŠ *ša i-*[*ma-qu-tu*]
> The men of battle wi[ll fall] at her feet. (370.90, cf. 369.44)

[29] Cf. the priests of Israel, who go out with the ark of God to ensure victory in battle, Jos 3.3, 6, etc.; 1 Sam 4.4, etc.?

This follows a statement of the priestess' part in preparation for war:

> *i-na* KASKAL-*ni i-tal-kum-ma i-pala-ḫu-ši*[...]
> When they go out on campaign they will give her reverence...(370.88)

The only certain direct speech attested in the Emar rituals is found at the beginning of the same sequence (lines 83-84).

4. The Gods of the Installations

The Storm God (^{d}IM/Baal)

Emar 369 is the installation of the high priestess of the storm god, and he is the principal deity of the ritual. Throughout the festival the name of the god is spelled ^{d}IM, and we have to look beyond the text itself for help in identifying what specific storm god name is intended. The evidence is not conclusive, but offers some ground for identifying ^{d}IM as Baal. C. Zaccagnini refers to new analysis by F.M. Fales that proves "convincingly" the alternative equation with Adad, but this work is not yet in print.[30]

The best tool for unmasking the Sumerian spelling is found in the collection of Emar personal names, complex as it is. In personal names, the storm god is usually written either ^{d}IM or ^{d}U, forms which can be interchangeable in a single text.[31] Although mixed names cannot be ruled out, theophoric personal names which include specifically Hurrian deities tend to be associated with Hurrian vocabulary, and we should at least look for Syrian deities in theophoric names which include Syrian-Semitic vocabulary.[32] This pattern is useful for distinguishing the Syrian storm god in theophoric names. First, the name of the Emar king, ^{d}IM-*ka-bar*/^{d}IM-GAL,[33] may be equivalent

---

[30] Carlo Zaccagnini, "Golden cups offered to the gods at Emar," *Or* NS 59 (1990) 518 n.4, 5. The article by Fales will appear in the *Mélanges P. Garelli*.

[31] For example, the name of the king of Emar is written ^{d}IM-*ka-bar* in text 42.8, but ^{md}U-GAL in line 20; the name of the diviner is written ^{md}IM-*ma-lik* in text 213.19, but ^{md}U-*ma-lik* in lines 12 and 21.

[32] This is the approach that E. Laroche takes when he interprets Emar names; see Laroche, "Les hiéroglyphes hittites de Meskéné-Emar: un emprunt d'écriture," *CRAIBL* 1983, 19-20.

[33] See Emar 15.29 and 42.8 for *-ka-bar*, 1.7 and often for the name with GAL.

to the form ᵐ*Ba-aḫ-lu-ka-bar*, giving us the West Semitic storm god Baal.[34] In addition, the name *Ba-'[a-l]a-ki-mi* (279.40) probably equals ᶠᵈU-*ki-mi* (279.22; 319.5), since the element *-ki-mi* is fairly rare (cf. ᶠ*Aš-tar-ki-mì*, 29.7). It is likely that Baᶜlu-kabar is also written EN-GAL in text 80.34, where the first witness is Zū-Aštarti DUMU EN-GAL. Zū-Aštarti, son of Baᶜlu-kabar, is the king of Emar who leads the list of witnesses in Emar 17.41 (cf. lines 1-2, 12-13, 17) and *RA* 77 text 2:43.

More information can be derived from the one type of theophoric name that has the form Zū-DN, "Belonging to DN."[35] This name type is very common at Emar and is significant because the gods Baal and Aštart dominate its use entirely, and Dagan/ᵈKUR is extremely rare.[36] Zū-Baᶜla[37] appears with

---

34 Emar 126.2; the name appears in the boundary description of a land sale, with no patronymic or modifier, so the equation cannot be certain. Note that in the bilingual seals from Emar, we find the equivalence, ᵐEN-GAL = *Ba-lu-*[*k*]*a-pa-*[*ra*]; Laroche, *Akkadica* 22 10, no.14. The name *Ba-'a-lu-ka* (336.14) may be an abbreviated form, though texts from Mumbaqat now show a divine name spelled ᵈ*Ba-aḫ-la-ka*, outside of personal names. W. Mayer, *MDOG* 122 47-48, suggests that the form could either be abbreviated from Baḫla-kabar or Baḫla-Ekalte, the latter based on the city-name. Abbreviation from the Ekalte city-name seems too limited to explain a name-type found also at Emar: cf. ᵈIM-*ka*, 109.44; 53.7(?); ᵈ*Da-gan-ka*, 2.36; 52.4, 32; EN-*ka*, 52.13, 21.

35 The very name type is West Semitic, from the determinative and relative pronoun /*d̲ū*/, "the one of." Manfred Krebernik says that at Ebla both *šu-* and *zu-* may be used to write the OAkk determinative pronoun /*šū*/, /*d̲ū*/; see Krebernik, *Die Personennamen der Ebla-Texte: eine Zwischenbilanz*, Berlin: Dietrich Reimer Verlag, 1988, 32. In Ebla names, the enclitic /*-m(a)*/ may be added; note the name *Zu-ma--da-mu*. This appears to represent a contrast to Ugarit, where /*d̲u*/ is rendered *du-ú* in the polyglot vocabulary, Ug 5 137 ii 29'; see Huehnergard, *Vocabulary*, 117. Arnaud states that /*d̲*/ is rendered with the signs DA, ZU, ZI, and ID at Emar; "Religion assyro-babylonienne," *AEPHER* 94 (1985-1986) 267.

36 To count these, I listed all the instances attested in Emar VI.3 and sorted them by associated patronyms, titles, and children (when the Zū-name is the patronym), to distinguish individual bearers of the names. The most reliable count comes from Zū-names that are followed by patronyms, Zū-DN DUMU PN. These should not be redundant, whereas a name found as a patronym may occur with multiple children.

37 The name ZU-Baᶜla raises special complications because one of the Hittite hieroglyphic seals renders ᵐ*ZU-Ba-la* as *Ya-di-ba-li*; see Laroche, *Akkadica* 22 11 (no. 30). The scribe for the seal has interpreted the ZU-sign as a logogram for the verb "to know." On the other hand, ᵐ*Zu-Aš-tar-ti* is rendered *Zu-wa-sa-tar-*[*ti*], reflecting the West Semitic pronoun. Given the predominance of Zū-Baᶜla and Zū-Aštarti among Emar names of this type, and the known association of these two deities in western Syria, it seems that the two names should have the same grammatical construction. Arnaud, *AuOr* 2 182 n.8, notes that a Hittite letter found at Emar mentions Zū-Baᶜla, and spells the name with *Zu-ú-*, as if reading /*zū*/. Arnaud suggests that the scribe might have mistaken what should be taken as an ideogram, but it seems more likely that the single example from the seals represents the mistake. I suspect that "Iadi-" does not reflect the original meaning and pronunciation of the name, and it may even be an error, mistaking a Semitic pronoun for a logogram. The name Iadi-Ilu (ᵐ*Ia-di-iḫ*-DINGIR^{meš}) is found at Ugarit (*Syria* 59 204ff; see Huehnergard, *Ugaritic Vocabulary*, 244), and a Hittite scribe might have seen this known Syrian element in the ZU-sign.

32 different patronyms, only two of which may represent the same person,[38] and Zū-Aštarti appears with 20 patronyms and only one possible repetition.[39] Zū-Eya and Zū-Anna have three examples each, Zū-Asdi has two, and Zū-Halma and Zū-ᵈKUR one each (for the latter, see 86.1, 9). The same pattern continues with the examples of Zū-names as patronyms, with titles only, or with no further identification.

The names Zū-Baʿla and Zū-Aštarti are almost always spelled syllabically,[40] and they indicate the existence of a cult at Emar for the west Syrian pair Baal and Aštart. These names are perhaps the strongest textual evidence for a strong Baal-Aštart cult in 13th-century Emar, and we will return to them when the question of Emar temples is discussed, below.

In the Akkadian texts, the name of the storm god is often spelled ᵈU-*ub* for "Teššub" in Hurrian personal names. These include the king of Carchemish, Ini-Teššub (201.1, 23) and his brother Hešmi-Teššub (18.2, 5, etc.; 19.1), as well as names for people who appear to live in the Emar area: Uri-Teššub,[41] Tuppi-Teššub,[42] and Mutri-Teššub.[43]

The Cult of Baal and Aštart, and the Chantier E Temples

I have indicated above that the popular names Zū-Baʿla and Zū-Aštarti may point to a cult for the divine pair Baal and Aštart at Emar. The texts from Emar themselves offer no hint of such a pairing, and the consort of ᵈIM is

---

The Akkadian of the bilingual seals appear to function with a set of scribal assumptions not found in the Akkadian texts:

- The names with ᵈIM are all Hurrian (with Teššub), and the logogram EN is reserved for both the DN "Baal" and the term "lord" (for ᵈIM, see no. 22, 41, 44).
- Dagan is always spelled with ᵈKUR (e.g. no. 19), though ᵈ*Da-gan* is common in the Akkadian texts.
- ᵈU can be the Akkadian storm god, Ad(d)a (e.g. no. 5, ᵐᵈU-UR.SAG = *A-tá-kar?-da*; no. 6, ᵐᵈU-*ra-pi-iḫ* = *A-ta-ra-pi-ya*). Adda does appear in names from the Akkadian texts: ᵐ*Ad-da*, 66.14; *Ad-da*, 110.6; ᵐ*Ad*ˀ*-du*, 256.2; ᵐ*Ri-ig-ma-Ad-da* from Karduniaš, 336.94.

38 *Ma*-[...], 52.55, and Madi-ᵈKUR, 120.19-20; *A-ḫi*-[...], 250.9-10, and Aḫi-Malik, 83.14, 15, 19.

39 EN-GAL, 80.34, may be the king ᵈIM-GAL, 17.1, etc.

40 Zū-Aštarti is always spelled *Zu-Aš-tar-ti*. There is one instance of Zū-ᵈIM, 14.29, and Zū-Baʿla is otherwise written *Zu-Ba-a'-la* (e.g. 14.27), *Zu-Ba-la* (e.g. 16.41), *Zu-Ba-a'-li* (32.23), and *Zu-Ba-aḫ-[la]* (108.2).

41 186.2, the *bēl abussi* (storehouse overseer); cf. 366.2?

42 261.11, 20, a wood-scribe from Šatappi.

43 252.9; 264.31.

Hebat in both the NIN.DINGIR installation and the offering lists (see above, Hebat). However, the excavations of Meskéné/Emar support the hypothesis that Aštart also was paired with ^{d}IM in 13th-century Emar.

The Emar which gave us the bounty of texts published by Arnaud existed for barely more than a century. Jean Margueron, the excavator, finds that the city was built almost from scratch on a manufactured tell during the reign of the Hittite king Muršili II, a massive project executed under supervision of Hittite architects and craftsmen, possible only with the resources of a major power.[44] Margueron and the epigraphers, Emmanuel Laroche and Arnaud, agree that archaeological and textual evidence show that Late Bronze Age Emar was built at the end of the 14th century (*c.* 1310?) and destroyed at the beginning of the 12th century (*c.* 1187?).[45] This means that the temple geography reflects the 14th-13th century religious situation much more closely than we could usually expect. The temples excavated at Late Bronze Emar were built not long before the Emar texts were written, and there were probably no pre-existing sacred sites to influence the placement of the new temples.

Two promontories stand atop the tell at Meskéné/Emar, one on the north side, toward the river, and the higher one at the west extreme of the city. A palace with texts involving the kings of Emar and relations with their superiors at Carchemish was found in chantier A on the north promontory.[46] The height at the west end of the tell revealed a pair of temples separated by a road, facing the city, and backed by an open space with basins cut into the surface, perhaps for making libations (chantier E).[47] These two temples produced the texts which led Arnaud and Margueron to assign the sanctuaries to Baal and

---

44 See Margueron, *CRAIBL* 1975, 210-211; *Syria* 52 (1975) 83-84; "Emar: un exemple d'implantation hittite en terre syrienne," in *Le Moyen Euphrate*, 285-312; *AAAS* 32 (1982) 242; "Aux marches de l'empire Hittite: une campagne de fouille à Tell Faq'ous (Syrie), citadelle du pays d'Aštata," in RAI 27, *La Syrie au Bronze Récent*, Paris: Editions Recherche sur les Civilisations, 1982, 61-62.

45 Arnaud, *Syria* 52 88-89.

46 Margueron, *AAAS* 32 234 and fig.2; see Arnaud, Emar VI.3, nos. 1-22.

47 See Margueron, *Syria* 52 62; *CRAIBL* 1975, 207-208; *Le Moyen Euphrate*, 308-310; *AAAS* 32 235-236 and fig.4.

Aštart.[48] Texts from the southern temple (Emar 42-62) include the three votive offerings from the king of Emar to the storm god (ᵈU, Emar 42), a list of the ᵍⁱˢTUKUL.MEŠ *ša* ᵈIM (45, line 1), a list of archers who receive bows for or at (*ana*) the temple of ᵈIM (52, line 1), and a small tablet mentioning the gold of ᵈIM (59, lines 1-2). In addition, text 43 records the treasure of ᵈINANNA URU.KI, "Aštart of the city" (line 1). A few tablets were discovered in the northern temple (Emar 63-67), but these are less helpful, being mainly lists of personal names. Excavations also uncovered a bronze bull and a male figure in bronze in the southern temple.[49]

Identification of the southern building as the sanctuary of the storm god is certainly warranted. The northern building is more difficult, but indirect testimony supports the tentative association with Aštart. First, in contrast to the diviner's archive in the temple M_1, the tablets from chantier E mention only two deities, Baal and Aštart-of-the-city. Then, the Emar texts in their entirety do hint at a Baal-Aštart cult in the city. The only installation rituals are for the priestesses of Baal and Aštart, and the common Zū-DN names occur with those two gods almost exclusively. The longest lists of personal names from the chantier E temples have the heaviest concentration of Zū-names of all Emar texts. Emar 52, from the southern building, has six separate men named Zū-Baᶜla, all with patronyms given.[50] Emar 65, from the northern building, mentions four Zū-Aštarti's and four Zū-Baᶜla's, all in the first position of the name-compounds. Although they do not appear to be combined systematically, all four Aštart names come first (lines 8, 17, 18, 28), with the Baal names after (lines 30, 33, 34, 35). Perhaps these are service-names, given to people dedicated to work in the temples of these deities.

Thirteenth-century Emar thus has a distinct cult for the gods Baal and Aštart, and more than that, a dual sanctuary for them which occupies the highest point of the tell, the place of honor in the geography of Emar

---

48 See Margueron, "Rapport préliminaire sur les deux premières campagnes de fouille à Meskéné-Emar (1972-1973)," *AAAS* 25 (1975) 77; Arnaud, "Catalogue des textes cunéiformes trouvés au cours des trois premières campagnes à Meskéné qadimé Ouest (Chantiers A, C, E, et trouvaille de surface)," *AAAS* 25 (1975) 92. Margueron is sure about the Baal temple and identifies the Aštart temple simply by its pairing with that of Baal. Arnaud says that some doubt must remain. See also Margueron, *CRAIBL* 1975, 208, and Arnaud, *Syria* 52 90.

49 Margueron, *Syria* 52 73.

50 Lines 5, 17, 19, 20, 55, 70; Zū-Baᶜla is never a father's name in the list.

temples.[51] This fact magnifies the tension we find between the status of Baal and that of Dagan in the varied pantheons of Emar.

Beyond Emar, the Baal/Aštart pair is not attested before the second half of the second millennium B.C.E.,[52] but a variety of sources attest the pair for that period. In the mythic texts of Ugarit, Aštart shares her position as Baal's consort with the more visible goddess Anat, setting the stage for the later fusion of the two in the first-millennium goddess Atargatis.[53] In the incantation against snakebite, KTU 1.100, the two goddesses are joined to form a compound name, *ʿnt wʿṯtrt*.[54] A second attestation may come from the myth of Elkunirša and Ašertu from Boghazkoy/Hattuša.[55] The four players are Elkunirša[56] and Ašertu (Ugaritic *ʾaṯrt*), dIM and dIŠTAR, not only a West Semitic but a specifically Canaanite pantheon, seen in the El/Asherah pair. dIM must be Baal in this context, and dIŠTAR should be Aštart, though we cannot rule out Anat.

A third source of evidence is Egypt. New Kingdom Egypt (the 18th and 19th dynasties, *c.* 1600-1200) expanded successfully into Palestine and Syria and in turn felt increased Semitic influence on its own culture. One manifestation of the new interchange was the appearance in the Egyptian pantheon of Syrian gods such as Baal and Rešep, Anat and Aštart.[57] Anat and Aštart take part in the Conflict of Horus and Seth as prospective wives of Seth, who is equated with Baal. Egyptian religion of this period followed normative practice, but took on foreign deities; for instance, there was a "priest (*hm-nṯr*)

---

51 See Margueron, *CRAIBL* 1975, 208. J.-L. Cunchillos says that the dominant temple at Ugarit is also Baal's, an interesting point of similarity if true; "Le dieu Mut, guerrier de El," *Syria* 62 (1985) 216.

52 Alalaḫ attests both dIM and INANNA/Ištar, but they should not be seen as a pair. dIM's proper consort is Hebat, as seen in the pantheon of Halab/Yamḫad. The Semitic pronunciation of dIM at Alalaḫ is probably the Akkadian Addu (see below).

53 See Nicholas Wyatt, "The Anat stela from Ugarit and its ramifications," *UF* 16 (1984) 327-329.

54 See A. Caquot, "Problèmes d'histoire religieuse," in Liverani, ed., *La Siria nel tardo bronzo*, 73.

55 Laroche, CTH 342; see E. von Schuler, "Beziehungen zwischen Syrien und Anatolien in der Späten Bronzezeit," in *La Siria*, 115; translation in *ANET* p. 519.

56 The name is understood as *ʾEl-qōnēʾ-ʾ(a)rṣ*, "El, creator of the earth." Note the compound divine name at Emar, dKUR EN *qu-ú-ni*, 373.5; 381.15; 382.16. The element *qu-ú-ni* tempts comparison with the term "creator." Emar does not fall within the zone of the operation of the Canaanite shift, but the title could be borrowed from further west. Dagan and El would play roughly equivalent roles as pantheon heads and father figures (note the title, dKUR *a-bu-ma*, "Dagan the father," in the *zukru*, 373.195).

57 K.A. Kitchen, "Interrelations of Egypt and Syria," in *La Siria*, 87.

of Astarte and Baal."[58] A New Kingdom Egyptian seal from Bethel identifies Aštart by name, and she faces a god who wears a helmet-crown and holds a scimitar -- probably Baal.[59] Finally, a stele from Abu Simbel lists offerings for gods that include the pair Seth and Astarte.[60]

During later times, we find the pair in Roman Palmyra, where Bolastar (*bwlʿštr*) was an early Bel-form,[61] and in the Phoenician pantheon recorded in Eusebius' source, Sakkunyaton. The sequence of Semitic deities in the latter moves from Chronos and Ouranos to Astarte and Zeus called Adodas.[62]

In all the cases where Baal and Aštart are paired, the cultural context is discernibly Canaanite, even when transmitted by a foreign medium.[63] We do not have third-millennium and early second-millennium sources to tell us how far back Baal (or the older Canaanite storm god) and Aštart can be found, but the pair shows no sign of belonging to inland sites in northern Syria. Neither Ebla nor Mari hint at such a connection, and Lambert traces into the west a different pair from early Mari, ᵈÍD and ᵈ*Aš-tár-ra-at*. He relates ᵈÍD ("river") to Ugaritic Yam's title, "judge river," though the coupling of Yam and Aštart is not found in known Canaanite texts.[64] The combination of Baal and Aštart at a site as far inland as Emar is quite unusual, and there is ground for suspecting western influence.

Aštart herself is already attested in the third millennium; she is the feminine aspect of the two-sided Semitic planetary deity Aštar.[65] Archi finds the feminine form at Ebla,[66] and Aštart is attested in Presargonic Mari.[67] She

---

[58] *Ibid*, 90. See also Rainer Stadelmann, *Syrisch-palestinensische Gottheiten in Ägypten*, Leiden: E.J. Brill, 1967, 34, on this tomb at Sakkara; Stadelmann concludes that this inscription shows there is a sanctuary of Baal and Astarte at this site.

[59] Stadelmann, *Gottheiten*, 43 and 105. The other possible identification for the male deity is Rašap.

[60] *Ibid*, 106.

[61] See Teixidor, *The Pantheon of Palmyra*, 9. "The spelling *bwl* instead of *bl* indicates that the association of Bel and Ishtar/Astarte had become a cultic formula at an early date."

[62] *Praeparatio Evangelica* 1.10.10:30-42. See Harold W. Attridge and Robert A. Oden, *Philo of Biblos, The Phoenician History*, Washington, D.C.: The CBA of America, 1981, 55.

[63] Even inland Palmyra appears to have derived many of its religious features from the west, via Arabian tribes; Teixidor, *Palmyra*, ix, 13, 18, etc. However, Emar shows that the western influence could be as early as the second millennium.

[64] W.G. Lambert, "The pantheon of Mari," *M.A.R.I.* 4 (1985) 535-536.

[65] See J.J.M. Roberts, *The Earliest Semitic Pantheon*, Baltimore: The Johns Hopkins University Press, 1972, 38-39; Lambert, *M.A.R.I.* 4 536-537. The male counterpart at early Mari is ᵈINANNA.UŠ, see Lambert, 537.

[66] *AAAS* 29-30 168.

[67] Roberts, 39; cf. Lambert, *M.A.R.I.* 4 535-536.

is found in western Syria of the second millennium at Ugarit.[68] However, the goddess became extremely popular in Mesopotamia under the masculine form Ištar,[69] and in Syrian peripheral Akkadian texts the borrowed form Ištar (/INANNA) is used to write the old name Aštart. At Emar, the West Semitic form appears almost exclusively in personal names such as Zū-Aštarti (above), otherwise spelled ^{d}*Iš*$_{8}$*-tár* or ^{d}INANNA, according to Mesopotamian custom.[70] The goddess *Aštartu ša ab(b)i* occurs in several forms, including the syllabic spellling of the divine name: [^{d}*A*]*š-tar-ti ša ab-bi* (153.2); [^{d}*Iš*$_{8}$*-t*]*ár a-ba-ú* (274.9); ^{d}INANNA *ša a-bi* (373.92; 384.2); ^{d}*Iš*$_{8}$*-tár ša a-bi* (452.5,17). These should represent the same deity.[71]

We should note the following mention of Aštart's temple affairs in Emar documents. One text is from the chantier E temple which appears to belong to Baal, an inventory of the treasure (*šu-kut-ti*) of ^{d}INANNA URU.KI, "Aštart of the city" (43.1). In texts from the archive of temple M_1, she appears in a request to perform her offerings, 265.10-11, and according to the list of temple personnel, 276.8, there is a NIN.DINGIR *ša* ^{d}*Iš*$_{8}$*-tár*.

Excursus: ^{d}*IŠTAR at Alalaḫ*

The use of the Mesopotamian writing for Aštart at Emar raises the question of who is ^{d}IŠTAR at Alalaḫ. Wiseman speculates that she is Išḫara, based on one case where the personal name Ummi-Išḫara is written *Um-mi-*DU(IŠTAR?)*-ra*,

[72] but DU may simply be a Sumerogram for Išḫara, with IŠTAR not involved at all.[73] Moreover, the sequence ^{d}IM ^{d}UTU ^{d}*Iš-ḫa-ra* in the treaty

---

68 *ʿṯtrt*; see de Moor, *UF* 2 195, 217-218; Wyatt, *UF* 16 327.

69 See Lambert, *M.A.R.I.* 4 536 and n.24 for explanation of the Mesopotamian use; see J. Renger, "Götternamen in der altbabylonischen Zeit," in D.O. Edzard, ed., *Heidelberger Studien zum Alten Orient*, Wiesbaden: Otto Harrassowitz, 1967, 164, for distribution in the OB period. W. Heimpel, "A catalog of Near Eastern Venus deities," *Syro-Mesopotamian Studies* 4 (1982) 13-14, 22, emphasizes that Ištar is directly related to the male form Aṯtar (Ebla's Aštar), and not thus linked to the female Aštart (Ugarit's *ʿṯtrt*).

70 Note the following Emar personal names that display the continued presence of the male deity Aštar: ^{f}*Aš-tar-ki-mì*, 29.7; ^{m}*Aš-tar-a-bu*, 33.1, cf. 111.11; ^{f}*Aš-tar*-É, 91.4; [^{m}*Ia*]*-ṣí-*^{d}*Aš-tar*, 97.4.

71 On *abû*, see the Appendix.

72 See Wiseman, *Alalakh*, 9, n.2, and AT 91 on page 54. Ilse Wegner, *Ištar-Šawuška*, 176, follows Wiseman, and gathers the following equations: AT 30:13 *Eḫ-li-*^{d}IŠTAR*-ra* = 91:7, 13 *Eḫ-li-*^{d}*Iš-ḫa-ra*; AT 91:13 ^{f}*Um-mi*-IŠTAR*-ra* = 88:5 ^{f}*Um-mi-Iš-ḫa-ra*. It would be helpful to have collated readings of the IŠTAR-names to see if the sign is really the same as those for IŠTAR without *-ra*.

73 Note Ebla's ^{d}BARA$_{10}$.RA for Išḫara; see Archi, *AAAS* 29-30 168. F. Pomponio, "I nomi divini nei testi di Ebla," *UF* 15 (1983) 146, notes the spellings ^{d}BARA$_{7}$, BARA$_{10}$, ^{d}BARA$_{10}$*-ra*, and ^{d}AMA*-ra*.

curse AT 346 separates Išḫara from the storm god by a male deity. If anything, Išḫara is paired with the Šamaš/^{d}UTU in this text, not ^{d}IM. Wilhelm says IŠTAR of Alalaḫ is Hurrian Šawuška,[74] allowing that she can be part of the western Hurrian pantheon (vs. the view of Haas, see below). A third possibility would be the West Semitic Aštart, following the later Emar equation.

Whatever the correct pronunciation of the logogram in second-millennium Alalaḫ, the goddess may have a heritage that predates any association with the storm god. Na'aman argues that IŠTAR is the city-goddess of Alalaḫ, and the prominence of ^{d}IM in the texts comes from the influence of Halab.[75] The excavations at Alalaḫ produced seventeen superimposed temples, which should belong to the city-god. IŠTAR's identification as that city-god is confirmed by the title on the Idrimi statue, ^{d}INANNA GAŠAN ^{uru}*A-la-la-aḫ*, "IŠTAR, mistress of Alalaḫ." Both Yarim-Lim and Idrimi set up their statues before IŠTAR, in the local temple.[76] If IŠTAR is the primary deity of Alalaḫ, independent of the storm god, perhaps she should have a north Syrian/West Semitic name.

The Storm God and Hebat

The religious texts from Emar present Hebat, not Ištar/Aštart, as the consort of ^{d}IM. These include the NIN.DINGIR installation, two god lists, and another ritual fragment. The *zukru* festival offering list included the *sikkānu* of Hebat and ^{d}IM of the *bīt Gadda* (see above). One god list from Emar begins with sets of divine spouses, 378.1-5:

1. [^{d}KUR] EN *bu-*[*ka-r*]*i*
2. ^{d}NIN.LÍL ⌜DAM$^{?!}$⌝ ^{d}KUR EN *bu-k*[*a-ri*][77]
3. ^{d}KUR.GAL (part of the Dagan set)
4. ^{d}IM *ù* ^{d}*Ḫé-ba-at*

---

[74] *Grundzüge*, 71.
[75] Na'aman's case works well with both the textual and archaeological evidence from Alalaḫ. However, I am hesitant to assign all the texts mentioning ^{d}IM to Halab without question. It seems difficult to prove that all the tablets with penalty clauses addressed to ^{d}IM are "genuine products of the court of Halab" (Na'aman, "The Ishtar temple at Alalakh," *JNES* 39 (1980) 211).
[76] For the whole argument, see Na'aman, *JNES* 39 209-214.
[77] The sign is more likely DAM than *ù*, which would involve repeating ^{d}KUR EN *bukari* without qualification.

5. ᵈ*É-a ù* ᵈ*Dam-ki-an-na* (cf. Enūma Eliš I:83-84)

Finally, both ᵈIM and Hebat receive offerings during the *ḫiari* of ᵈIM, Emar 463.25-28. The noun *ḫiari* also occurs at Alalaḫ and is thought to be a Hurrian loan (see *CAD* s.v. *ḫiari*), but it is not yet attested in a Hurrian text and might have a Semitic etymology.[78]

The goddess Hebat is the consort of the storm god of Halab in a tradition that works its way into the west Hurrian pantheon of Kizzuwatna and then the pantheon of Boghazkoy (see below). This Halab pairing also appears in the introduction to the level VII (OB) diplomatic text from Alalaḫ, AT 1:2-3. Hebat's name occurs in the name from OB Ebla, *Ig-ri-iš-ḫi-ib*,[79] the father of the Ebla king Ibitlim.[80] Although she becomes a prominent part of the Hurrian and Hittite pantheons, Hebat is attested very early in northern Syria, and may be of Semitic origin.[81] She should not be viewed as a Hurrian deity *per se*.

The contrast between the evidence of the religious texts and the evidence of the temple contents and the names indicates that 13th-century Emar was home to two separate traditions for the storm god and his circle.

ᵈIM as Pantheon Head

Naturally enough, the principal god of the NIN.DINGIR installation festival is ᵈIM, the god to whom the priestess is devoted. Emar's other dominant god, Dagan, fails to play any direct role. It seems that such an event should originate in a setting where Dagan was not the central figure. Further, the archaeological evidence shows us the temple and cult of ᵈIM set at the height of the 13th-century city. Although Dagan is the principal god of the Middle Euphrates region (see below), nearby pantheons place the storm god at the head, and these are potential sources of influence on both the NIN.DINGIR festival and Emar religion more broadly. Thus, it will be useful to examine the evidence for storm gods who lead pantheons in neighboring lands.

In the second millennium we find storm gods atop the pantheon in various lands north and west of Mesopotamia. The Hittite weather god,

---

78 *ḫiyaru* or **ḫayyaru*, "choice"? (Huehnergard, personal communication).
79 See Krebernik, 88 and 196.
80 See Haas, RAI 24, 65.
81 Haas, RAI 24, 65, speculates that the name might be related to the Semitic Ḥawwat (biblical Eve), though the phonological similarity does not seem very great. Hebat's origin remains unknown.

written ^{d}U and ^{d}IM, joined the sun goddess of Arinna at the highest rank,[82] though numerous forms of the storm god were venerated throughout the territories of Hatti. ^{d}IM/Teššub was the lone head of both east and west Hurrian pantheons (see below), with spouses Šawuška and Hebat, respectively.[83] Baal shows some tendency toward ascendency in the Ugaritic literary texts, though El still holds the supreme place.[84] Letters from Qatna found at El Amarna substitute "my storm god" (^{d}IM) for the usual greeting "my sun," a switch that probably shows the storm god's leading position in this city during the 14th century.[85] Preliminary evidence from 15th-century Mumbaqat/Ekalte indicates that the largest percentage of divine names in theophoric names are ^{d}IM and ^{d}EN, which W. Mayer interprets as Addu and Baḫla respectively.[86] The city-god of Ekalte contracts is Baḫlaka (a form of Baal), who may be distinguished in curses from ^{d}IM.[87]

Halab was an ancient cult-center of the storm god, and "the storm god of Halab" became important far beyond the bounds of the city-state itself.[88] This god was one of the northern Syrian deities encountered by Hattušili I (mid-16th century) in his campaigns southward,[89] and he thereafter became part of the

---

82 Laroche, *Recherches*, 108-109; see Haas, *Berggötter*, 25-26: in the early Hattian circle, these are Taru and Wurunšemu, the latter an earth-goddess, called sun-goddess at Arinna.

83 See Wilhelm, *Grundzüge*, 69-71; W.G. Lambert, "The Mesopotamian background of the Hurrian pantheon," in RAI 24, 129; cf. Haas, *Berggötter*, 34-35; Diakonoff, "Evidence on the ethnic division of the Hurrians," in M.A. Morrison and D.I. Owen, eds., *Studies on the Civilization and Culture of Nuzi and the Hurrians*, Winona Lake, IN: Eisenbrauns, 1981, 87.

84 This is a much-discussed topic. Marvin Pope offers a concise and balanced analysis in a recent article, "The status of El at Ugarit," *UF* 19 (1987) 219-230, especially 224-225.

85 EA 52:4; 53:6; see Moran, *El Amarna*: EA 52, n. 2. Bottéro, *RA* 43 8, notes that the storm god appears in the Qatna inventories.

86 Mayer, *MDOG* 122 47.

87 Mayer, in M. Dietrich, O. Loretz, and W. Mayer, *UF* 21 136-137, collects five Mumbaqat curses, invoking the following gods: MBQ-T 35:25-27, Baḫlaka (^{d}*Ba-aḫ-la-ka*); 36:14-19, ^{d}IM and Dagan (^{d}*Da-gan*); 41:17-20, Baḫlaka, Šamaš (^{d}UTU), and Dagan; 69:25-29, Dagan and Baḫlaka; 73:8-11, ^{d}IM and Dagan. Baḫlaka appears both before and after Dagan, and there are no texts that invoke both Baḫlaka and ^{d}IM, so the two are not demonstrably separate deities. Notice, however, that in the paired deities, ^{d}IM appears before Dagan twice, but Baḫlaka is placed after Dagan.

88 For full treatment of the second-millennium evidence for the storm god of Halab, treating texts from Hatti, Aššur, and Mari in the main, see H. Klengel, "Der Wettergott von Halab," *JCS* 19 (1965) 87-88. See also Ichiro Nakata, *Deities in the Mari Texts*, Columbia University PhD, 1974, 22-24.

89 Wilhelm, *Grundzüge*, 30; O.R. Gurney, *Some Aspects of Hittite Religion*, 13.

Hittite pantheon.[90] A Mari year formula from the reign of Zimri-Lim is based on consecration of a statue of the king for the storm god of Halab.[91] Ugaritic alphabetic lists of gods and offerings include *bˤl ḫlb*.[92]

The evidence from Alalaḫ is ambiguous. On one hand, the city-goddess of Alalaḫ does seem to be IŠTAR, and the political subjection of Alalaḫ to Halab/Yamḫad explains the prominence of the storm god. However, ^{d}IM is quite well assimilated into the religious scheme of Alalaḫ during the OB period, and may represent more than a superficial addition from outside.[93] Penalty payments in Alalaḫ sales documents are made to the temple of ^{d}IM, as well as to the palace and (once) to the temple of IŠTAR.[94] This role is reserved for ^{d}NIN.URTA at Emar, and seems to belong to the city-god. ^{d}IM is the first god listed in later Alalaḫ treaty curses (AT 2:77-78; 3:46, level IV), he is the most frequently attested god in theophoric names, with the moon god,[95] and the seals on one Alalaḫ legal document (AT 7, level VII) include four with titles *narām(ti)* DN, three of which have DN = ^{d}IM (the fourth is a woman, with ^{d}NIN.É.GAL).

Note that the Semitic form of the storm god in personal names is Ad(d)u. Wiseman finds that ^{d}IM = Adu/a in AT 41 (level VII), where the same name is spelled *Ir-pa-*^{d}IM (line 2) and *Ir-pa-da* (line 14),[96] and notes that Teššub rarely appears.[97]

Teššub and the Hurrian Pantheon

Although the established center at Halab provides a prominent home for an ancient Semitic cult with the storm god at its head, the Hurrian pantheon

---

90 Gurney, 4; cf. Laroche, *GLH*, 264 (Teššub); Haas, "Einführung in das Thema," in Haas, ed., *Hurriter und Hurritisch*, Konstanz: Universitätsverlag, 1988, 18-19 (a hymn to Teššub of Halab); E. von Schuler, in *La Siria*, 116; V. Souçek and J. Seigelova, "Der Kult des Wettergottes von Halap in Hatti," *ArOr* 42 (1974) 39-52; H.-J. Thiel and I. Wegner, "Eine Anrufung an den Gott Teššup von Halab in hurritischer Sprache," *SMEA* 24 (1984) 187-213 (his growing importance is attributed to the rise of Yamḫad, page 188).

91 Klengel, *Geschichte Syriens* I, 106, year formula no. 20. See also the Mari letter, A 1121 + A 2731, the new join published by B. Lafont, *RA* 78 9-10, especially lines 46, 49, 60.

92 J. de Moor, *UF* 2 191.

93 Again, see Na'aman, *JNES* 39 211.

94 ^{d}IM: AT 52, 54, 58, 95; the palace: AT 52, 54, 55, 56, 95; IŠTAR: 61. All of these are from level VII.

95 Wiseman, *Alalakh*, 10.

96 *Alalakh*, 45.

97 *Ibid*, 17.

probably remains the most visible storm god cult in northern Syria of the second millennium. The Hurrian pantheon is attested across northern Mesopotamia and Syria in this period, and encroaches on the ancient Hittite pantheon via the southern province of Kizzuwatna. Given the strength of Hurrian influence on the culture of northern Syria, we cannot consider the storm god's cult at Emar without examining the Hurrian version.

Evidence for the Hurrian culture is scattered across northern Mesopotamia and Syria, with a concentration of texts and quotations in the Hurrian language found at Boghazkoy/Hattuša. Hurrian cultural features are mingled with the local Hittite at Hattuša, with the Mesopotamian at Nuzi, and with the West Semitic at Alalaḫ, and unraveling the threads has been a long and difficult task.[98] There is increasing agreement that the Hurrian pantheon must be divided according to regions, and that some deities in the west derive from the Semitic Syrian pantheon. In particular, it must be determined whether there are Hurrian divine names in the new data from third-millennium Ebla.[99] Volkert Haas concludes there are not, and sets up a division between east and west Hurrian circles to explain the situation. The west includes Alalaḫ, Kizzuwatna, southeast Asia Minor, and northern Syria. Hattuša has a syncretic pantheon heavily influenced by the west Hurrian circle. The east includes Arrapḫa and Nuzi, from Lakes Van and Urmia to the Tigris River, and the Zagros Mountains. The eastern group is probably the more genuinely Hurrian, with sources in the Samarra inscription of Tišatal, the Nuzi personal names, and the first-millennium Urartu pantheon. From these, he constructs a core Hurrian pantheon of Teššub and Šawuška, Šimige, Kušuḫ, Kumarbi, and heaven and earth.[100] Mari and Mitanni stand between the two spheres, with Mari oriented more toward the west[101] and Mitanni to the east.[102] Ugarit is an exception, with Teššub and Šawuška placed at the head of the pantheon by a small Hurrian colony with origins in the Mitanni sphere.[103]

Major "Hurrian" deities with what may be pre-Hurrian attestation in northern Syria include Hebat, Išḫara, Adamma, and Kubaba.[104] Hebat is the

---

98 See Wilhelm, *Grundzüge*, 1-7, for background; cf. Haas, in *Hurriter und Hurritisch*, 20-21.
99 Haas, in RAI 24, 59.
100 *Ibid*, 60-62.
101 *Ibid*, 60. Teššub and Hebat are found at Mari; see J.-R. Kupper, "Dieux hourrites à Mari," *RA* 65 (1971) 171-172, and Kupper, "Les hourrites à Mari," in RAI 24, 118-119.
102 Haas, *Berggötter*, 35.
103 Haas, RAI 24, 66; *Berggötter*, 35.
104 Haas, RAI 24, 62-68: the "Substratgottheiten."

high goddess of the west Hurrian pantheon, known as far east as Mari, with weaker influence beyond that.[105] Išḫara and Adamma are found in third-millennium Ebla, with Hebat appearing in one second-millennium Ebla personal name (see above). These three deities appear in Emar festivals, which otherwise include only one reference to Hurrian gods (Šuwala and Ugur, 385.23).

Gernot Wilhelm reaches similar conclusions, but removes Alalaḫ from the west Hurrian circle, saying IŠTAR is Šawuška.[106] Hebat, Išḫara, and Adamma are definitely north Syrian.[107] In his early study of the Hittite pantheon, Emmanuel Laroche assumed Hebat was properly Hurrian, and Išḫara was a Sumerian goddess brought to the Hittites via the Hurrians,[108] but he assigned them western origins in his *Glossaire de la langue hourrite*, published after discovery of the Ebla archives.[109] Alfonso Archi says it is best to explain the presence at Ebla of gods like Adamma and Aštabi as adoption of these by Hurrian populations when they arrive in Syria.[110] Some scholars still call these gods "Hurrian"; this requires hypothesizing a Hurrian presence at Ebla as early as the mid-third millennium.[111]

This distinction of a Syrian-influenced substrate in a western Hurrian pantheon illuminates the pantheons of the Emar festivals. Most of the Emar festival gods that are shared by the Hurrian pantheon probably were worshipped in pre-Hurrian Syria. Moreover, the ᵈIM/Hebat pair of the NIN.DINGIR can be viewed as ancient Syrian and not exclusively Hurrian.

---

105 She is only in personal names in Arrapḫa and Mitanni; *ibid*, 65-66.
106 *Grundzüge*, 71-72.
107 *Ibid*, 78, based on the Ebla occurrences.
108 Laroche, *Recherches*, 131-132, cf. 47-48, 51.
109 *GLH*, 100, Hebat is west Hurrian; 126, Išḫara is Syrian; cf. Laroche, "Pantheon national et panthéons locaux chez les Hourrites," *Or* NS 45 (1976) 99. T. Jacobsen, "The Gilgamesh Epic: romantic and tragic vision," in Tzvi Abusch, John Huehnergard, and Piotr Steinkeller, eds., *Lingering Over Words*, HSS 37, Atlanta: Scholars Press, 1990, 237 n.9, suggests that the name Išḫara is likely borrowed from West Semitic **śᶜār* "barley," noting the identification of Išḫara with Sumerian Nisaba.
110 *AAAS* 29-30 171, quoting comments by Laroche at the 1977 Rencontre assyriologique; see also D. Stein, "Mythologische Inhalte der Nuzi-Glyptik," in Haas, ed., *Hurriter*, 173; A. Kammenhuber, *Or* NS 45 143, acknowledges that Hebat is a Syrian goddess from west of the Euphrates, as does J. Danmanville, "Hepat, Hebat," in *RlA* 4, 1972-1975, 328-329; see for Išḫara G. Frantz-Szabó, "Išḫara," *RlA* 5, 1977, 177.
111 M. Astour, "Les hourrites en Syrie du Nord: rapport sommaire," in RAI 24, 3; cf. F. Pomponio, *UF* 15 146.

5. The Background and Development of the Installations

It has been observed above that the two installation festivals display both strong similarities and fundamental differences. The similarities include a roughly parallel time scheme for both festival and annual allotment, a shared sequence of acts for performing offerings, equivalent dignitaries and assigned meat portions, and parallel sacred geography -- especially the *bīt* NIN.DINGIR and *bīt maš'arti*. These shared features probably reflect a closely related temple establishment in the 13th-century city excavated at Meskéné, and they would make sense in the context of the paired temples found in chantier E. However, the two installations do not appear to have originated in this setting. The storm god plays a minimal role in the *maš'artu* installation, and is certainly not treated as the husband of Aštart. Likewise, Aštart does not even appear in the NIN.DINGIR installation, where we find Hebat associated with ᵈIM instead. Other differences reflect the separate traditions of the NIN.DINGIR and *maš'artu* roles. The first comes from Mesopotamia, though the institution appears to be deeply rooted in Syrian culture by the Late Bronze Age. The second does not have any discernible Mesopotamian connection, and appears to function within a separate world of concern for military success.

The NIN.DINGIR Installation

The pantheon of the NIN.DINGIR installation has a second striking omission: Dagan, the high god of Emar. With the omission of both Aštart and Dagan, the festival suits neither the established pantheon of the Middle Euphrates, with Dagan at its head (see below), nor the Baal/Aštart combination given such architectural prominence in the Hittite-built city, favoring Hebat instead. These are traits that reflect an earlier time, and perhaps the pantheon of another city. Although Dagan is given no role in the festival, the authority of ᵈNIN.URTA and the elders, an old native institution, backs up the choice and enthronement of the new priestess. The *purû* (lots?) come from ᵈNIN.URTA, and the elders bow before her and give her gifts. The NIN.DINGIR festival belongs to an urban setting and temple cult; there is no hint of agricultural or rural concerns or locations.

While the western Baal/Aštart pair does not appear, other western characteristics are found: the anointing of Hebat's *sikkānu* is very like the anointing of the *maṣṣēbâ* in the biblical patriarchal narratives, and Gadda and

Šaḫru of ^{d}IM's circle may have West Semitic origins. The "NIN.DINGIR" herself and marriage to the god she serves may derive ultimately from the Mesopotamian institution of the NIN.DINGIR/*entu*, but the details of the installation festival seem deeply Syrian. Halab was a major Near Eastern center for the cult of the storm god ^{d}IM and may have been the original home of the ^{d}IM/Hebat pair, so a Halab connection for the Emar festival is a strong possibility. The institution of the NIN.DINGIR could have come to Syria in OB times, when Mari served as a powerful intermediary, or perhaps even earlier.

The maš'artu Installation

Like the NIN.DINGIR festival, the *maš'artu* installation has no active role for Dagan/^{d}KUR, though he does lead the pantheon for the cycle of feasting that fills the week between the detailed rites for the first and last days. The hierarchy for this week of feasting probably belongs to 13th-century Emar (see below). Ea appears at a key point in the festival, as the source of water when the *maš'artu* prepares to bathe Aštart, an appropriate function for the god of fresh waters. Otherwise, Aštart alone dominates this festival in her role as war-goddess (so, *Aštartu tāḫāzi*, in 370.20). Until the discovery of the Emar texts, the *maš'artu* was an unknown figure in ancient Near Eastern religion, and since her involvement in the NIN.DINGIR installation is not deep (and vice versa), her own ritual is probably based in a cult of Aštart that stood independent of the cult of the storm god. Again, there is no sign of rural/agricultural interests, and the centrality of preparation for battle might suit the concerns of the city-state center.

C. THE ZUKRU FESTIVAL

The *zukru* festival appears to have been a major ritual event in Emar, judging by its length and the scope of its activity, involving by far the most numerous offering materials in Emar ritual.[112] It is unique in that the action takes place outside the city, centering on the "gate of the stelae" (*sikkānātu*). Before the discovery of the Emar rituals, we have had no ancient Near Eastern

---

112 See 373.211: 700 lambs and 50 bullocks (read AMAR, not GUD).

attestation of a *zukru* festival, and the term itself is only known from one letter to Zimri-Lim of Mari, recently supplemented by a new join and republished by Bertrand Lafont.[113] The letter comes from a provincial official of Zimri-Lim, who relays requests from the kingdom of Yamḫad[114] for concessions to show gratitude for helping Zimri-Lim regain his throne at Mari. The first demand is that a *zukrum* (not specified as a festival) be given (*nadānum*) to ᵈIM *be-el Ka-al-la-su*ᵏⁱ, in conjunction with a land-grant (*niḫlatum*) consisting of a place called Alaḫtum.[115] The nature of the *zukrum* for Kallassu is not illuminated by the letter.[116]

1. The Plan of the Festival Text

Emar 373 (Msk 74292a plus fragments) is the principal witness to the *zukru* festival, a complex event that combines a long offering list for Emar's city gods, a calendar-based format that centers on the New Year (the 14th and 15th days of the first month, ⁱᵗⁱSAG.MU) of the 7th year of a 7-year cycle,[117] and an archaic ritual that takes place outside the city walls, apparently beyond the domains of temple and palace. Unfortunately, the beginning of Emar 373 is broken, and though Emar 375 clearly supplies that lack, it is severely

---

113 Lafont, *RA* 78 7-18.

114 The requests are communicated by means of prophecies from the *āpilum*'s of ᵈIM of Kallassu and ᵈIM of Halab.

115 See lines 3-10, 30-33.

116 Lafont (p. 11) understands the *zukrum* to be "un ensemble d'animaux mâles," derived from the root "être mâle," versus the *CAD* s.v. *zukru*, which was based on the earlier fragment without the join. Another possibility might be the root *zkr*, "to invoke," if the name of the festival (and offering?) refers to the act of devotion rather than the objects offered (see Akkadian *zakāru*, Hebrew *zākar*). The Emar festival involves the offering of many animals, but makes no special mention of males.

The reference to the *zukrum* in the Mari letter places this item at Kallassu, which may be relatively near Emar. Because the place called Alaḫtum is to be handed over to Kallassu, the two should be near each other, and another letter records that Hammurabi, king of Halab, later gives Alaḫtum (back) to Zimri-Lim; A 1257.3, see Lafont, 14-15. This exchange of territory suggests that both Alaḫtum and Kallassu should be somewhere between Mari and Halab, which would place them in the general region of Emar and the bend of the Euphrates. Lafont declines to accept this placement because the name should be known from other texts referring to this area, and chooses instead the region west of Halab, based on attestation of the name *Gal-la-su* at Alalaḫ. However, that seems an unlikely point of territorial exchange between Mari and Halab, and the names could belong to locations that are not on the major trade routes of Mari and Mesopotamia.

117 Arnaud wonders if the festival in fact took place every 70 years; *AEPHER* 92 233-234; *Hethitica VIII*, 9 n.2. For the 7-year cycle, compare the biblical jubilee (Lev 25).

damaged itself, and may come from a separate textual tradition that does not effortlessly join with 373. Dagan is spelled ᵈ*Da-gan*, in contrast to the usual rendering of the high god as ᵈKUR in the ritual texts: 375.2, 10, 17, 19.[118] Emar 373 uses only ᵈKUR, often with the epithet EN *bu-ka-ri*, "lord of the firstborn(?)."[119] Moreover, 375 provides no link-up with the calendar sequence we find when we first take up text 373.[120] We cannot be sure the month ⁱᵗⁱ*za-ra-ti* of 375.3 is really the month that opens 373.

On the other hand, these seem to be only the preliminaries to the *zukru* proper, which begins at 373.36:

> *i-na ša-ni-ti* MU.KÁM *zu-*[*u*]*k-ra* DÙ
> The next year they will perform the *zukru*...

Also, the plan of the text helps to reconstruct the broken parts: the offerings for the *zukru* are described first (373.1-65, and the list 66-167), and then the movements of the divine players (168-209), for the same period. A brief colophon closes the text (210-212). Thus, although there are significant breaks in the first part of the festival, the second is largely intact, and we have a reasonably complete version of the sequence. Only the opening is missing, again (168-173).

Several lines of evidence point toward this repeating format. First, the two sections cover different subjects, as mentioned already. Part one is entirely taken up with offerings, and processions are only included when sacrificial animals take part or attention is fixed on offerings:

373.15-16 Two bullocks (AMAR.MEŠ/*būru*) go in front of ᵈKUR.

23 The verb is lost at the end of the line, though the *šaššabētu ša bīt* ᵈNIN.URTA appear to be involved in the procession. The focus remains on the offering to them (24-26).

28 Gods are brought out (Š, *(w)aṣû*), one bullock and 10 sheep go in front of them.

---

118 See also 446.50, etc.; 447.8; 448.2, etc., all probably from annual calendar ritual; text 446 also uses ᵈKUR in lines 8, 99, cf. 54, KUR.

119 Compare Hebrew *bĕkôr*, Ugaritic *bkr*, and Akkadian *bukru* (*AHw*, "Erstgeborener," vs. *CAD*, "son, child"). Arnaud translates "bovins," apparently comparing Hebrew *bāqār*, Phoenician *bqr*, and Mari *bu-qá-ru* (ARM 2 131:39). E. Lipiński (personal communication) suggests comparison with either the latter or "firstfruits" (cf. Hebrew *bikkûrîm*).

120 Day 24, line 7; day 25, line 14.

35 Bread and beer go up to the city.[121]

40-41 The people (UN/*nišū*) go out to make offerings.

45-47 (^{d}KUR?, cf. line 46) is brought out, (one) bullock(?) and 10 lambs (go) ([*il-la-ku*], from lines 16, 28!) in front of ^{d}KUR.

58 The gods are brought up to the city (Š, *elû*), for offerings before the great gate (KÁ.GAL/*abullu*, 59-60).

61 (same as line 35?)

A second approach is comparison of the time sequence. It is not clear how lines 1-35 and 168-190 match up, but both probably cover the year before the actual *zukru* (see 373.36, 191). Perhaps the missing month of lines 7 and 14 is Niqali, as in line 185 (not Zarati, from 375.3), and the offering section has a more elaborate set of instructions for this period:

373.1-6 (Day 23?)

7-13 Day 24

14-35 Day 25

There is no break above line 168, but 168-173 should follow some introduction of the occasion for these events, and we are definitely missing some material between this and the end of the preceding offering list. However, lines 174-190 are fairly clear, and cover activities for the 6th year, before the *zukru* takes place in the 7th:

373.174-184 The 15th day (*i-*[*na* U$_4$.1]5.KÁM, line 176) of the first month of the 6th year, defined with respect to the *zukru* itself, offered (*nadānu*) in the 7th year.

185-190 An unknown day (in the break) during the month of Niqali.

The correspondence begins with lines 36 and 191:

373.36, 191: "During the next year," *i-na ša-ni-ti* MU.KÁM.

37-41, 191-192: Day 14 of the first month (^{iti}SAG.MU).

42-61 (or 64), 192-199: Day 15.

65: U$_4$.7.KÁM *ša* ^{ezen}*zu-uk-ri*, "for the seven days of the *zukru* festival," suggests that 200 and 202 in fact read *i-na* U$_4$.6.KÁM and *i-na* U$_4$.7.KÁM, referring to the sixth and seventh days of a seven-day festival, a pattern already found with the sequence of

[121] Read NINDA.MEŠ KAŠ$^{!}$.MEŠ, not AMAR.

years (174-175). Lines 200-209 then refer to days 6 and 7 of the seven days of line 65.

Further evidence is provided by examination of the items offered in lines 168-209. The occurrence of something (animals) "*ša* LUGAL" (from the king, cf. lines 16, 17, 20, etc.) and of NINDA.GUR$_4$.RA in lines 171-172 suggests that the short section from 168-173 may not belong to the second part of the repeating format. However, mention of offering in lines 174-209 either speaks in generalities or refers to the previous section:

373.178 "When they have offered, eaten, and drunk...," is circumstantial and general, perhaps referring to earlier instruction.

181 Cattle and vessels are purified (GUD.MEŠ DUG.ḪI.A).

187 Purified bullocks and lambs (AMAR.MEŠ SILA$_4$.MEŠ KÙ.GA) go in procession? (broken).

191 "The offered lambs," SILA$_4$.MEŠ *pa-a-da-ti*, are the seventy lambs for the seventy gods of Emar, lines 37-38.

196 Read NINDA(?).MEŠ *Šag-ga-ru*, "the 15th-day (*Šaggaru*)-loaves of all Emar will go up," not *ka-kà-ru*.[122]

199 The bread and meat which were before the gods go up into the city.[123]

200 "Offered lambs" again, with unknown referent.

204 "All the meat and bread," UZU NINDA.MEŠ *gáb-bi*.

In this section, the verbs *naqû*, *pa'ādu*, *šakānu*, and *qalû* do not appear except in reference to previous data (lines 178, 191, 200). The verb *zâzu* (D) occurs in lines 191 and 201; however, it is the most sweeping offering verb. Lines 174-209 of the *zukru* are not concerned with enumerating offerings.

Finally, two lines may refer to the earlier offering section directly:

373.194 SISKUR.MEŠ *ki-i ša i-na ṭup-pí ša-aṭ-ru*, "the offerings, just as written on the tablet"; this could refer to the first section.

---

122 The NINDA-sign shows only two clear verticals, but the *šag-* is certain, based on collation. The *zukru* festival does not use *kakkaru*-bread, and although the alternative reading would be unique, it fits the context (lines 192-199 cover the 15th day). Compare *u$_4$-mi Ša-ag-ga-ri*, without divine determinative, in 373.42, 176, and the writing ^{d}*Šag-gàr* of 195.

123 *ša pa-ni* DINGIR.MEŠ, somehow separate from 196, *ša gáb-bi* $^{uru.ki}$*E-mar*.

198 *pár-ṣi ki-i ša u_4-mi qa-du-ši-ma*, "the rites just as for the day of sanctification"; we do not know when the day of sanctification takes place -- presumably at the beginning -- but this demonstrates that the *zukru* has one, in common with all the other festivals.

As a conclusion to our discussion of the *zukru* calendar we should observe the similarity of the 14th and 15th day New Year to festival times prescribed for Israel in the Bible. According to Lev 23.5, the Passover feast begins at twilight on the 14th day of the first month, and the seven-day feast of Unleavened Bread begins on the 15th day (verse 6; cf. Num 28.16-17). The correspondence between this scheme and the seven-day core of the Emar *zukru* is remarkable. Certainly the middle of the lunar cycle is a significant sacred time throughout much of the ancient Near East, but its calculation varies considerably from text to text and culture to culture. At Emar, the annual calendar ritual 446 places only the New Year rites on the 15th day (lines 8, 45), versus days 17, 18 (and 19?) during the month of dNIN.KUR.RA (lines 58, 59, 67), days 7 and 8 during Adamma (lines 82, 83), days 14, 16 and 17 during Marzaḫani (lines 85, 86, 90), and day 8 during Halma (lines 101, 106). The ritual for the dead in the month of Abû has offerings for the 8th day (452.7, 8), the 14th, and the 16th days (see lines 9, 21), with day 15 possibly lost in the break. These represent only a few examples from Emar, and the issue of mid-month calculation in ancient Near Eastern ritual bears further study.

Other biblical references to the Passover likewise place it on the fourteenth day of the first month: Exod 12.6, 18; Num 9.3-5; Josh 5.10 (month not specified). Only Exod 12 includes the feast of Unleavened Bread as well, defining its bounds as the eve of the 14th to the eve of the 21st day, omitting the day 15 tradition. According to Lev 23.33 and 39 and Num 29.12 the feast of Tabernacles begins on the 15th day of the seventh month, exactly half the year from Unleavened Bread. In Deuteronomy, Unleavened Bread occurs in the month of Abib for seven unspecified days (Deut 16.1-8), and Tabernacles takes place seven days after harvest, with no mention of month or day (16.13-15). The tradition of the 15th day is reflected in festivals Jeroboam sets up at Bethel to compete with Judah, this time during the 8th month. Note that in Esth 9.17, events come to a head with a feast on the 14th day of Adar (and so, Purim, v.19).

2. The Language of the zukru

The backbone of the Emar festivals is formed by the two installations, the *zukru* festival, and the *kissu* festivals. Among them, the *zukru* festival stands out in terms of structure and composition, with its repetition, its link to the calendar, and its inclusion of the lengthy god-list for offering. The distinctiveness of the *zukru* runs deeply through the whole festival text and may be approached both via the words and items of the *zukru* that do not occur in the other festivals and via those common to the others but omitted from the *zukru*.

It is perhaps hardly worth comparing ritual personnel since one feature of the *zukru* is its near lack of them. As with the NIN.DINGIR installation (369.1-2), the sons of Emar initiate (if not carry through) the festival,[124] but no other ᵈIM festival personnel appear. Two groups make an appearance, both important to the question of the festival's social context. One is the UN(.MEŠ)/(*nišū*?), presumably the whole populace, who three times are assigned quantities of breadstuffs while similar foods (no meat) are offered to the gods.[125] Arnaud concludes this is a communal meal,[126] but this is not certain. The standard feasting terminology is absent,[127] and the portions are roughly equal to those given the gods. Distribution is not specified by TA.ÀM, "each." In lines 17-19, the assignment to the people is squeezed between two offerings to ᵈKUR (the second being meat), and in lines 27-31 it is apparently included in a total (line 31) that otherwise consists of offerings. Such indications suggest that the portions may be either offerings presented by the people or servings that symbolically allow the populace to dine alongside their gods. A fourth instance of UN in line 40 may suggest the former alternative:

---

124 373.174, ᵏᵘʳ*E-mar*, vs. 369.1 ᵘʳᵘ*E-mar*.

125 In this context, the verb is always *naqû* (vs. *pa'ādu*) when food is provided for the gods, and no verb is used with provision for the people; see 373.17-19, 29-30, 47-49.

126 Arnaud, in *Le Moyen Euphrate*, 254.

127 *akālu*/*šatû*; see above, and 373.187.

39 *i-na* u_4*-mi* EGIR-*ki*
40 *ša* ^{ezen}*zu-uk-ri* UN [*a*(?)-*na*(?)] DINGIR.MEŠ *ši-ni-*[*š*]*u*(?) *uṣ-ṣu-ú*
41 *ma-la al-lu-ti-im-ma i-pa-'a-a-du*

39 On the last(?) day[128]
40 of the *zukru* festival the people will go out twice(?) [to] the gods;
41 they will offer as much as those things(?).[129]

Here, the role of the people is to go outside the city to the place of the gods -- the gate of the *sikkānātu*, according to line 193 -- and make offerings to them.[130] Perhaps all the assignments to the people are for their particular offering to the gods. This concern for the participation of the whole community (whether direct or indirect) is indeed unique in the Emar ritual and might be an archaic feature which predates the established temple cults of the city, especially since the involvement is outside city-walls.[131]

The second group in the *zukru* festival is likewise unique in Emar ritual, a fact which again underlines the distinct social setting of the event, but this group represents the political center of Emar life, the palace. They are the enigmatic LÚ.MEŠ [*z*]*i*(??)-⌜*ir*(?)⌝-*a-ti ša* É.GAL-*lì*, 373.38, the broken text and the lack of parallels preventing us from knowing whether these are princes (if Arnaud's *zir'ātu*) or something else. Whatever the answer, their association with the palace is clear, and is evidently the complement to the role of the people. Whereas the people are given the right to make offerings, these palace men are each given[132] a sheep from its supplies for the occasion. The *zukru* is very likely an ancient Emar festival, but this need not preclude a strong role for the central government in the 13th-century version. The palace or the king repeatedly supplies materials for the offerings, over against "the

[128] The phrase *ina ūmi arki* in the NIN.DINGIR installation may refer to the last day of that festival (369.58-59). The term *arkû* is often the "latter" of two; it is not clear what time is indicated here.
[129] It is not clear whether *mala allūtimma* refers to the amounts described in lines 37-39, or to something else.
[130] A. Archi finds that the fundamental rite for the Hittite spring festivals is a procession to the stela (*ḫuwaši*, see above), ending with offering of bread and drink (cf. KUB XXV 25); see Archi, "Fêtes de printemps et d'automne et réintégration rituelle d'images de culte dans l'Anatolie hittite," *UF* 5 (1973) 19. The similarity between the Hittite and *zukru* practices shows the importance of stelae as (archaic?) non-urban religious shrines in both Asia Minor and northern Syria.
[131] With Arnaud, in *Le Moyen Euphrate*, 254.
[132] The verb is *nadānu*, appropriate for allotment to human recipients, as in the NIN.DINGIR installation.

city" (URU.KI) and the *bīt ili*.[133] Likewise, the palace deities Bēlet-ekalli, and Sîn and Šamaš *ša ekalli*, receive three sets of offerings, outside the pantheon lists,[134] and the only specific human participants are from the palace. In our recorded version, the palace is as central to the *zukru* as the people, though not through direct participation of the king. Part two of the festival mentions neither group, but focuses entirely on the leading gods of the rites.

The offerings and serving vessels of the *zukru* tend to be those of the calendar rituals and offering lists, not those of the other festivals. Examples are "Gerstenbrei," *pappāsu*, with determinative(?) ZÌ,[135] the vessels ^{dug}PIḪÙ/*pīḫu*,[136] ^{dug}ḪA,[137] and ^{dug}*ḫu-bar*.[138] ^{d}KUR's cart belongs specifically to the *zukru* at Emar.[139]

The unique character of the *zukru* festival is further expressed in the verbs regularly used for offering and procession. Where the other festivals rely on *naqû* for general offering, the *zukru* often uses *pa'ādu*.[140] Also, the verb *qalû*, "to burn", describes a type of offering not found in the other festivals (373.35, 60), and *šarāpu* occurs for burnt offering in 446.91 and 98(G) and often in the Anatolian rituals.[141] The verb *etēqu*, "to pass through," denotes the principal action of *zukru* procession: ^{d}KUR/Dagan repeatedly goes between the stelae of the gate of the *sikkānātu* in his cart.[142] They sometimes have another god (or gods) mount the cart with him.[143]

---

133 See for example lines 20-26 for all four.
134 Lines 27, 44(!), and 56.
135 373.55; 452.6, *passim*; 462.2, *passim*; 471.3, *passim*; with NINDA, only in the *zukru*, 373.17, *passim*.
136 373.7, *passim*; 452.1, etc.; 461.5; 463.5; 473.20.
137 This is not likely KU_6/*nūnu*, "fish," which appears without DUG in the NIN.DINGIR's ration, 369.90, and with the determinative for meat, UZU, in the ritual for the dead, 452.44; see for ^{dug}ḪA, 373.17, *passim*; 452.9, etc.; 461.7, 10; 462.34; 463.29, with *za-du*.
138 373.18, *passim*; 452.3, *passim*; 463.24.
139 ^{giš}MAR.GÍD.DA/*ereqqu*, 373.168, 179, etc.
140 373.9, *passim*; the middle *aleph* is marked in line 41, *i-pa-a'-a-du*.
141 471.33; 472.18, 24, 28(D) and 472.14, 15(G). Burning appears in both Hittite and Canaanite ritual, though R. Lebrun thinks that Hittite cremation of sacrifices probably has Syro-Canaanite origins; see "Les rituels d'Ammiḫatna, Tulbi et Mati contre une impurété = CTH 472," in Laroche et al, eds., *Hethitica 3*, Louvain: Peeters, 1979, 161. The Emar rites for the gods of Hatti thus reflect a cultural circle, whereby practices introduced to Kizzuwatna and then the Hittite capital from northern Syria return to Syria with their later conquests. Burning sacrifices in Syrian tradition is probably reflected in the *šrp*-offering at Ugarit; see A. Caquot, in *La Siria*, 74; de Tarragon, *Le Culte*, 60, 62-63.
142 373.179, 189, 197, 208.
143 Lines 180, ^{d}NIN.URTA; cf. 170, others?

The contrast between the *zukru* and the other major Emar festivals is even more striking when one looks at features shared by the latter that do not appear in the *zukru*. A cluster of ritual personnel belongs to both installations and the *kissu* set: the NIN.DINGIR's of ᵈIM and of the town of Šumi, the ˡᵘ́ḪAL and the singers (*zammārū*), the king of Emar receiving special portions, and the *nugagtu*.[144] Quite a few materials for offering appear in these three festivals but not the *zukru*:

wine and barley beer	KAŠ.GEŠTIN/*ḫamru*, KAŠ.ŠE
meat parts:	
ritual portion	GARZA/*parṣu*
ox-meat (beef)	UZU GUD
sheep-meat (mutton)	UZU UDU
the head	SAG.DU
marrow	UZU.Ì.UDU
breads:	
naptanu-bread	ⁿⁱⁿᵈᵃ*nap-ta-nu*
dried bread	NINDA UD.DU/*aklu ablu*
dried bread with fruit	NINDA UD.DU GURUN
oil	Ì.GIŠ/*šamnu*
aromatics	ŠIM/*riqqu*
(to people) "gift"	NÍG.BA/*qīštu*

A subset of these belongs to the festivals exclusively: *naptanu*-bread (probably; see above), the meats GARZA, SAG.DU, and UZU UDU, and the gift, NÍG.BA. The same sort of list can be made for ritual paraphernalia and allocation terminology:

vessels:
- *ḫizzibu*
- *kāsātu*, "cups"
- ᵈᵘᵍ*zadu*, (juglet for oil)

tables for offering
nignakku/incense burner
KÙ.BABBAR for payment

[144] See the NIN.DINGIR festival commentary for references to these and other terms found there.

^{giš}PA as a measure

Several verbs follow the same pattern, excluding the *zukru*:

šakānu

1. for setting out tables
2. for offering "before" (*ana pānī*) a god

mullû, filling cups

târu, D, returning an offering with divine property borrowed from a temple[145]

leqû, for payment

erēbu, both G and Š, for entering ritual locations

zamāru, with a god or gods as object

We can include two more features that fit the same *zukru* exclusion: the phrase *ina qaqqari* for table-setting follows the absence of this event from the *zukru*, and the *zukru* never uses the distributive marker TA.ÀM, having no (explicit) ritual feasting by sacred (temple?) personnel.

It is notable that we find no comparable set of ritual locations shared by the same three festivals. This is odd, if the common terminology reflects the temple cult of a single establishment. On the contrary, the association of these festivals seems to have a broader base.

In spite of the comprehensive distinctiveness of the *zukru* festival, there are a few important points of contact with the other festivals. It is celebrated by the "sons of Emar" (noted above), and includes an introductory sanctification (*qaddušu*, cf. 373.198) and the *kubadu* offering-ceremony (lines 171, 177). The palace and *bīt ili* storehouses and the *bīt tukli* (373.183) are familiar locations in the installations, and the stelae/*sikkānātu* are involved in both installations and in the *zukru* -- and nowhere else in Emar ritual. These features are some of the unique hallmarks of Emar religion and reveal a shared ritual heritage at some level.

145 See *leqû*, G, and *târu*, D, above; note 370.80; 385.11(F).

3. The Gods of the zukru Festival

Dagan, the Head of the Pantheon

The *zukru* festival is composed of two distinct parts, the ritual proper and the offering lists (lines 66-167, cf. 9-13). While the list mentions the whole range of Emar deities, the rest of the festival involves a limited group, omitting major figures such as ^{d}IM, Hebat, Aštart, ^{d}NIN.KUR, Ea, and Išḫara. Dagan and ^{d}NIN.URTA dominate the action, with Dagan clearly the central figure for the whole event. He heads the offering lists as well.

Most of the written evidence from Emar points to Dagan as the principal god of the region. He is invoked first in curses; he is by far the most popular god in Emar theophoric names; he leads the hierarchical offering lists; the *kissu* festivals are performed at his sanctuary in Šatappi, beginning with his own. Dagan's place in the *zukru* festival reflects his place at the head of the pantheon.

The Curses:

Two transactions conducted by kings of Emar close with curses on whoever alters the arrangements made in the given document (*ša a-wa-ti an-na-ti ú-na-kà-ar*, "whoever changes these words," 125.35-36, with curses in 35-41; cf. 17.32-33, curses in 32-40). Text 125 records king Pilsu-Dagan's purchase of a house, and invokes ^{d}*Da-gan*, ^{d}NIN.URTA, and Išḫara. Unfortunately, Emar 17 is broken in this section, since at least four or five deities are called on, and none of the divine names is certain. The text reads:

34 [^{d}*D*]*a*(??)-*gan ù* ^{d}NIN-x
35 [^{d}(x)]-x *ù* ^{d}x x x [x (x)] x
36 x ^{d}NIN.⸢É(?)⸣.[GAL(?)...]

In line 35, Arnaud sees [^{d}I]M, which fits the space, but the traces are not sufficient to confirm this, and it seems odd to put ^{d}IM after ^{d}NIN.URTA. One expects Išḫara from 125.38, but there is no room. The NIN-sign is clear in line 36, but not line 35.[146] ^{d}NIN.KUR fits neither set of traces, but ^{d}NIN.É.GAL would belong to the palace context, and might be read from the traces in the last line. The *zukru* palace gods ^{d}30 *u* ^{d}UTU *ša* É.GAL-*lì* should

[146] See Arnaud, ^{d}Nin-x-x.

be considered for the space in line 35, but the order would be the reverse of that in the festival.

The Emar curses are significant because their choice of gods draws on the leading gods in the pantheon and is likely hierarchical, though not necessarily exhaustive. Both texts give Dagan and ᵈNIN.URTA first and second place in a pantheon for kings, and do not appear to include ᵈIM, Aštart, or ᵈNIN.KUR.

Personal Names:

Evidence for the pantheon at Emar may also be drawn from theophoric personal names. When we add up the number of name-forms associated with each deity,[147] we find that Dagan/ᵈKUR is by far the most popular theophoric element.[148] There is little doubt that Dagan of the curses, the annual calendar ritual, and the *zukru* fragment 375 is the same god as ᵈKUR,[149] though we find some patterns in use. A few personal names are attested with the alternate forms, and at least two individuals can be shown to have names written both ways: the king of Emar Pilsu-Dagan has the theophoric element written *ᵈDa-gan* in almost all instances, but the text recording votive offerings to the storm god has *Píl-su-*ᵈKUR,[150] the scribe Iš-Dagan may be spelled with either *ᵈDa-gan* (96.15) or ᵈKUR (94.27; 97.25).

No other deity comes close to the popularity of Dagan/ᵈKUR in theophoric names, though Baal (Baʿla/ᵈIM/ᵈU) is probably second. Rašap (Rašap/Ra) and ᵈ30 (Sîn?) are the next in frequency. ᵈEN or EN often may

147 E.g. *Píl-su-ᵈDa-gan*, ᵐ*A-ḫi-*ᵈKUR, ᵐ*Ip-ḫur* ᵈKUR, etc. Note for the last name that in western names the G conjugation may be used for the expected D, so Ipḫur-Dagan would mean, "Dagan gathered"; William L. Moran, personal communication.

148 There are over 150 forms; the count comes from names published in Arnaud, Emar VI.3.

149 This was observed by Arnaud soon after he first examined the material from Emar; see "ᵈKUR," *RA* 68 (1974) 190.

150 Emar 42.2, 8. Lines 11 and 20 mention another figure who is both king of Emar and son of Baal-kabar (ᵐᵈU-GAL, line 20), ᵐ*BI-su-*ᵈKUR. Arnaud understands this to be a separate person (*Syria* 52 89), as does J.-M. Durand ("Hauts personnages à Emar," *N.A.B.U.* 1989, p.34; and *RA* 83 183-184, where he acknowledges the alternative described below). If this is true, *Bisu-Dagan must be Pilsu-Dagan's brother, since both have the same father. However, no such relationship is mentioned in line 11, where this name is introduced three lines after ᵐ*Píl-su-*ᵈKUR; the formula ŠEŠ-*šu* is common enough, cf. 2.32, 33. The line of Emar kings and princes can be followed via the witnesses to legal and sales documents, and no separate Bisu-Dagan is attested (see above, The king of Emar). It is more likely that this represents an alternative writing of Pilsu-Dagan, in a text that includes other unusual spellings: ᵈU for ᵈIM, ᵈIM-*ka-bar* for ᵈIM/U-GAL, *Píl-su-*ᵈKUR for *Píl-su-ᵈDa-gan*. Tsukimoto, *ASJ* 12, 180 n.25, analyzes the form as *pissu-* from *pilsu-*; cf. C.

stand in for Dagan rather than Baal, judging by elements that otherwise appear only with that deity.[151]

The Hierarchical Offering Lists:

While individual players and places from Emar proper are absent, the *zukru* is indeed a festival for the whole city of Emar, involving participation of the people as a group (UN/*nišū*?, line 19, etc.) and "all the seventy gods of Emar" (lines 37-38).[152] The festival has no personal place for the king or his court, but the event receives the full financial backing of the palace and its stores (see above). One purpose of the *zukru* festival seems to be to make offerings to all the gods of Emar in a systematic distribution. The list that regulates the distribution takes up over 100 lines in the middle of the *zukru* instructions (66-167). This presumably served as a unifying event for Emar and its environs, for both the political and the religious realms.

In contrast to many of the god- and offering-lists found at Emar, the *zukru* list seems to reflect an effort toward both completeness and order.[153] At

---

Zaccagnini, *Or* NS 59 518.

151 E.g. ^{m}*Ka-pí*-EN, 82.20; 279.9; ^{m}*Ka-pí-*^{d}*Da-gan*, 24.9; *Še-i*-EN, 65.27; *Še-i-*^{d}*Da-gan*, 52.24. EN = *bēlu* might represent Dagan in some names and Baal in others.

152 Compare *šbʿm.bn.ʾaṯrt*, "the seventy sons of 'Athirat," at Ugarit, KTU 1.4 VI 46.

153 Along with Emar 378, Arnaud places texts 379-384 in a separate group, "les listes sacrificielles." These are offering lists in the form of god lists, with minimal or no indication of what is given (e.g. 382, just numbers; 383, nothing), and fluid order. Unfortunately, the beginnings of 380, 381, 383, and 384 are broken, and they can give us no evidence for who takes first place. ^{d}NIN.KUR heads texts 379 and 382, but appears further down in two others, 380.6 and 381.5. Texts 379-382 are closely related, sharing many of the same gods:

All four lists	*Three lists*
^{d}NIN.KUR	^{d}NIN.URTA
^{d}INANNA *ta-ḫa-zi*	^{d}KUR EN *qu-ni*
(^{d}NÈ.IRI$_{11}$.GÁL) ^{d}EN KI.LAM	^{d}IM (381.7?)
^{d}NIN.É.GAL	^{d}EN SI.MEŠ/SI 2
^{d}*Iš-ḫa-ra*	
^{d}*É-a*	
^{d}KUR EN *da-ad-mi*	

Texts 383 and 384 seem to represent a somewhat different set of deities, but both are more severely damaged, and this judgment cannot be definitive.

Although these lists are related, they do not have a hierarchical format and do not tell us who are the lead gods. The gods in 379 appear to be labeled "the gods of the upper cities," DINGIR.MEŠ URU.MEŠ AN.TA, line 15, presumably referring to the Euphrates upstream. Since the four lists share so much, they might also share this source.

Another list that provides a sequence of gods is the inventory of sacred vessels in 274.1-10. This text begins with ^{d}NIN.URTA, followed by ^{d}KUR and ^{d}KUR ^{uru}*Tu-ut-tul* (lines 1-2). ^{d}IM receives a vessel via his temple (line 3). ^{d}NIN.URTA's prominence should be noted, and the first gods are generally major figures, but we cannot assume a strict hierarchy; the numbers of vessels do not come in rigorous descending order. Further deities are listed in 274.15-20 with a new set of materials, perhaps associated with Tuttul

the end of the *zukru* section dealing with offerings (lines 1-167), there is a list of deities in three groups, receiving decreasing amounts of cattle, bread, and drink.[154] Line 65 is the heading:

> U$_4$.7.KÁM *ša* ^{ezen}*zu-uk-ri* DINGIR.MEŠ [^{uru}]*E-mar gáb-bá i-pa-al-*[*la-ḫu*(?)]
>
> For the seven days of the *zukru* festival they will give cult to all the gods of Emar.

The gods in the first section of the list are shown to be most important by both placement and the larger offering, and the first three are the high gods of Emar, set in a confusing pattern that gives the storm god a place both above and below ^{d}KUR (see below).

We have two partial duplicates of the principal *zukru* festival god list. One is the short list of sheep offered on day 24 during festival preparations, 373.9-13, which roughly parallels the first twelve entries of the long list (lines 66-78). Also, the beginning of the god-list, Emar 378, closely follows the same order, though with a special interest in the spouses of the major gods. Here are the three lists set side-by-side:

373.9-13	373.66-78	378.1-13
[^{d}KUR EN *bu-k*]*a-ri*	^{d}KUR EN *bu-ka-ri*	[^{d}KUR] EN *bu-*[*ka-r*]*i*
		^{d}NIN.LÍL ⸢DAM(?)⸣ ^{d}KUR EN *bu-k*[*a-ri*]
		^{d}KUR.GAL
^{d}IM	^{d}IM	^{d}IM *ù* ^{d}*Ḫé-ba-at*
	^{d}KUR	
^{d}UTU		
[?]		
^{d}*É-a*	^{d}*É-a*	^{d}*É-a ù* ^{d}*Dam-ki-an-na*
^{d}30	^{d}30 *u* ^{d}UTU	^{d}30 *ù* ^{d}UTU

(line 20). This section is very fragmented, and the beginning is missing.

[154] One bullock, ten lambs, lines 66-85; five lambs, 86-102; two lambs, 103-136, and perhaps 137-150 (a right hand column, next to lines 174-190, Msk 74292a; only *a-na* [...])

^{d}NIN.URTA	^{d}NIN.URTA	^{d}NIN.URTA *ù* DINGIR.MEŠ *ša* É-*ti* ^{d}*Ša-aš-ša-bit-ti*
[?]	^{d}*A-lál* [*u* ^{d}*A-ma-za*]	^{d}*A-lál ù* ^{d}*A*-[*ma*]-*za*
[^{d}]EN KI.LAM	^{d}NÈ.IRI$_{11}$.GAL [EN KI.LAM]	^{d}NÈ.IRI$_{11}$.GAL EN KI.LAM
^{d}EN SI.MEŠ	^{d}NÈ.IRI$_{11}$.GA[L EN SI.MEŠ]	^{d}NÈ.IRI$_{11}$.GAL EN SI.MEŠ
^{d}NIN.KUR	^{d}NIN.KUR [^{d}*Ša-ag-ga-ar u* ^{d}*Ḫal-ma*]	^{d}NIN.KUR ^{d}*Ša-ag-ga-ar ù* ^{d}*Ḫal-ma*
[?]	^{d}NIN.É.GAL-*l*[*ì*]	^{d}NIN.É.GAL-*lì*
^{d}*Iš*$_{8}$*-tár ta-ḫa-z*[*i*]	^{d}*Iš*$_{8}$*-tár ša šu*(?)-[*bi*(?)]	(something, of the palace)

Observe that ^{d}KUR[155] and ^{d}IM head this pantheon, regardless of the ambiguous role of the repeated ^{d}KUR(.GAL) after ^{d}KUR EN *bu-ka-ri*. Ea is prominent, preceding deities such as ^{d}NIN.URTA, ^{d}NIN.KUR, and ^{d}*Iš*$_{8}$*-tár*, who have leading roles in other Emar texts. We will refer back to this pantheon as we deal with other evidence.

The cycle of offering and feasting in the *maš'artu* installation (370.45-68) also places both ^{d}KUR and ^{d}IM at the head of the gods, in the same order:

Day 2, ^{d}KUR, lines 46-47
Day 3, ^{d}IM, 49
Day 4, ^{d}NIN.URTA, 52-53
Day 5, DINGIR.MEŠ, 61-62
Day 6, ^{d}*É-a*, 64
Day 7, (in breaks), 66-68

^{d}NIN.URTA is advanced past Ea, which suits his importance in many Emar settings, though he only appears once, with ^{d}IM, in the feasting cycle insert (line 57 of 55-59) in the *maš'artu* installation. The association of ^{d}IM and ^{d}NIN.URTA belongs only to this context at Emar, somehow linked to the feast cycle; it appears in no other texts.

---

and 151-168, Msk 74290d + Msk 74304a.

155 ^{d}KUR is restored in two of three lists, but the presence of the special ^{d}KUR epithet (*bēl*)

Dagan is the ancient pantheon head of the Middle Euphrates. He is known from some of the earliest sources for the Semitic pantheon, including Sargonic period theophoric names,[156] third-millennium texts from Mari and Ebla, and a much quoted inscription of Sargon of Akkad, who credited Dagan with bestowing on him the lands of the west, from Tuttul to Ebla.[157] Dagan has a long-standing cult center at Tuttul, on the Euphrates River east of Mari, attested from Ebla and the Sargon inscription through late second-millennium Ugarit.[158] At Mari, he is the leading male deity at both official and popular levels,[159] present in texts from the late third millennium through the last king, Zimri-Lim,[160] with a cult center in Terqa, up-river toward Emar.[161] Dagan is equated with Mesopotamian Enlil[162] and Hurrian Kumarbi.[163]

Roberts finds that Dagan's identity with Enlil, the similarity between the names of his wife (Šalaš) and Adad's (Šala), and his paternal ties to the storm god[164] all indicate that Dagan himself is a storm god, and follows W.F. Albright in deriving the name from *dgn* "to be cloudy, rainy."[165] Wyatt applies this derivation to the specific problem of Ugaritic *bn dgn* and concludes that the title means "The Rainy One," and that Baal and Dagan are "hypostases of one divine reality"; Dagan is identified with Teššub, and Hadad is a Dagan title.[166] The Emar evidence does not support this thesis. The two gods are distinct and almost unrelated.

---

bukari in each case makes the restorations highly probable.

156 Roberts, *Pantheon*, 18.

157 See G. Pettinato, in Pettinato and H. Waetzoldt, "Dagan in Ebla und Mesopotamien nach den Texten aus 3. Jahrtausend," *Or* NS 54 (1985) 234; N. Wyatt, "The relationship of the deities Dagan and Hadad," *UF* 12 (1980) 375; a translation appears in *ANET* 268. Narām-Sîn and Hammurabi make similar statements; see UET 1 no. 275, *ANET* 268; and CH Prologue iv 24-27, *ANET* 165.

158 See Wyatt, *UF* 12 376; Pettinato, *Or* NS 54 237.

159 See H. Limet, "Le panthéon de Mari à l'époque des *šakkanaku*," *Or* NS 45 (1976) 92.

160 See Lambert, *M.A.R.I.* 4, 534, 538, and *passim*; J.-M. Durand, "Les dames du palais...," *M.A.R.I.* 4, 387.

161 For example, king Yasmaḫ-Addu's premier queen, Kunšim-matum, has special duties to pray for the king at Terqa and is probably the high priestess there, "wife of Dagan"; Durand, "Les dames," 396-397; 397, n.69, DAM + DN varies with NIN.DINGIR.RA for this title, the latter being generic, perhaps indicating simply *aššat ilim*, "wife of a god."

162 Lambert, *M.A.R.I.* 4, 538; cf. F.J. Montalbano, "Canaanite Dagon: origin, nature," *CBQ* 13 (1951) 387; Dagan is attested in personal names in Mesopotamia from the third millennium; see Waetzoldt, in Pettinato and Waetzoldt, *Or* NS 54 249. However, this does not constitute an active Mesopotamian cult.

163 Wilhelm, *Grundzüge*, 74.

164 Dagan-Baal at Ugarit, Kumarbi-Teššub among the Hurrians.

165 Roberts, *Pantheon*, 18-19.

166 Wyatt, *UF* 12 377-379; cf. C. L'Heureux, *Rank Among the Canaanite Gods*, Missoula,

It has been noted above that in Emar personal names, Dagan is spelled both syllabically and with the logogram ^{d}KUR.[167] Dornemann observes the same equivalence in the small set of texts from Hadidi/Azu, north of Emar on the Euphrates and a century or two earlier.[168] The divine name ^{d}KUR appears in the Mari Šakkanakku period[169] in a month name,[170] a temple name,[171] and the god-list T 142.[172] Durand argues that ^{d}KUR is not Dagan at Mari, based on identification of ^{d}KUR with the later ^{d}IGI.KUR in the OB period Mari calendar.[173] However, the case depends on two unproven links. First, we cannot be certain that ^{d}IGI.KUR is in fact equivalent to ^{d}KUR without more precise information on the earlier calendar. Second, though Dagan and ^{d}IGI.KUR are clearly separate month names in the OB calendar,[174] this is not clear for the month names Dagan and ^{d}KUR of the Šakkanakku period. One more pressing piece of evidence may come from the correlation of two early god lists which Durand has recently proposed: the resulting reconstruction would put ^{d}KUR (line 13) and ^{d}*Da-gan* (line 4) in the same list.[175] Durand suggests that Mari's ^{d}KUR be identified with ^{d}KU.RA, who is prominent in Ebla personal names, but we do not know what the actual pronunciation of the Sumerogram ^{d}KUR would have been, and the names may be wholely unrelated.[176] Whatever the origins of the spelling ^{d}KUR, the equation with

---

MT: Scholars Press, 1979, 13-14.

[167] Arnaud observed this immediately after the texts were discovered; see "^{d}KUR," *RA* 68 (1974) 190.

[168] R.H. Dornemann, "Tell Hadidi: an important center of the Mitannian period and earlier," in *Le Moyen Euphrate*, 219; cf. Dornemann, "Tell Hadidi: a millennium of Bronze Age city occupation," *AASOR* 44 (1979) 146; Robert Whiting is studying the texts. Azu is between Emar and Carchemish, and the texts come from the Late Bronze I, versus LB II at Emar.

[169] This is roughly equal to the Ur III period of Mesopotamia.

[170] D.O. Edzard, "Pantheon und Kult in Mari," in J.-R. Kupper, ed., *La Civilisation de Mari*, RAI 15, Paris: Société d'Edition "Les Belles Lettres," 1967, 57; Limet, *Or* NS 45 90, n.24; Sasson, in AOAT 203, 132.

[171] É ^{d}KUR, text 1:19 in Durand, "Sumérien et akkadien en pays Amorite," *M.A.R.I.* 1 (1982) 81.

[172] Georges Dossin, "Un 'panthéon' d'Ur III à Mari," *RA* 61 (1967) 99; cf. Lambert, *M.A.R.I.* 4 530.

[173] Durand, *M.A.R.I.* 1 85.

[174] Jack Sasson, "'Year: Zimri-Lim offered a great throne to Shamash of Maḫanum': an overview of one year in Mari. Part I: the presence of the king," *M.A.R.I.* 4 437.

[175] Durand, "La situation historique des Šakkanakku: nouvelle approche," *M.A.R.I.* 4, 161. The two lists are those of Dossin, *RA* 61 (T 142, above), and T 186 of Philippe Talon, "Un nouveau panthéon de Mari," *Akkadica* 20 (1980) 12-17.

[176] Durand, "Trois études sur Mari," in *M.A.R.I.* 3 (1984) 160-161. On Kura at Ebla, see

Dagan is clear by the time of our Emar texts.[177] Through most of the ritual texts, the writing ^{d}KUR is preferred, though the syllabic spelling appears in the *zukru* fragment Emar 375 and in the annual calendar rites, Emar 446.

Dagan also appears occasionally in Emar records kept at the temple M_1. Aḫi-ḫami is the *šangû*-priest of Dagan in the ration lists 279.21 and 319.4. A list of personal names records a *za-bi-ḫu ša* ^{d}KUR (336.108), the same temple official as the one found in 275.2 (see above).

Note: Dagan and ^{d}*IM*

It must be remembered that all of our evidence comes from a time span barely exceeding one century, and that regardless of the separate cults and their histories, we can say that we find in the 13th century widespread and active veneration of both ^{d}IM and Dagan. The two major festivals of the diviner's archive at Emar serve Dagan (the *zukru*) and ^{d}IM (the NIN.DINGIR installation), and though they have older roots, both events are known to us because of their importance in contemporary Emar; there is no sign that the festivals are defunct. Then, we find that the lists in the *zukru* and *maš'artu* festivals, along with Emar 378, make Dagan and ^{d}IM the first and second gods of a single pantheon. The best explanation for the contrast between the lists and the focus of the individual festivals is that the lists reflect a time when both gods serve as active heads for different Emar constituencies, a situation which evidently fits the 13th century.

Dagan of the *zukru* and the storm god of the NIN.DINGIR installation and the high Emar temples both appear to come from heritages where they function as pantheon heads. In 13th-century Emar, where these heritages meet, the confrontation seems to have been resolved by placing Dagan at the top, with ^{d}IM given the next position. Perhaps this suited the west Syrian tradition that Baal was of the younger generation, and "son of Dagan,"[178] though at Halab we find no such subordination.

A. Archi, "Les noms de personne Mariotes à Ebla (IIIème millénaire)," *M.A.R.I.* 4 54.

[177] At Emar, the equation between Dagan and ^{d}KUR in personal names is based on original Dagan, not ^{d}KUR, in at least one case: the Ebla name *Li-ma-*^{d}*Da-gan* is a type belonging particularly to Dagan/^{d}KUR at Emar (see Krebernik, *Personennamen*, 242). Compare *Li-mi-*^{d}*Da-gan* (Emar 52.12), *Li-'i-mi-*^{d}KUR (168.31), *Li-mi-i-Da-a* (15.30), *Li-mi-Da* (52.56), and *Li-mi-*DINGIR (171.5), ^{m}EN-*li-mì* (8.21), where DINGIR (Ilu/El?) and EN (Bēlu) are probably identified with Dagan. Abbreviated forms appear to derive from the same names: ^{d}*Da-gan-li* (3.21; 144.9), ^{d}KUR-*li* (90.25),*Li-*^{d}KUR (217.23), *Li-Da* (325.16), and *Li-*EN (79.14; 86.15). The practice of abbreviating the divine name is common at Emar, also noticeable in Rašap names; see especially *A-bi-*^{d}*Ra-ša-ap* (148.29) and *A-bi-i-Ra* (15.1). Durand, *RA* 83 166, observes the same phenomenon.

Along with the offering lists, the annual calendar ritual 446 and the (lunar?) calendar ritual 463 include sections that involve both gods, though their fields of activity remain mutually isolated. It may be that at least the collection of the ritual elements for these cycles likewise belongs to the 13th century.

^{d}NIN.URTA, the City God

^{d}NIN.URTA is shown to be a principal deity with an established place in local religion by his function in economic transactions and by the fact that he shares the spotlight with Dagan during the *zukru* ceremonies at the gate of the *sikkānātu* (see above). To judge by the position of ^{d}IM and ^{d}IŠTAR in sales documents at Alalaḫ (see above), that of Dagan at Hadidi/Azu, and that of ^{d}*Ba-aḫ-la*(*-ka*) at Mumbaqat/Ekalte, ^{d}NIN.URTA's exclusive role in such contexts appears to belong to the city god. The Mumbaqat texts are only partially published, but Mayer lists several sales of property belonging to Baḫla(ka) and the city of Ekalte, and he has published four of these, two of which make the god and the elders the sellers in the transactions.[179] A house is sold by Dagan and the $^{lú.meš}$AḪ.ḪI at Azu,[180] and ^{d}NIN.URTA and the elders are often sellers of property at Emar.[181] In the sales documents Emar 109.25-26 and 130.22-24, ^{d}NIN.URTA and the $^{lú.meš}$AḪ.ḪI(.A) are the recipients of the claim payments.

Beyond this evidence, Dagan's seal is on one of the Azu tablets,[182] and it seems that at Emar ^{d}NIN.URTA's seal carries official authority. Arnaud published three letters found at Ugarit which are from Emar (text 3, line 8), one of which argues a question of ownership in this way:

> *ù ṭup-pa ša* É*-ti-ši ša iš-tu* ^{na4}KIŠIB ^{d}NIN.URTA *ka-ni-ik na-ša-at*
> ...and she holds the tablet of her house which is sealed by the seal of ^{d}NIN.URTA.[183]

Similar authority seems to attend the seal of the king and the seal of ^{d}NIN.URTA in the legal document, Emar 203.22-23. P. Steinkeller observes

---

179 The published texts (Mayer, *MDOG* 122 55-62) are MBQ-T 22:12-15 and 35:9-12 (with the elders); and 21:4-7; 41:5-7. A catalog of texts from MBQ-T 31-81 (pp. 45-47) describes further sales documents of this type: MBQ-T 45, 47, 51, 57, 60, 67, 69, 73.

180 Text T-8, Dornemann, in *Le Moyen Euphrate*, 219.

181 E.g. Emar 1-4, 9, 126, 139, 144-155; cf. Leemans, *JESHO* 31 216.

182 Dornemann, 220.

183 Text 2, lines 8-10, in Arnaud, *AuOr* 2 183. See also Emar 123.9 and 202.17-18 for the seal of ^{d}NIN.URTA in legal documents.

that in Ur III and OB period Nippur, "judicial matters were Ninurta's domain,"[184] Ninurta being the city god, although Enlil leads the southern Mesopotamian pantheon from Nippur. ^{d}NIN.URTA's role in Emar economic and legal affairs suggests that he stands as city god as well, with Dagan still given primary place as head of the pantheon. Whatever the correct Semitic reading of the name ^{d}NIN.URTA at Emar, the writing might be accounted for by this parallel with the Mesopotamian pantheon. Since the Emar god has the same relationship to Dagan as Ninurta has to Enlil, the equivalence of Dagan and Enlil (see above) could lead scribes trained in the Mesopotamian system to use this Sumerian writing.

Lambert proposes a similar situation for Dagan and Itur-Mer at Mari. In southern Mesopotamia of the OB period, oaths were commonly taken by the city god and the ruler, so Lambert gathers various oaths from the Mari texts. More than one deity may be invoked, but the only god who is always included is Itur-Mer. Lambert concludes that Itur-Mer is the true (divine) "king of Mari."[185]

Which Syrian god would hold the position of city god at Emar? Arnaud wonders if ^{d}NIN.URTA might be Aštar, since we have the equivalences Ninurta = Aštabi and Aštabi = Aštar.[186] The name ^{d}NIN.URTA never appears in Emar theophoric names, so we might expect some Semitic equivalent that does.[187] Working from within the Emar texts themselves, we find two associations with other divine figures which could help identify ^{d}NIN.URTA. One is Išḫara, with whom he shares the *kissu* rite, 387, a table in Dagan's *kissu* festival (385.8), and a place in a royal curse (125.37-38). The other is a set of unidentified divine beings, the *Šaššabētu*, who belong to ^{d}NIN.URTA's temple (the *zukru*, 373.23, 43; the god list 378.7-8).

The pairing with Išḫara is one that might be expected for Dagan. Išḫara is associated with Dagan in Mesopotamia and Mari,[188] and she is identified

---

184 Steinkeller, *Sale Documents of the Ur III Period*, Stuttgart: Franz Steiner Verlag, 1989, 73 and n.209. There is also a "seal of Ninurta" at Nippur.

185 Lambert, *M.A.R.I.* 4 533-534.

186 Arnaud, "Religion assyro-babylonienne," *AEPHER* 96 (1987-1988) 175. Emar 378 might present a difficulty for this equation, since it includes the name ^{d}*Aš-tar* MUL (line 39) in the same god list as ^{d}NIN.URTA (line 7), [^{d}NI]N.URTA *ša iš-pa-*[*at*] and [^{d}NI]N.URTA *ša ma-k*[*a-li*] (lines 47-48).

187 Aštar would qualify: see Aštar-abu in 33.1 and 111.11(?); Aštar-kimi in 29.7; Aštar-bītu(É) in 91.4; and [Ia]ṣi(?)-Aštar in 97.4.

188 Lambert, "Išḫara," in *RlA* 5, 1977, 176-177; for Mari, see the offering list of Dossin, *Studia Mariana*, 1950, 44, 25.

with Šalaš at Hattuša,[189] Dagan's spouse in Mesopotamia.[190] This echo of the relationship of Dagan and Išḫara may somehow be linked to the unique pairing in one of the temple M_1 inventories: 282.6 reads *šu-kut-ti* d*Iš-ḫa-ra ù* dNIN.KALAM. The divine name/title "lord of the land" is prominent in ancient Syrian texts from Ebla and Mari. At Ebla, the title takes the form dBAD KALAM-*tim* and dBAD *ma-tum*, where BAD means "king" or "lord."[191] At Mari, the names dLU[GAL *ma-tim*] and d*Be-el-ma-tim* appear in the Šakkanakku period lists shown to be partial duplicates by Durand.[192] It is likely that these epithets were applied to whoever was identified as the chief god of the city or region.[193]

Could the Emar name dNIN.KALAM fit this pattern? Once we leave behind the special case of dNIN.URTA, the NIN-sign usually suggests a goddess, but the association with Išḫara means that we should at least consider the possibility that dNIN.KALAM is an alternative name for dNIN.URTA. Išḫara is paired with no deity other than dNIN.URTA in the Emar texts,[194] and if the unique name dNIN.KALAM represents an alternative writing for some more prominent Emar deity whose name begins with the NIN-sign, no goddess makes better sense than the male dNIN.URTA. dNIN.KUR would be the most prominent Emar goddess whose name is written with the NIN-sign, and we could suppose that the KALAM-sign might be a mistake for KUR, but she has no connection with Išḫara that would make this identification more than arbitrary. The Baal-names show that the equation NIN = Baʿlu does occur at Emar, albeit in a woman's personal name: f*Ba-la-bi*$_4$*-a*, daughter of f*Ku-'e-e*, is also written fdNIN-*bi-a*.[195] If dNIN.KALAM is dNIN.URTA, the title would suit the city god of Emar, and the NIN might have substituted for EN or

---

189 Haas, RAI 24, 62.
190 Roberts, *Pantheon*, 19.
191 Lambert, *M.A.R.I.* 4 529, n.4; he says Pettinato goes too far in making dBE = Dagan in all cases; Pettinato, *Or* NS 54 235, 244; see also Archi, *AAAS* 29-30 170.
192 Durand, "La situation historique...," *M.A.R.I.* 4 161-163; cf. Lambert, *M.A.R.I.* 4 528-529.
193 In the cases of Ebla and Mari, this is not necessarily Dagan; see Lambert, *M.A.R.I.* 4 529, n.4.
194 Text 379.3 includes Išḫara in the same line with d*Ud-ḫa* and dKUR EN *kara-ši*, but this list does not appear to give any special significance to the order or line-association. Rather, the writing appears to represent the compression of the text into a smaller space.
195 Emar 217.11 and 216.5, 9, 11, 20. The syllabic spelling appears with the variants f*Ba-a'-la-bi*$_4$*-a* (217.2, 14) and f*Ba-aḫ-la-bi*$_4$*-a* (218.1).

LUGAL by association with the usual divine name, ^{d}NIN.URTA.[196] Perhaps the pairing of Išḫara and ^{d}NIN.URTA follows the parallel roles of ^{d}NIN.URTA and Dagan as lords of Emar.

The link with the *Šaššabētu*-deities at Emar is specific and intriguing, but we can do little with the evidence until we discover the identity of these previously unattested figures. They seem to be set up as a separate group from "all the gods" (see the *zukru*, 373.14, 44, 193, 202); perhaps they may be underworld deities. The *Šaššabētu* appear in the *kissu* rites for Dagan[197] and at the beginning of the group *kissu* within the Dagan circle at Šatappi.[198]

Emar use of the Sumerian name ^{d}NIN.URTA is complicated by the fact that the name is used from Palestine to Hatti to represent deities who do not appear to have any real relationship to each other. In Hittite texts, ^{d}NIN.URTA is used for at least three dieties: Aštabi, Šuwala, and Tašmīšu, all Hurrian.[199] Of these, only Šuwala occurs in the local Emar festivals (the *kissu*, see above). In the Amarna letter EA 74:30-38, Rib-Adda of Gubla/Byblos complains to the king of Egypt that Abdi-Aširta of Amurru has invited troops located somewhere near to Gubla to assemble in the temple of ^{d}NIN.URTA to join him in an attack on the city.[200] Then, the Jerusalem letter EA 290:16 mentions a nearby town called É ^{d}NIN.URTA which has gone over to the side of Qiltu, a town south of Jerusalem. The West Semitic name Abdi-^{d}NIN.URTA appears in EA 84:39, referring to a man who is stationed in Egypt, probably from Gubla. We have no evidence to lead us to any reliable guess regarding the Semitic deity behind the Sumerian spellings in the Amarna letters. Given the wide use of the name ^{d}NIN.URTA in Syria and Anatolia for a variety of gods, we should hesitate to equate separate deities through the shared Sumerian writing, unless further evidence warrants. Emar's

---

196 Tsukimoto, *ASJ* 12 195; 196 n.5, finds a potential example of interchange between NIN and EN in the names ^{m}NIN-*li-mu* (HCCT-E 31, Text 9 obv.5) and ^{m}EN-*li-mì* (Emar 8.21; 9.20). See above for comment on this as a Dagan-name. Tsukimoto observes the set of names with ^{fd}NIN-*bi-a*, also.

197 Line 9 of text F, 385.21; line 3 of text G, cf. 385.12.

198 388.5-6, text F:

ù ^{d}*Ša-ša-bi-tu*$_{4}$ *iš-tu* É ^{d}K[UR(?)...]
it-ti ^{d}NIN.KUR *i-ša-ša-bu-ši* x [ ]

The related verb appears to be denominative.

199 Laroche, *Recherches*, 55, 60, 61; *GLH* 61, 174, 245, 259; Tašmīšu was assimilated to both Šuwala and Ninurta.

200 Moran, *El Amarna*: EA 74, n.10, observes that the lack of the determinative KI should indicate a real temple, versus the town in EA 290.

^{d}NIN.URTA is one more example, and may have no direct relationship to either the west Syrian or the Hurrian/Hittite deities. We should note the following appearances of ^{d}NIN.URTA in Emar temple records. Emar 275.4 includes the *za-bi-ḫu* of ^{d}NIN.URTA (see above), and at least the last entry in a list of men in crews (ERIM.MEŠ/*ṣābu*) refers to the É ^{d}NIN(?).URTA, "the temple of ^{d}NIN.URTA" (311.6).

The Goddesses

The *zukru* festival does not pair any goddess with Dagan, but it is appropriate to give brief attention to the female deities which have some association with Dagan and ^{d}NIN.URTA at Emar. In the god list Emar 378.2, the spouse of ^{d}KUR EN *bu-ka-ri* is the goddess ^{d}NIN.LÍL, according to the equation of Dagan and Enlil. This is ^{d}NIN.LÍL's only appearance at Emar, and the more prominent Emar goddesses in Dagan's circle are Išḫara, ^{d}NIN.KUR, and ^{d}EREŠ.KI.GAL. Išḫara is associated with ^{d}NIN.URTA at Emar, though she is linked to Dagan elsewhere (see above). ^{d}NIN.KUR's very name suggests a pairing with ^{d}KUR at some time in her history. ^{d}EREŠ.KI.GAL follows Dagan at the head of the *kissu* cycle at Dagan's cult center at Šatappi.

Išḫara's background in ancient Syria has been treated above (see the west Hurrian pantheon). She is an important north Syrian goddess with early influence in both Anatolia and Mesopotamia.[201] The situation for ^{d}NIN.KUR is the reverse: she is barely known in Syria at all. ^{d}NIN.KUR.RA is the goddess born to Enki and Ninšar in the Sumerian myth of Enki and Ninḫursag.[202] The only mention of the goddess in the west is from earliest Mari: ^{d}NIN.KUR (or $^{d.nin}$KUR) appears in the short list of deities from late Early dynastic time, T 66.[203] ^{d}NIN.KUR is a Syrian goddess who has apparently faded from the scene at Mari by the end of the third millennium. This is not the case at Emar, but prominent as she is, she remains a difficult figure in a pantheon with an abundance of major female deities (Aštart, Išḫara, ^{d}EREŠ.KI.GAL, ^{d}NIN.KUR, Hebat).

---

201 See for Mesopotamia, Lambert, *RlA* 5, 176-177; for Anatolia, G. Frantz-Szabó, *RlA* 5, 177-178.

202 *ANET* 39; cf. Lambert, "A list of gods' names found at Mari," in Durand and Kupper, eds., *Miscellanea Babylonica*, 188; a list found near Mari, TH 80:112, includes ^{d}NIN.KUR (line 6) and ^{d}NIN.KUR.RA (line 106), page 182.

203 Lambert, *M.A.R.I.* 4, 531; cf. 526 n.2.

It may be possible to identify ^{d}NIN.KUR through the company she keeps in the official Emar pantheon: ^{d}NIN.KUR ^{d}*Ša-ag-ga-ar ù* ^{d}*Ḫal-ma* (Emar 378.12). Volkert Haas observes that Išḫara is linked to an obscure set of almost unknown deities with Syrian origin, Halma, Tangara, and Tuḫḫiura.[204] The first two are not only attested at Emar, but are the very gods associated with ^{d}NIN.KUR in the above god list. The New Year's god, Šaggar,[205] is Tangara (with *š* and *t* for *ṯ*?).[206] Išḫara is given the title "mistress of the mountain" in the treaty between Ramses II and Hattušili III (13th century), from a link with a mountain near Tarsa in Kizzuwatna.[207] One wonders whether the Hittite name might reflect a connection with Syrian ^{d}NIN.KUR ("lady of the mountain"?) more than the Kizzuwatna mountain, or at least before it.

^{d}NIN.KUR is attested so early in Syria that there is no ground for assuming she is a deified epithet of Išḫara. The similarity between the names ^{d}KUR and ^{d}NIN.KUR, together with their occurrence in early Mari (though ^{d}KUR is not in T 66), suggests that ^{d}NIN.KUR's name does originate as the female counterpart to ^{d}KUR. It is interesting to find that ^{d}NIN.KUR plays a key part in ^{d}KUR's *kissu* festival set at Šatappi, but the role does not seem to be linked to ^{d}KUR specifically, since she goes through the same rite for the installation of the NIN.DINGIR of ^{d}IM.[208]

Both the apparent etymological connection to ^{d}KUR and the association with Išḫara through Anatolian sources show that ^{d}NIN.KUR, with Išḫara herself,[209] is an old earth goddess linked with the north Syrian Euphrates pantheon head Dagan/^{d}KUR. In the ritual from Emar, ^{d}NIN.KUR seems to play a special role in mourning, and in the NIN.DINGIR installation she oversees the transfer of the priestess to her new role, accompanying her through the period of mourning.

---

204 *Berggötter*, 101.
205 Šaggar is associated with Day 15 of the first month in the *zukru* (373.42, etc.) and the annual calendar rites, 446.45, ^{d}ḪAR.
206 See Frederick M. Fales, "A cuneiform correspondence to alphabetic *š* in West Semitic names of the I millennium B.C.," *Or* NS 47 (1978) 91-98, for /*ṯ*/ and /*ś*/ written with "*t*".
207 Haas, *Berggötter*, 99.
208 She is laid down at the beginning and raised at the end (see above).
209 Jacobsen, "The Gilgamesh Epic," 237 n.9, suggests a Semitic etymology for the name Išḫara from **ś'ār* "grain, barley," (see above). I.J. Gelb, "The language of Ebla in the light of sources from Ebla, Mari, and Babylonia," in Luigi Cagni ed., *Ebla 1975-1985. Dieci anni di studi linguistici e filologici*, Napoli: Istituto Universitario Orientale, 1987, 55, says Išḫara is from the same root as the Greek *iskara*.

^{d}EREŠ.KI.GAL rounds out the Dagan/^{d}KUR circle, appearing to serve as the earth-goddess of the Šatappi pantheon in the *kissu* set. She is mentioned only once otherwise at Emar, in a text that appears to refer to the sale of her temple in hard times (*ASJ* 10, text C, 3', 6', 10').[210] ^{d}EREŠ.KI.GAL is queen of the underworld in Mesopotamia. It is interesting to find Dagan closely associated with these two earth-goddesses who have strong ties with the underworld.

4. The Background and Development of the zukru Festival

The *zukru* festival is a study in contrasts to the installations. Baal/^{d}IM, Aštart, and ^{d}NIN.KUR have no part in the *zukru* outside the offering lists, and the principal gods are rather Dagan and ^{d}NIN.URTA. Moreover, the action of the ritual takes place outside the city walls, with no role mentioned for temples or their personnel, but the unique participation of "the people" (UN/*nišū*) in the offerings. The gate of the stone *sikkānātu*, outside the city, recalls the *ḫuwaši* cult in Anatolia, thought to be the oldest expression of Hittite religious practice.[211] Alongside the popular element, the *zukru* displays the full involvement and support of the palace and the central storehouse (*bīt tukli*/*bīt ili*). While the rites and offerings take place outside the city, all the participants nevertheless return at night; in its 13th-century incarnation, the festival belongs to the city community. However, it is not likely that a celebration which takes place outside the city at a non-urban shrine (the gate of the *sikkānātu*) came into being in an urban setting. Elements such as provision for return to the city at night and financial support from the institutions of the city probably reflect later adaptation to the city environment. The language of the *zukru* text is quite distinct from that of the temple festivals, but the offering terms are similar to those from the calendar rituals and lists, probably because they share palace and city storehouses.

---

210 A. Tsukimoto, *ASJ* 10 160-161.

211 Haas, *Berggötter*, 18-19. Arnaud describes the earliest history of the *zukru* in terms of a cult for two stones who represent ^{d}NIN.URTA (from 375.16) and Hebat (from 369 and the *zukru* offering list, 373.166). The *sikkānu* may indeed be shown to be an old feature in Emar religion by its place in the *zukru* festival, but the *zukru* description of Dagan going between the *sikkānātu* does not specify two stones, and Hebat is never associated with anyone but ^{d}IM at Emar... or in the ancient Near East generally. Read 373.179, *i-na be-ra-a*[*t* ^{na}]$^{4.meš}$*si-ik-ka-na-ti*, following line 168; not *be-ra-at* 2 $^{na4!}$*si-ik-ka-na-ti*. See Arnaud, *CRAIBL* 1980, 386; in *Le Moyen Euphrate*, 254 and n.45.

The separation from Emar's religious institutions, the involvement of the populace (at least peripherally), and the cult focused on standing stones outside the city all indicate the *zukru* festival's antiquity. There is no sign of significant foreign influence: the combination of Dagan and ^{d}NIN.URTA fits the local middle Euphrates pantheon attested for Mari and Hadidi/Azu, as well as Emar personal names and economic texts. The term "*zukru*" is attested for Kallassu, somewhere in the political sphere of Halab, perhaps even in the general region of Emar. While Arnaud attributes the archaic features of the *zukru* to "semi-nomadic" cultural influences on Emar,[212] I would prefer to say they are simply non-urban, or rural, until the question of influence from the south is more settled.

D. THE KISSU FESTIVALS

The *kissu* rituals of Šatappi are among the most prominent in the diviner's archive at Emar, attested in multiple copies and various formulations, but their basic purpose is nearly opaque. Emar 385-388 represent a cluster of tablets and fragments for a cycle of rites associated with the temple of Dagan in Šatappi, near Emar (see the commentary). These are identified principally by the title ^{ezen}*kissu*, "*kissu* festival," which appears at the head of all but one ritual:

385.1-2, the *kissu* festival of Šatappi, for (*ana*) Dagan,
385.27, the *kissu* festival of ^{d}EREŠ.KI.GAL,
386.1, the *kissu* festival of Ea,
387.1(J), the ^{ezen}LA, for Išḫara and ^{d}NIN.URTA,
388.1, text for rites associated with the *kissu* festivals.[213]

To these should be added one more reference to a *kissu* festival at the end of the *maš'artu* installation (370.113), which might be read at least two ways:

---

212 Arnaud, in *Le Moyen Euphrate*, 245-247, 254.
213 Emar 388.1 simply begins, *i-na* u_4*-mi ša qa-du-ši ša* $^{ezen.meš}$*ki-is-sí*, "On the sanctification day of the *kissu* festivals..." This could refer to the initiation of each one individually or to initiation of the whole set.

i-na ^{ezen}*ki-is-si ša*[^{d}*Iš*$_{8}$*-tár*(?)] x UDU ^{f}*maš-ar-tu*$_{4}$ TI-*qí*
At the *kissu* festival of [Aštart(?)] the *maš'artu* will get (x) sheep.[214]

i-na ^{ezen}*ki-is-si-ša* [x x (x)] *ù*(?) ^{f}*maš-ar-tu*$_{4}$ TI-*qí*
At her *kissu* festival... (and?) the *maš'artu* will get (it?).[215]

This *kissu* could either be the *maš'artu*'s, or that of some deity, perhaps her mistress Aštart.

All the Šatappi *kissu* rituals are included in text F (Msk 74286b), which provides the framework for ordering the *kissu* set and the strongest evidence of their unity. Many other fragments were found,[216] and each individual *kissu* is attested on at least two other tablets or fragments. No *kissu* for another deity was discovered, so it appears that the bounds of the Šatappi set were securely fixed.

The mention of the *kissu* in the *maš'artu* installation begins a second unit within the administrative section of the installation text, which seems to deal with allotments to the priestess (cf. 369.84-90, for the NIN.DINGIR). This conclusion is reinforced by the singular form of *leqû* in line 114 (TI-*qí*), the phrase *ana maš'arti* in lines 115 and 116, and the closing words of line 117, *i-na* MU.1.KÁM SUM, "they will give in one year" (cf. 369.90). The "*kissu* festival" is either an alternative name for the whole installation (^{ezen}*malluku* in lines 20, 41) or a separate rite specially associated with provision for the priestess.

Within the *kissu* cycle for Šatappi, the first and last rituals are considerably more complex than the three middle rites and display a distinctly different character. The rites for ^{d}EREŠ.KI.GAL, Ea, and Išḫara/^{d}NIN.URTA are not formed from a single mold, but each principally consists of offerings devoted to the deities of the individual festivals. By contrast, the first and last festivals involve more elaborate rites with a broader scope of interest.

Although the first *kissu* is dedicated to Dagan (385.2), the very title proclaims its role as flagship for the whole set: "Tablet of rites for (of) the *kissu* festival of Šatappi." Dagan's temple appears in each of the other

---

214 By this reading, the sign before UDU should either be a number (one?) or some part of the sheep. An advantage of this reading is that it provides an object for the verb *leqû*.

215 Arnaud reads *ù*, which fits the traces, but perhaps some object would be preferable, since there is little room for a second verb and accompanying object.

216 These are listed by Arnaud at the beginning of Emar 385-391, texts A through N; 389-391 cannot be placed with certainty.

individual festivals: É-*šú*, 385.38 ("his temple" in ᵈEREŠ.KI.GAL's festival); 386.21, cf. 19 (Ea); 387.21 (Išḫara and ᵈNIN.URTA).[217] The first *kissu* is structured very like the NIN.DINGIR installation, though the latter is more complex. Both begin with the heading *ṭuppu/i parṣi...*, followed by *enūma*, "when" the citizens of Emar/Šatappi (385) perform the festival. The *kissu* then has one day for sanctification, *qaddušu* (385.3-9), where the NIN.DINGIR installation has two days with two *qaddušu*-ceremonies (369.6, 22-28), but both include laying down ᵈNIN.KUR and setting four tables for the gods, the last two for underworld deities (369.24-25; 385.9). "The next day," *ina šanî ūmi*, follows the *qaddušu* (369.29; 385.10), leading to a period of feasting (*akālu/šatû*) -- only three days in the *kissu* (385.14), instead of seven. At the beginning of the last day (broken; cf. *ina ūmi arki*, 369.58B; U_4.4.KÁM, 385.21), ᵈNIN.KUR is made to rise.

The last festival, Emar 388, may not even be a proper *kissu*. It is linked to the initiation day of (all?) *kissu* festivals, but is not itself called a *kissu* and is not associated with a particular deity. The beginning of the ritual, which is best preserved, begins by placing ᵈNIN.KUR in the house of the *bēl bīti*, the ritual supplier, and shows a particular interest in his affairs. Fragmented lines from the rest of the text show a seven-day sequence (line 47), rites in the gate of the *sikkānu*'s (line 14), hints at procession (*ina pānīšunu*, line 31, with someone or something veiled, line 32?), and a wide variety of players, locations, and activities. Emar 388 does not have the limited focus of the middle three festivals, and its relationship to the set remains mysterious.

If the simplest *kissu* festivals represent the ritual in its purest form, the *kissu* may be fundamentally an offering rite devoted to a single deity.[218] The title itself should hold the key to the purpose and occasion of these festivals, since the texts offer no connection with the annual calendar or other fixed events.

---

217 The one possible reference to the temple in Emar 388 occurs in text F (line 5), the tablet for the whole set. After the DINGIR-sign, one winckelhaken is visible: *iš-tu* É ᵈK[UR(?)].

218 ᵈNIN.URTA is included in Emar 387 by association with Išḫara.

1. The kissu as "Throne"

The word *kissu*, always written *ki-is-sV*, looks very like a West Semitic form of *kussû*, "throne."[219] Does this interpretation work in the Emar texts?[220] Syllabic spellings of ^{giš}GU.ZA, "chair," indicate that the equation is not only possible but likely. There are only two examples: the month name ITI ^{d}NIN.KUR *ša ku-us-sí*, with the Akkadian *u*-vowel but no notation of a final long vowel, 150.38-39;[221] and the spelling *ki-is-sà-a* in the *maš'artu* installation (370.79, cf. 16), with the long final vowel but western "*i*" in the root. In the latter, the combination of bed and chair matches the gifts for the NIN.DINGIR in 369.70, and furniture in a ritual fragment, 372.12.

There is some evidence at Emar for each of the shifts necessary to derive *kissu* from *kussû*. The *ḫubu*-vessel (see above) should be the same as Akkadian *ḫābû/ḫāpû*, a pottery jug for storage,[222] but the long final vowel is entirely lost in Emar orthography.[223] Another important ritual noun shows *i/u*-vowel alternation in the root: the *kubadu* is spelled *ki-ba-dì* (446.95) and *ki-ba-da* (452.14) when in the phrase "day(s) of the *kibadu*." Two more Emar nouns appear to replace Akkadian *a/u*-vowels with "*i*". A "foreigner" is *ni-ka-ri* (Emar 20.13, 31; 80.13; HCCT-E 35:11),[224] for Akkadian *nakru*; compare

---

219 Note that the Akkadian *kussû* may be originally Semitic, not Sumerian. The word GU.ZA is a loanword in Sumerian, the native term being dúr-gar, from the verb "to sit." The final *-a* indicates loans in Sumerian. Semitic origin would mean that *kussû/kissu* need not come from Mesopotamia, but could be a western word, or could come from yet another language.

220 Arnaud originally guessed that *kissu* might be a Hurrian word (*AEPHER* 84 225), later proposing a comparison with the Hebrew *keseh*, full-moon, as a feast-day (*AEPHER* 92 233). One difficulty with interpretation as a lunar event would be discovering its relevance to the *maš'artu* installation; would this specify that her allotment must be bestowed at full moon?

221 The fragment Emar 13.10 (Msk 7235b) appears to have the same month written ^{d}NIN.KUR *ša* GU.ZA, though the GU-sign is compressed before ZA. This reading would make unlikely Durand's suggestion that Emar 150.38 reads ^{d}NIN.KUR *ša kuṣṣi*, "Ninkur d'hiver, de la venue du froid" (*RA* 84 63). The Emar lexical text, 544.33, 37, and 38 (Ḫḫ. IV) spells three types of chairs without the final vowel, *ku-us-sa*. Compare *ku-us-su* at Nuzi, TCL 9 1:4, 6, 7, (see *CAD* s.v. *kussû* 1a5'), and the *ku-us-su* in the Qatna inventories, I:75; see Bottéro, *RA* 43 17. Bottéro says this is not a chair, since the term is used of some ornaments on the solar disc in I:228. Perhaps "chair" should not be ruled out.

222 See *CAD*, *AHw* s.v. *ḫābû*; could the root vowel "*u*" be a result of the Canaanite shift, for /*ḫobu*/?

223 369.87; other ritual, 462.30; 465.3; 466.5; 484.4; temple inventories, texts 274, 305, 307; 363.1; 364.1-3 -- always *ḫu-bu*.

224 Tsukimoto, *ASJ* 12 198 and 200 n.11.

Mari *nikurtu* for *nukurtu*, "hostility" (*CAD* s.v. *nukurtu* a1'). In Emar 147.13, one edge of a piece of property is a *ki-pa-ú*, apparently the same root as Akkadian *kaba'u* (*CAD*, only lexical) and SB *kupû*, both "canebrake."[225]

Emar 387, the (*kissu*) festival of Išḫara and ᵈNIN.URTA, offers an alternate line of evidence for identification of the title. Instead of the expected "*kissu*," text J reads ᵉᶻᵉⁿLA (line 1).[226] The LA-logogram usually represents the Akkadian word *lalû*, "abundance, luxury," and does not suggest equivalence with any phonetic relative of the noun *kissu*.[227] Furthermore, the title in 387.1(J) does not imitate the form of the standard headings: it omits the divine reference, *ša* DN. Perhaps *lalû* is indeed the intended reading, and the festival for "the throne of the god" is identified as a festival of abundance, either abundance for the god or abundance following from the god's favor. The theme of plenty would suit the connection with the *maš'artu*'s supply in 370.113-117.

The meaning of the word *kissu* and the function of the festival remain uncertain, though the above discussion advances one hypothesis that might fit the evidence. The *kissu* set at Šatappi would have begun as enthronement rites for the major deities of the town, each consisting mainly of offerings for the god honored in the individual festival. By celebrating the throne and so the office of the gods, their various powers would be confirmed and invoked. These may not have been formed as a single set but were possibly joined under the auspices of Dagan and his temple at Šatappi. The use for the *maš'artu* installation remains the only evidence for *kissu* rites at Emar itself. They could be associated either with a god (Aštart?) or with the priestess herself, and the occasion might be either the installation festival itself or perhaps even an annual rite of provision.

Like the NIN.DINGIR installation, the *maš'artu* festival appears to take place after the death of the previous priestess, and so none of the *kissu*

---

[225] Durand, *RA* 83 173-174, 84 63, compares this text with ^{na4}*ga*$_{14}$(KA)-*ab-ú* in Emar 8.15 and Mari *gab'um* (ARMT XXVI/2, 295c), "hill, bluff," but the equation with *ki-pa-ú*, without the NA_4 determinative, should be considered only tentative. Of the above examples, the sound change is *a*>*i/u* before labial (*b*), except in the West Semitic *nikaru*; John Huehnergard, personal communication.

[226] [*i-na u*$_4$*-m*]*i qa-du-ši ša* ^{ezen}LA 1 ^{ninda}*ḫu-ki* [x DU]G KAŠ.ŠE.MEŠ 1 NINDA UD.DU *a-na qa-du-ši*, "On the sanctification day of the LA festival, one *ḫukku*-loaf, [x j]ars of barley-beer, and one dried cake (will be) for the sanctification" (lines 1-2); Arnaud does not mention *ša* and EZEN.

[227] The Emar lexical texts list the reading *la-lu-u* for the LA-sign; see Emar 537.142 (Syllabaire Sa).

evidence provides a specific date within an annual cycle. It is not even certain whether collection of the Šatappi rituals as a textual set (so, text F) indicates that they were celebrated together. The festivals might have been celebrated whenever need required petition of the gods' favor, individually or collectively. Installation of a major priestess might have represented such an occasion. Further illumination of the *kissu* rituals of Emar and Šatappi will depend on discovery of new text evidence.

2. The Language of the kissu Festivals

As mentioned above, the *kissu* festivals share much of the offering terminology of the installation festivals, over against the *zukru* and the rest of Emar ritual. We will examine these points of contact first and then move to the distinctive features of the *kissu* rites themselves.

It is not easy to pinpoint the features shared only by the *kissu* and the NIN.DINGIR festivals, since the one *maš'artu* tablet is incomplete, and we should not depend on argument from silence. Given the terminology that places them all in the same cultic sphere, it is surprising not to find the LÚ.MEŠ *ša qí-da-ši* in text 370, but their absence is not certain. While they do not appear in their feasters' role of the NIN.DINGIR installation, more or less replaced by the LÚ.MEŠ *ta-ḫa-zi*, the lúḪAL and *zammārū* -- the officials who are identified with the men of the *qidašu* in text 369 (see above) -- do take the first places in the apportionment section (370.108-109). During the festival proper, "the men of the battle" are not attested with genitive *ša*,[228] and it is possible that the reference at the end to people who eat and drink could be to the men of the *qidašu*, LÚ.MEŠ *ša* [*qí-da-ši*...] (line 110).[229]

A group of ration terms is found in the *kissu* and NIN.DINGIR festivals and not the *maš'artu*, but the ration section of that text is missing.[230] Likewise the verb *zâzu*, "to divide," is used for allotment to people (vs. gods) in the NIN.DINGIR installation and the *kissu*, but not the *maš'artu* text.

Comparison of the *kissu* texts with the NIN.DINGIR festival produces two items that may truly be outside the realm of the *maš'artu*. One is the

---

228 LÚ.MEŠ *ta-ḫa-zi*, see lines 62, 65, 68, 90, 91.

229 But see 388.43, *ša ta-ḫa-zi* [...].

230 The *kissu* references include *ḫaṣītu*-meat, intestines (*irrū*), ox and sheep hides, soured milk (GA.ḪAB/*kisimmu*), emmer (ZÍZ/*kunāšu*), and pigeons (TU.MUŠEN/*wattu*(?)). See Allotments, above.

slaughter and cooking of animals at the É EN É, "the house of the *bēl bīti*," which occurs on the shaving day for the NIN.DINGIR (369.14-15), on the first of the two days of ᵈEREŠ.KI.GAL's *kissu*,[231] and on the first day of the text for all *kissu*'s.[232] Then, we find the laying down (Š, *niālu*) and raising (Š, *tebû*) of ᵈNIN.KUR on the days of sanctification (*ina ūmi qaddušī*) and on the last days of the NIN.DINGIR installation (369.22-23, 60) and the *kissu* for Dagan (385.5, 21). These two ritual events are brought together at the beginning of the instruction for all *kissu*'s (?), 388.1-2, where ᵈNIN.KUR is laid down in the house of the *bēl bīti*. The extant tablet does not tell us when she is made to rise, but this likely belongs to one of the broken sections of the text.[233] ᵈNIN.KUR does not appear in what we have of the *maš'artu* text, and it may be that this installation omits her role in festival consecration. We cannot be sure.

Very little is found in only the *maš'artu* and the *kissu* festivals. The most significant are personnel: the female singer(s) (*zammirātu*) and the potter ((ˡᵘ́)BAḪÁR/*paḫāru*) appear together in the apportionment at the end of the last *kissu* ritual (388.67-69) and probably as recipients of allotments in the *maš'artu* installation.[234] Text 388.43 reads *ša ta-ḫa-zi*, but it is not certain this refers to the men featured in text 370. However, there is definitely a link between these festivals. The allotment section of the *maš'artu* installation records something the *maš'artu* takes *i-na* ᵉᶻᵉⁿ*ki-is-si*, "during the *kissu* festival," as if the installation included a *kissu* rite (see above).

The Emar *kissu* festivals themselves are not uniform. The Dagan *kissu* (385.1-26) has most in common with the NIN.DINGIR installation; only two offerings are different: ⁿⁱⁿᵈᵃ*ḫukku* (line 25) and the GUR-tu_4 of silver (line 27).[235] ᵈEREŠ.KI.GAL's festival (385.27-38) also shares NIN.DINGIR festival terminology but adds the *kirru* beer-container and 70 *ma-aš-ir-ta*

---

231 385.29; only slaughter, *nakāsu*.
232 388.10; only cooking, with many foods, Š *bašālu*.
233 Perhaps the *nakāsu-bašālu* preparation of food should be placed in the realm of ᵈNIN.KUR's cult as well. The NIN.DINGIR installation and the ᵈEREŠ.KI.GAL *kissu* make no mention of such a connection, but the association with festival openings would suit ᵈNIN.KUR's place.
234 370.59, the ᶠ·ᵐᵉˢ̌*za-mi-ra-*tu_4 eat and drink; line 116, the potter in the final ration list; both texts are broken.
235 Note: line 24 presents a unique ritual player: ˡᵘ́*ḫa-ar-ru-ta ša* DINGIR.MEŠ. The *-ūta* ending is odd for a masculine noun serving as subject of the verb *ir-ru-bu*, "will enter."

UZU.MEŠ, "70 *maš'irtu* (of) meats" (385.33, 34).[236] We have multiple texts of Emar 385: tablets C and F are like A (the main text); line 5(D) and lines 11-13 add further offerings not in 369, and line 13(G) includes the *Šaššabētu* of the *zukru* festival. The Ea *kissu* (386) is severely broken but seems quite close to the 385 texts, as is the ritual 394.26-44, the *ḫenpa*(=?) of oxen.

In contrast to the first three *kissu* festivals, the *kissu* for Išḫara and ᵈNIN.URTA displays many offerings and ritual actions not in the NIN.DINGIR texts. For example, the ritual players bathe Išḫara and ᵈNIN.URTA (*ramāku*, 387.3?),[237] and beat (knead?) flour with their hands (*maḫāṣu*, line 7); the men and women of the city "get" (*leqû*) something, they "seize(?)" (for *ṣabātu*) a servant-girl (GEMÉ/*amtu*), and bake (what they got?) with something sweet (*i-na ma-at-tuq-ti e-te-ep-pu-ú*; Gt, *epû*).[238] The whole ritual is dominated by similarly unfamiliar terminology. The closing instructions for all the *kissu*'s (388) begins with language right from the NIN.DINGIR installation: sanctification (*qaddušu*), the house of the *bēl bīti*, laying down ᵈNIN.KUR.RA, the *naqû-šakānu* offering sequence, and the *nugagtu* crying (lines 1-4), but as the focus shifts from ᵈNIN.KUR, new elements are introduced, and the balance of text 388 is as distinct as 387. These two therefore seem to be farther from the ritual language shared by the two installations and parts of the *kissu* set, and they represent another cultic sphere to be reckoned with.

3. The Gods of the kissu Festivals

The *kissu* festivals found in the Emar archives share the language of the temple cults in the festivals of Baal and Aštart, but lack Baal and Aštart themselves. Even the simplest rites that mention only the gods who receive the festival (ᵈEREŠ.KI.GAL, Ea, Išḫara and ᵈNIN.URTA) share characteristic terms: the EN É, the men of the *qidašu*, the *zammārū*/singers, the *šakānu*-

---

236 Compare Ugaritic *šʾir*, "meat," and Phoenician *šʾr*, "meat (for offering)"; E. Lipiński, personal communication.

237 Text F reads simply *i-ra-ma-ku-šu-nu-ti*. In Mesopotamia proper, the G stem of *ramāku* would be intransitive, with durative *irammuk*, and without object suffixes, which would appear only on the transitive D-stem. Emar 370.84, however, reads A.MEŠ *a-na ra-ma-ki* ᵈ*Iš₈-tár* GAŠAN-*ia lu-uḫ-bi-me*, "I will draw water for bathing Aštart my mistress." Comparison suggests that the verb in 387.3 is transitive with the object suffix referring to the gods.

238 All these occur in 387.18-21.

mullû sequence for offering, *naptanu*-bread and the GARZA portion of meat, and the *nignakku*/censer. The connection runs deeper than the association of ᵈNIN.KUR with the first and last rituals, though she brings with her a further set of ritual actions -- her lying down and rising, tables for the gods, and the *nugagtu*'s cries. Dagan, Ea, Išḫara, and ᵈNIN.URTA, as well as ᵈNIN.KUR, belong to an ancient Syrian pantheon; ᵈEREŠ.KI.GAL is unidentified, but may not be the Mesopotamian goddess. The envelope formed by introduction of multiple deities into the first and last texts (385.1-26; 388) should reflect some sort of complexity in formation of the set, probably incorporation of the larger sphere of Emar religion into a set that belongs essentially to the temple of ᵈKUR at Šatappi, outside Emar. It appears that the personnel for the *kissu* festivals come from Emar proper: the king, the ˡᵘ́ḪAL, and the chief scribe appear for their allotments (their influence is present, if not their persons), plus the men of the *qidašu* and the singers (as named separately). The *bēl bīti* (EN É) office may not be held by a single official. ᵈNIN.KUR is from Emar itself (her temple is in 369.65-66), so it appears that she must be brought to Šatappi if she is to be laid down there in Dagan's temple (385.5).

The *kissu* is another ritual term unknown before Emar, but the word probably is a non-Akkadian form of "throne," and the rites must belong to long-standing local religious practice, like the other major festivals. The location at a peripheral town, Šatappi, might have aided the preservation of the archaic pantheon found in the assignment of the individual rites.[239] With Dagan and ᵈNIN.URTA of the core *zukru*, the pantheon is at home in the Middle Euphrates, Dagan at its head. Arnaud suggests that the last temple found at Meskéné/Emar, temple M_2, may belong to Dagan. Given the strong link between Dagan's Šatappi cult and the Emar temple and ritual institutions, the Šatappi temple might rather be Dagan's major Emar-region temple.

[239] Arnaud concludes that the *kissu* festivals are organized around the hierarchy of the Šatappi pantheon; *AEPHER* 84 225.

E. THE OTHER EMAR RITUALS

1. The Rituals and Their Language

Arnaud describes the bulk of the remaining Emar ritual with the term "*ordo*," recalling the church's daily offices (Emar 446-470). This is the daily practice of the temple, where women are excluded and the diviners and scribes rule, in contrast to the festivals.[240] According to Arnaud, *Ordo* ritual imitates Mesopotamian practice to the point where it may even be an importation.[241]

Full treatment of these rituals belongs to a separate study, but it is nevertheless necessary to consider whether these constitute a separate category of Emar practice. In fact, there is ground for differentiating between the calendar ritual and lists from the festivals, though as observed above, the lines are not absolute. The format itself is perhaps the strongest trait: the predominant structural feature is repetition, either following the calendar or the recipients, human or divine. Although the *zukru* is linked to the calendar, it does not systematically cover the months of a year or days of a month. The best evidence from the ritual terminology comes from the content of offerings. Text 446, the annual calendar ritual, is a special case because it is dominated by procession and animal sacrifices, with almost no mention of other offerings.[242] Hurrian (ZÌ) *ši-na-ḫi-lu*[243] appears in the ritual for the dead in the month of Abû (452.7, *passim*), the offering lists,[244] and the rites for the Hittite gods,[245] as well as in various fragments. Other offerings that occur in the same set of rituals include ghee[246] and honey.[247] Generally, each of these rituals makes use of a set of offerings not at home in the festivals; the following are a sampling of some primary offering materials in the larger tablet fragments:[248]

---

240 Arnaud, in *Le Moyen Euphrate*, 258.
241 Arnaud, *CRAIBL* 1980, 384; cf. *Le Moyen Euphrate*, 258.
242 446.42, fruit; 62-63, *ḫukku*-bread; 92, *mar-za-ḫu ša mi-Ki*(?) [ninda]*na-ap-ta-na*; the last would be unique for [ninda]*naptanu*, which is always *nap-ta-nu/ni* in the festivals.
243 "Second," Laroche, *GLH*, 233; also at Nuzi.
244 462.1, etc.; 465.5; 466.8.
245 471.4, *passim* ; 472.16 *passim*; 473.4, *passim*.
246 Ì.NUN.NA/*ḫimētu*, 452.4, etc.; 463.9; 472.19.
247 LÀL/*dišpu*, 452.39, etc.; 463.9; 472.19.
248 A complete listing would be cumbersome, but the inclusion of some specific data seems appropriate, to give substance to the above observation.

452, ritual for the dead in Abû.

zì*ši-na-ḫi-lu*, lines 1, 3, *passim*
zìBA.BA.ZA/*pappāsu*, 3, 6, *passim*[249]
ZÌ.ŠE, barley-flour, 16, 28, *passim*
ninda*ṣabbuttu*, 33, 40, 41, 42
TU.MUŠEN/*wattu*(?), 6, 30, etc.

460, ritual for the *ša-aṭ*(?)*-ra-ḫi* of *Aštartu tāḫāzi* (dINANNA *iš*(?) MÈ).

KAŠ.ŠE.MEŠ, 2, *passim*
ninda*ḫukku*, 2, 10, 11
ninda*ra-ba-tu*$_4$ *ḫu-ki*, 22, 25, 30
ninda*ru-qam nu-ra-qu*, 17, etc.
ninda*kakkaru*, (16), 21, 24, 29
NINDA UD.DU (with or without fruit), 3, 8, 18
ninda*ma-Ku-ru*, (17), 21, 28
ninda*ḫalḫallu*, (16), 21, 28
ninda*zariu*, 2, 7
ninda*ṣubbuttu*, 4, 8

462, offering list.

zì*šinaḫilu*, 1, *passim*
zìBA.BA.ZA, 2, *passim*
(ninda)*tu-ru-be*, 2, *passim*[250]

463, ritual for "opening the doors" (*pí-it-ḫa* gišIG.MEŠ?).

ZÌ.ŠE (and variants), 2, 23, 28, 29
zì*pa-pa-sà*, 10, 13, 24 (ZÌ.ŠE *pa-pa-sà*), 28
TU.MUŠEN, 3, 6, 7

465, list fragment.

zìBA.BA.ZA, 5, 7, 9
tar-na-aš (container of oil), 6, 7

---

249 BA.BA.ZA appears as an offering in Hittite ritual; see Hoffner, *Alimenta*, 193: the BA.BA.ZA refers to a primary ingredient, not the bread itself; see also the glossary in Haas and Jakob-Rost, *AoF* 11 221.

250 Laroche, "Observations sur le rituel anatolien," 114, reads *durupu* in Emar 472.16 (Arnaud's numbering), etc., and proposes that this is an Akkadization of the rare Hittite word *tu-ru-up-pa-as*, KBo XV 10 + XX 42 *passim* (CTH 443). He compares Hurrian *turubi* and refers to Hoffner, *Alimenta*, 188.

471, ritual for the gods of Hatti.

- $^{\text{ninda.meš}}$*tu-ru-bu*, 3, *passim*
- ^{zì}*pa-pa-sà*, 3, *passim*
- ^{zì}*šinaḫilu*, 4, *passim*
- ZÌ.ŠE.MEŠ, 5, *passim*
- KAŠ.ŠE, 6, *passim*
- KAŠ.GEŠTIN, 9, *passim*

472, fragment of ritual for Hittite gods.

- ^{ninda}*tù-ru-bu*, 16, *passim*
- ^{zì}*šinaḫilu*, 16, *passim*
- ^{zì}BA.BA.ZA, 17, *passim*
- KAŠ.GEŠTIN, 25, *passim*
- KAŠ.MEŠ, 25, *passim*

473, same.

- ^{ninda}*tù-ru-bu*, 1, *passim*
- NINDA.ŠE, 4, *passim*
- ^{zì}BA.BA.ZA, 3, *passim*
- ^{zì}*šinaḫilu*, 4, *passim*

476, same

- NINDA.KUR.RA, 12, 16, 17, 19
- ^{ninda}*tù-ru-bi*, (2), 4, (6)

Note that the rituals for the gods of Hatti are included above, and their offerings have quite a bit in common with the calendar rituals and lists. However, some new offerings and vessels do appear in these rituals, especially outside the sections that are no more than offering lists (see 471.3-24; 472.33-72; 473.1-15).

471

- ^{dug}*ḫu-ur-ti-ia-lu*, 31, 32

472

- ^{dug}BUR.ZI/*pursītu*, 19-22, *passim*[251]
- NINDA.DÉ.A/*mersu* (cooked dish), 20
- MUNU$_6$.MEŠ/*buqlu* (malt), 21

[251] Laroche (*idem*) compares the Hittite ^{dug}BUR.ZI.TUM, from Boghazkoy.

IN.NU.DA.MEŠ/*tibnu* (straw), 22
ZÌ.DA *ḫur-ba-aš-šu*, 76
^{ninda}*tù-a-šu*, 78
^{ninda}*pu-ni-gu*, 78[252]

Moreover, the actions of offering are different from other Emar ritual. The fragment Emar 474.6-8 presents us with four verbs in a row which do not occur in the other Emar ritual:

line 6, *ú-DA-an-na-Bu*, (unknown)[253]
7, *ú-ka-sà-pu ú-bal-la-l*[*u*], they will break (bread), they will mix...
8, *ú-za-ar-ru-ú*, they will scatter[254]

The verb *kussupu* is used for breaking bread (^{ninda}*tù-ru-ba*) in 471.26-27 (cf. 472.74; 473.21), preceding a libation, ^{dug}GÚ.ZI *i-na-aq-qu-ú*. In the rest of Emar ritual, *naqû* covers all offering, and it only has a vessel for object in the rites for Hittite gods (see also 485.4?). Burning offerings (G ~ D, *šarāpu*) is more prominent in the rituals for Hittite gods than in the *zukru* and the annual calendar rite, the two other Emar events that include it.[255] The verb *šarāpu* (D) describes the offering *i-na* u_4*-mi ma-ḫi-ri-i* ("on the previous day"?) at the end of the ritual 471.28-33, and in Emar 472 the normal offering procedure joins burning (*šarāpu*) with presentation of foodstuffs.[256]

These practices both set apart Emar 471ff from the rest of Emar ritual and place the texts in the realm of Hittite ritual. In particular, the combination of breaking bread and making libation is a well-attested part of Hittite offering.[257] Burning offerings is known in Hittite ritual also,[258] though Lebrun

---

252 Laroche (*idem*) compares Hittite *punniki-* (Hoffner, *Alimenta*, 177-178).
253 Cf. *AHw* s.v. *ṭanāpu*, D, "beschmutzen"?
254 See *AHw* s.v. *zarû(m)* II, only G.
255 Arnaud says that the verb *šarāpu* is used to distinguish the burning that is typical of Hittite ritual from burning in local practice, expressed with *qalû* in the *zukru*; see *AEPHER* 92 235.
256 *šakānu*, with *ana pānī*; see lines 14, 18-22, 24-25; cf. 1?, 15, 28 for *šarāpu*.
257 See, for example, KBo XXI 34 + IBoT I 7 + CTH 699, Recto I.1-8, 9-14, 22-25, etc., in R. Lebrun, "Textes religieux hittites de la fin de l'empire," in Jucquois and Lebrun, eds., *Hethitica 2*, Louvain: Editions Peeters, 1977, 125-127; KBo XXIII 1 (and joins), CTH 472, Recto I 7-16, in Lebrun, *Hethitica 3*, 148-149; KBo XIX 128' Verso II 17-19, etc., in H. Otten, *Ein hethitisches Festritual*, StBoT Heft 13, Wiesbaden: Otto Harrassowitz, 1971, 2-3; cf. Otten and V. Souçek, *Ein althethitisches Ritual*, StBoT Heft 8, Wiesbaden: Harrassowitz, 1969, 36-37, Rs IV 5, etc.; G. Szabó, *Ein hethitisches Entsühnungsritual*, Heidelberg: Carl Winter, 1971, 20-21, Vs II 1-7, etc.; E. Neu, *Ein althethitisches Gewitterritual*, 12-13, 26-27; the 16th day of the AN.TAḪ.ŠUM festival (CTH 612) in O. Gurney, *Hittite Religion*, 32-33.
258 E.g. KBo XXIII 1, Recto I 48-50, II 1-16, *Hethitica 3*, 150-151.

believes the Hittite practice has Syro-Canaanite origins (see above). It may then be true that the Emar rituals for the gods of Hatti are copied from the practices of the Hittite lords.[259] An odd feature of this group is the absence of ritual personnel and ritual locations, not at all the norm for Boghazkoy Hittite ritual. The only human mentioned is ᵐ*Eḫ-li-it-te* (472.6), the only personal name in all Emar ritual, and the Hurrian term *ambašši (471.33*; 473.19; etc.) is not clearly a place.[260] It is tempting to suppose that the texts for Hittite gods do not even represent rituals actually performed at Emar, since there is little to define their place in the Emar cult. Nevertheless, these ritual texts do seem to have been composed at Emar, even if copied from Hittite practice. Compare the idioms for feasting,[261] presentation of offering,[262] and filling cups with beverage.[263] Standard Emar terms for wine and barley-beer, KAŠ.GEŠTIN and KAŠ.ŠE, are used throughout text 471, though KAŠ.GEŠTIN and KAŠ.MEŠ appear in the 472 offering list for the same pair (see above). Markers of time such as *ana pānī nubatti*,[264] "just before the evening watch," *ina ūmi šâšūma*,[265] "on that same day," and *ina ūmi šanî*,[266] "on the next day," belong to the temporal system of the festivals.[267] The perspective of the action is that of all the other rituals, expressed by 3mp verb forms. Perhaps the personal name Eḫlitte indicates an official for the Hittite overlords who was involved in the importation of these rites. Arnaud observes that such "religious imperialism" is unknown in the ancient Near East, making this an exceptional situation, and I would suggest that these rites are not central to practice by the local citizens.[268]

It does seem that we can properly separate the calendar rites and the lists from the festivals, and the rites for the gods of Hatti from all the rest, with appropriate cautions. However, the evidence at hand does not prove the

---

259 See Arnaud, *CRAIBL* 1980, 384.
260 473.19, *i-na* u_4*-mi a-ba-aš-ši* ? Laroche, *GLH*, 46, defines it as a cultic place or object, often joined to *keldi* in the Kizzuwatna traditions.
261 *ikkalū išattû*, "they will eat (and) drink," 471.25; 472.73; these are written syllabically, vs. other Emar ritual.
262 *a-na pa-ni* DINGIR.MEŠ *i-šak-ka-nu*, "they will place before the gods," 472.22, 25.
263 *umallû*, "they will fill," 472.19, with double accusative 7 ᵈᵘᵍGÚ.ZI KAŠ.MEŠ (not genitive?).
264 471.28; 472.18, 24, 28.
265 472.23, cf. 16, 26.
266 472.29, [i-na] U_4.2.KÁM.
267 See 369.20, 40, 62 for the first, line 59D for the second, and lines 7, 29 for the last.
268 See Arnaud, *Hethitica VIII*, 18-19.

Mesopotamian origins of the "*ordo*," nor its place in a temple cult set apart from the festival cult. The terminology that distinguishes the calendar rituals and the offering lists is not particularly Mesopotamian, and in fact introduces a number of previously unknown words that probably come from the local Syrian dialect:

446

$^{\text{lú.meš}}$*ga-ma-ru* (?), 16, 38

^{lú}*za-bi-ḫi*, 35, "butcher(?)" (western?)

$^{\text{lú.meš}}$*aḫ-ḫi-a*, "brothers(?)," of ^{d}Udḫa's temple, 36; also as recipients of the redemption payment in sales documents, e.g. 20.26

$^{\text{lú(.meš)}}$*nu-Bu-ḫa-an-ni*, 48, 78; cf. 14, 60, 80, 90 (no determinative); also 452.4, 17, *passim*; 458.6; 463.12(?)

Bi-ri-ki ša ^{d}IM, 49

bu-GA(*qá*?)*-ra-tu*$_4$, 85; little context; cf. Hebrew *bāqār*, "cattle"??; or, cf. 373.68, ^{d}KUR EN *bu-ka-ri*, "firstborn"

ṣa-du, 89, 90; also 452.20, 21; "rounds"?

É RI-RI-*ti*??, 91

$^{\text{lú.meš}}$*mar-za-ḫu ša mi-Ki*, 92; cf. ^{iti}*Mar-za-ḫa-nu*, 85[269]

447

^{uzu}*ni-pí*(?)*-šu*, 15; cf. Ugaritic *npš*, "throat," or some offering, in Gordon, *UT* glossary, no. 1681, 67 I:7 and RS 24 249:23

452

ḫu-us-si, in *ina ūmi ḫussi*, 1, "recollection"?; also 459.3

$^{\text{ninda.meš}}$*ka-ma-na-ti*, 18

ZÍZ(*kunāšu*) *ab-lu-ṣi*, 29

---

269 See *AHw* s.v. *marza'u*; *CAD* s.v. *marzi'u* (*marza'u*, *marziḫu*), "(a professional or religious group)," only Ras Shamra, "W Sem. word"; cf. Hebrew *marzēaḥ*, Ugaritic *mrzḥ*; see Eissfeldt, *Ugaritica* 6 187ff. The word *mi-ki* is obscure; note Moran, *El Amarna*, 239, EA 64 n.2, possibly read $^{\text{munus.meš}}$*mi-ki-tu*. This might then be a feminine form of *mikû* (unknown meaning).

ninda*ṣa-ab-bu-ut-tu*, 33; ninda*ṣa-bu-ut-*[*t*]*a*, 40; ninda.meš*ṣa-ab-bu-ta*, 41, 42; ninda*ṣa-bu-ta*, 41; 460.4, ninda*ṣu-bu-tu*$_4$
a-bi-i, 32 and *passim*; Hurrian (/Syrian) *abi*?[270]

454

wa-al-lu-ḫi, 7, 8; 461.8, *i-na u*$_4$*-mi wa-lu-ḫi ša* dIM
[*w*]*a-ar-di-ti*, 12

459

zìBA.BA.ZA *ḫu-ub-ri*, 7

460

ninda*za-ri-ú*, 2, 7 (*za-ri-i*); cf. 385 *kissu*, text E, 11
ninda*ru-qa nu-ra-qu*, 17, 29, cf. 24
ninda*qa-du-ú*, 18
ninda*ma-Ku-ru*, 21, 28, cf. 17
ninda*ḫal-ḫal-(lu)*, 21, 28, cf. 16; cf. 385 *kissu*, E, 12
ninda*ka-ka-ru* (*kakkaru*), 21, 24, 29, cf. 16
ninda*SI-PU*, 24, cf. 16, 22, 28
[Z]Ì.DA *qa-i-ti*, 32

463

pí-it-ḫa, 1; "opening"?

2. The Gods of the Other Emar Rituals

Once we have dealt with the major festivals and the god lists, a large group of ritual texts still remains. To review, the more important ones are:

-- the ritual texts 392-394 (Arnaud, "rituals divers")
-- the annual calendar ritual 446, and related fragments 447 and 448;
-- the ritual for the dead in the month of Abû, 452;
-- the offering lists for the *ša-aṭ*(?)*-ra-ḫi* rites of Aštart of the battle, 460, and unknown recipients, 462;

[270] See Laroche, *GLH*, 34, "Trou creusé en terre pour communiquer avec les puissances infernales," from Kizzuwatna traditions, borrowed from Akkadian *apu*/*abu* or Sumerian ab, "trou"; see Hoffner, "Second millennium antecedents to the Hebrew *ʾôb*," *JBL* 86 (1967) 385-401; *UF* 6 451 (compare Hebrew *ʾôb*?).

-- the rite that begins with opening doors, 463;
-- the rituals for the Hittite gods, 471-473 and fragments.

Among these, the last form an entirely separate group. Neither Dagan nor ^{d}IM (without epithet) appear at all, nor ^{d}NIN.KUR and ^{d}NIN.URTA, nor the Emar gods with some Hurrian-Hittite attestation, Ea, Išḫara, and Hebat. Rather, 471-473 include gods from the Hurrian-Hittite pantheon such as:[271]

Allanu/i (472.58; 473.8; 476.20): cf. Allani, Laroche, p. 44;
Hazi and Nani (472.58; 473.9; 476.21): cf. Hazzi and Namni, pp. 47, 55;
Hurraš, Hurra (472.58; 473.9; 476.20): cf. Hur-, p. 49;
Ištar *ša* Šamuḫa (472.38): p. 95;
Madi (472.60; 473.13): cf. Mati, p. 54;
Šanda (471.19; 472.70): cf. Šanta, p. 88;
Tenu (471.24; 472.72): p. 61;
^{d}IM ^{kur}Nirikka (472.17, 32): cf. ^{d}IM of Nerik, p. 114;
^{d}IM Piḫa'immi (472.24, 48): cf. Piḫaimiš/i, p. 71;
^{d}UTU *ša šamê* (471.10; 472.34; 473.6): cf. ^{d}UTU BĒL ŠAMÊ, p. 106;
VII.BI (472.8, etc.; 473.13; cf. 476.23, VII.VII.BI): p. 108, VII.VII.BI.

The rites for the gods of Hatti thus give us no information about the local Emar pantheon, since their pantheon is imported from the culture of Emar's overlords.

Evidence from the other rituals is some help, though the texts may serve a more limited portion of the Emar cult. The rituals 392-394 are quite broken, and each seems to be dedicated mainly to the affairs of a single god. Emar 392, the *imištu* (unknown meaning) of the king, and 394.26-44, the *ḫenpa* of the cattle, are both concerned with Dagan and his temple (392.3, 6, 11; 394.27, 30, 32, 34, 37). Text 393 revolves around the (^{d})Ar'uri, which is specially associated with ^{d}NIN.KUR (393.2, 3, 7), and 394.1-25 is broken and

271 References are to Laroche, *Recherches sur les noms des dieux hittites*, 1947. R. Lebrun, "Divinités louvites et hourrites des rituels anatoliens en langue akkadienne provenant de Meskéné," in *Hethitica IX*, Louvain-la-neuve: Peeters, 1988, 153, finds that the particular deities show a 13th-century god-list that could be contemporary with Hattušili III or Tudḫaliya IV, and which reflects Louvian-Cilician influence.

tells us little. Similarly, the list 460 is explicitly for the sanctification day of *Aštartu tāḫāzi* (lines 1, 6, 9).

The most useful information comes from the calendar rituals, 446, 452, and 463. Emar 446, the principal text for the annual calendar ritual, mentions many of the gods who appear in the festivals, but the two most active participants are ^{d}KUR/Dagan and ^{d}IM.[272] This association stands in contrast to the situation in all the major festivals, but conforms to the pattern of the official pantheon of the lists. Likewise, Emar 463 combines rites for Dagan (lines 1-8) with rites for ^{d}IM (lines 19-30?; lines 26-30 include Hebat). The ritual for the month of Abû, Emar 452, includes a list of gods whose *abû*'s receive offerings on the 25th through 27th days of the month, ^{d}NIN.KUR (452.33), Dagan (lines 40, 46), and Alal (line 50, cf. 41). Though she is not found in the ceremonies for the end of the month, various manifestations of Aštart dominate the earlier parts of the month: ^{d}*Iš*$_8$*-tár ša šu-bi*, lines 10, 14; ^{d}*Iš*$_8$*-tár ša bi-ri-*KA*-ti*, line 15; ^{d}*Iš*$_8$*-tár ša a-bi*, lines 5(!) and 17; and ^{d}*Iš*$_8$*-tár* alone in line 21. The mountain ḪUR.SAG *Ṣu-pa-ra-ti*, (line 29) recalls ^{d}INANNA *Ṣu-pá-ra-ti* of the god list, 379.6, and Latarak (^{d}LÚ.LÀL.MEŠ, line 55?) is part of Inanna/Ištar's circle in Mesopotamia.[273] Išḫara (line 42) and ^{d}NIN.URTA (line 25) appear once each. The main surprise is the storm god's absence.[274] He may be lost in the breaks, but the *maš'artu* installation (370) and the text for the offerings of Aštart (460) show that her cult can operate without the inclusion of ^{d}IM/Baal.

Note: Mesopotamian Gods at Emar

Just as the Emar scribes worked with rituals for a foreign Hittite/ Hurrian pantheon, they also adopted an independent set of Mesopotamian patron deities when dealing with texts from that land. Arnaud has collected the colophons of the Sumerian-Akkadian lexicographic and literary texts in Emar VI.4, no. 604. These generally include the name of the scribe, his title,

---

[272] Most of the Emar rituals use ^{d}KUR for the name Dagan. The *zukru* fragment 375 writes the name with the syllabic ^{d}*Da-gan*, lines 2, 3, 10, 17, and 19. Only text 446 uses both writings: ^{d}KUR, 446.99; cf. 8, ^{d}ḪAR, expected from line 45?; 54, *a-na* KUR; ^{d}*Da-gan*, 446.50, 62, 79, 96; cf. 447.8; 448.2, 4, 5, 18. For ^{d}IM, see 446.49, 90, 106, 109, 115.

[273] Latarak is Ištar's son in the Weidner list; see C. Wilcke, "Inanna/Ištar: A. Philologisch," *RlA* 5, 1976, 76 and 80. Latarak appears only once at Mari, in the ritual for Ištar (*RA* 35); cf. Nakata, *Deities in the Mari Texts*, 341.

[274] Read *a-*[*na*] ⸢DINGIR⸣.MEŠ *ú-za-a-zu*, in line 2.

and the gods he serves (ÌR DN..., "servant of DN..."). Nabû and Nisaba come first,[275] and only Mesopotamian gods play a part. Nabû is god of the scribal craft, with cult center in Borsippa near Babylon.

F. DEVELOPMENTS IN EMAR RELIGION

In order to understand properly the rituals found at Emar, we must consider their possible backgrounds. The patterns in the ritual type, the language used, and the pantheons served appear to reflect different settings in 13th-century Emar, but how did the distinct features of these settings come to be? What forces might have been at work to produce the situation found in the 13th century? These questions apply to the contents of any ancient archive. At Emar, we are faced with a city built and dominated by an outside power (Hatti), with rituals written in the language and writing system of another foreign culture (Babylonian/Assyrian), which show characteristics that fit neither, and which are internally diverse. Surely the festivals, at least, represent religious practices that come from the time before Muršili II conquered Emar and Aštata.

The task of looking behind the 13th-century final product is worthwhile but harder to control than description of the texts and their contents as they stand. I do not attempt minute deconstruction of the rituals and the culture, but rather a broad understanding of development and identification of the features that are clues to that development. As the body of knowledge for all ancient Syrian history, culture, and religion grows, the conclusions drawn may naturally be corrected and refined.

In undertaking to study the background of the Emar rituals, it must be remembered that the reality behind the collection made by the diviners is complex, reflecting different and interrelated cultural settings over time. It is not easy to distinguish what is definably old from what is simply a difference between urban and rural settings, for instance. The proposals offered here are based on two principal factors: the pantheon, which can be compared to fairly extensive information for ancient Syria, and cultural institutions that do not appear to have arisen in the context of 13th-century circumstances.

---

[275] 604.1.3-4; 2.1.4-5; 2.2.5; 5.6-7; 7.1.2; 7.2.7-8; cf. 3.2; 9.2.

1. Emar's Outside Contacts

Before examining possible developments in Emar religion that are suggested by the above study, it might be helpful to review the history of Emar's most significant outside contacts. Long before the Hittites captured Emar, the city was an important stop on the trade route from Mesopotamia to the Mediterranean that followed the Euphrates River westward until it turned north, and then crossed overland. Emar was placed at the point where the river route began or ended. Location alone put Emar in the way of outside contacts, always by trade, and often by military excursion. The Ebla archives show that Emar was probably independent in the middle third millennium, though within Ebla's sphere of interest.[276] It suffered the attacks of Sargon and Narām-Sîn of Akkad, with Ebla, along with early incursions from Mari. Emar was a dependant of Halab/Yamḫad during the reign of Mari's Zimri-Lim (early 18th century).[277] D. Beyer finds that the earliest seals found at Meskéné/Emar, from the 18th-17th centuries, reflect themes from the first dynasty of Babylon, showing one instance of Mesopotamian influence in nearly the same period.[278] P. Xella emphasizes the heavy Babylonian influence on northern Syria, and Ugarit in particular, during the Middle and Late Bronze Ages, finding indications of this in the Ugaritic ritual texts.[279]

We do not have textual evidence for the period between the Mari and the Emar archives, but the time included the decline of Yamḫad and the rise of the Hurrian-dominated kingdom of Mitanni, based in the region drained by the Habur River and northward, but reaching all the way across Syria at its greatest success.[280] Mitanni took control of Halab in about 1470 B.C.E.,

---

276 A. Finet, "Le port d'Emar sur l'Euphrate, entre le royaume de Mari et le pays de Canaan," in E. Lipiński, ed., *The Land of Israel: Cross-roads of Civilizations*, Leuven: Uitgeverij Peeters, 1985, 32.
277 See Finet, 34.
278 Beyer, "Notes préliminaires sur les empreintes de sceaux de Meskéné," in *Le Moyen Euphrate*, 270-271.
279 Xella, "L'influence babylonienne à Ougarit, d'après les textes alphabétiques rituels et divinatoires," in RAI 25, 321-338, especially 322-323. He finds the Mesopotamian influence in the sacrificial lexicon, the general structure of the ceremonies, the leading role of the king, and the liturgy following the lunar month. I wonder whether the last three features are unquestionably Mesopotamian, or, if they are originally Mesopotamian, how old that connection might be. It seems possible that the west might have its own calendar-based liturgical traditions, and religion which gives the head of the city-state a leading role.
280 Wilhelm, *Grundzüge*, 32-40. Na'aman believes that this Hurrian expansion was more political than a wave of invasion or emigration; see "Syria at the transition from the Old Babylonian period to the Middle Babylonian period," *UF* 6 (1974) 267-272.

reaching Mukiš/Alalaḫ at the same time.[281] Emar remained in the sphere of Mitanni under the terms of its treaty with Egypt, but by the end of the 14th century Mitanni's western holdings were threatened by both the Hittites and the rising Assyrians. The main outside cultural influence at Emar during this period came from the east.

After the Hittites took northern Syria in the second half of the 14th century, they set up vassal states at Carchemish and Halab. Emar's submission to the authority of Carchemish is reflected in the legal documents recording decisions by that city's kings (e.g. Emar 18, 19, 177).[282] Although contact with Mesopotamia and the east was certainly never cut off, the period of Hittite domination brought an important shift in Emar's orientation. It now belonged to an empire extending to the north and west, and it was situated at the eastern extreme of Hatti's Syrian provinces.[283]

2. Recent Developments

Several elements in the religion of the Emar ritual texts appear to be later than the core of the old festival cults. These are not foreign intrusions, for the most part; that is, they are not imports from Hurrian-Hittite or Mesopotamian religion, nor even immediately influenced by practices or language from the powerful neighboring cultures. It is not possible to date these changes with certainty, but we should take into account the tremendous upheaval caused by the Hittite conquest of Emar at the end of the 14th century and subsequent construction of a new city.

The one class of ritual that must have entered Emar practice under Hittite sovereignty is the ritual for the gods of Hatti. However, even these are not true imports but local compositions following Anatolian customs.

---

281 Wilhelm, 35.

282 The letter from the king of Ušnatu to the lord of Ugarit, RS 17.143, touches on Emar's position; see the discussion regarding Ini-Tešub, king of Carchemish, in Klengel, *Geschichte Syriens* I, 80-87.

283 Although Mesopotamian writing and scribal traditions had a continuing impact on the culture of Ugarit, perhaps the city does reflect a diminished Mesopotamian influence in other spheres. M. Yon and A. Caubet, "Ougarit, Mari, et l'Euphrate," *AAAS* 34 (1983) 33, observe that the material culture of Ugarit shows relatively little Mesopotamian influence during the Late Bronze Age. They find signs of Mesopotamian culture at Ugarit in some religious architecture and in funerary customs, as well as in the writing system (see pages 34-38).

Another key point of later religious change is the building of the Baal-Aštart temple complex at the high point of the Meskéné/Emar tell, setting them at the fore of the Emar pantheon in a way barely reflected in the texts. The pair is West Semitic, even Canaanite, and not a combination native to Emar. Emar temple style is the axial type known throughout Syria and Palestine, the one architectural feature of the city that follows a uniquely Syrian, non-Hittite pattern.[284] Perhaps this is a sign that the Hittites did not refrain entirely from interfering in matters of religious practice. In a city designed and built according to Hittite models, the distinctiveness itself is suspicious; it reflects an active, not a passive choice. Perhaps the temple style, like the Baal-Aštart pair, is slightly too western for Emar. The question should remain open at present, but it may be that the Hittite overlords left the temples to the local authorities, but nevertheless consciously or unconsciously served as a catalyst for stronger association with west Syrian/Canaanite religious culture, so that Emar became more closely linked to its western neighbors.[285]

The annual calendar ritual Emar 446 also displays western elements not found in the archaic local festivals. These include the "rounds(?)" of Baal and Aštart,[286] the scattering of seed, so reminiscent of the fertility image in the Baal cycle (lines 50-51), the prominence of burning the offerings (*šarāpu*), and the month [iti]*mar-za-ḫa-ni*, with its [lú.meš]*mar-za-ḫu (lines 85*, 92-93). Moreover, Dagan and Baal do not appear together as active players in the Emar festivals, and this may be a recent development. Arnaud describes the Emar "*ordo*" as distinctly Mesopotamian, even to the point of being copied (if not imported),[287] but this should remain a question. Text 446, at least, displays other western traits to go with its western deities, and the rites for the dead in Emar 452 need not belong to an exclusively Mesopotamian practice. Ugaritic ritual texts include the calendar format, which should not be considered exclusively, or at

---

284 Margueron, in *Le Moyen Euphrate*, 312.

285 The Hittites did have a strong presence in Ugarit. P. Vargyas explores the impact of the Hittite merchant community on the economic life of Ugarit; "Marchands hittites à Ugarit," *OLP* 16 (1985) 71-79. In a remarkable intervention, the Hittite king periodically banished Hittite merchants from Ugarit in order to eliminate damage to the local economy and to regulate commercial investments.

286 Lines 89-90; cf. *ʿṯtrt ṣwdt* at Ugarit, Nr. 177 in de Moor, *UF* 2 195.

287 *CRAIBL* 1980, 384.

least recently Mesopotamian.[288] Syrian religion may have had an established temple calendar of its own.

Finally, the official pantheon at Emar appears to combine Dagan and the storm god at its head in a way that is foreign to the Emar festival tradition. ᵈIM is certainly a god with a long heritage in Syria, but his cult nevertheless seems to be separate from that of Dagan at Emar. Other features of the systematic offering-lists that differ from the festivals and rituals are the high place of the sun and moon gods, who have little role in ritual, and the position of NERGAL, who is common in the offering lists but is otherwise absent in ritual. ᵈNÈ.IRI$_{11}$.GAL should be the same as Rašap, who is quite popular in personal names. Since the names speak for 13th-century popularity, this might suggest a more recent prominence.

---

288 See for example KTU 1.112, rites for the month(?) *ḫyr*, covering days 1, 3, 7, 8, 11, 13, 14, 15, 16, 17 (and broken), G. del Olmo Lete, "Ritual regio ugaritico de evocación/adivinación (KTU 1.112)," *AuOr* 2 (1984) 197-206. The day sequence for Emar 452 begins 1, 3, 8 (for 7?), 8, 14... .

V. CULTURAL AFFINITIES: PRELIMINARY OBSERVATIONS

The above commentary on Emar 369 and examination of the festival traditions from Emar touch on issues of cultural affinity at many points, and the reader should have gathered by now that the festival texts from Emar do not appear to derive directly from the neighboring cultures of Mesopotamia, Anatolia, or Canaan. This is not to say that Emar religion somehow escaped influence from any of these cultures; on the contrary, all of these probably left their imprint on the religion of Emar, leaving various distinctive traces that have been observed where appropriate, above. Nevertheless, the Emar festivals appear to represent established local Syrian practice.[1]

The purpose of this closing section is to review the broad outlines of foreign influence on Emar culture and the evidence for the Syrian character of the religious practice attested in the Emar festivals (and many other rituals). Problems in the relationship between Late Bronze Age Emar and other ancient Near Eastern societies will require detailed examination of many specific cultural features, involving issues of language, social organization, and more. Such detail and breadth is beyond the scope of this review. In order to place the Emar ritual in the context of the surrounding cultures, I have consulted the ritual corpora of Babylon and Assyria, Hatti (with its Hurrian component), and Ugarit. This reading has led me to conclude that Emar ritual is fundamentally independent of these ritual traditions, and the basis for this conclusion will be presented below. However, my examination of texts from these cultures has

[1] In this view, I am in fundamental agreement with Arnaud; see *Le Moyen Euphrate*, 252, and throughout his publications to date.

not been systematic, and these views are preliminary impressions. It is my hope that other scholars will refine and criticize the observations and generalizations which I hazard in the following discussion. Along with the consideration of other Semitic philologists, study of Emar ritual would benefit from the input of Hittitologists and specialists in sociological and anthropological approaches.

A. FOREIGN INFLUENCES AT EMAR

The principal foreign influences on Emar culture come from two directions: Mesopotamia and Anatolia. Northern Syria had experienced centuries of military and cultural invasion from its eastern neighbors by the 13th century B.C.E., leaving a multilayered legacy, and 13th-century Emar was experiencing the effects of current rule by the Hittite empire. Indications of both influences appear in the written and material evidence from Emar, and these may be sketched as follows.

1. Mesopotamian Influence

J. Margueron, the excavator of Meskéné/Emar, finds few indications of Mesopotamian influence on material culture at the site. He only discusses the large numbers of nails found at the entrance to the temple M_2, the last temple found at Emar. These appear to have belonged to a façade decoration that would resemble Mesopotamian use of nails in temple decoration.[2] Likewise, the seals from Late Bronze Emar showed little direct influence of Mesopotamian iconography, though D. Beyer observes that the Mari-period seals found at Emar display Mesopotamian themes.[3]

In aspects of life that involved writing, Mesopotamian culture had a major impact on Emar. The largest number of tablets found at Emar is written in Akkadian, including the legal and economic documents from daily life in Emar,[4] as well as extensive records for temple administration and instructions

---

2 See Margueron, in *Le Moyen Euphrate*, 305-308.
3 Beyer, in *Le Moyen Euphrate*, 268-271.
4 See Arnaud, *Syria* 52 88.

for performance of ritual. The scribal profession follows a Mesopotamian model, even to the point where the scribes proclaim their service to Mesopotamian deities in scribal colophons for the lexical and literary texts.[5] These lexical and literary texts come from Mesopotamian canons, though Arnaud suggests that the lexicography and some wisdom texts belong to a particularly Syrian branch of those traditions.[6] According to Arnaud, texts for magic and divination, a version of the Weidner god-list, and other literary texts (Gilgamesh, the Palm and the Tamarisk) appear to reflect an Assyrian scribal stream.[7] Roles and activities of local Emar religion and ritual are more difficult to pin down, but some may have developed from Mesopotamian practices transmitted to Syria in the more distant past. The NIN.DINGIR herself may come from such a heritage. In spite of the absence of substantial direct influence on Emar material culture for this period and the relative independence of the indigenous religious traditions, we should not underestimate the magnitude of the impact on Emar society produced by Mesopotamian writing in the realms of law, economic life, and religion.

2. Hittite Influence

Margueron treats at some length the Hittite influence on Late Bronze Emar in his study in *Le Moyen Euphrate*.[8] The most striking feature is the city itself, apparently built from scratch on a manufactured tell high above the Euphrates River as an outpost against the Assyrians, whose power was spreading from the east. One result of such a project was the creation of new sacred sites, to which the ancient religion of Emar must have adapted with some difficulty, since traditions of sacred locations were highly conservative in the ancient Near East. Perhaps this disturbance would explain why the only Dagan temple mentioned in the festival texts is at Šatappi, not Emar. The other principal Hittite features at Emar are architectural, which is not

---

[5] These include Nabû, the Babylonian god of the scribal craft. See Emar 604, the colophons, and Arnaud, *Le Moyen Euphrate*, 249. This is also true at Ugarit; see Huehnergard, *Akkadian of Ugarit*, 226, n.62.

[6] Arnaud, "Religion assyro-babylonienne," *AEPHER* 86 (1977-78) 185; *CRAIBL* 1980, 381-383.

[7] See Arnaud, *AEPHER* 85 209-211; in *Le Moyen Euphrate*, 250-251; *CRAIBL* 1980, 380-381.

[8] See pages 287-304.

unexpected since the Hittites built the city. Emar house design appears to follow a style known from Boghazkoy, and the "*bīt ḫilāni*" of the Emar palace-complex probably is patterned after a Hittite design.[9]

Arnaud writes that the tablets found at Emar which are written along the longer dimension represent a Syro-Hittite style, and Beyer similarly distinguishes a Hittite-style iconography on some cylinder seals.[10] The collection of Hurrian language treatises on hepatoscopy and medical prognostics appears to be based on the technical vocabulary of Boghazkoy,[11] and the two liver models found at Emar are like Boghazkoy examples.[12]

Altogether, the Hittite influence on Emar does not seem to have penetrated deeply into the Syrian culture -- much less so than the Mesopotamian. However, the blunt impact of Hittite city construction and political domination must have struck Emar life at many levels, forcing considerable adjustment.

B. SYRIAN FEATURES

Among the features of Emar culture that appear distinctly Syrian, religious practice stands out as most prominent.[13] This Syrian flavor is expressed in the pantheon, the character of the ritual traditions, and in the temple architecture.[14]

1. The Pantheon

The pantheon of the Emar festivals and of all the ritual texts except those for "the gods of Hatti" appears to belong to the region of Syria sometimes called the Middle Euphrates, and it should be considered essentially "local." Dagan is the principal god at Terqa downstream and at Hadidi/Azu upstream,

---

9 See *Le Moyen Euphrate*, 290; cf. Margueron, "Un '*ḫilāni*' à Emar," *AASOR* 44 (1979) 153-176. The *bīt ḫilāni* was not known previously from the Bronze Age, so this conclusion may be less certain.

10 Beyer, in *Le Moyen Euphrate*, 275-276.

11 See Laroche, in *Le Moyen Euphrate*, 244.

12 Arnaud, *AEPHER* 88 214-215.

13 Margueron observes this in *Le Moyen Euphrate*, 308.

14 For the last, *ibid*, 308-311.

as he is at Emar. Deities such as Išḫara, Ea, and Adamma have an ancient north Syrian heritage, and ^{d}NIN.KUR and ^{d}NIN.URTA seem to indicate gods who are deeply rooted in local religion. ^{d}IM and Ištar/Aštart are a special case, since both could have been known in this region by other names for centuries before the Late Bronze Age, but they appear in the 13th century under the names Baal and Aštart, a fact which indicates possible influence from western Syria. The particular combination of ^{d}IM and Hebat may come from Halab, the old center for this divine pair.

The contrast of the Emar pantheon to contemporary Anatolian and Mesopotamian pantheons can be seen in the rites for the gods of Hatti (Emar 471-473, etc.) and in the scribal colophons and canonical god lists from Emar. These texts offer sets of deities that are entirely different from the rest of the gods of Emar ritual.

2. Ritual Occasions

None of the major festivals from Emar has been found in the previously known collections of ritual texts of Anatolia, Mesopotamia, or elsewhere. Names such as the *kissu* and *zukru* are not known as ritual events even by oblique reference.[15] The *maš'artu* is an unknown figure, and although the NIN.DINGIR derives from the *entu* of Mesopotamia, the rites for her installation appear to reflect a long indigenous development. This is an argument from silence, but the absence of parallels must be remarked nonetheless. We see from the archives of the Emar diviner that he had access to scribal traditions from both Hatti and Mesopotamia, but we find no Hittite or Mesopotamian ritual texts.[16]

3. Details of Ritual Practice

Given the cultural contact between Emar and its powerful neighbors to the north and east, it is not surprising to find details in the Emar festival practice or terminology which may come from those neighbors. For instance,

---

[15] Recall the special case of the *zukru* in the Mari letter; see Lafont, *RA* 78 9, 11.

[16] Even insofar as the calendar ritual and offering lists might reflect a Mesopotamian ancestry, and the rites for the gods of Hatti follow Hittite practices, none of these has known Mesopotamian or Anatolian parallels in the specific sense.

the *naptanu* (ritual "meal") is an established Assyrian tradition,[17] and the *naptanu*-bread which is so prominent in the NIN.DINGIR installation offerings is only attested elsewhere in Assyrian texts (see above). From the north, we find the Hurrian term *šinaḫilu* used to describe flour in the calendar rituals and offering lists, and the *ḫubar*-vessel which appears often in the *zukru* offerings may be identical to the common *ḫuppar*-vessel of Hittite ritual. The words (MUŠEN) *aṭṭuḫi* (371.13) and *walluḫi* (454.7, 8; 461.8) may be Hurrian: the roots **atti* and *walli* (GLH 291), with the suffix of membership (Zugehörigkeitsadjektive) *=o=ǵ/ḫḫe*.[18] In the rites for the gods of Hatti we find the Hittite terms ᴰᵁᴳ*ḫurtiyali* and ᴺᴵᴺᴰᴬ*punniki-* (471.31, 32; and 472.78).[19]

However, when we look at the central players and places of the festivals, we find few parallels. In the NIN.DINGIR festival alone, several new ritual personnel are introduced: the men of the *qidašu*, the *ḫussu*-men, the ritual *bēl bīti*, the *maš'artu*, the *kawanu*-men, the *nugagtu*, and the *ḫamša'u*-men. The ˡᵘ́ḪAL and the *zammārū* are attested, but their roles do not fit the figures known from other texts, as might be said for the NIN.DINGIR herself. In the same installation, we discover new names for sacred locations: the *bīt(i) bēl bīti* (É EN É), the *bīt BuKKi* (of the NIN.DINGIR), the *bīt tukli*, possibly called the *bīt ili*, and the *bīt Gadda*. These represent just the most prominent among many new terms and uses. Such an abundance of new terms is particularly striking in texts that are written in remarkably good Akkadian by scribes who apparently did not lack familiarity with traditional Mesopotamian terminology.

Perhaps the deepest indication of an indigenous reality underlying the Akkadian description is found in the language which communicates the component actions of the rituals. When comparing the Mesopotamian ritual traditions, the differences appear in the choice and use of Akkadian verbs for similar or equivalent ritual actions.

The late first-millennium Babylonian rituals gathered by F. Thureau-Dangin reflect practices from the first half of the millennium and before, as

---

17 See MVAG 41/3, pages 60-66; Karl F. Müller, *Das assyrische Ritual, Teil I: Texte zum assyrischen Königsritual*, Leipzig: MVAG 41/3, 1937.

18 G. Wilhelm, personal communication; note that the word **atti-* seems to be a topographical expression in one use at Nuzi (A. Fadhil, *Studien zur Topographie und Prosopographie der Provinzstädte des Königsreichs Arrapḫe*, Mainz am Rhein: Verlag Philipp von Zabern, 1983, 263-264), and Wilhelm suggests that this would make sense as the definition for a type of bird.

19 Wilhelm, personal communication.

seen by the involvement of the *šangû* and *bārû*, who are rare in Hellenistic temple practice.[20] They comprise a good base for examining Babylonian ritual terminology because they come from the temple archives of Uruk in the south. In this Babylonian ritual tradition, the sequence of animal-sacrifice and presentation of meat is expressed by *naqû* followed by *ṭeḫû* (D, "to bring near, present"),[21] a verb not found in Emar ritual. This combination is frequently followed by libation (verb, *naqû*),[22] an action not specified in the Emar festivals. When tables are set with food (in itself, not necessarily a Mesopotamian action), the verb *šakānu*, "to place," may be used to describe setting out the food,[23] as at Emar, but the tables themselves are "placed" with the verb *kunnu*[24] or "prepared" (*rakāsu*).[25] The verb *kunnu* is also used for setting drinks on the tables.[26] Other Babylonian offering verbs include the idiom *riksu rakāsu*, "to prepare offerings,"[27] and *qerēbu* (G or D, "to bring near, present"),[28] neither one found at Emar.

When the parallel between actions is closest, as is the case with offering, the contrast in terminology should be most significant, but the Babylonian rituals are also characterized by many actions or verbs that are completely foreign to our Emar ritual corpus. Examples include scattering flour, seed, etc., with verb *šarāqu*,[29] the mouth-washing ceremony *mīs pî*,[30] fumigation with verb *ḫâbu*,[31] offering water with verb *našû*,[32] and the repeated taking of

---

20 François Thureau-Dangin, *Rituels accadiens*, Paris: Editions Ernest Leroux, 1921; G.J.P. McEwan, *Priest and Temple in Hellenistic Babylonia*, Wiesbaden: Franz Steiner Verlag, 1981, 8-9, 15.

21 See RAcc, page 12, II:3-6; 14 II:33-34; 24 Rev 5; 34 10-11; 36 Face 20-21.

22 RAcc page 36 Rev 6; 38 9-10, 12, 21-23.

23 RAcc page 10 I:18; 24 Rev 3-4; 34 Face 7-9.

24 RAcc page 10 I:17; 30 III:24-25; cf. 12 II:2; 38 Rev 21. The Mari ritual for Ištar published by Dossin, "Un rituel du culte d'Ištar provenant de Mari," *RA* 35 (1938) 1-13, appears to be a much earlier representative of the same tradition of Babylonian offering terminology. It uses the idiom *ina meḫret* DN *kunnum* for offering: I:21-22; IV:35. The Mari ritual also uses *izuzzum* (see below) for taking up a ritual station, I:9, 16, 19, etc. Ritual players include the king (II:8, etc.), the lamentation priests (*kalûm*, II:19; Rev III:3-5, 14), the *šangûm*, and the *pašīšum* (both Rev IV:20), the last three being characteristic Babylonian temple personnel.

25 RAcc page 24 Rev 3-4; 38 Rev 9.

26 RAcc page 34 Face 7-9; cf. 10 I:19; 12 II:7; 32 IV:1-2; 42 Rev 7.

27 RAcc page 16 III:17; 42 Rev 4, 6; 44 6.

28 RAcc page 75 7; 76-77 34-35, 42, 50, Rev 3; 79 39, 42; 90 25; 92 6, 8, etc.

29 Aromatics, RAcc page 10 I:10; 42 18; 46 20; sand, 10 I:13; flour, 24 Rev 3-4; 30 III:27; 34 Face 10; seed 40 16; bread, dates, and flour, 44 7.

30 RAcc page 12 II:8; 16 III:24; 30 III:23.

31 RAcc page 12 II:12-13; 16 III:21, 26.

32 RAcc page 32 IV:23-24; 34 13; 90 33; 91 20.

ritual stations with verb *izuzzu*.[33] Again, these represent an argument from silence, less compelling than comparison of offering terminology, but producing a cumulative impression of contrast.

Assyrian ritual presents a similar situation. The offering verbs *qerēbu* and *rakāsu* appear in Assyrian ritual also,[34] as does the verb *izuzzu* for taking ritual stations.[35] We find the Assyrian offering idiom, *silqa apālu*,[36] "to offer boiled meat," and the sequence *(w)abālu-šakānu* for bringing gifts and presenting them before the god (*ana pān Aššur*).[37] Assyrian texts use the verbs *karāru*[38] and *ṣalā'u*[39] for "to put, place." None of these appears in Emar ritual, in spite of the fact that some of the literary and divination texts from the diviner's archive show an Assyrian character. Both Babylonian and Assyrian ritual make frequent reference to spoken liturgy: prayers, incantations, or songs. Emar ritual may include speech, but the traditions for recording the instructions omit this almost entirely.

Comparison with Hittite and Hurrian ritual is made somewhat more difficult by the shift to non-Akkadian and non-Semitic languages. Ritual personnel, locations, materials for offering, etc., might reveal equations if Emar showed any tendency to use Hittite or Hurrian ritual terminology, but few shared terms emerge. Some parallels appear through Hittite use of Akkadograms and Sumerograms (e.g., the NIN.DINGIR; see the commentary), but viewed as a whole, the components of Emar and Hurrian-Hittite ritual seem essentially distinct.[40] The strongest contrast between the basic frameworks of Emar and Hittite ritual can be seen in some activities from Hatti which have no part at all in Emar. The most prominent may be the Hittite practice of "breaking" bread for offering, which appears in a wide variety of rituals from Hatti, even including the Emar rites for the Hittite

33 People, RAcc page 92 8; gods, 100 10-11; 101 4, 6, etc.

34 KAR 139 Vs 3; MVAG 41/3 page 8 I:38, 40; 10 I:41. Both of these are Middle Assyrian.

35 MVAG 41/3 page 14 III:11 (MA); page 64 III:42 (NA).

36 MVAG 41/3 page 10 II:14 (MA).

37 MVAG 41/3 page 14 III:6 (MA).

38 MVAG 41/3 page 10 II:27; 14 III:9 (MA); KAR 215 I:11 (NA).

39 MVAG 41/3 page 10 II:28; 14 II:46.

40 Some useful references for broad comparison include H.G. Güterbock, in RAI 20, 125-132, for the temple and temple personnel; H.A. Hoffner, *Alimenta Hethaeorum*, for foodstuffs; and Haas and Wilhelm, *Hurritische und luwische Riten aus Kizzuwatna*, AOATS 3, Neukirchen-Vluyn: Neukirchener, 1974, for offering terminology in Hurrian rituals, as well as Laroche's *GLH*.

gods.[41] Other characteristic practices include "drinking (to)" a god,[42] hand-washing,[43] and purification by burning birds.[44] One feature that sets Hittite ritual apart from both Emar and Mesopotamian ritual is the primary role of both the king and queen in most Hittite ritual.[45] Singer observes that the standard format for Hittite festival texts involves step-by-step instructions for the rites, text for the recited liturgy, and a section for administration of materials, etc.[46] The first and third elements are closely paralleled by the form of the NIN.DINGIR installation at Emar, but Emar consistently lacks any recorded liturgy, as mentioned above.

Ugarit provides a collection of ritual and temple texts that comes from roughly the same period as the Emar rituals, yet the two groups do not display any marked affinity. The king dominates most Ugaritic ritual,[47] and terms for ritual personnel and offerings do not resemble those from Emar, on the whole. Compare the offering-types, *šrp wšlmm*, *šnpt*, *dbḥ*, *ṯ*ᶜ*(y)*, and *ḫḏrǵl*, among others.[48] De Tarragon classifies Ugaritic ritual into two main types, purification of the king and transfer of divine statues, placing CTA 32 in a separate category.[49] This is not the world of Emar ritual.

---

41 See above, Other Emar Rituals; The Rituals and Their Language, including the note with Hittite ritual references for breaking bread followed by libation.

42 See Lebrun, "Textes religieux," in *Hethitica 2*, 127, Kizzuwatna ritual CTH 699, I:38, 42, 47; Singer, *KI.LAM* I, page 79 III:12-18; 80 III:33-39, 47-51, etc.

43 See Singer, *KI.LAM* I, page 72 (KBo X 26) I:24-27; I:43-II:4; cf. page 73; H. Otten, StBoT 13 (KBo XIX 128), page 2-3 Vs I:17-19; cf. page 16-17; E. Neu, StBoT 12, page 24-25 Rs III:11'.

44 See G. Beckman, *Hittite Birth Rituals*, 117 n.308, burning birds is "seemingly characteristic of Hurrian-influenced texts at Bogazkoy." Compare, Haas and Wilhelm, AOATS 3, page 154-155 (KUB XV 31) Vs II:1-5, etc.; Lebrun, CTH 472, in *Hethitica 3*, page 150 Ro I:48-50.

45 See Lebrun, *Šamuḫa*, 43, and Lebrun, "Les hittites et le sacré," 170, for comment. For examples in texts, see Lebrun, "Textes religieux," in *Hethitica* 2, 103, etc.; Neu, StBoT 12, 10-11; Otten and Souçek, StBoT 8, 16-17, etc.; Singer, *KI.LAM* I, page 72 (KBo X 26) I:43-II:4, etc.; page 90.

46 Singer, *KI.LAM* I, 52.

47 See the Commentary above, on the king of Emar.

48 On *šrp wšlmm*, see Dietrich and Loretz, "Neue Studien zu den Ritualtexten aus Ugarit (I)," *UF* 13 (1981) 77-88; de Tarragon, *Le culte à Ugarit*, 59-63. On *šnpt*, see del Olmo Lete, "The cultic literature of Ugarit," in RAI 32, 159 and translation; de Tarragon, 64-65. On *dbḥ*, see del Olmo Lete, *UF* 19 (1987) 12; de Tarragon, 56. On *ṯ*ᶜ*(y)*, see de Tarragon, 58-59; del Olmo Lete, "Ugaritic *ṯ*ᶜ, *ṯ*ᶜ*y*, *ṯ*ᶜ*t*; nombre divino y accion cultual," *UF* 20 (1988) 30-33. On *ḫḏrǵl*, see del Olmo Lete, RAI 32, 159 and translation. For all of these terms, also consult Paolo Xella, *I Testi Rituali di Ugarit I*, Roma: Consiglio Nazionale delle Ricerche, 1981, via the glossary.

49 De Tarragon, 78-90 and 98-112, with 92-97 on CTA 32. Rituals for transfer of divine statues include CTA 33, UT 2004, and Ug. 5 no. 9.

This whirlwind tour through the ritual traditions of Emar's ancient neighbors does not do justice to the issues raised in comparing any one of them, but it would be folly to take up these problems in depth in a study focused on the Emar texts themselves. Each of the above comparisons merits separate study. It is hoped that this broad overview will give some substance to my observation that Emar ritual does not seem to share the language or religious traditions of any of its known neighbors. Thus, the ritual very likely reflects traditions native to north-central Syria that were previously unattested because we lacked written evidence for ritual practice in that part of the ancient Near East.

4. Temple Architecture

Excavations at Meskéné/Emar uncovered four temples for the city which the Hittites built, and all of them display roughly the same form: construction of rooms and entry along a single axis (more precisely, Margueron's "*in antis*" form). Moreover, each is associated with an open space that is not integrated into the architectural scheme of the temple rooms, but is simply juxtaposed to the temple with separate access and orientation.[50] The *in antis* form belongs to the Syrian axial temple architecture that appears in various forms at Megiddo,[51] Shechem,[52] Hazor,[53] Mardikh/Ebla,[54] Alalaḫ (level IV),[55] and Mari,[56] among others.[57] The Emar temples do not have the single-room, thick-

[50] Margueron, *Le Moyen Euphrate*, 308-309.

[51] See P. Matthiae, "Unité et développement du temple dans la Syrie du Bronze Moyen," in RAI 20, 62, temples 4040, 5269, and 5192, in stratum XV-XIV, area BB, *c.* 2000; cf. M. Ottosson, *Temples and Cult Places in Palestine*, Uppsala: Boreas, 1980, 53, the *migdal*-type of level VII B and A, MB II; Matthiae, 65, temple 2048.

[52] Ottoson, 57-58; Temple I A and B, *migdal*-type, MB IIC (*c.* 1650-1550).

[53] Ottoson, 59-60; *migdal*-type, Area A, MB II - LB I; cf. Matthiae, 65-67, "temple 3," *c.* 1700.

[54] Matthiae, 49; Temple D, elongated Syrian style, thick walls (cf. *migdal*), axial, "à antes," open front, *c.* 1900-1800; cf. Ottosson, 53.

[55] Matthiae, 61; the level IV temple has axial form, comparable to Hamah J, Amuq J, and Mardikh III; cf. Ottosson, 34, "Breitraum" style. Matthiae, 55, says the level VII temple also has axial form.

[56] Margueron, "Quelques remarques sur les temples de Mari," in *M.A.R.I.* 4, 496; only the early second-millennium temple of Dagan (fig. 10) has the axial Syrian form; cf. R. Dornemann, "The excavations at Ras Shamra and their place in the current archaeological picture of ancient Syria," in G.D. Young, ed., *Ugarit in Retrospect*, Winona Lake, IN: Eisenbrauns, 1981, 62, Mari and Alalaḫ have a mix of Syrian and non-Syrian forms.

[57] Margueron, in *Le Moyen Euphrate*, 308, suggests temples from Tell Chuera of the third millennium, Tell Fray and Mumbaqat of the late second millennium, and Tell Taynat of the early first millennium.

walled structure of the *migdal*-type; their walls are not extremely thick, and temple M_1 has additional rooms off the side of the cella. However, all the Emar temples have the large, elongated cella with an axial entrance. This Syrian religious architecture makes a striking contrast to the Hittite architecture which dominates the city and follows the same tendency toward independence in religious practice that we find in the rituals.

VI. CONCLUSION

A. THE NIN.DINGIR INSTALLATION

The NIN.DINGIR (*ittu*?) is the high priestess of the storm god at Emar. She is put into office in a ceremony that in part involves marriage to the god, as would be appropriate for the EN/*entu*/NIN.DINGIR as known in OB period Mesopotamia. However, the festival which celebrates her installation is filled with features not characteristic of the Mesopotamian institution. For example, her official temple residence is the *bīt* (*BuKKi ša*) NIN.DINGIR, not the Mesopotamian *gipāru*.

The occasion for the installation is apparently the death of the previous NIN.DINGIR, and the festival pays respect to the old priestess while initiating the new. The NIN.DINGIR can be the daughter of any Emar citizen, and it is "the sons of Emar" who initiate the festival, which is remarkably free of involvement of the central government -- the king and his palace court. The elders, not the king, appear to provide a stamp of approval from the civic leadership by bowing before her and giving gifts. These traits may indicate that the festival reflects a religious heritage at Emar which is not tied to the centralized royal establishment, although the installation certainly belongs to the temple cult of ^{d}IM in Emar proper, in contrast to the *zukru*'s placement outside the city. The whole festival tradition of Emar seems to reflect origins in a religious practice that has a wider base of participation in the local population. This characteristic may belong to essentially non-urban or non-sedentary societies, and it could point to influence from non-sedentary Syrian cultures. At least, the religious institutions of Emar appear to have maintained ties with a heritage that predates the dominance of royal government.

The NIN.DINGIR rites move through nine days, during which the new priestess makes a gradual transition from the household of her father to that of ^{d}IM, through daily processions to the temple of ^{d}IM and return to her father's house. The last day of the installation introduces explicit wedding imagery, when the NIN.DINGIR leaves her father's house veiled and embraced "as a bride." However, the events and symbols from the rest of the festival may belong more to installation for sacred service than to marriage:

1. She is anointed twice by oil on the head, a purification rite that marks consecration of priests in the Bible (cf. the *pašīšu*-priest of Mesopotamia, "anointed"?), as well as change in legal status through manumission or marriage in second-millennium Syrian texts.
2. The new priestess is "shaved" (*gallubu*). This is a purification rite of passage that especially pertains to consecration of priests and not to marriage, as far as we know.
3. The NIN.DINGIR is enthroned before the final day, in conjunction with obeisance from the city-elders and gifts from the elders and her brothers. Enthronement manifests her actual "installation" (*malluku*), which is then celebrated for seven days. The term *malluku* is used for the installation of the *maš'artu*-priestess as well, and this definition of the occasion does not appear to belong to marriage. (The *maš'artu* is not wedded to Aštart.)
4. On the enthronement day, the goddess ^{d}NIN.KUR takes up residence in the father's house and stays there through the final day of the installation festival, when her departure just precedes the final departure of the new priestess. In the intervening period, there are seven days of offerings and feasting at the temple residence of the NIN.DINGIR, while she remains at her father's house with ^{d}NIN.KUR. The feast (*šūkultu*) appears to be associated with the enthronement of the priestess (line 51, *uššab*), which took place in the evening on the installation day (line 40). ^{d}NIN.KUR's participation has a close parallel in the *kissu*, "throne," festivals, where again she is made to lie down and later rise to depart from Dagan's temple (385) and the house of the *bēl bīti* (388). The role of ^{d}NIN.KUR in the NIN.DINGIR festival may be particularly associated with mourning the previous priestess, and this aspect of the installation falls outside the realm of marriage custom and imagery.

Only on the last day does the "wedding" begin, with a set of events that begin with the departure of the priestess (above) and end with her climbing onto her bed. Does this finale mean that the NIN.DINGIR installation is a "sacred marriage rite"? She is indeed married to the storm god, but we have no indication of rites intended to promote fertility. No marriage partner is provided for her bed, and when she ends the celebration by getting into bed, the priestess may be finalizing her transition to residence in the household of dIM rather than preparing for consummation of a sacred marriage.

The NIN.DINGIR installation belongs to the cult of the storm god, whose consort is Hebat, not Aštart, though the temples of Baal and Aštart apparently were situated at the highest spot in Late Bronze Age Emar. Emar's cult of the storm god seems to reach back beyond the association in the city of Baal and Aštart to the cult for dIM and Hebat which belonged to the major storm god center at Halab.

B. THE EMAR FESTIVAL TRADITION

The Emar pantheon, the ritual texts as units and in their component parts, and the Emar temple architecture all indicate that we have a new body of information for religious practices native to north central Syria of the Late Bronze II Age. Emar religion and culture has some affinities with the cultures of its neighbors, but it remains distinct from all of them. The religious traditions represented in the Emar festivals and other ritual texts will begin to fill in the gap in our knowledge of second-millennium Syrian religion for the broad region between Mari and Ugarit, supplementing the earlier archives from Ebla.

Emar's festival tradition reflects complex origins that appear to pre-date discernible 13th-century religious traits. In particular, placement of Dagan and dIM together at the head of the pantheon is not found in the festivals beyond the offering lists of the *zukru* and *maš'artu* festivals. This gives us reason to suspect that these lists are later than the core of each celebration and are based on the needs of festival performance for Emar in the 13th century. Secondly, as mentioned above, the association of Baal and Aštart appears to be fairly new to Late Bronze Emar and is not reflected in the great installation rituals of the storm god and Aštart (369 and 370).

The religion of Emar should become a starting point for fresh examination of ancient Syrian religion, with the hope that this new evidence will help us to better understand the culture of this land between the empires.

APPENDIX: RITES FOR THE DEAD AT EMAR

Emar text 452 (Msk 74146b), classed as "*ordo* liturgique mensuel" by Arnaud, may be a cycle of rituals centering on rites for the dead. This conclusion is based in the first place on an offering made on the 25th day *ina bāb kimāḫi*, "at the gate of the grave." Then, the rites for the 25th, 26th, and 27th days of the month are primarily oriented toward the *abû*'s of various sacred locations, recalling discussion of similar terms in relation to the dead.[1] The entire cycle occurs in the month of Abû, spelled the same way as the *a-bi-i*'s at month's end.[2] This appendix represents only a preliminary discussion of the text, which merits further evaluation. Consideration of the organization and character of the whole text will precede closer examination of the latter portion.

1. The Framework of Emar 452

Msk 74146b contains 55 long lines, though one large piece is broken from the upper right portion of the tablet, so that the middle lines of the ritual are severely damaged. The ritual is given no title but is headed by the temporal phrase *i-na* [iti]*A-bi-i*, "during the month of Abû." The rites for this month are separated into days, each begun with the phrase *ina* X (number) *ūmi* and marked by horizontal lines above and below. Emar 452 concerns itself with special days and does not involve summation of all offerings for the month. The closest parallel may be the Ugaritic ritual texts which likewise begin with a month name and are organized about a scheme of special days, especially KTU 1.112, which starts with the same first, third, and eighth days.[3] Offerings comprise the principal activity through Emar 452, but the text is more than an offering list. For example, the mid-month days involve processional rites, though much of the context is unfortunately lost. Although

---

[1] See especially H.A. Hoffner, "Second millennium antecedents to the Hebrew *ʾôb*," *JBL* 86 (1967) 385-401.
[2] Collation shows the five horizontals of the I-sign where Arnaud reads the similar ḪÉ (so *a-bi-ḫé*).
[3] See G. del Olmo Lete, "The cultic literature of Ugarit," 158; cf. *AuOr* 2 197-206.

the Ugaritic texts provide a significant point of comparison, the Emar ritual does not appear to be borrowed directly from any other known ritual tradition.

The Emar rites for Abû give special consideration to the middle of the month and to days 25 to 27, with lesser rites provided for other days. The whole text may be organized as follows:

1. Lines 1-8 describe offerings on the *ūmi ḫussi* (first), the third, and the eighth days, as in the Ugaritic ritual KTU 1.112. No other rites are involved on these days. The *ūmi ḫussi* might be "the day of remembrance" if the cognate is Akkadian *ḫasāsu* as glossed by West Semitic *zkr* ("to remember") in EA 228:18.[4] Alternatively, Ugaritic *ḥdṯ*, "new moon," is temptingly close to the Emar word, and should even have an *u*-vowel in the root (cf. Hebrew *ḥōdeš*). The phonetic equivalence, however, would be difficult to explain. Ugaritic *ṯ* is usually expressed in Akkadian as *š*, and **ḫudšu* is not expected to become *ḫussu* or *ḫuzzu*.[5]

2. Lines 9-27 cover the mid-month days from the 14th to the 19th and describe both offerings and other ritual events. Unfortunately, the full nature of these more complex rites is obscured because of the damage to the tablet, but the following should be observed:

-- line 10, NINDA.MEŠ KAŠ.MEŠ; from other Emar ritual, the one verb that should follow is *uqaddašū*, "they will sanctify," the action that commonly initiates Emar rituals.

-- lines 19-20, two Š forms of *erēbu*, "to enter."

-- lines 21, 25, 27, Š and G forms of *(w)aṣû*, "to depart." These are verbs of procession which occur in several other Emar rituals (see above). Perhaps such procession is associated with what lines 20 and 21 call the *ṣâdu*, "rounds(?)."

-- line 26, *epēšu*, "to do, perform." This verb occurs elsewhere in Emar ritual with objects *zimaru*, "song," with the *kubadu*, and with named festivals (e.g. the *zukru*, 373.36, etc.).

---

4 See *CAD* s.v. *ḫasāsu* 3 for the Akkadian verb as "to remember." The verbs in EA 228, a letter from Canaanite Hazor, are rendered *liḫšuš-mi* and *yazkur-mi*.

5 For *ṯ* as *š*, see Huehnergard, *Ugaritic Vocabulary*, 186-189, and observe the noun *qidšu*, "sanctuary" (page 173).

3. Line 30 (day 20) resembles the first days in that it involves only an offering. Lines 28-29 may belong to the same category, but any date is lost in the break.

4. Rites for the 25th, 26th, and 27th days occupy lines 31-52, the second major focus of the month's events. As with the mid-month period, days 25 to 27 involve more than simple offerings, but none of the additional activities from the middle of the month reappear here. This part of the ritual will be reviewed below.

5. The new month arrives in lines 53-55, with offerings and purification of the city.

Days 25 to 27 show the strongest indications of concern for the dead, but the rest of the ritual offers a hazier picture. Several features of that remaining text should be observed.

The month name Abû resembles the widely attested Mesopotamian month Abu, which has particular association with the *kispum* rites for the dead in the OB period and with the underworld of the Maqlû incantations.[6] An Emar will is dated to the month of [iti]*A-ba-i* (15.35, cf. [iti]*A-ba*-x, 456.2), apparently the same name. Given the equivalent spellings, the month name and the *abû* of the offerings on days 25 to 27 surely represent the same word.

While days 25 to 27 outline various offerings made at several specified temples and sacred sites, *none* of the offerings made outside those days indicates a location, but only the recipient. One primary location for the ritual might be assumed and left unnamed. The one description of locale is associated with the processional rites of the mid-month period: in line 26, some event occurs *arki bīt* [d]NIN.URTA, "behind the temple of [d]NIN.URTA." J.-C. Margueron has suggested that Emar temple architecture included an open space beside or behind the temple proper, with separate access; perhaps this illuminates the unexpected preposition *arki*, though equation of text and material find is always problematic.[7] Repeated reference to the *bīt ili* indicates

---

6 For a comprehensive treatment of the *kispu(m)* see Akio Tsukimoto, *Untersuchungen zur Totenpflege (kispum) im alten Mesopotamien*, AOAT 216, Neukirchen-Vluyn: Neukirchener, 1985, and pages 40-51 on the OB *kispum* in the month of Abu. On the underworld aspects of the month of Abu, with regard to the Maqlû series, see Tzvi Abusch, "Mesopotamian anti-witchcraft literature: texts and studies. Part I: The nature of *Maqlû*: its character, divisions, and calendrical setting," *JNES* 33 (1974) 261 n.35.

7 See Margueron in *Le Moyen-Euphrate*, 308-311.

a source of particular offerings and does not tell us where the rite is taking place.[8]

Besides the above appearance of ᵈNIN.URTA's temple, the one deity named before day 25 in our extant text is the goddess Ištar/Aštart. Compare:

> *Aštartu ša abi*, lines 5, 17;[9]
> *Aštartu ša šubi*, lines 10, 14;
> *Aštartu ša BiriGāti*(?), line 15.

All three forms occur in other Emar lists. Line 21 says, "on the 16th day is the *ṣâdu* of Aštart," without epithet, and the end of the text mentions Latarak, Ištar's son in Mesopotamian tradition.[10] The mountain Ṣuparati recalls the divine name ᵈINANNA *Ṣu-pá-ra-ti* in one Emar god list (379.6). In its larger framework, at least, Emar 452 thus seems to belong to the sphere of Ištar/Aštart. While Ištar is by no means an underworld goddess, she becomes entangled in the world below in the stories of her descent, and her request to Gilgamesh in that epic might reflect not only Gilgamesh's place as an underworld deity, as shown by Abusch, but also her own links to that realm.[11]

Offerings are made to the mountains Šinapši in lines 6, 8, and 30, and Ṣuparati in line 29. It is not certain whether these carry any overtones of the underworld.[12]

2. Days 25 to 27

Without days 25 to 27, we might never ask whether the rest of Emar 452 has connections with rites for the dead. These three days introduce several features not found elsewhere in the month's ritual.

Offerings are made throughout these three days at specified sacred sites, beginning and ending with the with *bīt tukli*, known at Emar as an important source of materials for offerings, interchangeable in one text with the *bīt ili*

---

[8] Lines 3, (17), 29, 31, 47, 54; see The *bīt tukli* and the *bīt ili*, above.
[9] Collation shows that *a-bi* in line 5 is smudged, but an intentional erasure does not seem likely (vs. Arnaud).
[10] See Wilcke, "Inanna/Ištar," 76-80.
[11] See T. Abusch, "Ishtar's proposal and Gilgamesh's refusal," *History of Religion* 26 (1986) 143-187.
[12] The term *šinapši* is attested from Boghazkoy as a sacred place (the *šinapši*-house), an epithet of Teššub and Hebat, and as a mountain (1273/v 2'; KUB XXXII 52 Rs?4); see Haas and Wilhelm, *Hurritische und luwische Riten aus Kizzuwatna*, 37-38.

(see above). Other locations include the palace (line 39) and the temples of ᵈNIN.KUR (line 33), Dagan (lines 40, 46), Alal (lines 41, 50), Išḫara (line 42), and one unknown deity (line 48, lost in the break). The temple of Aštart is omitted, as is the temple of ᵈNIN.URTA, though the *bīt tukli* storehouse may be in that temple area (see above). Most of these offerings are given further precision by the phrase *ana abî* before the temple name (all but lines 41 and 42). Use of the verb *naqû*, "to offer," in lines 32, 39, and 46 eliminates the possibility of a human recipient, and the relation of the *abû* to offering is defined in line 46 by the compound preposition *ana pānī*, "before."

Days 25 to 27 are also marked by performance of two offerings defined by the new Emar ritual term, *kubadu*. They perform (*epēšu*) a great (GAL) *kubadu* "at the gate of the grave" (*i-na* KÁ KI.MAḪ) on the 25th day and a lesser (TUR) *kubadu* "before the *abû* of Dagan's temple" on the 27th day, each apparently consisting of the preceding list of foodstuffs (lines 34-35, 43-46). These examples of the *kubadu* show no hint of distinction as a preparatory rite for offering, though perhaps such a call for offering as *kubadu* involves a major sacrifice *with* the presentation ritual.

On days 25 and 26, five different offerings are headed by *ṣabbuttu*-bread, not otherwise found in this ritual (lines 33, 40, 41 twice, 42). Day 26 begins with some offering for "all the gods" *adi dalāti*, "as far as the doors of ..." (something), after which the doors are barred. Any further point of reference is unfortunately lost. Finally, there is singing for the gods on the 27th day (line 48). None of these features appear in the rest of the text.

As observed in introduction, two elements of this ritual section indicate particular connection with the dead: these are the great *kubadu* performed "at the gate of the grave" (line 35) and the repeated offerings to or at the *abû* of various sacred locations. Mention of the grave, KI.MAḪ/*kimāḫu*, both produces direct evidence for funerary concern and raises difficult problems. What and where is this "grave"? The very lack of specificity in the description seems to define the location as *The* Emar Grave, and reference to a "gate" adds to the impression of a significant construction. We might assume this is the royal tomb, but at Emar this cannot be taken as given. The king is conspicuously absent as an active participant in this text and in most Emar ritual, and this *kimāḫu* may not belong to the palace so much as to the city as a whole. The only other temple and deity receiving offerings on the 25th day is the temple of ᵈNIN.KUR, who may have a special function in the mourning aspect of the NIN.DINGIR installation. Perhaps "the grave" is associated with ^{d}NIN.KUR, though this is only speculation.

While the *kubadu* at the grave points directly toward funerary interest, the *abû*'s are what pull together all the rites for these three days in the month of Abû. Arnaud translates the term "mer" (sea), based on pairing of *Aštartu ša abi* with the god ^{d}*Ya-a-mi* in the long *zukru* festival god list (373.92). Identification of this god with Ugaritic Yammu, (double *-mm-*) should not be considered certain, and even if correct, other terms offer closer comparison with the Emar word *abû*.

Two principal options come to mind. The Hurrian *abi* (*a-a-bi*) is a pit for communication with underworld beings, in which offerings are placed to lure them up.[13] On the other hand, Semitic *ab(u)* simply means "father" and could refer to ancestors. Both alternatives have been discussed in connection with the Hebrew *ʾôb*, spirit of the dead, and Ugaritic *ʾilʾib* (*ʾilu ʾabi*(?)), ancestral deities.[14] The Emar recipient of offerings is always spelled *a-bi-i*, marking a final long vowel,[15] except in the annual cycle 446.79, *a-bi*. The Aštart name is generally spelled *a-bi* when the deity is written as Mesopotamian ^{d}INANNA or ^{d}*Iš*$_{8}$*-tár*, but one sale document appears to read [^{d}*A*]*š-tar-ti ša ab-bi*, with a doubled consonant that could mark the plural, "fathers." Note the name DINGIR *a-ba* in one Emar offering list (380.17), which might link the Ugaritic and Emar terms.

Whereas the Hurrian attestations of *abi* consistently portray this as a pit which is dug or cut into the ground, none of the Emar occurrences indicate such a character, and the one use in line 46 of our text uses the preposition *ana pānī*, "before." In light of the one Aštart name, I have a slight preference for the derivation from *abu*, "father," though a distinct term may have developed that designates a physical shrine. Whatever the correct definition, the *abû* surely has a special relation to the goddess *Aštartu ša abi*, named twice in our text. Aštart's prominence in the Abû-month rites as a whole might after all carry funerary overtones.

---

13 See Hoffner *JBL* 86 385; Laroche, *GLH* 34.

14 See Hoffner, *JBL* 86; Klaas Spronk, *Beatific Afterlife in Ancient Israel and in the Ancient Near East*, AOAT 219, Neukirchen-Vluyn: Neukirchener, 1986, 253 (as "father"); J. Ebach and U. Rüterswörden, "Unterweltsbeschwörung im Alten Testament. Untersuchungen zur Begriffs- und Religionsgeschichte des *ʾōb*, I," *UF* 9 (1977) 57-70; "II," *UF* 12 (1980) 205-220 (cf. *apu*, "pit").

15 Collation shows the same spelling for line 50, where Arnaud's copy lacks the final *-i*.

3. Summation

The 25th through 27th days of the Emar rites for the month of Abû appear to involve funerary-type offerings made throughout the city at a selection of temples and special locations. The Emar offerings are not restricted to royalty or the palace, as we might expect from the focus of many other known ancient Near Eastern ritual. Perhaps the *abû* are ancestor figures (or stelae?) that would have stood in many temples and sacred sites, from the temple of Dagan to the *bīt tukli* storehouse to the royal palace -- just as the *ʾilʾib* are prominent in so many and diverse god- and offering-lists at Ugarit.

BIBLIOGRAPHY

Abdallah, Fayssal. "La femme dans le royaume d'Alep au XVIIIe siècle av. J.-C.," in J.-M. Durand, ed., *La femme dans le Proche-Orient antique*, RAI 33, 1987, 13-15.

Abusch, I. Tzvi. "Mesopotamian anti-witchcraft literature: texts and studies. Part I: The nature of *Maqlû*: its character, divisions, and calendrical setting," *JNES* 33 (1974) 251-262.

--------. "Ishtar's proposal and Gilgamesh's refusal," *History of Religion* 26 (1986) 143-187.

--------. *Babylonian Witchcraft Literature*. Atlanta: Scholars Press, 1987.

Archi, Alfonso. "Fêtes de printemps et d'automne et réintégration rituelle d'images de culte dans l'Anatolie hittite," *UF* 5 (1973) 7-27.

--------. "Les dieux d'Ebla au IIIe millénaire avant J.C. et les dieux d'Ugarit," *AAAS* 29-30 (1979-80) 167-171.

--------. "Les noms de personne Mariotes à Ebla (IIIeme millénaire)," *M.A.R.I.* 4 (1985) 53-58.

--------. "Die ersten zehn Könige von Ebla," *ZA* 76 (1986) 213-217.

--------. "Imâr au IIIeme millénaire d'après les archives d'Ebla," *M.A.R.I.* 6 (1990) 21-38.

Arnaud, Daniel. "Emar," *RA* 67 (1973) 191.

--------. "^dKUR," *RA* 68 (1974) 190.

--------. "Les textes d'Emar et la chronologie de la fin du Bronze Récent," *Syria* 52 (1975) 87-92.

--------. "Catalogue des textes cunéiformes trouvés au cours des trois premières campagnes à Meskéné qadimé Ouest (Chantiers A, C, E, et trouvaille de surface)," *AAAS* 25 (1975) 87-93.

--------. "Religion assyro-babylonienne," *AEPHER* 84 (1975-76) 221-228.

--------. "Religion assyro-babylonienne," *AEPHER* 85 (1976-77) 209-215.

--------. "Religion assyro-babylonienne," *AEPHER* 86 (1977-78) 183-190.

--------. "Traditions urbaines et influences semi-nomades à Emar, à l'âge du bronze récent," in Jean Margueron, ed., *Le Moyen-Euphrate, zone de contacts et d'échanges*, Actes du Colloque de Strasbourg (10-12 mars 1977). Strasbourg: Université des Sciences Humaines de Strasbourg, 1980, 245-264.

--------. "Les textes suméro-accadiens de Meskéné (Syrie) et l'Ancien Testament," *Bulletin de la Société Ernest-Renan*, 1979, in *RHR* 197 (1980) 116-118.

--------. "La bibliothèque d'un devin Syrien à Meskéné-Emar (Syrie)," *CRAIBL* 1980, 375-387.

--------. "Religion assyro-babylonienne," *AEPHER* 89 (1980-81) 305-312.

--------. "Les texts suméro-accadiens: un florilège," in Beyer, ed., *Meskéné-Emar*, 1982, 43-51.

--------. "Religion assyro-babylonienne," *AEPHER* 92 (1983-84) 231-237.

--------. "La Syrie du moyen-Euphrate sous le protectorat hittite: l'administration d'après trois lettres inédites," *AuOr* 2 (1984) 179-188.

--------. *Recherches au pays d'Aštata, Emar VI.1, 2: textes sumériens et accadiens, planches*. Paris: Editions Recherche sur les Civilisations, 1985.

--------. "Religion assyro-babylonienne," *AEPHER* 94 (1985-86) 261-272.

--------. *Emar VI.3: textes sumériens et accadiens, texte*, 1986.

--------. *Emar VI.4: textes de la bibliothèque, transcriptions et traductions*, 1987.

--------. "La Syrie du moyen-Euphrate sous le protectorat hittite: contracts de droit privé," *AuOr* 5 (1987) 211-241.

--------. "Les hittites sur le moyen-Euphrate: protecteurs et indigènes," in *Hethitica VIII, Acta Anatolica E. Laroche Oblata*. Louvain-la-neuve: Peeters, 1987, 9-27.

--------. "Religion assyro-babylonienne," *AEPHER* 96 (1987-88) 174-178.

Artzi, Pinḥas. "The influence of political marriages on the international relations of the Amarna-Age," in Durand, ed., *La femme...*, RAI 33, 1987, 23-26.

Astour, Michael. "Les hourrites en Syrie du Nord: rapport sommaire," in *Les Hourrites*, RAI 24, *RHA* 36 (1978) 1-22.

Balkan, Kemal. "Betrothal of girls during childhood in ancient Assyria and Anatolia," in Harry A. Hoffner and Gary M. Beckman, eds., *Kaniššuwar: A Tribute to Hans G. Güterbock*, *AS* 23. Chicago: The Oriental Institute, 1986, 1-11.

Beckman, Gary M. *Hittite Birth Rituals*, 2nd ed. Wiesbaden: Otto Harrassowitz, 1983.

--------. "Three tablets from the vicinity of Emar," *JCS* 40 (1988) 61-68.

Beyer, Dominique. "Notes préliminaires sur les empreintes de sceaux de Meskéné," in Margueron, ed., *Le Moyen-Euphrate*, 1980, 265-283.

Beyer, ed. *Meskéné-Emar: dix ans de travaux, 1972-1982*. Paris: Editions Recherche sur les Civilisations, 1982.

Bottéro, Jean. "Les inventaires de Qatna," *RA* 43 (1949) 1-40.

Burkert, Walter. *Structure and History in Greek Mythology and Ritual*. Berkeley: Univ. of California Press, 1979.

--------. *Homo Necans: The Anthropology of Ancient Greek Sacrificial Ritual and Myth*. Berkeley: Univ. of California Press, 1983.

--------. *Greek Religion: Archaic and Classical*. Oxford: Basil Blackwell, 1985.

Caquot, André. "Problèmes d'histoire religieuse," in M. Liverani, ed., *La Siria nel tardo bronzo*. Roma: Centro per le antichita e la storia dell'arte del vicino oriente, 1969, 61-76.

Carre-Gates, M.-H. "Alalakh levels VI and V: a chronological reassessment," *Syro-Mesopotamian Studies* 4/2, 1981.

Cavigneaux, Antoine. "Le nom akkadien du grain," *N.A.B.U.* 1989, 33 (no. 52).

Charpin, Dominique. "Nouveaux documents du bureau de l'huile à l'époque assyrienne," *M.A.R.I.* 3 (1984) 83-126.

--------. "Les archives du devin Asqudum dans la résidence du 'Chantier A'," *M.A.R.I.* 4 (1985) 453-462.

--------. *Le clergé d'Ur au siècle d'Hammurabi (XIXe-XVIIIe siècles av. J.-C.).* Genève-Paris: Librairie Droz, 1986.

--------. Tablettes présargoniques de Mari," *M.A.R.I.* 5 (1987) 65-127.

Cook, Arthur B. *Zeus: A Study in Ancient Religion* Vol.2. New York: Biblo and Tannen, 1965.

Cross, Frank M. *Canaanite Myth and Hebrew Epic.* Cambridge, MA: Harvard University Press, 1973.

Cunchillos, J.-L. "Le dieu Mut, guerrier de El," *Syria* 62 (1985) 205-218.

Cutler, B., and MacDonald, J. "On the origin of the Ugaritic text KTU 1.23," *UF* 14 (1982) 33-50.

Danmanville, J. "Hepat, Hebat," *RlA* 4 (1972-75) 326-329.

Darga, Muhibbe. "Über das Wesen des *ḫuwaši*-Steines nach hethischen Kultinventären," *RHA* 27 (1969) 5-24.

Delcor, M. "Le personnel du temple d'Astarté à Kition d'après une tablette phénicienne (CIS 86 A et B)," *UF* 11 (1979) 147-164.

Deller, Karlheinz, and Fadhil, Abdulillah. "NIN.DINGIR.RA/*ēntu* in Texten aus Nuzi und Kurruḫanni," *Mesopotamia* 7 (1972) 193-213.

Deller, K., Mayer, W.R., and Sommerfeld, W., "Akkadische Lexikographie: *CAD* N," *Or* NS 56 (1987) 176-218.

Diakonoff, I.M. "Evidence on the ethnic division of the Hurrians," in M.A. Morrison and D.I. Owen, eds., *Studies on the Civilization and Culture of Nuzi and the Hurrians, in Honor of Ernest R. Lacheman on his Seventy-fifth Birthday.* Winona Lake, IN: Eisenbrauns, 1981, 77-89.

Dietrich, Manfried. "Das Einsetzungsritual der Entu von Emar (Emar VI/3, 369)," *UF* 21 (1989) 47-100.

Dietrich, M., and Loretz, Oswald. "Bemerkungen zum Aqhat-Text. Zur Ugaritischen Lexikographie (XIV)," *UF* 10 (1978) 65-71.

--------. "Neue Studien zu den Ritualtexten aus Ugarit (I)," *UF* 13 (1981) 63-100.

--------. "Die ugaritischen Gefässbezeichnungen *ridn* und *kw*," *UF* 19 (1987) 27-32.

Dietrich, M., Loretz, O., and Mayer, W. "*Sikkanum* 'Betyle'," *UF* 21 (1989) 133-139.

Dijkstra, Meindert, and de Moor, Johannes C. "Problematical passages in the legend of Aqhatu," *UF* 7 (1976) 171-215.

Dornemann, Rudolph H. "Tell Hadidi: a millennium of Bronze Age city occupation," *AASOR* 44 (1979) 113-151.

--------. "Tell Hadidi: an important center of the Mitannian period and earlier," in Margueron, ed., *Le Moyen-Euphrate*, 1980, 217-234.

--------. "The excavations at Ras Shamra and their place in the current archaeological picture of ancient Syria," in G.D. Young, ed., *Ugarit in Retrospect: Fifty Years of Ugarit and Ugaritic*. Winona Lake, IN: Eisenbrauns, 1981, 59-69.

Dossin, Georges. "Un rituel du culte d'Ištar provenant de Mari," *RA* 35 (1938) 1-13.

--------. *Studia Mariana*. Leiden, 1950.

--------. "Un 'panthéon' d'Ur III à Mari," *RA* 61 (1967) 97-104.

Douglas, Mary. *Purity and Danger: An Analysis of Concepts of Pollution and Taboo*. New York: Frederick A. Praeger, 1966.

van Driel, G. *The Cult of Aššur*, Studia Semitica Neerlandica 13. Assen: van Gorcum and Company, 1969.

Dunand, Maurice. "Byblos et ses temples après la pénétration Amorite," in Hans-Jörg Nissen and Johannes Renger, eds., *Mesopotamien und seine Nachbarn*, RAI 25. Berlin: Dietrich Reimer Verlag, 1982, 195-201.

Durand, Jean-Marie. "Sumérien et akkadien en pays Amorite," *M.A.R.I.* 1 (1982) 79-89.

--------. *Textes administratifs des salles 134 et 160 du palais de Mari*, ARMT XXI. Paris: Paul Geuthner, 1983.

--------. "Trois études sur Mari," *M.A.R.I.* 3 (1984) 127-180.

--------. "Le culte des bétyles en Syrie," in Durand and J.-R. Kupper, eds., *Miscellanea Babylonica: mélanges offerts à Maurice Birot*. Paris: Éditions Recherche sur les Civilisations, 1985, 79-84.

--------. "La situation historique des Šakkanakku: nouvelle approche," *M.A.R.I.* 4 (1985) 147-172.

--------. "Les dames du palais de Mari à l'époque du royaume de Haute-Mésopotamie," *M.A.R.I.* 4 (1985) 385-436.

--------. "Hauts personnages à Emar," *N.A.B.U.* 1989, 33-35.

--------. Review of Arnaud, *Emar VI.1-3*, *RA* 83 (1989) 163-191, 84 (1990) 49-85.

--------. "La cité-état d'Imâr à l'époque des rois de Mari," *M.A.R.I.* 6 (1990) 39-92.

Durand, J.-M., and Joannes, Francis. "*kubuddâ'u* à Mari et à Emar," *N.A.B.U.* 1990, 53-54.

Ebach, J., and Rüterswörden. "Unterweltsbeschwörung im Alten Testament. Untersuchugen zur Begriffs- und Religionsgeschichte des *ʾōb*, I," *UF* 9 (1977) 57-70; "II," *UF* 12 (1980) 205-220.

Edzard, D.O. "Pantheon und Kult in Mari," in J.-R. Kupper, ed., *La civilisation de Mari*, RAI 15. Paris: Société d'Edition "Les Belles Lettres," 1967, 51-71.

Fadhil, Abdulillah. *Studien zur Topographie und Prosopographie der Provinzstädte des Königsreichs Arrapḫe*. Mainz am Rhein: Verlag Philipp von Zabern, 1983.

Fales, Frederick M. "A cuneiform correspondence to alphabetic *š* in West Semitic names of the I millennium B.C.," *Or* NS 47 (1978) 91-98.

--------. "Notes on the royal family of Emar," in *Mélanges P. Garelli*, forthcoming.

Falkenstein, Adam. "'Wahrsagung' in der sumerischen Überlieferung," in *La divination en Mésopotamie ancienne et dans les regions voisines*, RAI 14. Paris: Presses Universitaires de France, 1966, 45-68.

Farber, Walter. "Tamarisken-Fibeln-Skolopender," in Francesca Rochberg-Halton, ed., *Language, Literature, and History: Philological and Historical Studies Presented to Erica Reiner*, New Haven: American Oriental Society, 1987, 85-105.

Finet, André. "La place du devin dans la société de Mari," in RAI 14, 1966, 87-93.

--------. "Les autorités locales dans le royaume de Mari," *Akkadica* 26 (1982) 1-16.

--------. "Le port d'Emar sur l'Euphrate, entre le royaume de Mari et le pays de Canaan," in E. Lipiński, ed., *The Land of Israel: Cross-roads of Civilizations*. Leuven: Uitgeverij Peeters, 1985, 27-38.

--------. "Šamaš IGI-KUR, l'oeil-du-pays," *M.A.R.I.* 4 (1985) 541-543.

Frantz-Szabó, G. "Išḫara," *RlA* 5 (1977) 177-178.

Frayne, Douglas R. "Notes on the sacred marriage rite," *BiOr* 42 (1985) 5-22.

Friedrich, Johannes. "Ein Sonderfall partitiver Apposition beim hethitischen Personal Pronomen," *AfO* 18 (1957-58) 127.

Garelli, Paul. "Les temples et le pourvoir royal en Assyrie du XIVe au VIIIe siècle," in *Le temple et le culte*, RAI 20. TE ISTAMBUL: Nederlands historisch-archeologisch Instituut, 1975, 116-124.

Gelb, Ignace J. "Sumerian and Akkadian words for 'string of fruit'," in G. van Driel et al, eds., *Zikir Šumim: Assyriological Studies Presented to F.R. Kraus on the Occasion of his Seventieth Birthday*. Leiden: E.J. Brill, 1982, 67-82.

--------. "The language of Ebla in the light of sources from Ebla, Mari, and Babylonia," in Cagni, Luigi, ed., *Ebla 1975-1985. Dieci anni di studi linguistici e filologici*. Napoli: Istituto Universitario Orientale, 1987, 49-74.

van Gennep, Arnold. *The Rites of Passage*. Chicago: Univ. of Chicago Press, 1960.

Gonnet, Hatice. "Rituel des fêtes d'automne et de printemps du dieu de l'orage de Zippalanda," *Anadolu* 19 (1975-76) 123-164.

Güterbock, Hans G. "The Hittite temple according to written sources," in *Le temple et le culte*, RAI 20, 1975, 125-132.

--------. "Hethitische Götterbilder und Kultobjekte," in R.M. Boehmer and H. Hauptmann, eds., *Beiträge zur Altertumskunde Kleinasiens: Festschrift für Kurt Bittel*. Mainz am Rhein: Verlag Philipp von Zabern, 1983, 203-217.

Gurney, Oliver R. *Some Aspects of Hittite Religion*. Oxford: The University Press, 1977.

Haas, Volkert. "Die Unterwelts- und Jenseitsvorstellungen im hethitischen Kleinasien," *Or* NS 45 (1976), RAI 21, 197-212.

--------. "Substratgottheiten des westhurrischen Pantheons," in *Les Hourrites*, RAI 24, 1978, 59-69.

--------. *Hethitische Berggötter und hurritische Steindämonen: Riten, Kulte und Mythen*. Mainz am Rhein: Philipp von Zabern, 1982.

--------. "Einführung in das Thema," in Haas, ed., *Hurriter und Hurritisch*, Konstanzer altorientalische Symposien II, Xenia 21. Konstanz: Universitätsverlag, 1988, 11-26.

Haas, and Jakob-Rost, Liane. "Das Festritual des Gottes Telipinu in Ḫanḫana und in Kašḫa: ein Beitrag zum hethitischen Festkalendar," *AoF* 11 (1984) 10-91, 204-236.

Haas, and Wilhelm, G. *Hurritische und luwische Riten aus Kizzuwatna*, AOATS 3. Neukirchen-Vluyn: Neukirchener, 1974.

Hawkins, J.D. "Karkamiš," in *RlA* 5 (1980) 426-446.

Healey, J.F. "The underworld character of the god Dagan," *JNSL* 5 (1977) 43-51.

--------. "The Ugaritic dead: some live issues," *UF* 18 (1986) 27-32.

--------. "The 'pantheon' of Ugarit: further notes," *SEL* 5 (1988) 103-112.

Heltzer, Michael. "Problems of the social history of Syria in the Late Bronze Age," in Liverani, M., ed., *La Siria nel tardo bronzo*. Roma: Centro per le antichità e la storia dell'arte del vicino oriente, 1969, 31-46.

--------. *The Rural Community in Ancient Ugarit*. Wiesbaden: Dr. Ludwig Reichert, 1976.

Hoffner, Harry A. "Second millennium antecedents to the Hebrew *ʾôb*," *JBL* 86 (1967) 385-401.

--------. *Alimenta Hethaeorum: Food Production in Hittite Asia Minor*, American Oriental Series 55. New Haven: American Oriental Society, 1974.

Huehnergard, John. "Five tablets from the vicinity of Emar," *RA* 77 (1983) 11-43.

--------. *Ugaritic Vocabulary in Syllabic Transcription*, Harvard Semitic Studies 32. Atlanta: Scholars Press, 1987.

--------. *The Akkadian of Ugarit*, Harvard Semitic Studies 34. Atlanta: Scholars Press, 1989.

Jacobsen, Thorkild. Moran, W.L., ed. *Toward the Image of Tammuz and Other Essays on Mesopotamian History and Culture*. Cambridge: Harvard University Press, 1970.

---------. *The Treasures of Darkness: A History of Mesopotamian Religion*. New Haven: Yale University Press, 1976.

--------. "The Gilgamesh Epic: romantic and tragic vision," in Abusch, Tzvi; Huehnergard, John; and Steinkeller, Piotr, eds., *Lingering Over Words: Studies in Ancient Near Eastern Literature in Honor of William L. Moran*, Harvard Semitic Studies 37. Atlanta: Scholars Press, 1990, 231-249.

Kammenhuber, A. "Neue Ergebnisse zur hurrischen und altmesopotamischen Überlieferung," *Or* NS 45 (1976), RAI 21, 130-146.

--------. *Materialen zu einem hethitischen Thesaurus*, Lieferung 6. Heidelberg: Carl Winter, 1977.

Kitchen, K.A. "Interrelations of Egypt and Syria," in Liverani, ed., *La Siria nel tardo bronzo*, 1969, 77-95.

Klein, Harald. "*Tudittum*," *ZA* 73 (1983) 255-284.

Klengel, Horst. "Zu den *šībūtum* in altbabylonischer Zeit," *Or* 29 (1960) 357-375.

--------. *Geschichte Syriens im 2. Jahrtausend v.u.Z.*, I, Deutsche Akademie der Wissenschaften zu Berlin Institut fur Orientforschung 40. Berlin: Akademie-Verlag, 1965.

--------. "Der Wettergott von Halab," *JCS* 19 (1965) 87-93.

Koehler, Ludwig, and Baumgartner, Walter. *Hebräisches und aramäisches Lexikon zum Alten Testament*. Leiden: E.J. Brill, 1967, 1974, 1983.

Kramer, Samuel N. *The Sacred Marriage Rite*. Bloomington: Indiana University Press, 1969.

--------. Bottéro, Jean, ed. *Le Mariage Sacré*. Paris: Berg International Editeurs, 1983.

Krebernik, Manfred. *Die Personennamen der Ebla-Texte: eine Zwischenbilanz*, Berliner Beiträge zum Vorderen Orient 7. Berlin: Dietrich Reimer Verlag, 1988.

Kupper, Jean-Robert. "Dieux hourrites à Mari," *RA* 65 (1971) 171-172.

--------. "Les hourrites à Mari," in *Les Hourrites*, RAI 24, 1978, 117-128.

--------. "La cité et le royaume de Mari: l'organisation urbaine à l'époque amorite," *M.A.R.I.* 4 (1985) 463-466.

Kutsch, Ernst. *Salbung als Rechtsakt im Alten Testament und im Alten Orient*, *ZAW* Beiheft 87. Berlin: Alfred Topelmann, 1963.

Labat, René. *Manuel d'épigraphie akkadienne*, 5th ed. Paris: Librairie orientaliste Paul Geuthner, 1976.

Lafont, Bertrand. "Le roi de Mari et les prophètes du dieu Adad," *RA* 78 (1984) 7-18.

Lambert, W.G. "The Mesopotamian background of the Hurrian pantheon," in *Les Hourrites*, RAI 24, 1978, 129-134.

--------. "A list of gods' names found at Mari," in Durand and Kupper, eds., *Miscellanea Babylonica*, 1985, 181-189.

--------. "The pantheon of Mari," *M.A.R.I.* 4 (1985) 525-539.

Laroche, Emmanuel. *Recherches sur les noms des dieux hittites*. Paris: Librairie Orientale et Americaine, 1947.

--------. *Catalogue des textes hittites*, Etudes et Commentaires 75. Paris: Editions Klincksieck, 1971.

--------. "Panthéon national et panthéons locaux chez les Hourrites," *Or* NS 45 (1976), RAI 21, 94-99.

--------. *Glossaire de la langue hourrite*, *RHA* 34-35. Paris: Editions Klincksieck, 1976-77.

--------. "Emar, étape entre Babylone et le Hatti," in Margueron, ed., *Le Moyen-Euphrate*, 1980, 235-244.

--------. "Les hiéroglyphes de Meskéné-Emar et le style 'Syro-hittite'," *Akkadica* 22 (1981) 5-14.

--------. "Documents hittites et hourrites," in Beyer, ed., *Meskéné-Emar*, 1982, 53-60.

--------. "Les hiéroglyphes hittites de Meskéné-Emar: un emprunt d'écriture," *CRAIBL* 1983, 12-23.

--------. "Observations sur le rituel anatolien provenant de Meskéné-Emar," in Imparati, Fiorella, ed., *Studi di storia e di filologia anatolica dedicati a Giovanni Pugliese Carratelli.* Firenze: Elite (edizioni librarie italiane estere), 1988, 111-117.

Lebrun, René. *Šamuḫa: foyer religieux de l'empire hittite*, Publication de l'Institut Orientaliste de Louvain 11. Louvain-la-neuve: Institut Orientaliste, 1976.

--------. "Deux textes hittites représentant la version impériale tardive de fêtes anatoliennes," in Guy Jucquois and R. Lebrun, eds., *Hethitica 2.* Louvain: Editions Peeters, 1977, 7-23.

--------. "Textes religieux hittites de la fin de l'empire," in *Hethitica 2*, 1977, 93-153.

--------. "Les hittites et le sacré," in Julien Ries et al, eds., *L'expression du sacré dans les grandes religions, I. Proche-Orient ancien et traditions bibliques.* Louvain-la-neuve: Centre d'histoire des religions, 1978, 155-202.

--------. "Considérations sur la femme dans la société hittite," in E. Laroche et al, eds., *Hethitica 3.* Louvain: Peeters, 1979, 109-125.

--------. "Les rituels d'Ammiḫatna, Tulbi et Mati contre une impureté = CTH 472," in *Hethitica 3*, 1979, 139-164.

--------. "Divinités louvites et hourrites des rituels anatoliens en langue akkadienne provenant de Meskéné," in *Hethitica IX.* Louvain-la-neuve: Peeters, 1988, 147-155.

Leemans, W.F. "Aperçu sur les textes juridiques d'Emar," *JESHO* 31 (1988) 207-242.

Levine, Baruch A. "Ugaritic descriptive rituals," *JCS* 17 (1963) 105-111.

--------. "The descriptive ritual texts from Ugarit: some formal and functional features of the *Genre*," in Carol L. Meyers and M. O'Connor, eds., *The Word of the Lord Shall Go Forth.* Winona Lake, IN: Eisenbrauns, 1983, 467-475.

L'Heureux, Conrad E. *Rank Among the Canaanite Gods: El, Ba'al, and the Repha'im*, Harvard Semitic Monographs 21. Missoula, MT: Scholars Press, 1979.

Limet, Henri. "Le panthéon de Mari à l'époque des *šakkanaku*," *Or* NS 45 (1976), RAI 21, 87-93.

Lipiński, Edouard. "*Skn* et *sgn* dans le sémitique occidental du nord," *UF* 5 (1973) 192-207.

Liverani, Mario. "*Kbd* nei testi amministrativi ugaritici," *UF* 2 (1970) 89-108.

Mallul, Meir. "'*Sissiktu*' and '*sikku*' -- their meaning and function," *BiOr* 43 (1986) 20-36.

Margueron, Jean. "Les fouilles françaises de Meskéné-Emar (Syrie)," *CRAIBL* 1975, 201-213.

--------. "Quatre campagnes de fouille à Emar (1972-1974): un bilan provisoire," *Syria* 52 (1975) 53-85.

--------. "Rapport préliminaire sur les deux premières campagnes de fouille à Meskéné-Emar (1972-1973)," *AAAS* 25 (1975) 73-86.

--------. "Un < <*ḫilani*> > à Emar," *AASOR* 44 (1979) 153-176.

--------. "Emar: un exemple d'implantation hittite en terre syrienne," in Margueron, ed., *Le Moyen-Euphrate*, 1980, 285-312.

--------. "Rapport préliminaire sur les 3e, 4e, 5e, et 6e campagnes de fouille à Meskéné-Emar," *AAAS* 32 (1982) 233-249.

--------. "Aux marches de l'empire hittite: une campagne de fouille à Tell Faq'ous (Syrie), citadelle du pays d'Aštata," in *La Syrie au Bronze Récent*, RAI 27. Paris: Editions Recherche sur les Civilisations, 1982, 47-66.

--------. "Architecture et urbanisme," in Beyer, ed., *Meskéné-Emar*, 1982, 23-39.

--------. "Quelques remarques sur les temples de Mari," *M.A.R.I.* 4 (1985) 487-507.

Matsushima, Eiko. "Le lit de Šamaš et le rituel du mariage à l'Ebabbar," *ASJ* 7 (1985) 129-137.

--------. "Le rituel hiérogamique de Nabû," *ASJ* 9 (1987) 131-175.

--------. "Les rituels du mariage divin dans les documents accadiens," *ASJ* 10 (1988) 95-128.

Matthews, Victor H. "Government involvement in the religion of the Mari kingdom," *RA* 72 (1978) 151-156.

Matthiae, Paulo. "Unité et developpement du temple dans la Syrie du Bronze Moyen," in *Le temple et le culte*, RAI 20, 1975, 43-72.

Mayer, Walter. "Die Tontafelfunde von Tall Munbāqa 1984," *MDOG* 118 (1986) 126-131.

--------. "Der antike Name von Tall Munbāqa, die Schreiber und die chronologische Einordnung der Tafelfunde: Die Tontafelfunde von Tall Munbāqa 1988," *MDOG* 122 (1990) 45-66.

McEwan, Gilbert J.P. *Priest and Temple in Hellenistic Babylonia*, Freiburger Altorientalische Studien 4. Wiesbaden: Franz Steiner Verlag, 1981.

Menzel, Brigitte. *Assyrische Tempel.* Rome: Biblical Institute Press, 1981.

Mettinger, Tryggve N.D. *King and Messiah: the Civil and Sacral Legitimation of the Israelite Kings.* Lund: C.W.K. Gleerup, 1976.

Meyer, J.-W. and Wilhelm, G. "Eine spätbronzezeitliche Keilschrifturkunde aus Syrien," *DamM* 1 (1983) 249-261.

Michalowski, Piotr. "Third millennium contacts: observations on the relationships between Mari and Ebla," *JAOS* 105 (1985) 293-302.

Montalbano, Frank J. "Canaanite Dagon: origin, nature," *CBQ* 13 (1951) 381-397.

de Moor, Johannes C. "The Semitic pantheon of Ugarit," *UF* 2 (1970) 187-228.

--------. "The ancestral cult in KTU 1.17:I.26-28," *UF* 17 (1986) 407-409.

Moore, George C. "GIŠTUKUL as 'oracle procedure' in Hittite oracle texts," *JNES* 40 (1981) 49-52.

Moran, William L. *Les lettres d'El-Amarna: correspondance diplomatique du pharaon.* Paris: Les Editions du Cerf, 1987.

--------. "Emar notes," *N.A.B.U.* 1988, 24-25.

Morrison, J.S. "The classical world," in Loewe, Michael, and Blacker, Carmen, eds., *Oracles and Divination.* Boulder, Colorado: Shambhala, 1981, 87-114.

Müller, Karl F. *Das assyrische Ritual, Teil I: Texte zum assyrischen Königsritual*, MVAG 41/3. Leipzig, 1937.

Na'aman, Nadav. "Syria at the transition from the Old Babylonian period to the Middle Babylonian period," *UF* 6 (1974) 265-274.

--------. "The chronology of Alalakh Level VII once again," *AnSt* 29 (1979) 103-113.

--------. "The Ishtar temple at Alalakh," *JNES* 39 (1980) 209-214.

Nakata, Ichiro. *Deities in the Mari Texts.* Columbia University PhD, 1974.

Neu, Erich. *Ein althethitische Gewitterritual*, StBoT 12. Wiesbaden: Otto Harrassowitz, 1970.

--------. *Althethitische Ritualtexte in Umschrift*, StBoT 25. Wiesbaden: Otto Harrassowitz, 1980.

Nilsson, Martin P. *The Minoan-Mycenaean Religion.* New York: Biblo and Tannen, 1971.

Noth, Martin. *The Laws in the Pentateuch and Other Essays.* Philadelphia: Fortress Press, 1967.

Nougayrol, Jean. "Trente ans de recherches sur la divination babylonienne (1935-1965)," in RAI 14, 1966, 5-19.

del Olmo Lete, G. "Ritual regio ugaritico de evocación/adivinación (KTU 1.112)," *AuOr* 2 (1984) 197-206.

--------. "The cultic literature of Ugarit: hermeneutical issues and their application to KTU 1.112," in Karl Hecker and Walter Sommerfeld, eds., *Keilschriftliche Literaturen*, RAI 32. Berlin: Dietrich Reimer Verlag, 1986, 155-164.

--------. "Catalogo de los festivales regios des Ugarit (KTU 1.91)," *UF* 19 (1987) 11-18.

--------. "Ugaritic *ṯʿ*, *ṯʿy*, *ṯʿt*: nombre divino y accion cultual," *UF* 20 (1988) 27-33.

Oppenheim, A. Leo. Erica Reiner, ed., *Ancient Mesopotamia: Portrait of a Dead Civilization.* Chicago: The University of Chicago Press, 1977.

Otten, Heinrich. *Ein hethitisches Festritual (KBo XIX 128)*, StBoT 13. Wiesbaden: Otto Harrassowitz, 1971.

Otten, H., and Souçek, V. *Ein althethitisches Ritual für das Königspaar*, StBoT 8. Wiesbaden: Otto Harrassowitz, 1969.

Ottosson, Magnus. *Temples and Cult Places in Palestine.* Uppsala: Boreas, 1980.

Pardee, Dennis. "A new Ugaritic letter," *BiOr* 34 (1977) 3-20.

Parke, H.W. *Greek Oracles.* London: Hutchinson University Library, 1967.

Pecchioli Daddi, Franca. *Mestieri, Professioni e Dignità Nell'Anatolia Ittita.* Roma: Edizioni Dell'Ateneo, 1982.

Pettinato, Giovanni, and Waetzoldt, Hartmut, "Dagan in Ebla und Mesopotamien nach den Texten aus 3. Jahrtausend," *Or* NS 54 (1985) 234-256.

Pomponio, F. "I nomi divini nei testi di Ebla," *UF* 15 (1983) 141-156.

Pope, Marvin H. "The cult of the dead at Ugarit," in Gordon D. Young, ed., *Ugarit in Retrospect: Fifty Years of Ugarit and Ugaritic.* Winona Lake, IN: Eisenbrauns, 1981, 159-179.

--------. "The status of El at Ugarit," *UF* 19 (1987) 219-230.

Pope, M.H., and Tigay, Jeffrey H. "A description of Baal," *UF* 3 (1971) 117-130.

Renger, Johannes. "Götternamen in der altbabylonischen Zeit," in D.O. Edzard, ed., *Heidelberger Studien zum Alten Orient.* Wiesbaden: Otto Harrassowitz, 1967, 137-171.

--------. "Untersuchungen zum Priestertum in der altbabylonischen Zeit," *ZA* 58 (1967) 110-188; 59 (1969) 104-230.

--------. "Heilige Hochzeit. A. Philologisch," *RlA* 4 (1972-1975) 251-257.

--------. "Ortliche und zeitliche Differenzen in der Struktur der Priesterschaft babylonischer Tempel," in *Le temple et le culte*, RAI 20, 108-115.

Roberts, J.J.M. *The Earliest Semitic Pantheon: A Study of the Semitic Deities Attested in Mesopotamia Before Ur III.* Baltimore: The Johns Hopkins University Press, 1972.

Roth, M. "Age at marriage and the household: a study of Neo-Babylonian and Neo-Assyrian forms," *Comparative Studies in Society and History* 29 (1987) 715-747.

--------. *Babylonian Marriage Agreements: 7th - 3rd Centuries B.C.*, AOAT 222. Neukirchen-Vluyn: Neukirchener, 1989.

Saggs, H.W.F. *The Might that was Assyria*. London: Sidgwick and Jackson, 1984.

Sapin, J. "Quelques systèmes socio-politiques en Syrie au 2e millénaire avant J.-C. et leur évolution historique d'après des document religieux (légendes, rituels, sanctuaires)," *UF* 15 (1983) 157-190.

Sasson, Jack M. "The calendar and festivals of Mari during the reign of Zimri-Lim," in Powell, Marvin A. and Sack, Ronald, eds., *Studies in Honor of Tom B. Jones*, AOAT 203. Neukirchener: Neukirchen-Vluyn, 1979, 119-141.

--------. "'Year: Zimri-Lim offered a great throne to Shamash of Maḫanum': an overview of one year in Mari. Part I: the presence of the king," *M.A.R.I.* 4 (1985) 437-452.

von Schuler, Einar. "Beziehungen zwischen Syrien und Anatolien in der Späten Bronzezeit," in Liverani, ed., *La Siria nel tardo bronzo*, 1969, 97-116.

Sigrist, M. "Miscellanea," *JCS* 34 (1982) 242-252.

Singer, Itamar. *The Hittite KI.LAM Festival*, I, StBoT 27. Wiesbaden: Otto Harrassowitz, 1983.

--------. II, StBoT 28, 1984.

Sivan, Daniel. *Grammatical Analysis and Glossary of Northwest Semitic Vocables in Akkadian Texts of the 15th-13th C.B.C. from Canaan and Syria*, AOAT 214. Neukirchen-Vluyn: Neukirchener, 1984.

von Soden, Wolfram. "Kleine Bemerkungen zu Urkunden und Ritualen aus Emar," *N.A.B.U.* 1987, 25 (no. 46).

Sollberger, Edmond. "The temple in Babylonia," in *Le temple et le culte*, RAI 20, 1975, 31-34.

Soubeyran, Denis. "Une graphie atypique de Saggarātum?," *M.A.R.I.* 3 (1984) 276.

Souçek, Vladimir. "Die hethitischen Feldertexte," *ArOr* 27 (1959) 379-395.

Souçek, V., and Siegelová, Jana. "Der Kult des Wettergottes von Halap in Hatti," *ArOr* 42 (1974) 39-52.

Soyez, Brigitte. "Le bétyle dans le culte de l'Astarté phénicienne," *MUSJ* 47 (1972) 149-169.

Spronk, Klaas. *Beatific Afterlife in Ancient Israel and in the Ancient Near East*, AOAT 219. Neukirchen-Vluyn: Neukirchenner, 1986.

Stein, Diana L. "Mythologische Inhalte der Nuzi-Glyptik," in Haas, ed., *Hurriter und Hurritisch*, 1988, 173-209.

Steinkeller, Piotr. *Sale Documents of the Ur III Period*. Stuttgart: Franz Steiner Verlag, 1989.

Stol, Martin. *On Trees, Mountains, and Millstones in the Ancient Near East*. Leiden: Ex Oriente Lux-Med. XXI, 1979.

Szabó, Gabriella. *Ein hethitisches Entsühnungsritual für das Königspaar Tutḫaliya und Nikalmati*. Heidelberg: Carl Winter, 1971.

Talon, Philippe. "Un nouveau panthéon de Mari," *Akkadica* 20 (1980) 12-17.

de Tarragon, Jean-Michel. *Le culte à Ugarit d'après les textes de la pratique en cunéiformes alphabétiques*. Paris: J. Gabalda, 1980.

Teixidor, Javier. *The Pantheon of Palmyra*. Leiden: E.J. Brill, 1979.

Thiel, H.-J., and Wegner, Ilse. "Eine Anrufung an den Gott Teššup von Halab in hurritischer Sprache," *SMEA* 24 (1984) 187-213.

Thureau-Dangin, François. *Rituels accadiens*. Paris: Editions Ernest Leroux, 1921.

van der Toorn, Karel. "The significance of the veil in the ancient Near East," 1991 Society of Biblical Literature Annual Meetings, Kansas City.

Tsevat, Matitiahu. "The husband veils a wife (Hittite Laws, 197-98)," *JCS* 27 (1975) 235-240.

Tsukimoto, Akio. "Eine neue Urkunde des Tili-Šarruma, Sohn des Königs von Karkamiš," *ASJ* 6 (1984) 65-74.

--------. *Untersuchungen zur Totenpflege (kispum) im alten Mesopotamien*, AOAT 216. Neukirchen-Vluyn: Neukirchener, 1985.

--------. "Sieben spätbronzezeitliche Urkunden aus Syrien," *ASJ* 10 (1988) 153-189.

--------. "Akkadian tablets in the Hirayama collection (I)," *ASJ* 12 (1990) 177-259.

Turner, Victor. *The Ritual Process: Structure and Anti-Structure*. Chicago: Aldine Publishing Co., 1969.

Vargyas, P. "Marchands hittites à Ugarit," *OLP* 16 (1985) 71-79.

de Vaux, Roland. *Ancient Israel: Its Life and Institutions*. New York: McGraw-Hill, 1961.

Wegner, Ilse. *Gestalt und Kult der Ištar-Šawuška in Kleinasien*, AOAT 36. Neukirchen-Vluyn: Neukirchener, 1981.

Whiting, Robert M. *Old Babylonian Letters from Tell Asmar*, *AS* 22. Chicago: The Oriental Institute, 1987.

Wilcke, Claus. "Inanna/Ištar: A. Philologisch," in *RlA* 5 (1976) 74-87.

Wilhelm, Gernot. *Grundzüge der Geschichte und Kultur der Hurriter*. Darmstadt: Wissenschaftliche Buchgesellschaft, 1982.

Wiseman, Donald J. *The Alalakh Tablets*. London: The British Institute of Archaeology at Ankara, 1953.

Wyatt, Nicholas. "The relationship of the deities Dagan and Hadad," *UF* 12 (1980) 375-379.

--------. "The 'Anat stela from Ugarit and its ramifications," *UF* 16 (1984) 327-337.

Xella, Paolo. *I testi rituali di Ugarit, I,* Testi. Roma: Consiglio Nazionale delle Ricerche, 1981.

--------. "L'influence babylonienne à Ougarit, d'après les textes alphabétiques rituels et divinatoires," in *Mesopotamien und seine Nachbarn*, RAI 25, 1982, 321-338.

Yon, Marguerite, and Caubet, Annie. "Ougarit, Mari et l'Euphrate," *AAAS* 34 (1983) 33-41.

Zaccagnini, Carlos. "Golden cups offered to the gods at Emar," *Or* NS 59 (1990) 518-520.

INDICES

A. AKKADIAN/SYLLABIC WORDS

B. SUMERIAN LOGOGRAMS

C. GODS

D. EMAR TEXTS